MODI
THE CHALLENGE OF
2024

MODI
THE CHALLENGE OF
2024
THE BATTLE FOR INDIA

MINHAZ MERCHANT

AMARYLLIS

AMARYLLIS

An imprint of Manjul Publishing House Pvt. Ltd.
• C-16, Sector 3, Noida, Uttar Pradesh 201301, India
Website: www.manjulindia.com
Registered Office:
• 10, Nishat Colony, Bhopal 462 003 – India
Distribution Centres
Ahmedabad, Bengaluru, Bhopal, Chennai, Hyderabad,
Kolkata, Mumbai, Noida, Pune

MODI – The Challenge of 2024: The Battle for India by Minhaz Merchant

Copyright © Minhaz Merchant, 2023

Minhaz Merchant asserts the moral right to be
identified as the author of this work

This edition first published in India in 2023

ISBN 978-93-5543-338-1

Contents

Author's Note   *ix*

SECTION ONE: MODI

1. The Making of a Prime Minister   3
2. 2019: Storming to Victory   29
3. The Second Coming   36
4. After Two Years in the Himalayas   56
5. 2024: The Year of Reckoning   69
6. Matters of State   80
7. Modi: The New Vajpayee?   98

SECTION TWO: OPPOSITION

8. Waiting for Rahul   115
9. Role of the Gandhi Dynasty   130
10. Heralding Corruption   136

SECTION THREE: ECONOMY

11. Bouncing Back After a Global Crisis   143
12. Smart Cities and Climate Change   164
13. India, the Startup Hub   181

SECTION FOUR: CHINA

14. A Historical Turning Point   191
15. 1979: The Defining Year   204
16. The Untold Covid Story of Wuhan   213
17. Nehru's China Blunder   226

SECTION FIVE: GEOPOLITICS

18. Unwrapping the Middle East Puzzle   241
19. Russia-Ukraine and the Saxon-Slav Conflict   250

SECTION SIX: SECULARISM

20. Fear of the "Other"   263
21. Hinduism Needs Reform Too   276
22. Adityanath's 80:20 Formula   288
23. Why Indian Secularism is Different
   from Western Secularism   295
24. Behind Kashmir's Veil   305
25. Come One, Come All   318

SECTION SEVEN: LIBERALISM

26. True-Blue Liberals   331

SECTION EIGHT: BRITAIN

27. Disunited Kingdom   349

SECTION NINE: PAKISTAN

28. A State of Terror   367
29. "Terror and Talks Can't Go Hand in Hand"   380

SECTION TEN: MEDIA

30. Shining the Light on India   389
31. A Simmering Anger   401

Index   409

Author's Note

This book is not a biography of Prime Minister Narendra Modi. I met Modi for the first time in 2012 to invite him to a townhall I was organising with the Association of Democratic Reforms (ADR) at Mumbai Press Club.

A year later, Modi, who was then Gujarat chief minister, asked me if I would write his biography. I declined politely and suggested the names of a few authors. Andy Marino, a London-based writer with a PhD in English literature, was finally picked for the job. The book was published in March 2014. It remains an objective account of Modi's life and work.

This book is different. It focuses on Modi's first two five-year terms as prime minister. After almost a decade in power, how successful has Modi been in reforming the economy? Is his foreign policy in an increasingly complex world establishing India as a major global power? In 2014, when Modi took office as prime minister, India's economy was the world's tenth largest. Today it is the fifth largest.

But amidst significant achievements, there have been disappointments as well. Institutional governance has weakened. Transparency has reduced. Discourse has coarsened. The Opposition must share some of the blame. It has often reduced Parliament to a farce.

All of this has diverted attention from the government's achievements: water on tap, last-mile electrification, sanitation, massive infrastructure building, digitisation, free health insurance, and deployment of technology across domains.

This book focuses on social reform as well and redefines the true meaning of secularism and liberalism. It assesses India's freedoms across religion, democracy and media over the decade of Modi's prime ministership.

As India's G20 presidency ends on 30 November 2023, Modi will swing into General Election mode. The Rajasthan, Chhattisgarh, Madhya Pradesh and Telangana assembly elections will provide clues ahead of the 2024 Lok Sabha election.

If Modi secures a third term as prime minister, he will be the first Indian leader since Jawaharlal Nehru to win three successive five-year prime ministerial terms.

The Opposition knows that possibly the only way to stop Modi is to present a united front against him in 2024. But can the clashing personalities of Rahul Gandhi, Mamata Banerjee and Arvind Kejriwal be accommodated under a single political umbrella?

A pressing issue for Modi is the need to build a strong second line of leadership for the future. Home Minister Amit Shah, Uttar Pradesh Chief Minister Yogi Adityanath and Assam Chief Minister Himanta Biswa Sarma are seen as forming a core inner leadership in a third-term Modi prime ministership backed by a technocratic cabinet team including External Affairs Minister S. Jaishankar, Finance Minister Nirmala Sitharaman and others.

The 2024 Lok Sabha election could determine the course of Indian politics for the next decade. With India set to be the world's third largest economy by 2026–27 behind the United States and China, 2024 could prove an historic turning point.

Minhaz Merchant
August 2023

Section One

MODI

ONE

The Making of a Prime Minister

WHAT STRUCK ME ABOUT NARENDRA MODI WHEN I MET HIM FOR THE first time in 2012 were his eyes. They bore into you. The gaze is unflinching.

We met in Mumbai. Modi, then Gujarat's chief minister, was in town for a BJP conclave. His office had suggested a closed-door meeting. Only his press secretary Jagdish Thakkar would be present. I was curious to know more about Modi. After exchanging pleasantries, I invited him to a Mumbai Press Club event where, following his speech, journalists would ask him questions.

Modi's gaze didn't waver. "But who will translate for me?" he asked. "I'm comfortable speaking in Hindi."

"Not a problem," I said.

Modi's face crinkled into a smile. The steely gaze softened. "Okay, Minhazbhai, you organise it. Let me give it a thought."

We then spoke about the country's political situation. In 2011–2012, the Anna Hazare movement was in full swing. Corruption scams involving the Congress-led UPA government were unravelling. Modi himself was not yet a leading national figure. He was focusing on the next Gujarat assembly election scheduled for December 2012.

If he won a third successive term as chief minister, would he emerge as a potential prime ministerial candidate from the BJP? Congress president Sonia Gandhi, for one, thought he well could. She had kept an eye on him since 2007 when he won his second consecutive assembly election. She was quick to label him *maut ka saudagar* for complicity in the 2002 Gujarat riots. But few others in the Congress, and even fewer in the BJP, regarded him, in the first half of 2012, as a serious contender for the prime ministership.

Lal Krishna Advani was the natural heir to Atal Bihari Vajpayee. If the BJP won a majority in the 2014 Lok Sabha election, Advani was the party's obvious candidate for prime ministership. He had served as deputy prime minister to Vajpayee in the National Democratic Alliance (NDA) government and was co-founder of the BJP. Besides, Advani had been a parliamentarian since 1970, first nominated to the Rajya Sabha from Delhi. Modi had been confined to state politics ever since he was parachuted into the chief ministership of Gujarat in October 2001. He lacked experience but not ambition.

✍

A year before I met Modi I had invited Advani, in March 2011, to speak at the Mumbai Press Club and take questions from journalists. The Association of Democratic Reforms (ADR), a leading advocacy group, was my partner in the event. I assembled a distinguished three-member panel to quiz Advani after his speech before throwing the floor open to questions from nearly 200 journalists gathered in front of us.

The panel we put together on the dais comprised N. Ram of *The Hindu*, Kumar Ketkar (then editor of *Maharashtra Times*, now a Congress-nominated Rajya Sabha MP), and Uday Shankar, then head of Star TV and now a global media entrepreneur. The economist Ajit Ranade, co-founder of ADR, was my co-moderator.

Advani was gracious as ever. He took questions from the panel and then from the journalists who packed the main hall of the Press Club, spilling out into the adjoining open area. A large TV screen relayed the event live. With the Congress-led UPA government engulfed in corruption scandals in 2011, Advani knew he had a real shot at the prime ministership in the forthcoming 2014 Lok Sabha election. Modi knew that too. He had organised Advani's *rath yatra* in 1990, three years after joining the BJP from the RSS. He was aware of Advani's national appeal cutting across demographics.

The Sonia Gandhi-led Congress, however, showed scant respect for Advani in Parliament. It extracted an apology from him on the floor of the House for declaring the Congress' 2009 general election victory "illegitimate". Sonia realised early on that Modi was different. He had succeeded in turning Gujarat into a BJP bastion – a proto-Hindutva laboratory that paid huge electoral dividends.

Sonia had once, way back in the late 1980s, told Dr Subramanian Swamy, then a good friend of her husband Prime Minister Rajiv Gandhi, that she was wary of Swamy because unlike other Indian politicians Swamy, was ruthless like a Sicilian. Dr Swamy recently related this story on his social media platforms with glee. By then he had become the *bête noire* of the Gandhi family, launching a series of corruption cases against Sonia, Rahul Gandhi and Priyanka Gandhi-Vadra.

Sonia saw in Modi the same ruthlessness – a ruthlessness Advani lacked. Her instincts told her that Modi, not Advani, would present the real danger to the Congress in 2014.

Through much of 2012, Modi kept a relatively low profile. He knew the December 2012 Gujarat assembly election would be a critical inflection point for his national political ambitions. And national political ambitions he clearly had. When our closed-door meeting in 2012 was over, Modi said softly: "Come to Gandhinagar. We will talk."

∽

And so it was that I found myself in Gandhinagar in early 2013. Modi was in high spirits. He had just won a resounding third term as chief minister of Gujarat in the December 2012 assembly poll. The decks were now cleared for the final push towards a larger national role.

As we spoke, Modi discussed the idea of a biography on him. "There has been so much misinformation about my life, especially over the Godhra riots," he said. "A book that tells the real story of my life is necessary. Why don't you write it?"

I smiled and shook my head. "I've written the biography of former Prime Minister Rajiv Gandhi," I said. "One prime ministerial book is enough."

I explained that it was important for an editor or author not to be typecast. Modi nodded. "Think about it though," he said.

I then suggested that if he wanted a neutral and completely objective examination of his life and work, perhaps a foreign author could be invited to write the book.

Modi liked the idea. When I returned to Mumbai, I got in touch through common associates in London with the British author Andy Marino. A PhD in English literature, Andy took on the assignment with enthusiasm. I introduced him to Modi in Gandhinagar and left them to get on with the project. Published in March 2014 by HarperCollins, the book titled *Narendra Modi: A Political Biography* quickly became a bestseller. It remains one of the most dispassionate accounts of Modi's life and political career.

ॐ

Meanwhile, by June 2013, the die was cast. At the BJP's national executive council meeting in Goa, party president Rajnath Singh declared Modi campaign head for the forthcoming 2014 Lok Sabha election. Not everyone was pleased. Advani boycotted the meeting. In Modi, he saw a formidable rival as the party's prime ministerial candidate. The BJP had not announced its choice as yet. But as campaign head, Modi got down to work. The next few months, he knew, would be crucial.

Shortly after Modi returned to Gandhinagar from the BJP's national executive council meeting in Goa, I met him at his chief minister's office.

Modi had spent the past several weeks in August 2013 campaigning for the BJP. As campaign head he addressed multiple rallies across the country. The strain appeared to be telling on him. Sitting at his large office table, he looked uncharacteristically tired.

There was nobody else present at our meeting. I told Modi that I was speaking from a strictly neutral position. I said he was making a mistake campaigning up and down the country, putting in the hard yards, without an assurance that he would be appointed the BJP's prime ministerial candidate. Let others campaign too, I said, if they wanted the top job.

Modi appeared surprised at my vehemence. "You're addressing several election rallies a day," I continued. "At the end of it all, others will benefit. Stop doing everybody else's work for them unless the party nominates you as the prime ministerial candidate – or you decide you don't want the job."

Modi said nothing. He knew the Congress was imploding. The economy had tanked. There was policy paralysis. Corruption scandals were erupting. Campaigning was getting into full swing in August 2013. The BJP knew it had more than a fair chance of winning the May 2014 general election. Whoever the party chose as its prime ministerial candidate could well be prime minister in another nine months.

The choice for the BJP had by now narrowed down to Advani and Modi. I retained a soft corner for Advani. He had been a regular columnist along with several other writers, including K. Subrahmanyam, Shashi Tharoor and Henry Kissinger, for over a decade in my first media startup, Sterling Newspapers Pvt. Ltd.

I knew almost no one else in the BJP except Advani and now Modi. But I believed, as did many, that the overriding need was to evict the UPA2 government—enmeshed in serious corruption scams—from power. I had no particular affinity for the BJP. But in practical terms, it seemed to me the only political formation that could defeat the discredited Congress-led UPA.

There was ferocious opposition, however, within the party to Modi as the BJP's prime ministerial candidate. The opposition came, principally from the party's old guard led by Advani and Murli Manohar Joshi. It is difficult to imagine today, given Modi's complete command over the BJP, that he had to struggle to win approval from the party's top leadership barely months before the 2014 Lok Sabha election.

At one stage Advani threatened to resign from the BJP if Modi was named the party's prime ministerial candidate. It took calls from the RSS *Sarsanghchalak* Mohan Bhagwat to make him change his mind.

✑

And yet Advani remained resolutely opposed to Modi's prime ministerial candidature. In the process, as the BJP bickered, the Congress-led UPA government was seemingly being let off the hook. The Anna Hazare anti-corruption movement had lost momentum. Arvind Kejriwal was about to break away from Anna and launch the Aam Aadmi Party (AAP), with a wink and a nudge from the Congress to divide the pro-BJP vote.

Would the anti-corruption movement end in a whimper? Would the corrupt shenanigans in the AgustaWestland, 2G and coal scams go unpunished? With hindsight, a decade later, that is exactly what has happened. The BJP in government has been far less keen to bring the corrupt to book than when it was in the Opposition.

But in early August 2013, with the Advani camp unwilling to relent in its opposition to Modi, I took the liberty to write an open letter to Advani whose regular column, titled *The Opposition*, I had edited and published for over ten years in one of my media firm's magazines. The Congress was then in power and we wanted to give every shade of political opinion a platform and a voice. Other Opposition leaders, including the late Madhu Dandavate and IK Gujral, were also our monthly columnists.

The purpose of the open letter was to respectfully tell Advani that Modi, and not him, had the best chance of ending a decade of UPA misgovernance. There was nothing personal in this. I believed – and still do – that Advani in different circumstances, at a different time, would have perhaps made a better prime minister than Modi. But these were extraordinary times. This is what I wrote to Advani:

Respected Shri Advaniji,

I am taking the liberty, sir, of writing to you at a critical juncture in Indian politics. This is the most important inflection point since 1977 when, following the revocation of the Emergency, you first became a minister. But first some background.

In mid-1980, when the BJP did not yet exist, I requested you to write a monthly column for a magazine I had just launched. The column was titled "The Opposition" and you instantly and generously agreed.

I was just 25 years old and you had just completed your term as Information & Broadcasting Minister in the short-lived Janata government led by Prime Minister Morarji Desai.

Your column, published in our magazine alongside articles by leaders like IK Gujral and Madhu Dandavate, was designed to give a voice to the Opposition in Indira Gandhi's and Rajiv Gandhi's governments spanning the 1980s. It proved among the magazine's most popular columns and continued well into the 1990s.

The NDA government took office in 1998 and you became Deputy Prime Minister. My publications were as critical of the BJP-led NDA government during 1998–2004 as they had been of earlier Congress governments.

The first principle of journalism is to be constructively

adversarial with the government of the day and give the Opposition an equal platform for debate and dissent.

The second principle of journalism is to maintain "arm's length" from the government except for professional work. Hence, despite our decades-old editorial relationship, I did not contact you between 1998 and 2004 when you were Home Minister and then Deputy Prime Minister.

Indeed, you explicitly referred to this on 28 March 2011 when you addressed the inaugural **Face the Press** programme at the Mumbai Press Club which I moderated along with Ajit Ranade of the Association for Democratic Reforms (ADR) and three panelists: N Ram of *The Hindu*, Kumar Ketkar[1] of *Maharashtra Times* and Uday Shankar of Star TV[2].

This is how you prefaced your outstanding speech on Democracy and Accountable Governance at the event which was televised live:

"When I received this invitation from Minhaz Merchant in February 2011, I felt really honoured that he had thought of me and said he would like me to be the first speaker in this series, though I told him that it would have been more appropriate if the Prime Minister, Dr Manmohan Singh, had been called for the inaugural Face the Press."

Though Dr Manmohan Singh was in fact the chief guest at the launch of my biography of the late industrialist Aditya Birla, I had no hesitation in choosing you to be the first national leader to address the inaugural **Face the Press** event. I have always regarded you as one of India's most distinguished statesmen.

As you know, sir, the 2014 general election can throw up three possible outcomes: NDA 3, UPA 3 or UF 2.

And as the pre-eminent leader who, along with Atal Bihari Vajpayee, founded the BJP in December 1980 and took the

[1]Kumar is now a Congress MP in the Rajya Sabha.
[2]Uday Shankar is co-founder of a media venture.

party's Lok Sabha tally from 2 seats in 1984 to 182 seats in 1998, you know better than anyone else how critical the next 10 months leading up to the 2014 Lok Sabha poll are.

The only way an NDA 3 government can be formed in 2014 is if the BJP nominates a strong, decisive prime ministerial candidate.

He must satisfy four criteria: **one**, he must be incorruptible; **two** he must have a record of good governance; **three**, he must have the support of the party cadre; and **four**, he must be a vote-multiplier.

Every opinion poll in the past three months has shown that only one of the BJP's state-level and central leaders can deliver the Lok Sabha majority the BJP needs: Narendra Modi.

As the most respected leader in the BJP, your mentorship of the party's next prime ministerial candidate could decide the outcome of the 2014 general election and set the course of Indian politics for the next decade.

The three-day BJP National Executive meeting in Goa which begins on June 7 presents you an historical opportunity to make the right choice for India.

Yours truly
Minhaz Merchant

The BJP's president at the time was Rajnath Singh. He had been instrumental in ensuring Modi was declared campaign head at the BJP's national executive council meeting in Goa in June 2013 in the teeth of fierce opposition. He now played a key role in convincing the Advani camp to finally back down. But it took that final intervention from the RSS in September 2013 to seal Modi as the BJP's prime ministerial candidate.

Uncertainty over, six months of hard campaigning lay ahead.

Watching the drama unfold, Sonia and Rahul Gandhi were worried. They knew an implacable Modi presented a far bigger electoral threat to the Congress in the 2014 Lok Sabha poll than the mild-mannered Advani. Personal attacks on Modi from the Congress' well-oiled ecosystem of politicians, journalists, activists, lawyers, academics and civil society now took on a sharper tone.

I met Modi again in Gandhinagar to discuss progress on Andy Marino's book shortly after Modi was appointed the BJP's prime ministerial candidate. While Andy was writing the book, I had agreed to co-publish it in a joint venture with HarperCollins India. Modi was meanwhile campaigning around the country. He had stopped by in Gandhinagar for a few days before going back on the campaign trail. Despite the feverish activity around him, he maintained his usual Zen-like calm as we spoke. Modi recalled the day when, as a 17-year-old, he left home to wander around in the Himalayas, talking to, learning from, and eating with, monks.

He returned home two years later, packed his bags and, at 19, left his family to join the RSS. Modi's parents were distraught. But their 19-year-old son was adamant. He would not return home. His life and work would now belong to the RSS.

As he spoke of those early days, Modi looked out at the space adjoining his office. It had a traditional Gujarati swing. Modi gazed wistfully at it as if he would one day prefer sitting there in quiet monk-like contemplation once the hurly burly of politics was over for him.

Before leaving, I handled him a typed sheet of paper. It contained a list of distinguished foreign and economic policy experts who could be part of his advisory councils if and when he won the general election. He studied the list for a minute, nodded and said: "But these are very big people."

"You'll need all the advice you can get," I replied. "Besides, apart from addressing election campaign rallies for the next few months, it might be a good idea to publish a white paper on foreign and economic issues."

Modi shook his head. Speaking mostly in Gujarati he said: "Prime Minister Manmohan Singh *saab* has a large Prime Minister's Office (PMO). At this stage I don't want to appear to be interfering on, especially, foreign policy issues."

Within months, however, Modi shed his reticence. In rally after rally he attacked the Congress on its policy on Pakistan, on dynastic politics, on corruption and on terrorism. The Gandhis were the principal target but Manmohan Singh came in for sharp criticism as well as a puppet prime minister remote controlled by Sonia and Rahul.

In January 2014, I met Modi again, this time at his official residence. Not once during these interactions, at his office or his home, was any member of the Citizen's Action Committee (CAC), then run by Prashant Kishor, later renamed I-PAC, or anyone from Modi's election team, present. The campaign strategy of the BJP *per se* didn't interest me. It's important in journalism to not only be politically neutral but to be seen to be politically neutral. That is why I avoided contact with any of Modi's cabinet ministers – then and since. To this day, of the over 2,500 people Prime Minister Modi follows on Twitter, I am one of the very few who has never followed him back.

As we sat in Modi's residential study in January 2014 came the news that Arvind Kejriwal and a group of rowdy Aam Aadmi Party (AAP) members were driving down the Ahmedabad highway towards Modi's home in an effort to confront him over allegedly fake encounter cases by the Gujarat police.

Modi reacted calmly to the news. "Let him come," he shrugged, continuing our conversation. In the event, Kejriwal was stopped by the police several miles before he reached the high-security zone where Modi lived.

Kejriwal led the Opposition's invective against Modi. In a politically astute move, Kejriwal stood against Modi in Varanasi in the 2014 Lok Sabha election. He was beaten by nearly 4 lakh votes, narrowly escaping losing his deposit. Later, Kejriwal would base his nascent political career as Delhi chief minister by routinely abusing Modi, calling him a "psychopath" and a "coward". It would take years for Kejriwal to realise that this abuse was fetching him diminishing returns. His relationship with Modi mellowed but remained volatile.

Kejriwal made peace by apologising for defaming the late Arun Jaitley, the former finance minister and defence minister in Modi's Union cabinet, ending the criminal case Jaitley had filed against Kejriwal. The transformation of Kejriwal from an opportunist – who used anarchy and abuse as political strategy – into a relatively mature politician whose party won the Punjab assembly election in a landslide in March 2022, took several years. And even then the gene of opportunism and anarchy never wholly left him.

ॐ

All this lay in the future. For now, on 26 May 2014, as India's newly elected prime minister, Modi's task had just begun. Shortly after his inauguration in front of South Asian leaders, including then Pakistani Prime Minister Nawaz Sharif, Modi got down to work. The first briefings he received over the next few days were from the finance ministry. The details shocked him.

The economy was in far worse shape than he had imagined. Banks were bleeding. Large Non-Performing Assets (NPAs) lay hidden in bank and corporate balance sheets. GDP growth had stalled. Inflation was high and rising. Foreign exchange reserves had fallen to a little over $300 billion, covering barely eight months of imports. Corruption in defence acquisitions was rampant.

Modi toyed with the idea of publishing a white paper on the parlous state of the economy. He decided not to because, as he revealed in several interviews later, foreign investment would have been affected.

I had written on many occasions that this was a mistake. I touched upon Modi's missteps in his first year as prime minister at an event in May 2015 organised by the Mumbai Press Club.

According to one report[3], "To understand the political economy the nation has seen in the past year, The Press Club, Mumbai, held a face-to-face discussion on *One Year of Modi Sarkar* between Rajdeep Sardesai and Minhaz Merchant. 'Has Narendra Modi changed the face of Indian politics? To be fair to him, he has brought a lot of visible energy to the government in the past one year,' said Rajdeep Sardesai. 'Contrast his prime ministership with that of Manmohan Singh. It was not that Manmohan Singh did not go to other countries. In fact, when he went to Germany, we got far more investments from the Germans but the overall choreography has created a sense of energetic dynamism which has infused a sense of hope among industry and people. A sense that you finally have a leader.'

"Sardesai also opined that the PM's strength could be his biggest weakness; namely the concentration of power around one person. 'The PM's strength is that he is very good at executing projects but he also needs to understand that he alone cannot get everything done. We are seeing that he is understanding this slowly. He needs the support of people like Mayawati, Mamata Banerjee, etc., to pass his legislations,' he said. Sardesai added that the bureaucracy has been used to a certain way of functioning and they are now trying to come to terms with the PM's dynamism and way of working.

"Minhaz Merchant, meanwhile, opined that private equity investment has increased, which he called an indication of the hope people still hold in Modi's leadership. Merchant also expressed surprise over the Congress targeting Modi with the line *suit-boot ki sarkar*. 'Modi has actually been keeping industrialists at arm's length and not allowing them to get any unlawful benefits,' he

[3]e4m, 20 May 2015.

said. Sardesai also agreed with Merchant that even industrialists who thought that the Modi sarkar would lead to quick benefits have been made to wait till the various schemes reach fruition.

"Among the issues that Merchant criticised the Modi government in its first year were regressive taxation and, what Merchant said, was the lack of a proper and strict foreign policy in relation to Pakistan. Sardesai added that it will be very important for Modi to ensure that the concentration of power around his personality does not lead to a lack of initiative among the bureaucracy and his own ministers due to fear.'"

Modi's first-term prime ministership began in a flurry of activity. Foreign policy was a priority. Fixing the broken economy was another. But there was a complication. Though the Congress had plunged from 206 Lok Sabha seats in the 2009 general election to 44 seats in 2014, it had left behind an ecosystem of loyalists across the bureaucratic spectrum.

The ecosystem had been carefully built over decades of dominant Congress rule. Between 1947 and 2014, the Congress had been in power at the Centre for fifty-five out of sixty-seven post-independence years. Its loyalists included Left-leaning academics, historians, activists, bureaucrats, lawyers and journalists. The ecosystem, promoted, patronised and protected by the Congress, enjoyed power and privilege without oversight or accountability. Marxist historians dictated the political and social narrative. Text books reflected a quasi-colonial mindset. Dozens of educational institutions were named after members of the Nehru-Gandhi family. So were roads, airports, sealinks, parks, colleges, planetariums, libraries, museums and welfare schemes.

Much of this dynastic narcissism took place after Nehru's death. Nehru himself was a visionary in several respects. He established the Indian Institutes of Managements (IIMs) and Indian Institutes of Technology (IITs), built steel plants in a plundered post-colonial country bereft of infrastructure, and crafted a nuanced foreign policy. He failed, however, to read both Pakistan and China correctly. Nehru erred grievously by granting over-generous terms to Pakistan in the 1960 World Bank-midwifed Indus Waters Treaty (IWT). He underestimated China's latent hostility that led to the 1962 Sino-Indian war. India's defeat broke Nehru's spirit. He died 19 months later, in May 1964.

Nehru's daughter Indira Gandhi took the wrong fork in the road, leading the country towards economic socialism. It cost India dearly. In the two decades between 1966, when Mrs Gandhi assumed office, and 1984, when she was assassinated, India's average economic growth rate ambled along at just over 3 per cent a year. During the same period, the tiger economies of Southeast Asia, ranging from Singapore, Thailand and Malaysia to the Philippines, Taiwan and Indonesia, grew at an average of over 8 per cent a year. Those two lost decades were to prove costly for India's economy. Mrs Gandhi was prime minister for the entire period between 1966 and 1984 except for the short post-Emergency interregnum in 1977–79.

Fast-forward to 2014. Modi's first three years in office produced robust economic growth. In 2014–15, GDP rose 7.4 per cent; in 2015–16, it surged by 7.9 per cent; and in 2016–17, despite the disruption caused by demonetisation in November 2016, GDP still increased by 8.2 per cent, later revised downwards to 7.4 per cent.

But warning signs had started flashing. The full effect of demonetisation, which squeezed lakhs of small cash-reliant firms out of business, was felt in 2017–18. The introduction of the Goods and Services Tax (GST) in July 2017 caused further disruption. GDP growth in 2017–18 sagged to 7.2 per cent. Worse was to follow. The economy began to stall in 2018–19 with growth plunging to 6.8 per cent. By 2019–20, the news was even grimmer: in the last financial year before the Covid pandemic struck, GDP growth fell to 4.2 per cent, later revised downwards to below 4 per cent.

Demonetisation and GST bludgeoned the micro, small and medium enterprise (MSME) sector. Jobs were lost as small businesses shut shop. Towards the end of the sixth year of Modi's prime ministership in March 2020, India's economic growth seemed to have hit a nadir. It hadn't. A perfect storm was brewing. It would strike the Indian economy with gale force in March 2020 as the Covid-19 pandemic swept the world, plunging India's economy into its worst crisis in over half-a-century.

✍

But back in February 2019, other thoughts occupied Modi's mind. Campaigning for the 2019 Lok Sabha election, Modi again crisscrossed the country, addressing hundreds of rallies. His *ma-beta* charge against the Congress, used so effectively in the 2014 campaign, had morphed into a more forceful assault on political dynasts and their corrupt, corrosive sense of entitlement.

Congress President Rahul Gandhi had meanwhile shed his reticence and attacked Modi ferociously. Emboldened by the Congress' victories in the Rajasthan, Madhya Pradesh and Chhattisgarh assembly elections in December 2018, Rahul used the taunt *chowkidar chor hai* throughout the electoral campaign. Modi had earlier declared himself the *chowkidar* (guardian) of the country, protecting it from the machinations of corrupt dynasts. Rahul turned the epithet against the incumbent prime minister.

Citing the ₹ 59,000-crore Rafale fighter jet deal as proof of corruption in the Modi government, Rahul's attack was relentless – and unsuccessful. When the results of the general election were announced on 23 May 2019, the Congress had won a mere 52 Lok Sabha seats, an increase of eight seats over its 2014 tally. The BJP swept back to power with 303 seats.

Rahul took responsibility for the party's second successive humiliating defeat and resigned as Congress president. But he continued to call the shots in what now seemed, more than ever, a family enterprise rather than a political party.

Modi had more urgent matters to worry about than the implosion in the Congress. After the Pulwama terrorist attack by the Pakistan-backed Jaish-e-Mohammad terrorist group on 14 February 2019, Modi had ordered an air strike deep into Pakistan on a terrorist training camp in Balakot. The attack, following the September 2016 surgical commando ground strike across the Line of Control (LoC), displayed a new muscularity in India's approach to Pakistan.

With China too, earlier inhibitions gradually gave way to a stronger line on Beijing's provocations along the Line of Actual Control (LAC). Matters would escalate with China in eastern Ladakh. But for the moment Modi basked in the glow of the BJP's landslide victory in the May 2019 general election. A packed political and legislative agenda lay ahead.

೭ఞ

How much had Modi changed at the start of his second term in 2019 since I first met him in 2012?

He was now a global statesman with an international profile. After the results of the 2019 Lok Sabha election were declared, all eyes were on Modi's new cabinet. Would there be major changes? With former Finance Minister Arun Jaitley terminally ill (he passed away in July 2019), former External Affairs Minister Sushma Swaraj suffering from serious ailments (she died in August 2019) and former Defence Minister Manohar Parrikar having succumbed to cancer in March 2019, Modi had lost over a short period of five months the services of three of his four most important ministers.

Traditionally, the four senior ministers who serve on the powerful Cabinet Committee on Security (CCS) hold the home, defence, finance and external affairs portfolios. Without Jaitley, Swaraj and Parrikar, who held three of those four portfolios,

Modi faced a challenge of talent and experience at the top end of his cabinet. He shuffled Home Minister Rajnath Singh – the only survivor among the big four—to defence. BJP party president Amit Shah was inducted as home minister. Nirmala Sitharaman, who had been elevated to finance minister after Jaitley took ill, retained her portfolio. The surprise addition to the big four was S. Jaishankar, a former foreign secretary who was appointed external affairs minister. It would be the first time a bureaucrat – an Indian Foreign Service (IFS) officer – had been given charge of the critical foreign ministry.

Jaishankar is an erudite and principled man. Context and disclosure are required here. Jaishankar's late father, K. Subrahmanyam, served for several years as head of the Institute for Defence Studies and Analysis (IDSA). He is credited with establishing India's nuclear doctrine. Subrahmanyam was a contributing editor in my first media startup for a decade and a columnist for another ten years in my second media startup before he sadly passed away in 2011.

His son Jaishankar had a distinguished career in the foreign service. In August 2016, when he was foreign secretary, Jaishankar requested a private meeting with me. I flew down from Mumbai for the day. We met at his official Delhi residence for a little over two hours. India's future strategy with respect to China and Pakistan was the principal focus of our discussion (which must remain confidential as it was off the record). The idea was to create a strategic blueprint for a policy on Pakistan and China.

A former ambassador to Washington and Beijing, Jaishankar speaks Mandarin, Russian, Hungarian, Japanese (his wife is Japanese), Tamil, Hindi and of course impeccable English. Though entirely unconnected with our conversation, India's surgical strike across the LoC in September 2016, a month after my meeting with Jaishankar, following a terror attack on the Uri army camp, showed the Modi government's determination to take Pakistan-abetted terrorism head-on. After my meeting with Jaishankar, I was driven to the prime minister's residence on 7 Lok Kalyan Marg. Security in the three-bungalow complex is tight. Modi holds key meetings here.

After his retirement as foreign secretary, Jaishankar briefly served with the Tata Group as a strategic advisor. Meanwhile, following his landslide victory in the May 2019 general election, Modi mulled inducting technocrats with specific domain knowledge into his cabinet. No one was more surprised than Jaishankar himself when he received a phone call that the prime minister was considering him for the key foreign minister's post. It was unprecedented. Never before had a former foreign secretary been appointed foreign minister.

Jaishankar has proved one of the standout ministers in the Modi cabinet. He was confronted, within a year of being sworn in, with China's aggression along the LAC in the spring of 2020. Amid the early diplomatic effort mounted by the ministry of external affairs (MEA) to defuse the standoff, Jaishankar found time to write a meticulously researched book *The India Way: Strategies for an Uncertain World*. In it, he made a key point about India's geopolitical challenges and opportunities:

> As the world moves towards greater diversification the case for enhanced participation in global value chains will strengthen further. India can move more purposefully in this direction but it must balance that with building up its domestic capabilities. A more capable India that will emerge as a result of greater self-reliance will surely also have more to offer. Far from turning its back on the world, India is actually preparing to participate more but with better preparation. After all, Atmanirbhar Bharat does coexist with Vasudhaiva Kutumbakam (the world is a family).
>
> Rising in the midst of global turbulence, a lot will depend on India's ability to distinguish itself from others. The last

few years have demonstrated a growing Indian capacity to contribute to the global discourse and make a difference to international outcomes. We have significantly shaped the connectivity debate and backed that up with a plethora of projects, including in our immediate neighbourhood. A single-minded campaign against terrorism has brought that issue into sharp focus in key world forums. Where maritime security and humanitarian assistance and disaster relief (HADR) situations are concerned, India has emerged as a key player, especially in the Indian Ocean.

At the political level, our confidence in overcoming the hesitations of history has opened up new space. Strategic clarifications have helped to exploit that more effectively. Overall, the Indian persona is much more in evidence in a variety of ways. Overall, our footprint has visibly grown in Africa, as also in many other regions where past connections were weaker. Indeed, this combination of significant engagement and deeper collaboration that extends across continents prepares us for a global mindset. The world may be on the threshold of a new decade; but India is ready for the next phase of its own evolution.

The world we are poised to enter is a subject of intense argumentation. It is further complicated by transformational changes in politics, economics and technology. Coming to terms with the declining shelf-life of the old-post-1945 order is itself difficult. It is a still bigger challenge to fully recognise the elements which drive the one in the making. Assumptions of various dimension are being questioned, at home as well as abroad. What we can just about agree upon is that the world is in the midst of a real transition. And our reading of the directions we head is influenced by our own preferences, interests, viewpoints and hopes.

Many of Jaishankar's thoughts reflect Modi's evolving worldview, especially in the transformed geopolitical environment following the Russia-Ukraine war.

✍

After taking office as Prime Minister in May 2014, Modi was proactive in building close links with the Gulf states, Japan, the United States and the littoral nations in the South China Sea. Now, following his inauguration for a second term in May 2019, Modi focused on domestic issues. Newly appointed Home Minister Amit Shah was tasked with piloting two key laws in parliament: the J&K Reorganisation Bill and the Citizenship (Amendment) Act (CAA). Both would prove deeply controversial.

The Citizenship (Amendment) Act has two clear objectives, one stated, the other unstated. The stated objective is to offer citizenship rights to Hindus, Sikhs, Jains, Buddhists, Parsis and Christians who faced persecution in Pakistan, Bangladesh and Afghanistan and arrived in India as illegal refugee-migrants before 31 December 2014. The unstated objective is to polarise the Hindu electorate by leaving persecuted Muslim refugee-migrants out of the CAA's warm citizenship embrace.

The CAA, however, is not targeted at India's 210 million resident Muslims who retain full Constitutional rights. Its messaging is aimed squarely at India's 1.10 billion Hindus. Beneath the BJP's emollient arguments in Parliament on CAA lies electoral ambition. CAA and the National Register of Citizens (NCR) are majoritarian electoral weapons designed for use in the 2024 Lok Sabha election.

The actual merits and demerits of the CAA have not been fully decoded. Consider first what the gazette notification on the CAA issued by the Ministry of Law and Justice says. Here is the critical clause 2: "In the Citizenship Act, 1955 (hereinafter referred to as the principal Act), in section 2, in sub-section (1), in clause (b), the following proviso shall be inserted, namely: Provided that any person belonging to Hindu, Sikh, Buddhist, Jain, Parsi or Christian community from Afghanistan, Bangladesh or Pakistan, who entered into India on or before the 31st day of December, 2014 and who has been exempted by the Central Government by or under clause (c) of sub-section (2) of section 3 of the Passport (Entry into India) Act, 1920 or from the application of the provisions of the Foreigners Act, 1946 or any rule or order made thereunder, shall not be treated as illegal migrant for the purposes of this Act."

Clause 3 makes the intent of the CAA even clearer: "After section 6A of the principal Act, the following section shall be inserted, namely: '6B. (1) The Central Government or an authority specified by it in this behalf may, subject to such conditions, restrictions and manner as may be prescribed, on an application made in this behalf, grant a certificate of registration or certificate of naturalisation to a person referred to in the proviso to clause (b) of sub-section (1) of section 2.'

In short, stateless and paperless refugees who entered India before 31 December 2014, will get near-automatic citizenship—as long as they belong to the six non-Muslim religions identified in Clause 2.

Whether Article 14 of the Constitution on the validity of classification of groups holds or not will be adjudicated by a larger Constitution Bench. One way of defusing opposition to the CAA is by simply replacing the following 10 words in Clause 2 of the Act: "...belonging to Hindu, Sikh, Buddhist, Jain, Parsi, or Christian community..." with the following four words: "...belonging to persecuted minorities...".

But what about the National Population Register (NPR) and the National Register of Citizens (NRC)? The government has announced that providing information under the NPR is both a constitutional requirement and entirely voluntary. But won't the NPR lead to the ominous NRC? The government knows the nationwide NRC will not be approved in the Rajya Sabha with even allies opposing it.

The NRC is designed to weaponise the CAA. Without the

NRC, the CAA—especially with modified wording—is neutered. Shah has said categorically that he won't withdraw the CAA. But if the Supreme Court nudges him, will he tweak those 10 key words? Once anti-CAA sentiment has had its desired polarising effect over a sufficiently long period, he may. As for the NRC, though unworkable in practice, it will remain on the BJP's agenda like an electoral Sword of Damocles right up to May 2024. It is a strategy Modi has perfected over the years.

∞

But it was as a teenager that Modi first began to crystalise his thoughts. Andy Marino, author of *Narendra Modi: A Political Biography,* spent weeks interviewing Modi and attending his rallies. Among his most insightful observations was how a teenage Modi's two-year-long journey through India shaped his character and political future:

> Exactly what Narendra Modi did between the ages of seventeen and nineteen, where he went and why, remains obscure. Scraps of information from his walkabout, however, can help assemble a rough itinerary and give a theme to his meanderings. Sitting at home today, he smiles and waves away questions about those years of wandering. But some hints emerge. More than anything else, it was a pilgrimage in the footsteps of Swami Vivekananda. By the time he left home, Narendra had devoured most of the Swami's literary works, lent to him by a Vadnagar local, Dr Vasantbhai Parikh. Vivekananda had made a deep and, it would turn out, a permanent impression on the young man.
>
> Narendra set out from home, carrying very little. He owned few clothes anyway, and what money he had put away from what he had earned – not only from his father's tea stall but also from lugging containers of cooking oil for a few paise a time for a local businessman – would be barely

enough to sustain him for two weeks, never mind two years.
But it is good to be poor when young because it offers
the priceless opportunity to learn not to be dependent on
money. This would prove to be one of the most valuable
lessons Narendra learned during his period of uncertainty.
It would pay dividends later on, hardening or inoculating
Modi against temptations presented by a career in the chaotic
world of Indian politics.

Young Narendra initially made his way to West Bengal
and to the Belur Math, on the west bank of the Hooghly
river near Calcutta (as it then was), sometime in the early
summer of 1968. The Math is the principal temple-monastery
and headquarters of Vivekananda's Ramakrishna Mission,
established at the end of the 19th century, although the
present building was built only in 1935. At the time Narendra
visited, Swami Madhabanandaji Maharaj was its president.
Unfortunately for Narendra, he discovered the Math was
strictly a postgraduate institution and the Swami told him if
he wanted to study there, he would first have to complete
his college education.

After a short stay of about a week at the Math, and an
exploratory sojourn in Calcutta and its hinterland, Narendra
headed north. Whether he paid his way by working or was
dependent on alms is lost in the mist of time, but at one
point he found himself, travelling via Siliguri, as far north-east
as Guwahati or even further, and deep in a 'remote jungle'.
There, miles from civilization, he stumbled across a hermit
or mendicant with whom he struck up a friendship. The
man was 'very thin, it seemed that he had transparent skin'.
There was little sense of urgency in Narendra's journeying,
and he spent about a month helping in the ascetic's garden
plot, spending time discussing 'spiritual matters', before he
decided to move on.

Eventually, Narendra arrived at the other monastery

Swami Vivekananda had set up, the pleasant bungalow of the Advaita Ashram near Almora, in the foothills of the Himalayas. It makes sense that he would have made his way north after Calcutta before heading west again on a fresh path, picking his way across Bihar and Uttar Pradesh into what is now Uttarakhand, because he had already crossed India once, form the west, after leaving Gujarat.

Narendra's adventure was an exploration. But was he seriously seeking to become a monk at this point, or was he simply a little lost and unsure of what direction his life should take? At Almora he could at least absorb some more of Vivekananda's influence, although the answer he received from the monks was the same as in Calcutta: graduate from college and then try again.

Eventually, after at least another year of wandering, Narendra returned to Gujarat and the final location associated with Swami Vivekananda, the Ramakrishna Mission in Rajkot. His route there took him via Delhi and then south through Rajasthan. He wished to see new places and not retrace his steps. He skirted the Himalayas as far north-west as Himachal Pradesh, then a Union Territory, a place Modi still adores and whose electoral charge he would get over 20 years later as BJP general secretary. Not quite nineteen, Narendra was still on his own discovery of India. Many ideas formed in those impressionable years. They have stayed with him, he admits. But he prefers today to talk of the future, of his vision for India, governance, development and economic reforms.

At the Rajkot Mission, as if playing his role in a mystic parable, Narendra was turned away from the monkish life for a third time. Swami Atmasthanandaji Maharaj, who arrived in 1966 and incidentally still remains there, was the one who finally told Narendra that he should forget about becoming a Ramakrishna monk, that he was fundamentally unsuited to it. This is certain, because Modi himself admitted it when he returned to the Belur Math in Kolkata in 2013 and met the Swami there. In fact, Modi thanked him for his wise guidance of many years before.

The monks were astute in 1969, and identified in young Narendra what he could not yet see in himself: that whichever quest he was on, it was not one that would be best answered in the life of an ascetic monk. Swami Atmasthanandaji told him that his destiny lay elsewhere, and elsewhere he should seek it. From that point onwards Narendra changed course. The making of Modi was about to begin.

2019: Storming to Victory

THE SHEER SCALE OF THE BJP-LED NDA'S VICTORY IN THE 2019 LOK Sabha elections was unprecedented. The BJP was confronted by a powerful BSP-SP-RLD mega-alliance in Uttar Pradesh. It was expected to cut the BJP down to size. It didn't: the BJP won 62 out of 80 Lok Sabha seats. In Jharkhand, another Congress-led *gathbandhan* failed as well. In Karnataka, the Congress-JD(S) alliance was soundly defeated.

In states like Madhya Pradesh, Chhattisgarh, Rajasthan and Gujarat, where the BJP appeared to have reached saturation point, the party repeated its 2014 parliamentary sweep. The biggest story of the 2019 general election, of course, was West Bengal, where the BJP ended the Trinamool Congress' eight-year-long monopoly with 18 of the state's 42 Lok Sabha seats.

The BJP-led NDA's landslide victory in the 2019 general election was historic for several reasons. This was the first time since Independence that a non-Congress-led government had won two successive five-year terms. That led to several inferences. First, the 2019 Lok Sabha election marked the end of the old order—the calcified ecosystem populated by the entitled, the self-important, and the out-of-touch.

Second, the scale of the BJP's win marked a tectonic shift in the electoral plates that had bedrocked Indian politics since 1947: a decisive consolidation of the Hindu vote. The Congress and its allies based their electoral arithmetic on the fact that if they locked-in the 20 per cent Muslim and Christian vote (which often votes in blocs), and drew away a slice of the secular, liberal, Left-leaning Hindu vote, the party would be assured of a vote share of around 35 per cent.

In a first-past-the-post (FPTP) parliamentary electoral system, that's usually good enough to win a comfortable majority in the Lok Sabha. It worked exactly to plan through the 1970s and 1980s. The Congress won 43.68 per cent vote share and 352 seats in 1971, 42.69 per cent vote share and 374 seats in 1980, 48.12 per cent vote share and 414 seats in 1984 and 35.66 per cent vote share and 244 seats in 1991.

This is when the Congress first began to misread the national mood. Its vote share in the 1996 Lok Sabha election, post-Babri Masjid, dropped to 28.80 per cent. Its seat tally plummeted to 140. The Congress had always assumed that the Hindu vote was so divided that it would not support a "Hindu nationalist" party like the BJP.

It was right. Though Atal Bihari Vajpayee formed the BJP-led NDA government in 1998 and 1999, the BJP's vote share never went above 30 per cent. In 1998, it was 25.59 per cent. In 1999, it slid to 23.75 per cent. In 2004, it dipped further to 22.16 per cent and in 2009, its vote share fell to 18.80 per cent. The Congress' assumption seemed to have been borne out: despite Babri Masjid, Ayodhya and the Ram Mandir, the 80 per cent Hindu vote seemed simply too divided to hurt the Congress electorally.

But what exactly is the Hindu vote? Broadly, Brahmins and other upper castes (Thakurs, Nairs, Menons, Kayasths, etc.) make up 25 per cent of the Hindu vote. Dalits comprise another 25 per cent. OBCs, EBCs and the rest make up the middle 50 per cent. The Congress believed Dalits would not vote for a Brahmin-dominated party like the BJP. The middle 50 per cent would vote on regional and linguistic grounds. And of the 25 per cent upper castes, while the BJP would get a large slice, it would not be enough to break through the 30 per cent vote share barrier.

An OBC *chaiwala* called Narendra Modi upended these elitist calculations in 2014. He kept the BJP's upper caste vote intact, drew in OBCs and EBCs, and made inroads with Dalits. As a result, the BJP in 2014 for the first time in its history crashed through the 30 per cent vote share barrier. The BJP-led NDA took overall vote share to nearly 39 per cent. In an FPTP electoral system, that was enough to give the BJP and NDA 282 and 336 seats respectively in the 2014 Lok Sabha.

In the run-up to the 2019 general election, the Congress realised the folly of its decades-old strategy. It was too late. Years of resentment among moderate Hindus at being taken for granted by the Congress and its allies finally boiled over. That simmering anger helped coalesce the Hindu vote in 2019 for the BJP-led NDA across upper castes, OBCs and Dalits, smashing through the 40 per cent vote share barrier. The NDA's nearly 45 per cent vote share in 2019 was, extraordinarily enough, not far removed from the Congress' vote share (48.12 per cent) in Rajiv Gandhi's landslide victory in 1984. The BJP on its own recorded 37.4 per cent vote share, a historic high that helped it to win 303 Lok Sabha seats. The NDA secured a record 353 seats.

Modi won the 2019 Lok Sabha election for other equally important reasons. Many villages received electricity for the first time in their lives. With free LPG cylinders, women were spared the hazard of cooking on polluting wood fires, never mind the expensive refills. Their villages, again for the first time, got paved roads and toilets. The poor received access to universal health insurance, bank accounts and subsidies that were transferred digitally into those new accounts without corrupt middlemen siphoning off their share.

Rahul Gandhi's defeat in Amethi at the hands of the feisty Smriti Irani in May 2019 meanwhile set the alarm bells ringing—

but the Congress remained tone-deaf as far as the dynasty's supreme control of the party was concerned.

✎

Shah meanwhile took to his new job with gusto. The home ministry under Rajnath Singh had been reactive rather than proactive. It was successful in fighting Naxal terrorism in central India. But as the man who had played a large role in securing the prime ministerial candidacy for Modi in the teeth of opposition from the BJP's senior leaders, Rajnath was overshadowed by Jaitley and Swaraj in Modi's first term.

With Shah taking over home, Rajnath applied himself to defence with renewed vigour. He would play a key role during the long standoff in eastern Ladakh between Indian and Chinese troops. But for much of the second half of 2019, it was Shah who occupied centre stage in Parliament. Shah has been Modi's confidant for two decades. He served as home minister in Modi's Gujarat government. Known to be a hard taskmaster and Modi's loyal second-in-command, Shah handled the J&K issue with an iron fist.

Four years after Article 370 was read down in 2019, J&K is undergoing a transformation. Private investment in tourism, hospitality, infotech, infrastructure, hydro-electric power, fast-moving consumer goods (FMCG), pharmaceuticals and agriculture is growing rapidly. Movie theatres have returned to the Kashmir Valley more than 30 years after Islamist terrorists, backed by Pakistan, shut them down in 1990.

The cumulative effect of changes in J&K has not pleased the families who monopolised power in the Valley for 70 years. Sporadic terror attacks by Pakistan-backed jihadis continue on police, civilians, panchayat leaders, Kashmiri Pandits and the BSF. With elections, the next phase in J&K's evolution will be closely watched.

While 2019 ended relatively quietly, despite the controversial legislations on J&K and the CAA followed by the Supreme Court's verdict in favour of the Ram Temple, 2020 would bring problems by the bucketful. US President Donald Trump arrived in India in February 2020 even as riots broke out in Delhi over the CAA. The foreign media, hostile to Modi from the start – *The Economist* had endorsed Rahul Gandhi as prime minister in May 2014 – quickly got down to business. Here was an opportunity, in front of the American presidential party and the accompanying foreign media, to portray Modi's India as an ultra-nationalist Hindu majoritarian state where dissent was being ruthlessly silenced.

Do Indians pay more attention to the Anglo-Saxon media than they should? Many still care about India's image abroad. They watch the BBC and CNN, read *The New York Times* and *The Guardian* and worry about India's global reputation. Indians are obviously right to care about every rape, every caste atrocity, every communal riot, and every action that suppresses dissent.

India is a complex country. Nowhere else in the world do you find dehumanising poverty, social discrimination and casual violence co-existing with world-class entrepreneurs, outstanding scientists and dedicated social workers. This paradox is difficult for foreign correspondents to understand. Western journalists know that rapes and violent crime are as prevalent in their affluent countries as they are in India. They read strong daily criticism of the Modi government in Indian newspapers and watch prime time TV anchors mocking Modi's economic policies. They surf news portals tearing apart the government's foreign policy. And they see fact-checking sites exposing the government's faultlines.

India's democracy has so many octopus-like arms among the bureaucracy, Opposition-ruled states, the police, NGOs, activists and journalists that it is in no imminent danger. But editors back in New York and London want stories that work on the principle that bad news about India makes good editorial copy. Indian journalists writing for American and British newspapers give their editors what they want: stories of rape, riots, casteism and communalism. Much of this is legitimate journalism. Where it is not is in the failure to construct a balanced narrative.

For a wealthy democracy, America has intractable problems of its own – racial violence, police brutality and fatal inner-city shootings. India's problems therefore need to be contextualised. India annoys many in the West: here's a country that was not expected to make it. India was supposed to Balkanise after Independence. How could post-Independence India, with a teeming population impoverished by 190 years of British rule, a toxic caste system, and simmering Hindu-Muslim tension, become the world's fifth largest economy?

The West, thoughtful foreign journalists know, grew rich after the 1750s on the back of the brutal transatlantic slave trade from Africa to America and invasive, exploitative colonialism in Asia which fuelled the Industrial Revolution. Poor, colonised, benighted India in 1947 had a literacy rate of 12 per cent, life expectancy of 32 years and a GDP of ₹2.70 lakh crore. Today literacy in India is nearly 80 per cent, life expectancy 70 years and GDP over $3.75 trillion, larger than the GDP of former colonial power Britain.

It wasn't meant to quite work out that way, write bemused foreign journalists. Western businessmen and investment bankers now line up in Delhi with billions of dollars in foreign direct investment (FDI) in the world's third largest economy and the fastest-growing consumer market, bursting with world-class tech startups.

But what about dissent and democracy? Indian politics and society are undergoing a metamorphosis. The old elite with its ossified colonial mindset is being challenged by a rising new elite. The old elite embraces dynasty, practises nepotism and works in closed, incestuous circles. India is a noisy, open democracy. It gives everybody an opportunity to defame it. That, as I have often said, is as it should be. It is India's true strength.

Foreign journalists meanwhile are puzzled. Most are middle-level careerists who head their newspapers' South Asian bureaus. An Indian posting is a stepping stone to a top editorial job back home or in a larger bureau in Europe, China or the United States.

For these mid-career journalists, India is a challenge. Most know they'll be transferred out of New Delhi in a few years even as they are finding their feet in the country. For example, Simon Denyer, the *Washington Post*'s former New Delhi bureau chief with whom I appeared in 2012 on a *Times Now* debate on then Prime Minister Manmohan Singh's famed silences, was sent off to Beijing before he had a chance to do extended reportage out of India. Besides, as we agreed in that particular debate, foreign journalists cater to an audience that knows little about India and is easily swayed by undercooked foreign reportage.

Francois Gautier, the French editor-in-chief of *La Revue de l'Inde*, puts all of this in historical perspective: "The British set upon establishing an intermediary race of Indians whom they could entrust with their work at middle-level echelons and who could one day be convenient instruments to rule by proxy, or semi-proxy. The tool to shape these British clones was education. In the words of Macaulay: 'We must at present do our best to form a class, who may be interpreters between us and the millions we govern; a class of persons, Indians in blood and colour, but English in taste, in opinions, in morals and in intellect.' The unfortunate element of course is that Western journalists now quote Indian intellectuals when they pillory India: 'See we are not saying anything, Indians themselves are saying it'."

THREE

The Second Coming

IN 2019, MODI BECAME ONLY THE FOURTH INDIAN PRIME MINISTER AFTER Jawaharlal Nehru, Indira Gandhi and Manmohan Singh to win a full second consecutive term. It was clear from the inauguration, however, that Modi 2.0 would be different. Gone was the elaborate ceremony of May 2014 with South Asian leaders in attendance. The inauguration in May 2019 was brisk and businesslike. The government quickly got down to work. With a majority of 303 seats in the 543-seat Lok Sabha, the BJP's political and socio-cultural agenda would now be placed on the fast track.

Newly appointed Home Minister Amit Shah drove that agenda. The J&K Reorganisation and Citizenship Amendment bills topped his post-election list of priorities. The Supreme Court's verdict in November 2019 allowing the Ram Temple to be built on the disputed Babri Masjid site in Ayodhya armed the BJP with three arrows in its electoral quiver ahead of key state assembly polls in 2020. The first arrow was J&K's changed status following the revocation of Article 370. The second was the controversial Citizenship (Amendment) Act. And the third was Ayodhya. The politics of polarisation was now set in stone.

The anti-CAA protests, the clampdown in J&K and the Supreme Court order on the Ram Temple in Ayodhya deepened the cleavage between communities. The Shaheen Bagh blockade, leading to the Delhi riots in February 2020, vitiated the communal atmosphere. Amidst all this, Covid-19 emerged as the most serious public health crisis in a century. By April 2020, the full extent of the pandemic was apparent. Lockdowns worldwide severely damaged economies. A global recession loomed. Europe was hit by a series of deadly Covid waves in 2021. The United States reported mounting fatalities. Life and work, post-pandemic, recovered in 2023 but they would never be quite the same again.

The global Covid-19 pandemic threw Modi's agenda into disarray. The economic and human toll was unprecedented. Amit Shah was hospitalised after testing positive for the virus. Several lawmakers succumbed to the disease.

∽

The news of a potentially deadly virus had begun to filter out of China in the third week of January 2020. Secretive links between Chinese authorities, biological laboratories in Wuhan and subverted US scientists aiding intellectual property theft by China were revealed in the US media.

Modi was quick to spot the danger the virus presented. The first infection in India from the as yet unnamed virus had been recorded in Kerala on 30 January 2020. President Trump was arriving in India in the last week of February. The Shaheen Bagh protests against the CAA were an additional worry for Modi. The riots that engulfed Delhi couldn't have come at a worse time with superspreaders infecting large crowds.

Modi then made a decision that became as contentious as demonetisation: imposing a complete lockdown of the country with just four hours' notice. All economic activity ceased overnight at midnight on 24 March 2020. Millions of migrant workers from various states were stranded: no trains, buses, taxis or trucks. The total national lockdown – the harshest in the world – made the economy seize up. GDP growth was already faltering. For the January-March 2020 quarter, GDP growth had slowed to 3.1 per cent. When the April-June 2020 results were announced, the full extent of the damage caused to the economy by the lockdown became apparent: GDP shrunk in the quarter by 23.9 per cent.

The MSME sector was already reeling from the effects of demonetisation in November 2016 and an overly complex rollout of the Goods and Services Tax (GST) in July 2017. Job losses mounted. Growth momentum stalled. The lockdown made things immeasurably worse. Despite all-round misery among migrant workers and the destruction of small businesses during the lockdown, Modi's own popularity, defying the odds and political logic, rose.

According to a study published in *Mint* (22 September 2020), 17 months after the 2019 general election when anti-incumbency is often high, 76 per cent of respondents across socio-economic demographies said Modi had handled the Covid crisis well. An equal proportion felt that the prime minister's management of the economy was good or excellent. Surveys in 2021 and 2022 confirmed the trend: despite job losses, Covid fatalities and Chinese aggression along the LAC, Modi remained popular across demographics. The phenomenon was similar to the popularity of former US president Ronald Reagan. However badly Reagan's economic performance was, criticism bounced off him. The media gave him the monicker: Teflon President.

In India, Modi had an additional asset. He was deified. During the lockdown, he grew a long beard. His mannerisms took on a saintly ouevre. The greater the trouble India faced, the more he seemed revered in a nation susceptible to worship. The Supreme Court's verdict in November 2019 in favour of the Ram Temple in Ayodhya added to Modi's mystique. Shrewdly, its inauguration was set for January 2024, on the eve of the next Lok Sabha election.

As I wrote in my 2022 book, *Iqbal Singh Chahal: Covid Warrior,* the pandemic brought about rare coordination between the Prime Minister's Office (PMO) and the Brihanmumbai Municipal Corporation (BMC). Commissioner Chahal recounts an incident during the pandemic that reveals how proactive Modi was as a decision-maker, often tackling problems even at 1.00 am. Says Chahal:

Cipla had received a licence from the Indian government and the Drug Controller General of India (DCGI) to manufacture Remdesivir and Tocilizumab in India in Silvasa. The vaccine was still months away. It was around 7.00 pm on Friday evening, 26 June 2020. Cipla's then CEO Nikhil Chopra phoned me. He said he had imported intermediates from China to manufacture Remdesivir. The intermediates had landed at Mumbai's international airport's air cargo division.

Now, this consignment could be used to manufacture one lakh Remdesivir vials for the entire country. But the Indian government had, meanwhile, banned 59 Chinese apps following the border clash in the Galwan Valley in eastern Ladakh on 15 June. Within weeks, orders were issued to ban key Chinese products in the country. The Union government further ordered that containers with Chinese products lying at Indian ports should meanwhile not be offloaded. Air cargos from China too, should not be released but sent back.

When Nikhil Chopra called me, he said his intermediates to manufacture one lakh doses of Remdesivir had arrived from China but the principal commissioner of customs had refused to release the consignment. He said customs had received orders from the government. Chopra told me Cipla's licence would be of no use as only two countries in the world have the pharma intermediates needed for this drug – China and the US. Washington had put a ban on the export of this intermediate. If China's intermediates go back from Indian customs, Chopra said, there will be zero local output of the drug.

Chahal was worried. He knew he had to act quickly. He described how events unfolded and Modi's crucial intervention:

I went to my office later on Saturday and called Nikhil Chopra. I told him that the finance secretary of India is concerned about China potentially creating some problem with the intermediates. You are a world-class company, I said. Don't you have a high-tech lab in which you can identify a possible virus in the intermediates before you process it? Chopra replied that Cipla has one of the best labs in the world. It could identify any virus or contamination in the consignment. I requested Chopra to send me an email certifying this.

The mail arrived at 9.15 pm on Saturday, 27 June. It stated that Cipla had the capability to identify any contamination or virus in these intermediates. There will be no problem if the intermediates are handed over to Cipla. It was like a guarantee. There was a young IAS officer, Shrikar Pardeshi, in the PMO. I had met him when he was a collector in Nanded. Elections were on and I had gone there as an observer on behalf of the Election Commission of India. Later, we worked together in Delhi. I sent an urgent email in his name as joint secretary to the PMO. I explained the entire situation in the mail. I also said that if the intermediate is released, it will not only benefit Mumbai but the whole of India. I enclosed Cipla's mail validating its confidence in identifying any potential contamination in the intermediates.

Across India, lakhs of patients were using Remdesivir. So roughly one lakh doses in those critical times, June-July 2020, the first peak of the pandemic, could save thousands of lives. I literally begged the PMO to make an exception for these intermediates from China. After the young PMO officer received my mail, I spoke to him on the phone at around 10.00 pm and requested him that whenever the prime minister is available, please tell him to read this mail. It is the urgent request of the commissioner of the BMC. Please just read this. After that, whatever his decision may be, it will be accepted, but first please read this mail. The PM should be aware of this dire situation.

It was past midnight, I learnt later, when the young PMO

officer showed my mail to the PM. The PM is very diligent. He works late every night. He read the mail just before 1.00 am. It was Saturday night. I was already asleep by 12.30 am. Next morning, at 9.00 am I received a call from Vinayak Azad, then the principal commissioner of customs, air cargo. He told me that instructions have been issued and we have released the intermediate consignment half-an-hour back as a special case. This was Sunday morning, 28 June, almost exactly 2 weeks after we lost 20 soldiers in the Galwan Valley clash with the People's Liberation Army (PLA).

To confirm this overnight development, I called Nikhil Chopra. He said, yes Cipla's officer was on his way to the airport cargo section and the consignment will be with the company in another 30 minutes. All I can add is: hats off to the PM. I salute him for taking it upon himself, at a time of a war-like situation with China, to take a decision at 1.00 am that could save, and did save, thousands of lives. Not many knew about this till now. The PM deserves the country's salutation.

꩜

The key to the 2024 Lok Sabha election lies in vote shares translating into seats. The road to Delhi passes through Lucknow and Ayodhya in Uttar Pradesh. The 2022 UP assembly election decided several issues. First, it was a test of Chief Minister Yogi Adityanath's popularity in India's largest state which accounts for 80 seats in the Lok Sabha. Second, it proved to be a referendum on UP's record on law and order under Adityanath. By winning a second successive term, he has emerged as a future national leader in a post-Modi era. Third, the UP poll was a test of Priyanka Gandhi-Vadra's political acumen.

As the Congress party's leader in-charge of UP, Gandhi-Vadra's lacklustre performance in UP cast her future political role in doubt. At 51, time is not on her side. She has dabbled in politics for over 20 years without delivering results. She has never held a constitutional post. With the 2024 Lok Sabha poll looming, this was Gandhi-Vadra's last opportunity to prove her critics wrong. The Congress' disastrous performance, plunging from a vote share of 6.25 per cent in the 2017 assembly poll to 2.33 per cent in 2022, was one more failure in Gandhi-Vadra's on-off political career.

The 2022 Uttar Pradesh assembly election answered two other questions as well. One, does Yogi Adityanath have the staying power to move to a larger national role? Clearly he does. Two, will UP's brand of hard Hindutva resonate in the 2024 Lok Sabha election? Equally clearly, it will.

In the 2019 Lok Sabha election, the BJP won over 37 per cent vote share. With few allies left, Modi knows he must lift the party's own vote share up to 42–3 per cent to ensure a comfortable majority for the BJP in the 2024 Lok Sabha poll. The Opposition, though fractious, is likely to unite tactically in 2024. It will forge alliances at national and state levels. It knows that a BJP victory in 2024 could end many of their family fiefdoms. Along with the Congress, virtually every party is dynastic: SP, RJD, NC, JD(S), NCP, TMC, DMK, BJD, AIMIM, SAD and BRS. Only the Left and the BJP remain untethered to dynastic rule.

Fifteen years of Modi as prime minister could, by 2029, erode decades of dynastic entitlement. For the Opposition, the 2024 Lok Sabha poll is therefore existential. It represents the last chance for many leaders in the Opposition to reclaim power and remain relevant. By 2029, the citadel of the old ecosystem could be broken beyond repair. The tactics of minority appeasement and vote bank politics may no longer work. Entitlement and privilege will recede. Dynasty will atrophy. The corroded bureaucratic and academic ecosystem, built brick by brick by corrupt politicians, is in danger of being dismantled, brick by brick.

The obvious jeopardy for the BJP is that it will appropriate some of the Congress' bad habits. This is already evident. Modi is worshipped as Indira Gandhi was in the early 1970s. Sycophancy in the BJP is rampant. Power is centralised. New talent finds it difficult to rise through the party's ranks. This is Modi's biggest challenge. His tenth year in power, leading up to campaigning for the May 2024 general election, will be crucial to his legacy.

Assuming he wins the 2024 Lok Sabha election, Modi will be 78 when the May 2029 general election rolls along. He would have already equalled Jawaharlal Nehru's record of winning three consecutive five-year prime ministerial terms. Will he fight the 2029 Lok Sabha poll for an unprecedented fourth time? No Indian prime minister – not Jawaharlal Nehru, not Indira Gandhi – has fought and won four general elections.

In a live interview on *India Today* Television in September 2019 with the network's consulting editor Rajdeep Sardesai, I said if Modi won the 2024 general election, he could well step aside in 2029 after 15 years as prime minister.

Sardesai was surprised. In India politicians do not voluntarily step aside unless they lose an election. I explained to Sardesai that Modi had wandered in the Himalayas for two years after walking out of his Vadnagar home in Gujarat at the age of 17. Modi lived in caves and ate with monks. He told me during our several meetings that he did not have a meal at the same place more than once. Modi lived like a rishi.

I said to Sardesai in that television interview that Modi could, at 78, decide to go back to a spiritual life. The next morning, *India Today* headlined the story: "In 11 years, PM Narendra Modi will retire to the Himalayas, author and senior journalist Minhaz Merchant claimed on India Today TV's show."

In its online story, *India Today* went on to write:

Minhaz Merchant, author and senior journalist, on Tuesday, claimed that the Prime Minister will give up power by 2029 and head to the Himalayas to live the life of a monk. 'At the age of 18, he went to the Himalayas and at the age of 80, I can guarantee you, he will again go to the Himalayas. He is not going to hang on to power. He will live like a monk,' said Minhaz Merchant, who wrote a biography on former Prime Minister Rajiv Gandhi.

Talking to India Today TV Consulting Editor Rajdeep Sardesai, Minhaz Merchant said, 'This transition will take place if he wins the 2024 elections. There is every possibility that before the 2029 elections, he will step aside.' Minhaz Merchant said this in response to a question on idol worshipping of PM Modi by a section of society.

All of this—as I said clearly to Sardesai and which *India Today* reported faithfully—depended on the political circumstances in 2024 and 2029. What shape would the Congress be in? Would other Opposition leaders have risen to challenge Modi? Most importantly, I said, would Modi have groomed a successor? Amit Shah? Yogi Adityanath? Another dark horse?

Obviously, as I told a bemused Sardesai, Modi would have to first win the 2024 Lok Sabha election before even thinking of 2029. Modi is not given to long-term projections. He lives in the present.

India is one of the world's most devout countries. Studies have shown that over 90 per cent of Indians are religious, pray regularly and visit temples, mosques, churches and gurudwaras frequently. Modi has used religion as an electoral scimitar more effectively than any previous Indian leader.

The Ram Mandir's scheduled opening to devotees in the first quarter of 2024 will cause an upsurge in religious sentiment. The electoral impact cannot be underestimated. At the Ram Temple's ground-breaking ceremony in August 2020, Modi prostrated himself in front of the giant idol of Lord Ram. The messaging could not have been clearer. When devotees pour in from early 2024 to pray in the grand Ram Temple complex, the optics will electrify a large section of devout Hindus. But are there enough of them to make an electoral difference?

That in fact is the second weapon in Modi's electoral armoury: building the BJP's membership. This now accounts for over 120 million people who are BJP members. At an average of three members of voting age per family, that works out to 360 million committed BJP voters. The number of eligible voters in the 2019 Lok Sabha election was 811 million. In 2024, the number is expected to rise to over 900 million.

In theory, the BJP thus has a lock on 360 million of this 900 million-strong electorate – giving the party potentially a near 40 per cent vote share even if no new members join the BJP before 2024. India's population is estimated to be 1.40 billion in 2024. Around 79 per cent or 1.10 billion are Hindus. Over 25 per cent of these Hindus are Dalits and could vote for non-NDA regional parties. Another small slice of Hindus, roughly 10 per cent, are traditional Congress and Left-leaning voters.

Of the 900 million likely eligible voters in 2024, the BJP could strategically focus on BJP-leaning Hindu voters. With 360 million eligible voters already members or supporters of the BJP (counted along with voting-age family members), that leaves relatively few who sit on the fence. The task in front of the party is to target this segment, however small, in the run-up to the 2024 Lok Sabha poll. It could tip the scales.

In essence, therefore, to achieve a 45 per cent vote share in 2024, the BJP needs to win 285 million voters out of around 630 million voters from 900 million eligible voters, adjusted proportionately downwards, assuming an expected turnout of 70 per cent. That is unlikely to be a difficult task, given the likely outpouring of sentiment around the inauguration in early 2024 of the Ram Temple, especially in the Hindi heartland. In politics though, it is folly to take anything for granted. Modi knows this.

The BJP won 31 per cent vote share and 282 seats in the 2014 Lok Sabha poll. It won 37 per cent vote share and 303 seats in 2019. Crossing the 45 per cent barrier in 2024 would be historic. No prime minister in Independent India has won more than 48 per cent vote share in a general election. These are the winning vote shares since India's first Lok Sabha election in 1952:

1952: Nehru (44.99 per cent)
1957: Nehru (47.78 per cent)
1962: Nehru (44.72 per cent)
1967: Indira Gandhi (40.78 per cent)
1971: Indira Gandhi (43.68 per cent)
1977: Morarji Desai (41.32 per cent)
1980: Indira Gandhi (42.69 per cent)
1984: Rajiv Gandhi (46.86 per cent)
1989: VP Singh (17.79 per cent – National Front government with allies)
1991: Narasimha Rao (36.40 per cent)
1996: Deve Gowda (8.08 per cent – Janata Dal formed United Front government with allies)
1998: Atal Bihari Vajpayee (25.59 per cent)
1999: Atal Bihari Vajpayee (23.75 per cent)
2004: Manmohan Singh (26.53 per cent)
2009: Manmohan Singh (28.55 per cent)
2014: Narendra Modi (31.00 per cent)
2019: Narendra Modi (37.36 per cent)

༄

A key weapon in Modi's electoral armoury is welfare benefits. The number of people, especially among the poor, impacted by dozens of schemes launched by Modi could be a game changer. So where could it all go wrong for Modi? The short answer: the economy. Modi's macro-economic management has retreated into protectionism and over-regulation, making statutory compliances pointlessly cumbersome. While agriculture and labour reforms are structurally sound, their implementation remains uncertain. Key reforms like the 2016 Insolvency and Bankruptcy Code (IBC) have not lived up to their early promise.

The Direct Tax Code (DTC) aimed at personal tax reform has not been implemented. The Committee set up to recommend the DTC submitted its report in 2019. The report has been ignored. The bureaucracy remains unreformed. Institutional governance has deteriorated. The government's communications strategy oscillates between indifferent and poor. The jumbo-sized Union cabinet lacks domain expertise in key portfolios though, to be fair, several ministers have latterly shown an excellent grasp of complex issues.

The Indian media, denied access to the prime minister, has meanwhile broken into two halves. One half acts as a virtual propaganda arm of the government. The other half functions as a critic, as it should in a democracy, but often deals in false narratives and rarely offers concrete solutions. The foreign media is as hostile as ever, scavenging for stories in India's underbelly. Reports on India's successful space programme and tech revolution rarely find their way into the international media.

Modi's foreign policy has been an odd mix. He has shrewdly built a transactional relationship with the Sunni Arab Muslim world led by Saudi Arabia and the United Arab Emirates. Modi's outreach to Southeast Asia, however, has met with limited success. The Act East policy remains theoretically sound. India has historical cultural ties with Southeast Asia, stretching from Malaysia and Singapore to Cambodia and Indonesia. Apart from religion – both Hinduism and Buddhism – the region has a significant Indian-origin diaspora.

A large number of Indians arrived in Southeast Asia as indentured workers from the British Empire. Voluntary migration from especially Tamil Nadu followed. Wealthier Indian professionals and entrepreneurs have increasingly set up operational bases in countries like Singapore where the ease of doing business is higher than in India. E-commerce major Flipkart, for example, for long operated under Singapore's jurisdiction. Several Indian-origin leaders occupy senior positions in the city-state's political establishment.

India's decision to stay out of the Regional Comprehensive Economic Partnership (RCEP) was predicated on China's outsized influence in the group. The decision caused several East Asian countries to question the seriousness of India's Act East policy. However, most members of the RCEP like Japan, New Zealand and Australia, besides the ASEAN 10, already have pre-RCEP trading agreements with India. India's supposed trading disadvantage by staying out of the RCEP may thus be overstated. Besides, India can join the RCEP at any time of its choosing, as the 15-member bloc has confirmed. By signing FTAs with Australia and the United Arab Emirates (UAE) and negotiating trade deals with Britain, the Gulf Cooperation Council (GCC), Canada and the European Union (EU), India has shown clear intent on expanding trade globally.

India's G20 presidency, which runs up to November 30, 2023, has allowed Modi to enhance India's global clout as well as burnish his international leadership. The G20 summit in September 2023 in New Delhi will be attended by a galaxy of world leaders, including US President Joe Biden and Chinese President Xi Jinping.

The elephant in the room, China, however complicates matters. Beijing has disputes with several littoral countries in the South China Sea. As India's contest with China deepens, Modi must use this leverage both economically and diplomatically. Moreover, as his second term draws to a close, Modi has the opportunity to strengthen alliances with Southeast Asia and in particular ASEAN, which continues to view China with both suspicion and trepidation.

The battle between China and India has long-term geopolitical implications for the evolving world order. An alliance between the US-led coalition of Western democracies and India, including the Quad, is aimed squarely at countering China's aggression. Under the Biden administration, New Delhi's tilt towards Washington is now irreversible.

The Biden presidency is being watched carefully by Indian policymakers as it unfolds its geopolitical doctrine. There is a hard-core Left in the Democratic party that is critical of Modi's "Hindu nationalist" government. Its influence though may be less than is popularly believed. Following his acquittal for the second time by the Senate in February 2021, Donald Trump had hinted he would run for president again in November 2024 – the US Constitution allows him to do so. With civil and criminal cases ranged against him in various courts, the road back could be long and hard. Trump shrugged off such worries on 15 November 2022 when he announced he would run in 2024. With Trump-backed Republicans faring poorly in the November 2022 midterm elections, however, Trump's grip on the Republican party has loosened.

Biden, who at 82 is likely to run again in 2024, has long experience of dealing with India as former President Barack Obama's vice-president. US foreign policy has a continuity that rises above presidential changes. There is broad consensus in the US establishment that a US-India alliance, along with "middle powers" like Britain, France, Germany, Japan, Canada, Australia and South Korea, is necessary to counter the hegemonic threat China poses in the Indo-Pacific and beyond. The Quad and AUKUS form complementary alliances aimed at weaponising this strategy.

Ironically, some of Modi's foreign policy worries in his second term centre around South Asia. The relationship with Nepal has been fraught. Bangladesh is deeply uncomfortable with the Citizenship (Amendment) Act and delays in signing the Teesta river accord. Sri Lanka's strategic tilt towards China is another localised worry. Bhutan's *entente cordiale* with China is a red flag. None of these problems are unsurmountable. India's rise as a global power this decade is seen as inevitable by its neighbours. As with the Maldives and Nepal, relationships can fall and rise quickly in the neighbourhood.

The China-Pakistan nexus remains a long-term geostrategic concern. India and China did not share a land border until 1950. China's military invasion of Tibet that year changed the geopolitical equation with India forever. Tibet remains a festering sore between India and China. After India granted the Dalai Lama refuge in 1959, that sore has become an open wound. Every action China has subsequently taken, including the 1962 war and illegal annexation of Aksai Chin, has its roots in Beijing's simmering anger over the Dalai Lama's presence in India which constantly draws attention to China's brutal occupation of Tibet.

Since 1962, Indian policymakers have been paralysed with the fear of alienating Beijing. The Dalai Lama is not allowed to make political statements as a condition for staying in India. Emboldened by Indian timidity, China issues periodic statements discrediting the Dalai Lama. Maintaining a diplomatic silence on Tibet hasn't appeased China. It has encouraged Beijing to claim Arunachal Pradesh as South Tibet. China routinely objects to the Dalai Lama travelling to Arunachal.

Just as India's first Prime Minister Jawaharlal Nehru misread China in the 1950s, Modi misread China in his first term. China respects strength. It treats weakness with contempt. India's appeasement diplomacy was seen as a weakness that Beijing exploited ruthlessly. Chinese incursions along the LAC are part of Beijing's strategy to test India's resolve. In the past, successive Indian governments have quietly accepted China's salami-slicing of India's border areas so as to not risk a confrontation with Beijing. That is exactly the reaction China expected.

Galwan on 15 June 2020, changed the India-China dynamic. The fierce battle on narrow ridges between Indian troops and soldiers of the People's Liberation Army (PLA), resulting in fatalities on both sides, made Beijing reassess India's intent. India's build-up along the LAC of over 50,000 troops, attack helicopters, air defence systems, predator drones, battle tanks and fighter jets has telegraphed a warning to China: India doesn't seek war but is prepared for it.

Tibet is China's second-most sensitive issue. Taiwan is the first. China has tried to bully India into silence over the One-China policy which accepts Taiwan as an inseparable part of China. Does China reciprocate by accepting the One-India policy – including Pakistan occupied Kashmir (PoK) and Chinese-occupied Aksai Chin? It does the exact opposite. At every forum and at every opportunity, China condones and protects Pakistan's state sponsorship of terrorism in J&K. For India to remain ambivalent on the One-China policy – as it has since 2010 – is no longer tenable. Modi must bite the bullet on both Tibet and Taiwan. They are China's two blind spots.

India needs to urgently increase trade with Taiwan. Two of the largest contractors for Apple iPhones – Foxconn and Pegatron – are expanding their production facilities for iPhones in India. Both are Taiwanese. The imperative for trade and investment with Taiwan has never been greater. India shouldn't over-estimate China's truculence. Nor should it underestimate Beijing's determination to reunify Taiwan with the mainland.

China is a toxic power. Its closest allies are rogue nations: Pakistan and North Korea. It does not obey global rules and has refused to abide by the 2016 verdict of the United Nations Convention on the Law of the Seas (UNCLOS) that found in favour of the Philippines on Beijing's transgressions in the South China Sea. China's alliance with Russia has increased after the Ukraine war, albeit as a senior economic partner, deeply alienating the US-led West.

When cornered, the legendary Chinese strategist Sun Tzu said, use deception. He wrote his famous treatise *Art of War* 2,500 years ago. China's leaders still revere Sun Tzu. What else did he write in the treatise? First, a leader must be "inscrutable and serene". He must craft plans that are "unfathomable" to the enemy. Sun Tzu advocated a nuanced mix of deception and diplomacy to overcome the enemy.

The Chinese have employed all the tools in Sun Tzu's playbook. They used deception to make rapid incursions along the Line of Actual Control (LAC). They remain inscrutable during military-to-military talks between Generals from both sides. Their future intent in disputed areas in Ladakh is unfathomable. But they have allowed diplomacy and disengagement to proceed as they probe India on how far it can be pushed. Beyond the standoff lie larger geopolitical questions.

Beijing views India as not only a regional rival but a future global adversary allied with the West and a confluence of Indo-Pacific "middle" powers like Japan, Australia and South Korea. India is a crucial pivot in this anti-China alliance. It has a large and expanding military. Its economy – despite indifferent macro-economic management – will be the third-largest in the world well before 2027. By Purchasing Power Parity India's GDP is already the world's third largest. India's geography places it in command of the vital Indian Ocean Region (IOR) which China covets. Its youthful demography contrasts sharply with an ageing China, a consequence of Mao Zedong's one-child policy.

President Xi Jinping is the principal culprit in China's aggressive policy across Asia. More than any other recent Chinese leader, he has made China a more authoritarian state at home and a more expansionary one overseas. He has protected Pakistan, a state sponsor of terrorism, at every global forum while blocking India's entry into the Nuclear Suppliers Group (NSG). Xi, however, has bitten off more than he can chew. Dissent against him in China in the first year of his unprecedented third five-year term is rising. His legacy, the Belt and Road Initiative (BRI), has stalled. The Covid-19 crisis has peeled away the veneer of invincibility around him.

After several centuries, India emerged in mid-2023 as the world's most populous country, ahead of China. That has drawn the attention of the world to India's economic, military and market potential. Size matters though quality obviously does too. As I wrote[4]: "After more than 300 years, India is once again the world's most populous country. China is not pleased. Beijing's foreign ministry spokesperson Wang Wenbin was quick to claim that China still had over 900 million people of working age. He tactfully didn't mention that this number was declining rapidly.

"How rapidly? According to a United Nations report published on 19 April 2023, the most startling revelation is that China's total population will halve from the current 1.43 billion to just over 700 million in 2100. India's population, in sharp contrast, will still be 1.40 billion in 2100, having peaked at 1.60 billion in 2050 before plateauing. Crucially, the average Chinese, already nearly 40 years old, will be over 55 in 2100. The average Indian today is 28 and will still be only 40 in 2100.

"What will be the impact of this on workforce productivity? As Roshan Kishore, the data editor of *Hindustan Times*, pointed out on 21 April 2023, "The 2022 World Population Prospects (WPP) data – the basis of the United Nations (UN) report released on 19 April 2023 – shows that India is expected to have outgrown China in 2023 not just in terms of overall population but also working-age (15–59 years) population. 'India's lead vis-a-vis China's working-age population will become 1.5 times by 2048 and then reach two times by the year 2076. By 2100, till when WPP projections are available, India's working-age population will be 2.3 times that of China's. *Ceteris paribus* (all other things remaining the same), this should give a huge economic advantage to India vis-a-vis China'."

[4]*Business World*, 6 June 2023.

Given China's unpredictable leadership, what should India do? Follow Sun Tzu's advice: be patient, be inscrutable, be deceptive and above all keep your plans unfathomable. Modi has deployed some of Sun Tzu's advice to the Middle East. His outreach early in his first term continues to pay rich dividends deep into his second term. The détente between the Saudi-led Gulf states and Israel fits comfortably into Modi's diplomatic and security doctrine in the region. Modi had paid less attention to post-Brexit Britain than previous prime ministers. That is changing as the two countries hammer out a free trade agreement (FTA) with the affable British Prime Minister Rishi Sunak establishing a good equation with, Indian policymakers. Modi's interaction with the European Union (EU) too has intensified over trade and security cooperation, especially after the Russia-Ukraine war reordered the EU's economic and strategic priorities in Asia.

The presence of large numbers of migrants and refugees from the Middle East in Western Europe has led to the growth of radicalised Islamist pockets across the continent, especially in France and Germany. The Islamist threat, morphing across the volatile Middle East and feeding into an unstable Talibanised Afghanistan, has led increasingly to funds, terrorists and weapons finding their way into India.

∽

With important state elections due towards the end of 2023, Modi's attention has turned inwards. Following the 2021 West Bengal assembly election, the BJP increased its tally from three seats to 77 seats. This subsequently declined due to deaths, defections and bypoll losses. Modi recognises that the path to power does not always lie in igniting majoritarian sentiment. Local issues and parochial pride, as Bengal showed, matter.

For decades under Congress governments, secularism was the social credo. Indian secularism evolved in post-Independent India, changing its characteristics from Nehru to Modi. The electoral trajectory of the BJP began with LK Advani's *rath yatra* to Ayodhya in 1990. The Hindu nationalism project was put on steroids. Events followed one another quickly. The demolition of the Babri Masjid, communal riots and serial bomb blasts in Mumbai within a period of three months between December 1992 and March 1993 shocked Indians. A period of relative calm descended. The BJP's political rise was established in 1998 when it took office at the Centre, 14 years after it had won just two seats in the 1984 Lok Sabha election. It won 182 seats in the 1998 general election and repeated that performance in 1999.

To what extent has majoritarianism and Hindutva helped the BJP capture power? Vajpayee was regarded as a consensual leader. Modi's rise changed the social discourse. Hindutva was now the dominant political force. BJP leaders were no longer defensive about Hindutva, frequently citing the Supreme Court's December 1995 observation that Hindutva was a way of life.

Modi's muscular Hindutva challenged the political order. Communal cleavages deepened. India was a nation increasingly divided along ideological lines. The Congress and regional parties like the TMC, JD(U), SP, Shiv Sena and NCP have tried to stitch together an Opposition front to counter Modi's Teflon persona. Modi meanwhile has taken his global statesman role seriously. He has left much of the polarisation project to Home Minister Amit Shah and UP Chief Minister Yogi Adityanath.

That draws criticism from the Hindutva faithful. They rail against Modi's newfound "secularism". It isn't quite true of course. Modi has simply mastered the art of compartmentalising his Hindutva. At his election rallies, Hindutva emerges, amidst cries of Jai Shri Ram, Bharat Mata Ki Jai and Vande Mataram. In the chanceries of the world, however, Modi is the consummate global consensus-maker, his tone measured, his bearing statesmanlike.

FOUR

After Two Years in the Himalayas

MODI HAD LEFT HOME IN 1967 AT THE AGE OF 17. HOW MUCH DID that experience impact his personality and worldview? Modi journeyed across India for two years, spending much of that time in the Himalayas before returning home. Overjoyed to see him, his mother asked him to unpack his few belongings and settle down back home. A 19-year-old Modi sought her and his father Damodardas' blessings before telling them that he had come home not to stay, but to pack his remaining personal effects and join the RSS for life. His parents could do nothing to change his mind. It was 1969. For the next 18 years, Modi washed the clothes of RSS *pracharaks*, cleaned toilets and did other menial work. In 1987, the RSS sent him to join the BJP. Within 14 years, he was chief minister of Gujarat and 13 years later, prime minister.

A little over a decade after joining the BJP, Modi in 1998 was put in charge of several north Indian states. He was 47 and clearly a rising star. Vajpayee had just begun his term as prime minister. Within months India tested a nuclear device at Pokhran in May 1998. I happened to be on a short vacation with the family in New York.

The news of the Pokhran nuclear test came in that afternoon, US time. Surfing the news channels, I was shocked at the tone of the reportage. On CNN, ABC, CBS, NBC and Fox, anchors hectored India for this unpardonable sin. How dare India, a non-NPT member, test a nuclear device? The United States had 6,000 nuclear warheads but it regarded upstart India's nuclear test as an affront to the world order.

The Indian point of view was totally absent from US media. American military experts, security officials and defence hawks all came together on TV to denounce India. President Bill Clinton was urged to impose immediate economic and technology sanctions on India which he did days later.

Annoyed by the one-sided coverage, I called CNN from my hotel room. "Please get the Indian point of view on the nuclear test on your programme," I said to an editor in the newsroom. She replied that she had no idea whom to contact.

"Talk to the Indian ambassador, Naresh Chandra, in Washington," I suggested. "You need balance in your story on India's nuclear test."

Eventually the network did get Chandra and other Indian viewpoints on air but the coverage remained skewed. While President Clinton was a friend of India, Vajpayee had been prime minister for just two months. The two leaders hadn't developed a rapport. Indian diplomacy was lacklustre and defensive. In Washington, India lacked clout. American newspapers were as biased as the TV networks. *The New York Times* and *The Washington Post* eviscerated India over the nuclear test. The tone was febrile.

Back home, the reaction to the nuclear test was euphoric. But there was also bitterness in India over the hostile reaction in the West, especially in the US and Britain. And yet, like our diplomats, Indian media remained defensive. Even harsh US economic sanctions – entirely unfounded – evoked only tepid criticism.

On my return to India from New York, I phoned the editor-in-chief of *The Times of India* under whom I had worked years ago. He told me to quickly write a strong op-ed on the Indian nuclear test and the West's reaction to it. He agreed that Western media reportage smacked of hypocrisy and arrogance. Here's an excerpt from what I wrote in *The Times of India* on 16 June 1998 in an op-ed titled *"The NPT Game Is Up – India Must Set The Agenda Now"*:

> India's nuclear test has shaken the edifice of nuclear hegemony carefully constructed by the five 'original' nuclear weapon powers (the P-5). Their duplicity in denying the same right to other countries—a responsible nuclear weapons programme—that they arrogate to themselves stands exposed in the glare of international debate that will now increasingly focus on the P-5's double standards. By testing its nuclear device, India broke no laws, domestic or international. It is the P-5 nations who have been in consistent breach of the law by reneging on two of their legal obligations under the nuclear non-proliferation treaty (NPT). First, that they would not abet the transfer of nuclear technology to a third country (China did so clandestinely to Pakistan, Iran and North Korea). And second, that they would work towards eliminating their own nuclear arsenals. Strategically, India was absolutely justified in pursuing its nuclear option to a logical end—testing and eventual weaponisation.

India is today an acknowledged nuclear weapons power. NSG membership remains under negotiation but the US, so viscerally opposed to the Indian nuclear test in 1998, is at the forefront pushing India's case. Back in 1998, however, opinion in the US was hostile to an extraordinary degree. Even Congress MP Shashi Tharoor, then executive assistant to UN Secretary-General Kofi Annan, was opposed to India's nuclear test. Shortly after the Pokhran test, Tharoor—a former Contributing Editor (foreign affairs) in my media firm—arrived in Mumbai on a personal visit. At a private lunch with me, Tharoor argued passionately against

India's "nuclear adventurism". It took all of two hours for me to demolish the foundation of Tharoor's argument which in effect, as I told him, defended nuclear apartheid. I am glad that today, as an Indian parliamentarian, Tharoor's views on India's nuclear strategy have changed.

As expected, the direct consequence of Pokhran-II was Pakistan's own nuclear test a month later. Pakistan periodically rattles the nuclear sabre, calling it Islamabad's weapon of last resort. And yet, it is an empty threat—a bluff. In a statement issued in 2015, Pakistan's then national security advisor Sartaj Aziz said India shouldn't take his country for granted. Pakistan, he added grimly, has nuclear weapons. Other members of the Pakistani establishment have made similar statements in the recent past. But as Pakistan's army chief knows perfectly well, Islamabad cannot use its nuclear stockpile—not even the small tactical battlefield nuclear weapons Pakistan has developed. The reason is simple: a retaliatory nuclear strike by India would cripple Pakistan.

Farooq Abdullah, the former chief minister of Jammu and Kashmir, had this to say about Sartaj Aziz's nuclear threat in an interview[5]: "When a senior diplomat, a former foreign minister, talks about nuclear weapons, it's crazy. May I remind Sartaj Aziz about Hiroshima and Nagasaki? Does he want to bomb Jammu and Kashmir? India also has a bomb. When I went to Pokhran after the tests were conducted, I remember Vajpayee's words. He said we aren't the ones to use this first, we have this as deterrence, only to tell people, don't take us for granted. We can defend ourselves. I want to tell Aziz, don't think of the bomb because innocents will die. Sartaj Aziz *saab*, you too will die if the bomb falls."

Modi has remained steadfast in enhancing India's nuclear deterrent with long-range missiles that can be fired from land,

---

[5]*The Times of India*, 27 August 2015.

sea and air. India's nuclear triad, along with the Russian-made S-400 advanced air defence system, has greatly strengthened India's offensive and defensive capability.

Following the war in Ukraine, the alignment of interests among China, Russia, Pakistan and Turkey is seen as a geopolitical challenge for India in the region. In contrast, in Afghanistan the Taliban is proving a poisoned chalice for Pakistan. For two decades the Pakistan army ran with the Taliban hares and hunted with the American hounds. That option is closing.

The narrative around India's national interest is frequently compromised by a domestic constituency of internal saboteurs. They come from diverse professional backgrounds: politics, law, journalism, academia and activism. They have a single-point agenda: to discredit India at every forum, Indian and international. They inveigle farmers, co-opt Islamist groups and harness Left academics to mount a multi-cornered assault on India's narrative as a rising power. India, these saboteurs say, is anything but a rising power. It is instead, they insist at global Hinduphobic conferences, a semi-dictatorship. There is no freedom of expression. Human rights are abused. Islamophobia is rampant.

As Modi knows, this enemy within is more insidious than detractors outside. It carries a patina of credibility by virtue of being Indian. The charge of racism cannot be levelled against it. It serves as the perfect proxy. To understand the intellectual synapses of the alliance between agenda-driven Indian detractors (as opposed to legitimate critics) and Western Indiaphobes it is necessary to understand its historical roots.

❧

The Mayflower Pilgrims, a group of 74 men and 28 women, set sail from Southampton to escape religious persecution in their native England. They landed in Cape Cod, North America, in November 1620. At the time, the North American continent had a population of over seven million indigenous Indians.

The English pilgrims were among the first Europeans to set up a permanent colony in Plymouth in today's Massachusetts.

The foundation of white America was laid. Over the next four centuries—1620 to 2020—the population of indigenous Indians in North America dwindled from seven million to a little more than four million today.

The population of Europeans in the continent, meanwhile, rose rapidly. In 1900, 89 per cent of 76 million people who lived in the United States were white. The rest were African-Americans—shipped to North America as slaves by European slave traders since the 1600s—and indigenous Indians who suffered periodic massacres at the hands of European colonist-settlers. Dubbed Red Indians, they were confined to reservations.

The US published its first census in 1790. On 12 August 2021, the US Census Bureau published the much-awaited 2020 census, delayed for a year by the Covid-19 pandemic. The results sparked a furious debate across America. For the first time in over 300 years when the European colonist-settler population in North America overtook the population of indigenous Indians and African-American slaves, whites are today close to slipping below 50 per cent of the US population of 332 million.

Non-Hispanic whites now comprise 57.8 per cent of Americans, down from 2010 when they accounted for 63.7 per cent of the US population. It is the first time that the non-Hispanic white population has dipped below 60 per cent since the US census began in 1790. Forecasters believe that the US will become a non-white majority country by as early as 2040. The geopolitical implications of these rapid demographic changes in the world's most powerful country could be far-reaching. The balance of power is shifting from the Atlantic Ocean to the Pacific. China's rise has been toxic for its neighbours and the wider world but India must prepare for a fundamentally altered world order over the next decade.

Former British Prime Minister Tony Blair sounded an early warning, using America's shambolic retreat from Afghanistan as a symbol of fraying Western power. Blair wrote on the website of the Tony Blair Institute for Global Change on 21 August 2021: "Look no further than Pakistan's prime minister (Imran Khan) congratulating the Taliban on their 'victory'. Although many of those espousing Islamism are opposed to violence, they share ideological characteristics with many of those who use it. Islamism is an ideology utterly inconsistent with modern societies based on tolerance and secular government. Yet Western policymakers can't even agree to call it 'Radical Islam'. We prefer to identify it as a set of disconnected challenges, each to be dealt with separately. And for Britain, out of Europe and suffering the end of the Afghanistan mission by our greatest ally, the United States, with little or no consultation, we have serious reflection to do. We are at risk of relegation to the second division of global powers."

The West needs India as a counterweight to China. But a strong India, beyond a point, is not entirely in the West's interests. Washington, the inheritor of the Mayflower Pilgrims' objectives in the New World, knows that the swift demographic ethnic changes taking place in the US could embellish India's strategic power. In the late 2020s, the world's three largest economies will be the US, China and India. As the 400-year-old geopolitical and cultural link between Europe and America loosens, the US will increasingly look to India to counterbalance China's push for global supremacy by 2049. That year will mark the centenary of the founding of the People's Republic of China.

India, which would have celebrated the centenary of its Independence two years earlier, will play a pivotal role in determining, along with a multiracial US, the balance of global power in the second quarter of the 21st century. Detractors of the Modi government in Western academia and policy think tanks aren't pleased. For them, a successful partnership with New Delhi revolves around managing India's rise as a global power under Modi's prime ministership without losing their ability to influence India's strategic policies.

~

One of the strongest criticisms levelled against Modi is that he has a rubber-stamp Union cabinet. No minister dares contradict him. Modi's own larger than life persona dominates the BJP. He is the party's key election campaigner, domestic policymaker and global statesman.

Modi remains personally exceptionally popular but that is for a complex amalgam of reasons. He has cultivated a persona that places him above the fray. If things go wrong with the economy, Modi is given the benefit of the doubt by the average voter who blames the lingering effects of the Covid pandemic or the Russia-Ukraine war for India's economic performance. China's continuing occupation of slices of Indian territory is blurred by the surging "pride" over the bravery of Indian soldiers in the clash with Chinese troops in the Galwan Valley.

This works well for Modi – for the moment. And the moment could last right up to 2024 when the Ram Mandir in Ayodhya is inaugurated. Unless there is a dramatic development that upends Modi's carefully choreographed moment, the BJP could well sweep the 2024 Lok Sabha election for a third successive term. But Modi, a keen student of history, knows the perils of complacency.

Rewind to Indira Gandhi. In 1972, shortly after the Bangladesh war, she appeared impregnable. A cult developed around her. The Congress had a 352-seat majority in the Lok Sabha. Mrs Gandhi's cabinet was filled with a smattering of talented ministers but also many time-servers. Sycophancy was rampant. Congress president DK Barooah infamously declared, "India is Indira and Indira is India". Mrs Gandhi didn't bother to demur. She probably believed him.

The similarity with Modi is uncanny. In his second term as prime minister, Modi has been deified. No op-ed or TV interview begins or ends without a minister referring to the "inspiring leadership of Modiji".

Bad news awaited Indira Gandhi in her second term as elected prime minister. Jayaprakash Narayan had launched a civil disobedience movement in 1974 against Mrs Gandhi's growing autocracy. A year later Mrs Gandhi made a fatal mistake. She reacted to an adverse judgment by the Allahabad High Court on 12 June 1975 invalidating her 1971 Lok Sabha election victory from Rae Bareli against Raj Narain and debarring her from contesting elections for six years over a fairly minor electoral malpractice of using government machinery during the poll. Mrs Gandhi imposed the Emergency on 26 June 1975.

When it was revoked in March 1977, the Congress was thrown out of power and Mrs Gandhi, after 11 years as prime minister—nine of them legitimately—barely escaped imprisonment.

The Congress is in decline today because it is no longer a cadre-based political party but a private family business. The Gandhis are the only shareholders. The others serve at their pleasure, including party president Mallikarjun Kharge. Even thoughtful Congress leaders dare not defy the Gandhis as recent events have shown. They want regular inner-party elections but when pressed will dutifully say that veto power on all decisions resides with the Gandhis. This isn't just sycophancy, it is servitude.

But the BJP shouldn't rejoice. It is dangerously close to emulating the Congress. The deification of Modi must stop. He should receive honest advice, however unpalatable, not advice ministers think he wants to hear. By 1975, Indira Gandhi was receiving feedback from Siddartha Shankar Ray, the former chief minister of West Bengal and union cabinet minister, that was both inaccurate and self-serving. It led to the Emergency and her downfall. Modi needs ministers who are competent, have domain knowledge and aren't afraid to disagree constructively with him.

Despite the rigours of the Covid pandemic and the Russia-Ukraine war, Modi has done much to commend himself in the past nine years: welfare, financial inclusion, electrification, infrastructure, defence indigenisation, tap water, health insurance, direct subsidy benefits, food security, sanitation and digitisation. On foreign policy he has had more hits than misses. On the macro economy, direct tax reform, privatisation and regulation, he has his work cut out.

When Modi completes his second term in office in May 2024, he will have been prime minister for ten years. If he wins a third term in 2024 and completes his tenure in 2029, Modi will have been PM for 15 consecutive years. Add to that over 12 years as CM of Gujarat and Modi would have held a Constitutional office for an unprecedented 27 years.

Modi turns 73 in September 2023. He will be 79 in 2029. If Modi avoids Indira Gandhi's mistakes deep into her second term, victory in 2024 is likely. But sycophancy within the BJP must end or history may be tempted to repeat itself.

∽

As May 2024 approaches, Modi faces another dilemma. He has built his entire political career on criticising—and rightly so—the nepotism and entitlement of political dynasts. Apart from targeting the Gandhis of the Congress, Modi is unsparing of the Yadavs of the Samajwadi Party (SP) and Rashtriya Janata Dal (RJD), the Karunanidhis of the DMK, and the Abdullahs and Muftis of respectively the National Conference (NC) and People's Democratic Party (PDP). He is less vocal about other dynastic political families like the Pawars, Patnaiks and Thackerays for strategic and electoral reasons.

Modi knows his strengths are predicated on doubling down on a nationalism that borders on majoritarianism. This has alienated Muslims who comprise 15 per cent of India's electorate. Along with Christians and other minorities, nearly 20 per cent of India is non-Hindu. The 2002 riots in Gujarat polarised communities. Muslims comprise only 9 per cent of Gujarat's population but many voted for the BJP in its historic landslide win in the 2022 assembly election. Gujarat has long served as a laboratory for the BJP's majoritarian project. Modi soon realised that the Gujarat model could not be replicated nationally. There were entrenched minority interests in Delhi's ecosystem, in West Bengal and in Kerala. He would have to tread carefully.

Throughout his two terms, Modi has rarely spoken out on rising communal violence. He has let the narrative play out. The old ecosystem, nurtured for years on Left-Congress entitlement and privilege, treated Modi with scant respect. To them, he was an *arriviste*, son of a *chaiwala*. Abuses poured forth from the

Opposition, activists and media. The attacks were choreographed with brutal efficiency.

In late December 2018, just four months before the 2019 Lok Sabha poll, matters did not look propitious for the BJP. The party had lost three state assembly elections in quick succession to the Congress: Rajasthan, Chhattisgarh and Madhya Pradesh. Not surprisingly, opinion polls in January 2019 predicted a close general election.

Modi swung into campaign mode. As he had done in 2014, he travelled tirelessly across the country, addressing over 150 rallies. But the Congress was now in full voice. Party president Rahul Gandhi, buoyed by Congress' sweep of three states (though the win in Madhya Pradesh was razor-thin and the state would be lost a year later to the BJP) attacked Modi relentlessly.

For the first time, Modi appeared defensive and tired. Rahul had meanwhile rediscovered his Kashmiri Brahmin roots and begun to visit temples. The soft Hindutva tactic had worked in the Gujarat assembly election in December 2017 when the BJP was reduced to 99 seats in the 182-seat assembly before defections from the Congress took it back up to three digits. But in Gujarat—the prime minister's homegrown laboratory of Hindu nationalism—temple-hopping had served Rahul and the Congress well. Now as campaigning for the May 2019 Lok Sabha election entered its last lap, Rahul was in full cry. He called Modi corrupt, slammed demonetisation, excoriated the hasty rollout of GST, taunted Modi over the BJP's triple state assembly losses, accused him of corruption in the Rafale fighter jet deal and pilloried his economic mismanagement.

Other Opposition leaders, spearheaded by West Bengal Chief Minister Mamata Banerjee and Delhi Chief Minister Arvind Kejriwal, attacked Modi over Hindu majoritarianism. The old ecosystem sprung back to life with a string of petitions in the Supreme Court on the Ram Temple, Rafale and the allegedly mysterious death of a Bombay High Court judge BM Loya.

Rahul's advisors included several foreign educated technocrats. They told him privately in February 2019 that the BJP would win no more than 150 seats. The Congress, they said, could win 170 seats and, with like-minded allies, could form the government in May 2019.

On 14 February 2019, the narrative changed overnight. Terror struck Pulwama, 30 kms south of Srinagar in J&K. This was the deadliest attack by Pakistan-sponsored Jaish-e-Mohammad (JeM) terrorists on Indian soil in years. After the Uri terror attack in September 2016, India had retaliated strongly. Elite commandos crossed two kilometers deep into the LoC over a front of 70 kilometers to destroy several Pakistani terror modules without a single Indian casualty.

Praised for launching the surgical strike across the LoC within days of the terror attack on Uri, the pressure now mounted on Modi to act decisively against Pakistan's terror infrastructure. The Pulwama attack had enraged public opinion. The risks inherent in a retaliatory military strike on Pakistani soil were enormous. But if he didn't act, the damage to Modi's reputation as a leader tough on terror would be incalculable.

Time was of the essence. A response delayed beyond a few weeks would signal indecisiveness. National Security Advisor Ajit Doval, the three chiefs of the army, air force and navy, and the high-level Cabinet Committee on Security (CCS) met several times to draw up a plan of action.

Modi was conscious of the electoral impact of an Indian military response to Pulwama. A successful counter-strike would buttress his campaign with barely weeks left for the crucial 2019 Lok Sabha election. A botched strike would have the opposite effect. Not responding was not an option.

For Modi though, the principal consideration was ensuring that Pakistan-abetted terror was punished and the cost of future terror strikes made unaffordable. Pakistan, he told the NSA and service chiefs, must pay a heavy price for Pulwama. In a series of high-powered meetings Modi stressed that electoral considerations were irrelevant. Pulwama represented an act of war by Pakistan against India.

The Balakot strike by the Indian Air Force deep inside Pakistan on 27 February 2019 transformed the mathematics of the 2019 general election. Analysts and pollsters had predicted a close election, giving the BJP 250–260 Lok Sabha seats, slightly short of a simple majority. When the election results were announced on 23 May 2019, the BJP had emerged triumphant with 303 seats.

FIVE

2024: The Year of Reckoning

AS HIS SECOND FIVE-YEAR TERM COMES TO AN END AND THE 2024 Lok Sabha election nears, Modi has emerged as the shrewdest Indian political leader since Indira Gandhi. The two couldn't have come from more different backgrounds. Indira Gandhi was born into privilege in 1917. She studied in Sommerville College at Oxford University but left without a degree. Indira married a young Parsi, Feroze Gandhi, in 1942 at the height of the freedom movement.

In 1959, at the age of 41, Indira was installed by father Jawaharlal Nehru as Congress president. She had never held an institutional post before nor did she have significant administrative experience. Dynastic politics in Independent India was thus officially launched in 1959. It would, like a virus, spread to virtually every other political party over the next few decades and infect India's body politic.

Living in the luxury of Teen Murti House, Nehru's prime ministerial residence, Indira revelled in her role as her widowed father's official hostess at diplomatic banquets. She was estranged from husband Feroze, a fiery parliamentarian who frequently challenged his father-in-law in Lok Sabha debates and ran the Congress party's newspaper *National Herald*. Feroze died of a heart attack in 1960, days before he was to turn 48.

In January 1966, Indira Gandhi found herself as prime minister following Lal Bahadur Shastri's death in Tashkent. She would occupy that office—with a short 19-month interruption following revocation of the draconian Emergency she had imposed on the country in 1975—for a total of 16 years, just nine months short of her father's tenure as prime minister.

Modi's circumstances – and rise to power – were a polar opposite. He grew up in the small Gujarati town of Vadnagar. He left home at 17, joined the RSS at 19, was seconded to the BJP at 37, became general secretary looking after six states at 48, was appointed chief minister of Gujarat at 51 and—against fierce opposition from within the party and abuse from the Congress—won office as prime minister at 63.

Modi served as chief minister of Gujarat for over 12 years across three terms. He won three successive assembly elections in 2002, 2007 and 2012. When Prime Minister Atal Bihari Vajpayee visited Gujarat after the 2002 Godhra riots, he reprimanded the newly installed chief minister. Modi had assumed office just four months ago. Follow "raja dharma", Vajpayee told Modi. Sitting beside Vajpayee at the crowded press conference, Modi replied he was doing just that. Vajpayee nodded, then said to the assembled journalists, "The chief minister is doing the same (following raja dharma)."

The media played the first part of the interaction—Vajpayee's reprimand—over and over again. It quickly went viral on the internet. Modi's response and Vajpayee's supportive reply were both cut out. The demonisation of Modi had begun. Despite being acquitted by the Supreme Court of complicity in the 2002 Gujarat riots that killed 790 Muslims and 254 Hindus, many still believe Modi did not do enough to control the carnage.

The riots were sparked by a mob of Ganchi Muslims at the Godhra railway station. They burnt to death 59 Ramsevaks returning by train from Ayodhya. After Modi became prime minister in 2014, the taint of the 2002 riots was used in election after election—assembly and Lok Sabha—by the Opposition and sections of the media to tarnish his credentials as a leader. Those tactics failed electorally but they achieved one collateral purpose: the gradual Vajpayee-fication of Modi.

Vajpayee began his leadership of the BJP, when the party was founded in December 1980, as a fiery Hindutva proponent. Consider this excerpt from a speech Vajpayee delivered in Assam in 1983: "Foreigners have come here and the government does nothing. What if they had come into Punjab instead? People would have chopped them into pieces and thrown them away."

The Nellie massacre of Bengali Muslims in Assam took place soon after Vajpayee's speech.

While LK Advani was regarded as the BJP's hardline leader who encouraged party workers to bring down the Babri structure, Vajpayee cultivated a softer image. Yet his speech just one day before the Babri structure was demolished on 6 December 1992, laid bare his true feelings on the issue: "Sharp and pointed stones have come out. No one can sit there. The ground has to be levelled. It has to be made fit for sitting. Arrangements for a yagya (of the Ram temple) will be done, so there will be some construction."

Two months after the Gujarat riots, in April 2002, Vajpayee, now the prime minister, said this at a BJP national council meeting: "We should not forget how the tragedy of Gujarat started. The subsequent developments were no doubt condemnable. But who lit the fire? How did the fire spread? Wherever Muslims live, they don't like to live in co-existence with others, they don't like to mingle with others; and instead of propagating their ideas in a peaceful manner, they want to spread their faith by resorting to terror and threats. The world has become alert to this danger."

Vajpayee was careful to cloak his thoughts in poetry, long silences and pacifist prose. So, in Parliament in May 2002, Vajpayee declared: "I accept the Hindutva of Swami Vivekananda but the type of Hindutva being propagated now is wrong and one should be wary of it."

Like most Indian leaders, Vajpayee realised early in his career that you can govern a complex country like India only from the centre. The extremes—right and left—aren't sustainable. In public therefore Vajpayee drifted from the right towards the centre just as Jawaharlal Nehru, Indira Gandhi and others had drifted from the left towards the centre.

What about Modi's own ideological trajectory? Over the past nine years, Modi has evolved from a state leader to a national leader to a deified leader and finally to a world leader. In doing so, Modi has used Vajpayee's playbook: hard Hindutva warrior during elections; pro-poor messiah at home; and sober global statesman abroad. Thus we see Modi's fiery version in election campaign rallies. That is followed by a messianic touch: providing free food and subsidies to 80 crore distressed Indians. And finally, a statesmanlike role in global affairs as leader of the G20.

All three avatars are visible in Modi as he gears up for the 2024 Lok Sabha election. Vajpayee took the BJP from two Lok Sabha seats to 182 seats in 1998. He became the longest-serving non-Congress prime minister in 2004. Modi has effortlessly passed Vajpayee's record of six years as prime minister by doing exactly what Vajpayee did: moving from the hard right towards the centre-right where governance has greater longevity.

And yet India in 2024 will not mirror the India of 1998. A new generation of voters will have come of age. They see no contradiction between centre-right nationalism and aspirational consumerism. As 2024 looms, Modi is attempting what no other BJP or even Congress prime minister has done: win three consecutive Lok Sabha elections. But didn't Nehru win three successive Lok Sabha elections? He did. In 1952, 1957 and 1962. But of course, he didn't complete his third term.

To surpass Nehru's electoral record, Modi will have to not only win in 2024 but complete his third term in office. For someone once reminded of doing *raj dharma*, that could be a moment to savour.

The Congress long enjoyed a quasi-colonial existence after 1947. The British were evicted but not their institutions, manners, prejudices, favouritism, greed and elitism. Nehru liked the description of him as Indian in dress and English in manner. He could be effete with the British, especially the Mountbattens, and was susceptible to flattery.

The colonial Indian Civil Service (ICS) became the Indian Administrative Service (IAS)—a steel frame now long rusted. Minorities were appeased, not empowered. Private industry was shackled even as the rest of Asia raced ahead. Governance was paternalistic rather than pragmatic. The poor were patronised with slogans like *garibi hatao*. Instead of liberalising the economy, Indira Gandhi's socialist government, through the 1960s and 1970s, straitjacketed it.

Companies were discouraged from scaling up. Most remained small to avoid the Monopolies and Restrictive Trade Practices (MRTP) Act. Regulation was overbearing. Tax rates rose to more than 97 per cent in the highest-income bracket. The black economy proliferated as Indians sent their unofficial income by *hawala* to secret Swiss bank accounts rather than pay tax. What is being tortuously uncovered today by court investigations as illicit money laundering had its early origins in the socialist India of the late 1960s.

Is Modi becoming another Indira? He has her political instincts. But is he now, like her, a protectionist and an enthusiastic over-regulator? The short answer: possibly. Modi's slogan "be vocal about local" has protectionism encoded within it. I wrote an article in the *Hindustan Times* in September 2020 that the slogan should be rephrased: "be vocal about both local and global". In short, make India self-reliant but also make India an export hub and make the world India-reliant. That is true liberalisation. It too is the orientation Modi's new forward-looking trade and economic policy is now taking.

The prime minister's address at the centenary of the Aligarh Muslim University (AMU) in 2020 seemed to launch a kinder, softer version of Modi. By calling Islam an integral part of India's cultural heritage, Modi went even further than Vajpayee. According to a translation of Modi's speech[6] as reported by a leading daily, the prime minister adopted a conciliatory tone on religious identity.

He said: "The policies made by the government reach every section irrespective of their religion. Bank accounts of over 40 crore poor have been opened without any discrimination. Without discrimination, more than two crore poor were provided pucca houses. More than eight crore women were given gas connections without discrimination. Around 50 crore people got free treatment of up to ₹5 lakh under the Ayushman scheme without any discrimination. What belongs to the country belongs to every countryman and every citizen should be benefited. Our government is working with this spirit.

"AMU's founder Sir Syed had said that growth of the country is above the caste and religion of the people. He had also given an example and said that for the body to remain healthy, every body part should be healthy. Sir Syed had also said that religion should not be the reason for anyone's backwardness. India is on the path where no citizen would be left behind because of their religion and everyone would get equal opportunities so that everyone can fulfil their dreams."

Hardline supporters of Modi fear that Modi's "soft secularism" is as electorally motivated as Rahul Gandhi's "soft Hindutva". They believe both are ideologically corrupt. Modi's attempt to woo Muslims, they say, is counter-productive: Muslims see through the hypocrisy of the AMU speech and anyway vote en masse against the BJP just as most Hindus see through Rahul's temple-hopping and vote against the Congress.

Modi, Muslims believe, remains an implacable Hindutva warrior.

---

[6]22 December 2020.

His actions, they say, belie his words. The CAA, the revocation of J&K's special status and the building of the Ram Mandir in Ayodhya where the demolished Babri structure stood, all point in one direction: hard Hindutva.

What explains Modi's personal popularity despite the perfect storm of problems that periodically buffet India's economy and national security? A large part has to do with the psyche of the average Indian voter. Modi's understanding of the Indian mind was acquired at an early age. His teenage wanderings in the Himalayas, eating and living with monks, sadhus and ordinary villagers, gave him rare insights. During a varied career in the RSS—from doing menial jobs to fixing organisational issues—Modi learnt much about human nature.

He realised that religion played an oversized role in most Indians' lives. Religion could have both political and psychological uses. In Gujarat as chief minister, he employed religion to win and keep power. But an equally powerful tool was the psychological impact of religiosity on individuals. In no other country are religious figures treated as reverentially as they are in India. The transmogrification of Prime Minister Modi to Saint Modi began with the ground-breaking ceremony of the Ram Temple in Ayodhya. By identifying himself with Lord Ram, Modi raised himself in popular imagination to a saintly person. The year-long untrimmed beard was symbolic: Modi was signalling penance, sharing the pain and distress of poor Indians who had lost livelihoods during the Covid pandemic.

A saint can have foibles. But most Indians think that people with Godly souls have noble intentions, irrespective of outcomes. That is why respondents in surveys continued to back Modi despite the insensitive treatment of migrant workers during the first pandemic lockdown. Modi cultivated an air of being a father figure. His rhetoric was softer, more persuasive than aggressive. But Modi is not turning into a Vajpayee or a saffron version of Nehru as many of his Hindutva supporters fear. Modi's belief in Hindutva remains as strong as ever. Only the dressing has changed.

The Congress-Left ecosystem hasn't fully understood Modi's strategy. It attacks him personally and venomously. Rahul continues to taunt him. NGOs have sharpened their attack on him. The foreign media is irredeemably hostile. All these attacks roll off Modi's new saintly skin. Instead of weakening his popular appeal, they appear to strengthen it.

Indians admire martyrs. That is one reason why Modi has deliberately avoided actively pursuing cases that could send the Gandhis to jail over, for instance, the alleged ₹3,000-crore *National Herald* scam or prosecuted Robert Vadra over a decade-old land corruption allegation. The lessons of Indira Gandhi's 1980 election victory are fresh in Modi's mind. She lost power in the 1977 general election shortly after the Emergency was revoked. She was relentlessly attacked by the media and the Janata government between March 1977 and December 1979. She spent hardly any time in jail. But Indians promptly voted her back to office in January 1980.

✻

Modi has made himself about "trust". Indeed, the most common reaction to him among middle-class and poor voters is that they trust him. Modi has spoken very rarely about his family. In my interactions with him, he skirted over his relationship with his father, his mother (who passed away aged 99) and his brothers. In a tribute to his mother on her 99th birthday in June 2022, Modi however laid bare his innermost feelings in an emotional blog post[7].

> My mother was born in Visnagar in Mehsana in Gujarat, which is quite close to my hometown Vadnagar. She did not get her own mother's affection. At a tender age, she lost my

---

[7]*The Times of India*, 19 June 2022.

grandmother to the Spanish Flu pandemic. My mother did not have much of a childhood due to these struggles – she was forced to grow beyond her age. She was the eldest child in her family and became the eldest daughter-in-law after marriage.

Like clockwork, my father used to leave for work at four in the morning. His footsteps would tell the neighbours that it is 4 am and Damodar kaka is leaving for work. Another daily ritual was to pray at the local temple before opening his little tea shop. Mother was equally punctual. She would also wake up with my father and finish many chores in the morning itself. From grinding grains to sifting rice and daal, Mother had no help. While working she would hum her favourite bhajans and hymns.

During rains our roof would leak, and the house would flood. Mother would place buckets and utensils below the leaks to collect the rainwater. Even in this adverse situation, Mother would be a symbol of resilience. Even today, mother takes only as much food in the thali as she can eat and doesn't waste even a morsel.

Today many years later, whenever people ask her if she is proud that her son has become the country's prime minister, mother gives an extremely deep response. She says, 'I am as proud as you are. Nothing is mine. I am a mere instrument in the plans of God.' You must have noticed that Mother never accompanies me for any government or public programme.

She has accompanied me on only two occasions in the past. Once, it was at a public function in Ahmedabad when she applied tilak on my forehead after I had returned from Srinagar where I had hoisted the national flag at Lal Chowk completing the Ekta Yatra. That was an extremely emotional moment for Mother because a few people had died in a terror attack in Phagwara at the time of the Ekta Yatra. She became extremely worried.

The second instance is when I first took oath as Gujarat's Chief Minister in 2001. The oath-taking ceremony held two decades ago was the last public event that Mother attended with me. Since then, she has never accompanied me to a single public event.

When I decided to leave home, mother already sensed my decision even before I told her: I would often tell my parents that I wanted to go out and understand the world. I would tell them about Swami Vivekananda and mention that I wished to visit the Ramakrishna Mission Mutt. This went on for days. Finally, I revealed my desire to leave home and asked them for their blessings. My father was extremely disheartened, and in irritation he told me, 'As you wish'. I told them that I would not leave home without their blessings. However, mother understood my desires, and blessed me, 'Do as your mind says.' To assuage my father, she asked him to show my horoscope to an astrologer. My father consulted a relative who knew astrology. After studying my horoscope, the relative remarked, 'His path is different. He will go only on the path the Almighty has chosen for him.'

A few hours later, I left home. By then, even my father had come to terms with my decision and gave me his blessings. Before leaving, mother fed me curd and jaggery for an auspicious new beginning. She knew that my life would become extremely different henceforth. Mothers may be extremely adept at controlling their emotions but always find it hard when their child leaves home. Mother was teary-eyed but there were immense blessings for my future.

After moving to Delhi, my meetings with her are even fewer than before. Sometimes when I visit Gandhinagar, I call on her for a short while. However, I have never felt any discontent from mother over my absence. Her love and affection remain the same, her blessings remain the same.

Mother often asks me. 'Are you happy in Delhi? Do you like it?' She keeps assuring me that I should not worry about her and lose focus on the larger responsibilities. Whenever I speak to her on the phone, she says, 'Never do anything wrong or anything bad with anyone and keep working for the poor.'

Heeraben Modi passed away peacefully after a short illness on 30 December 2022.

SIX

Matters of State

IN 2007, THE CONGRESS-LED UPA 1 GOVERNMENT WAS IN FULL FLOW. Despite winning just 145 seats in the 2004 Lok Sabha election—only seven more than the BJP—the Congress had been propped up by the Left's 59 MPs and other UPA allies. Hamid Ansari, a retired Indian Foreign Service (IFS) officer, was plucked out from the National Commission for Minorities in 2007 by the Congress and elected vice-president of India. He was re-elected in 2012 for a second term under the UPA 2 government.

Ansari suited the Congress' ideological purpose. On assuming office in 2004, the party had sought to establish itself as the principal protector of minorities. With Ansari as vice-president, the strategy seemed to pay off. Against the grain, the Congress won 206 seats in the 2009 Lok Sabha poll. Ansari was keen on a third term in 2017. Sensing opposition from the BJP-led NDA government, he quietly withdrew from the race.

Between 1990 and 1992, Ansari served as India's ambassador to Iran. The period was a penumbra in Indian politics. Prime Minister VP Singh had resigned in November 1990 after 11 months in office. Prime Minister Chandra Shekhar served for seven months till June 1991 before giving way to Prime Minister PV Narasimha Rao. Weeks before, former Prime Minister Rajiv Gandhi had been assassinated by a woman suicide bomber from the Liberation Tigers of Tamil Eelam (LTTE).

Thus in a frantic period of less than two years, India had

sworn in three prime ministers and witnessed the assassination of one former prime minister. No one in Delhi's political establishment was paying much attention to what Ambassador Ansari was up to in Iran.

What was he up to? RK Yadav, a former senior officer in India's intelligence agency Research and Analysis Wing (R&AW), wrote a book titled *Mission R&AW*. Published in 2017, it bared Ansari's role in Iran. Yadav said Ansari severely compromised India's intelligence operations in Iran. He refused to cooperate when a RAW agent in Tehran was kidnapped by Iran's intelligence agency. Narasimha Rao was prime minister. Atal Bihari Vajpayee, then leader of the Opposition, prevailed upon Rao to persuade Iran to release the RAW agent. Ansari though had caused long-term damage to India's intelligence network in Iran.

As Yadav wrote in his book, "Most of the operations of R&AW received a setback after this incident since its operatives became insecure due to inaction of Ansari. R&AW operatives had penetrated inside the Qom religious centre to monitor the activities of some Kashmiri elements whose activities were detrimental to the security situation in Jammu and Kashmir but this incident made them abort further infiltration inside that centre at that juncture."

Given his track record in Iran, it was not surprising that Ansari accepted an invitation to attend a conference hosted by the radical Islamist Popular Front of India (PFI) in September 2017, weeks after stepping down as vice-president of India. The group was banned by the Modi government in September 2022.

In a virtual conference organised in 2021 by the Indian American Muslim Council (IAMC), an Islamist body, Ansari echoed worn-out tropes: the rise of "Hindu nationalism" and the "emergence of trends and practices that dispute the well-established principle of civic nationalism". Ansari went on to say: "This interposes a new and imaginary practice of cultural nationalism. It seeks to present an electoral majority in the guise of a religious majority and monopolised political power. It wants to distinguish citizens on the basis of their faith, give vent to intolerance, insinuate otherness, and promote disquiet and insecurity. Some of its recent manifestations are chilling and reflect poorly on our claim to be governed by rule of law. It's a question that has to be answered. These trends need to be contested and contested legally and contested politically."

Other participants in the 2021 IAMC conference were American lawmakers well known as anti-Indian lobbyists, many on the payroll of Pakistan's Inter-Services Intelligence (ISI). The tell-tale marks of this cabal are everywhere: among sections of the media, hard-Left activists and lawyers, Opposition leaders tasked with disrupting Parliament, retired army officers who write newspaper op-eds based on misleading defence data, former IFS bureaucrats and track-2 specialists with vested interests.

It's obviously important to ventilate diverse views. A democracy would be intellectually parched without fierce dissent. The problem is when facts are manufactured to fit a pre-fixed narrative. Governments need to be criticised. The Modi government must be held to account and its policies scrutinised. But selective criticism based on fixed facts often lapses into propaganda.

✑

When he entered Parliament for the first time in May 2014 as prime minister, Modi had prostrated himself on the steps of the Lok Sabha. It was a conciliatory gesture to the old established order that, with minor interruptions, had ruled India for the previous 67 years. Modi was in effect saying: I'm new to Delhi; I know the elite still think of me as a mere *chaiwala*; but with the Lok Sabha election over, we need to put aside our differences and cooperate with one another to create a new India.

The reaction was swift and dismissive. The old political elite, smarting from its defeat in the 2014 Lok Sabha election, sneered at Modi's rustic ways. When Modi put on a personally monogrammed pinstriped suit, Congress leader Rahul Gandhi mocked him with the "suit-boot sarkar" taunt. Modi 1.0 was still burdened with self-doubt. The old elite continued to treat him with withering contempt. By 2019, it was clear that Modi had in five years not changed Lutyens' Delhi even though his ministers now occupied large swathes of it. But Lutyens' Delhi was never about real estate as about a bent of mind.

Modi 2.0 emerged as a changed leader after winning a landslide in the May 2019 Lok Sabha election. Major Bills were tabled and passed in Parliament. The Covid-19 pandemic reversed the momentum abruptly. CAA rules were not notified for years. The Uniform Civil Code (UCC) remains a work in progress. Months ahead of the 2024 General Election, Modi faces three clear challenges: the economy, inflation and jobs. The production-linked incentive (PLI) scheme is one of the government's most innovative economic initiatives. It has the potential to transform India into an export manufacturing hub even as China's labour costs rise and foreign companies diversify their supply chains to move production capacity out of China.

A critical task for Modi in the run-up to 2024 is to refresh governance. The prime minister won his mandate on the promise of minimum government, maximum governance. The opposite has often been the case. The BJP is already acquiring some of the traits of the old elite. In UPA 1 and 2, the Gandhi family and a tight circle of acolytes called the shots. In the Modi government, the prime minister, the home minister and a few insiders decide key policies.

Members of the old Congress-led Lutyens' elite had humble origins. They climbed up the slippery social, economic and political ladder till most had obliterated all evidence whence they had emerged. Who after all remembers that Sonia Gandhi, now living in a government-owned Lutyens' bungalow valued at over ₹600 crore, was sent to England to study English nearly

60 years ago, aged 17, by a family whose modest background in Italy mirrored Modi's own?

Rahul Gandhi inherited a party that had lost several former Congress leaders since the 1990s. Many formed breakaway Congress clones: Sharad Pawar (Nationalist Congress Party), Mamata Banerjee (Trinamool Congress) and YS Jagan Mohan Reddy (YSR Congress). Recognising Congress' historical brand value, all three have retained it as a suffix.

The Gandhis run a political party with valuable financial assets, but restless loyalists. They rebel occasionally but are quickly brought to heel. The three Gandhis have divided management duties among themselves. Sonia Gandhi is the final authority. No Congress leader dares to defy her. Priyanka Gandhi-Vadra plays the role of peacemaker among squabbling Congress leaders. She makes sure, though, that everyone knows that underneath her velvet glove lies an iron fist. Rahul Gandhi's role is clearly defined: to attack Prime Minister Narendra Modi personally at every opportunity. Gandhi knows that the party's best electoral hope is to damage the prime minister's credibility.

Congress President Mallikarjun Kharge poses no challenge to the Gandhi troika's authority. At 81, Kharge provides the family with a political shield. He takes responsibility for electoral losses and allows the Family to take credit for poll victories. Sonia shrewdly recognises that however hard Mamata Banerjee and Sharad Pawar try, the numbers for the potpourri of regional parties may not add up to 272 in the 2024 Lok Sabha poll. But at 53, Rahul has time on his side. Banerjee is 69, Pawar 81, and Modi 72.

Kejriwal, at 53 the same age as Rahul, remains the dark horse. But Kejriwal's attempt to claim the Congress' Opposition space came up against a road block in the Gujarat and Himachal Pradesh assembly elections in December 2022. His appeal to a new generation of aspirational middle-class Indians cannot, however, be underestimated. For Kejriwal, 2029, not 2024, is the target.

India is at an inflection point. The great cities of Mumbai, Kolkata and Chennai were colonial projects. Before 1700, India's thriving trading economy was centred around coastal towns like Surat. The British shifted the balance of power towards cities from where they could both trade profitably and tax the hinterland. India's small towns and villages slipped into vassalage. The collector would come to collect taxes, consigning rural India, steadily but surely, to poverty and famine.

After 1947, the levers of power stayed with a postcolonial elite. It paid lip service to Mahatma Gandhi's truism that India lives in its villages. India has around 6 lakh populated villages in which more than 800 million people live. They have for decades remained poor and largely out of sight. That is changing. This has important political implications. Congress built its post-Independence electoral constituency on the basis of a largely illiterate and impoverished rural India, a legacy of colonial rule. BJP's electoral successes have been founded on a social and economic transformation in what in popular characterisation is known as New India or more accurately Bharat.

Several Indian politicians remain out of touch with the subtle shift in the balance of economic and cultural power between India and Bharat that signifies a shift in the balance of political power. Modi was quick to notice the change. His focus on welfare benefits has been aimed squarely at small towns and villages across India: last-mile electrification, water on tap, digitised subsidy transfers, health insurance and rural housing. The rural middle class may be small in number but rural India is also aspirational India—the future urban middle-class.

Richard Verma served as US ambassador to India from 2014 to 2017. An Indian-American, Verma addressed students of an Indian university in 2021. Here's what he said: "I look out at the year 2030, for example, and I see an India that may lead the world in almost every category... [The] most populous nation, the most college graduates, the largest middle class, the most cellphone and internet users, along with the third largest military and third largest economy, all coexisting in the world's largest democracy...The journey to global leadership has begun."

The young students at Jindal University's School of Banking and Finance listened with rapt attention. The message they were hearing from a distinguished former diplomat who had travelled widely in India as US ambassador and met the country's entrepreneurs, NGOs, activists, journalists, politicians and ordinary people, was very different from the downbeat assessment they often receive from the media—Indian and Western.

Was Verma being overly optimistic? Do facts bear out his projections? By the early 2030s, as Verma correctly pointed out, India will have the world's largest middle-class that is both aspirational and young. For Western and Indian companies that is demographic nirvana: size, youth, ambition. Companies such as Apple have begun shifting some production of iPhones from China to India. Foreign direct investment (FDI) is at record highs. India is the world's third largest startup hub after the US and China and well ahead of Britain and Japan. The West welcomes the investment opportunities India offers. It embraces India as a member of the confluence of democracies arrayed against China. And yet it knows that India will continue to follow a policy of strategic autonomy—or nuanced neutrality—that it showed during the Russia-Ukraine war.

Many of Modi's welfare projects for the poor contributed significantly to his victory in the 2019 Lok Sabha election. And yet many are still a work in progress. Why, for example, has open defecation continued despite the rise in coverage of toilets across India from 43 per cent before 2014 to a reported 98 per cent today? The answer: culture and religion. Toilets in some villages have been converted into storerooms. Many lack sewage connections and are unusable. On rural electrification, last-mile connectivity remains a problem. For free LPG cylinders, refills are often unaffordable for many poor families as fuel prices rise. In health insurance, top hospitals have been reluctant to empanel themselves, citing low rates set for various surgical and non-surgical treatments after the Covid pandemic.

All of this captures the scale of what Modi is attempting to do—and largely succeeding—though the job is yet half-done. Many of the pro-poor welfare schemes the Modi government has initiated since 2014 should have been initiated and completed by past governments.

In an insightful article in *Business Standard* on 3 November, 2021, R. Jagannathan, Editorial Director of *Swarajya* magazine, wrote: "Modi is a socio-political venture capitalist at work. From Swachh Bharat to Ujjwala to the latest Atmanirbhar Bharat, Modi has launched one new scheme almost every two months in his tenure. Swachh Bharat and Ujjwala were huge successes, apart from the reformative Jan Dhan-Aadhaar-Mobile trio, direct benefit transfers, and the bankruptcy code. In this term, GST will deliver with some tweaks, and for ordinary people Nal-Se-Jal (water from tap) will be hugely beneficial. Taken separately, Ujjwala, Saubhagya (providing last-mile power connections to the home), Swachh Bharat, Ayushman Bharat and Nal-Se-Jal are separate initiatives. Taken together, they empower the homemaker and improve health outcomes.

"Modi has formalised the Indian economy like no one else before him. With GST, the push for tax compliance and the extension of social security benefits to many more workers (often on self-help), Indian business has taken a big leap towards formalisation. Micro and small companies, currently paying extortionate rates in the informal lending markets, will now get loans through the account aggregator initiative. But Modi's formalisation goes beyond firms and companies. The poor have been conscripted too. Between Jan Dhan, DBT and Unified Payments Interface (UPI), more Indians are now part of the formal financial sector than ever before. With the e-Shram portal for migrant labour, blue collar gig economy workers are being visibly formalised as well."

The Modi government inherited a crisis-ridden economy in 2014—spiralling inflation, high fiscal deficit and low GDP growth. Modi's first five years focused on "micro-economic reforms"—principally welfare schemes—but less so on macro-economic reforms. The task now is to take welfare schemes to their conclusion by ironing out wrinkles in their execution and refocus on the broader economy, especially growth, jobs and inflation.

✍🏻

No Indian prime minister since Indira Gandhi has attracted as much adulation—or as much revulsion—as Narendra Modi. Indira Gandhi's first term, from 1966 to 1971, was a mixed bag. She nationalised banks, abolished princely privy purses, battled crippling food shortages, and presided over a socialist rate of economic growth that averaged 3 per cent a year.

Modi rode to power in May 2014 on a wave India had witnessed only twice before. The first was in March 1977 when the Congress was swept out of power in the Lok Sabha election following the revocation of the Emergency and the Janata Party's Morarji Desai installed as independent India's first non-Congress prime minister. The second was after the assassination of Indira Gandhi in October 1984 which lifted Rajiv Gandhi two months later to the biggest electoral landslide in the history of independent India. The Congress won more seats (over 400) in December 1984 than it had won under Jawaharlal Nehru and Indira Gandhi.

But those two electoral waves followed unusual events—one, the Emergency, the other, a prime minister's assassination. The wave that took Modi to victory in 2014 was preceded by an anti-corruption movement against the scam-tainted Congress-led UPA government—but it was not on the scale of the epochal events of 1977 and 1984.

By winning the first single-party majority since Rajiv Gandhi's triumph in 1984, expectations from the Modi government were high. Modi has been excellent in executing big-ticket development projects and enhancing welfare benefits. But on structural economic reforms, his record is mixed. The land acquisition bill remains in suspended animation. Farm laws were repealed in the face of farmers' protest. Several infrastructure projects are moving at a snail's pace because laws around acquiring land are opaque and complex. The implementation of labour laws has been slow and halting.

The Insolvency and Bankruptcy Code (IBC) is meanwhile in danger of being blindsided by India's somnolent judicial system. Recognising the urgency to give the IBC more teeth, the government has amended it to ensure it does not go the way of previous debt structuring schemes. The amendments have helped but more needs to be done to make the IBC the game changer it was designed to be.

Among the biggest disappointments of Modi's first five years in office was the lack of urgency shown on public sector divestment. PSUs simply bought each other's shares to fulfil budget divestment targets—there was no serious attempt to privatise loss-making government-owned companies like MTNL, BSNL and other chronic loss-makers. As in Gujarat, Modi placed his faith in the public sector and the bureaucracy. It was only after Air India's privatisation, well into Modi's second term, that public divestments gathered pace with a successful sale of equity by Life Insurance Corporation (LIC), one of the world's largest insurance companies.

The late Finance Minister Arun Jaitley's six Union Budgets from 2014 to 2018 (including the interim Budget in July 2014) were uninspiring. He tinkered with tax slabs—but did not establish a new tax paradigm, such as the direct tax code (DTC) that previous Congress finance ministers attempted. The constant tampering with import duties took India several steps back into an earlier protectionist era. It was left to Finance Minister Nirmala Sitharaman, who has grown into her job, to cut corporation tax, repeal the unconscionable retrospective tax law, and begin delivering on some of Modi's promised macro-economic reforms.

The government's tentacles have meanwhile grown, not receded. Compliance requirements for companies are now more onerous, and paperwork more tiresome. The governance of regulatory institutions too has wobbled—SEBI, RBI and TRAI are three specific examples. SEBI has stalled several market-friendly investment measures. The RBI had issued circulars that are dilatory and cumbersome to implement. TRAI's changes in broadcasting rules have complicated rather than simplified viewers' choices.

Much progress, however, has also been made. The PM Gati Shakti Master Plan promises to transform India's infrastructure. Roads, bridges and tunnels in Ladakh and J&K have bolstered both India's defence capability and connectivity between previously inaccessible regions. The Border Road Organisation (BRO) has worked in difficult conditions to improve infrastructure at rapid pace.

Governance needs to be simplified and improved. Modi believes far too much time is spent on multiple election campaigns, leading to less time devoted to governance. He wants to compress the Lok Sabha election and 28 state assembly elections into one mega poll. Modi says the plan will achieve four key objectives.

First, it will cut down the high cost of holding elections. The 2019 Lok Sabha poll cost the exchequer over ₹8,000 crore. Political parties and their candidates collectively spent another ₹50,000 crore, mostly in unaccountable black money. Cutting costs by holding one combined election for the Lok Sabha and the state assemblies will thus not only cut expenses all round but reduce the circulation of unaccounted cash.

Second, and most important, merged elections will allow political leaders to focus on governance over their five-year terms rather than campaign every few months for state assembly polls. Third, voter turnout will rise. With just one election every five years and two choices (Lok Sabha and state assembly), more voters will be encouraged to exercise their franchise. Fourth, the pressure on security forces will lessen, freeing them up for duties in areas where insurgencies fester.

Opposition leaders have pointed out the practical difficulties in implementing the prime minister's proposal. These were echoed by former Chief Election Commissioner SY Quraishi, who wrote in *The Hindu*[8]: "First, how will 'One Nation, One Election' work in case of premature dissolution of the Lok Sabha, for instance, as happened in the late 1990s when the House was dissolved long before its term of five years was over? In such an eventuality, would we also dissolve all State Assemblies? Similarly, what happens when one of the State Assemblies is dissolved? Will the entire country go to polls again? This sounds unworkable both in theory and in the practice of democracy."

In his column in *The Economic Times*[9], economist Swaminathan Aiyar suggested a way out by holding one general election every five years and polls to all state assemblies together in the middle of the five-year Lok Sabha term: "The first need is a fixed government term for five years, and this will require amending laws. After an election, every legislature should elect a prime minister or chief minister for five years.

"That leader should stay in office for a full term even if defections reduce his party or coalition to a minority. Problem: if elections are held only once in five years, voters have little chance in between to show their dissatisfaction. The solution is to hold state elections in the middle of the fixed Lok Sabha term. This will mean alternating central and state elections every two-and-a-half years. This will give the fullest scope for focusing on state-specific issues in one set of elections, and on central issues in the other."

There is a fundamental flaw in both Quraishi's and Aiyar's proposals. The idea of fixed-term, five-year Lok Sabha and

[8] 19 June 2019.
[9] 23 June 2019.

assembly terms is antithetical to parliamentary democracy and India's federal structure. If a government at the Centre or in the states loses its majority due to defections or loses the confidence of the House for any other reason, that government has no business staying in office under the guise of a five-year fixed term. If a government loses a trust vote in Parliament or in a state assembly, that legislative body must be dissolved and fresh elections called.

This isn't likely to lead, however, as some would think, to legislative chaos. The number of times a government has lost a vote of confidence in the Lok Sabha over the past 25 years can be counted on the fingers of one hand – mostly during the Gowda-Gujral-Vajpayee years in the 1990s.

Even if a state government does lose its majority, through political machinations, there would typically, in a five-year period, be a maximum of three or four mid-term elections across India. In order to synchronise their next election with other state assemblies, those mid-term polls would give the assembly concerned a truncated term till it goes to the polls again with the rest of the states at the end of the remaining five-year cycle. We would thus have at most a few mid-term elections across a five-year timeframe while preserving the democratic sanctity of parliamentary and assembly majorities.

How do other nations approach the problem? In a controversial move in 2011, Britain opted for a fixed five-year term for parliament. The imbroglio over Brexit showed how ill-judged that decision was. David Cameron stepped down as prime minister in 2016, shortly after the Brexit referendum's shock result. Ideally, Britain's House of Commons should have conducted a floor test at the time. If the Conservative Party had lost the trust vote, the House should have been dissolved and a general election called immediately.

Instead Britain's five-year fixed-term legislation witnessed a parade of prime ministers – David Cameron, Theresa May, Boris

Johnson, Liz Truss and Rishi Sunak. Legislating a five-year fixed term for the House of Commons stood common sense on its head. Recognising the folly, Britain in April 2022 dissolved the 2011 legislation and reverted to a system that had served it well for centuries.

The United States has an orderly system with the Presidential and Congressional elections alternating every two years in November. But the US is not a parliamentary democracy like India or Britain and therefore not strictly comparable. The Opposition in India worries that "One Nation, One Poll" will become a quasi-presidential system like America's, benefiting Modi because of his popularity as a mass leader. That might skew assembly poll results where Modi rather than local candidates would draw votes.

∽

While improving governance increasingly occupies Modi, realpolitik is never far from his mind. By appointing a polarising Chief Minister, Yogi Adityanath, Modi in 2017 took UP's festering communal cauldron head-on. For decades, the Samajwadi Party (SP), Congress and BSP used religion and caste to divide UP. With captive vote banks of Yadavs, Muslims and Dalits, the SP and BSP dominated UP's electoral politics. By choosing a 44-year-old, five-term Gorakhpur MP Yogi Adityanath, a Thakur, as chief minister, Modi put politics first. If anyone could deliver UP's 80 Lok Sabha seats in 2019, Modi and Shah believed, it was likely to be Adityanath. As one BJP leader said wryly: "When you pick Yogi Adityanath to lead the biggest state, you do not have to shout from the rooftop that you stand with Hindus and Hindutva."

Following the BJP's landslide victory in UP in 2017, the appointment of Adityanath as chief minister however ruffled several feathers in India and abroad. *The New York Times*, for example, was apoplectic: "Emboldened by a landslide victory in recent elections in India's largest state, Uttar Pradesh (Mr Modi's) party named a firebrand Hindu cleric, Yogi Adityanath, as the state's leader. The move is a shocking rebuke to religious minorities, and a sign that cold political calculations ahead of national elections in 2019 have led Mr Modi's Bharatiya Janata Party to believe that nothing stands in the way of realizing its long-held dream of transforming a secular republic into a Hindu state.

"Mr Adityanath has made a political career of demonizing Muslims, thundering against such imaginary plots as 'love jihad': the notion that Muslim men connive to water down the overwhelming Hindu majority by seducing Hindu women. Mr Modi's economic policies have delivered growth, but not jobs. India needs to generate a million new jobs every month to meet employment demand. Should Mr Adityanath fail to deliver, there is every fear that he – and Mr Modi's party – will resort to deadly Muslim-baiting to stay in power, turning Mr Modi's dreamland into a nightmare for India's minorities, and threatening the progress that Mr Modi has promised to all of its citizens."

The New York Times, horrified that a Hindu monk can lead a state, should look inwards. The inflammatory, ultra-conservative rhetoric of some of America's Christian evangelists in the Republican party make Adityanath appear secular in contrast. The rise of far-right, racist politicians in France (Marine Le Pen) and Italy (Giorgia Meloni) show how well India has handled its plural agglomeration of communities, castes, regions, languages and ethnicities. Foreign media like *The New York Times* and *The Economist* are quick to judge but slow to understand India's complexity.

Adityanath's history-making victory in the 2022 UP assembly election quietened some of those foreign voices. The monk-CM's national ascent seems assured. But in the unfortunate preponderance of caste and religion in UP, one of India's most backward states, where does development figure? It clearly remains at the top of Modi's agenda in the remaining months of his second term. But the BJP has also adopted in Uttar Pradesh the Opposition's decades-long vote bank polarisation model. What the Opposition's didn't do, fatally, is follow it up with good governance and economic development. In the fullness of time, that has backfired. Modi and Adityanath cannot afford to make the same mistake in India's largest state.

Adityanath's landslide win in 2022 to secure a second successive term as CM overcame five inimical factors. First, he broke the 37-year trend of UP switching governments every five years. That was a clinical demolition of history. Second, by in effect dropping out of the race, BSP's Mayawati tactically converted the multi-cornered contest into a straight shoot-out between the BJP and SP. Binary contests carry dangers for the incumbent with vote shares coalescing rather than splitting. By winning in UP, though with fewer seats than in 2017, Adityanath showed that his double engine with Modi was firing on all cylinders ahead of 2024.

Third, the narrative that the farmers' agitation had angered Jats in western UP to form an iron wall with the SP's Muslim-Yadav vote bank to stop the BJP was laid to rest. The BJP fared far better in western UP than most expected, giving it the momentum to push through to a clean majority in the assembly. Fourth, the belief that "bodies floating in the Ganga river" during the lethal second wave of Covid-19 in the summer of 2021 would erode Adityanath's reputation for tough crisis management proved false. This was partly because the earlier narrative was itself bloated and partly because the UP government quickly got the situation under control.

Fifth, Adityanath was fighting friendly fire from within sections of the BJP. Internal dissent against his style of working peaked in early 2022. It took decisive intervention from Modi to quell the dissent before it got out of hand. The strategy deployed to overcome these five hurdles and lead the BJP to victory can, with caveats, be extrapolated to determine which issues will matter to the Indian voter in the 2024 Lok Sabha election and the best way to deal with them.

Law and order is key. Adityanath has dismantled the mafia raj that UP suffered from for decades. Delivering free rations and other welfare benefits digitally to the poor without corrupt middlemen siphoning them off has given the Adityanath government significant leverage over the electorate in the run-up to 2024 where UP's 80 Lok Sabha seats will be crucial. Digitally allocated subsidies are religion-agnostic: poor Muslims benefit as much as poor Hindus.

Infrastructure has meanwhile improved across the state. Several projects—airports, roads, housing and metros—were incomplete legacies of previous governments. The Adityanath government pushed them through to completion, especially expansion in the number of operational airports.

One of the least understood contributory factors in Adityanath's win was the female factor. The BJP's vote share lead over the SP across the state was significantly greater among women than men. There were three reasons for this. First, women felt safer amidst improved law and order. Second, providing free gas cylinders, enhancing rural electrification, putting water on tap and building toilets helped the BJP gain the confidence of women voters. Third, the triple talaq law provided a level of comfort among Muslim women with the BJP. Anecdotal evidence points to Muslim women discreetly, and often secretly, having voted in polling booths for the BJP while their menfolk remain loyal to the SP.

Some granular numbers offer further clues. The share of youth voters of total voters in the 2017 UP election was 28.73 per cent. In 2022, that ratio dropped to 22.93 per cent. Fewer younger voters—most affected by joblessness—cushioned the BJP just as women voters, including Muslim women, bolstered it.

The big loser in UP was the Congress. It was always a big

player in the state. But UP-in-charge Priyanka Gandhi-Vadra addressed more campaign rallies in UP (213) than even Adityanath (206). Despite that, the Congress made little impression in the state. For the Gandhis, that is not a happy augury for 2024.

Why does Yogi Adityanath frighten the Opposition as much as he dismays the foreign press? The natural successor to Modi of course is Home Minister Amit Shah. But 2029 is a long way away. By then Shah will be 64. The man who today worries the Opposition the most is Yogi Adityanath. He will be 57 in May 2029.

Congress President Sonia Gandhi was among the first to spot the threat Modi, then relatively unknown, posed. The 2002 riots had polarised Gujarat. After Modi's victory in the December 2002 Gujarat assembly election, the knives came out. Sonia bided her time, waiting till the 2007 assembly elections before delivering her taunting verdict on Modi: *maut ka saudagar*. For the next seven years Modi faced a relentless inquisition over the 2002 riots. It resulted in the BJP-led NDA sweeping to power in 2014 and again in 2019.

Is Adityanath next in the line of fire? He has long been in the cross hairs of the Opposition. In Adityanath, the Opposition sees a long-term electoral threat potentially as serious as the one Modi posed in 2012 after he won his third successive Gujarat Assembly election. While Adityanath is not Modi, he runs India's most complex state with a population exceeding the combined population of Britain, France and Germany. There are similarities as well. Like Modi, Yogi has a ruthless streak. He is already the monk young Modi once was.

SEVEN

Modi: The New Vajpayee?

IN THE EARLY YEARS OF INDEPENDENCE, PRIME MINISTER JAWAHARLAL Nehru was the soft-spoken, erudite globalist while Home Minister and Deputy Prime Minister Sardar Vallabhbhai Patel played the iron-fisted strongman. When the BJP came to power in 1998, Prime Minister Atal Bihari Vajpayee was the gentle persuader. Home Minister and Deputy Prime Minister LK Advani was the executor.

Is history repeating itself today? Ironically, the harshest critics of Prime Minister Narendra Modi who have vilified him since 2002 now look fearfully at Amit Shah and Yogi Adityanath. They hope, if the BJP wins the 2024 Lok Sabha election, that Modi stays Prime Minister and doesn't retire to the Himalayas before 2029. The prospect of Amit Shah or Adityanath as Prime Minister unnerves them so much that they are prepared to put up with Modi 3.0 as the new Vajpayee – internationalist, moderate, statesmanlike.

Curiously, much the same happened with Vajpayee. He was vilified by the Congress and its allies as communal. In December 1984, when Vajpayee, then the 58-year-old BJP president, was defeated in the Lok Sabha election by Madhavrao Scindia in Gwalior, the Congress rejoiced at the electorate's rejection of a Hindutva icon.

Vajpayee was replaced as BJP president by LK Advani in 1986. With just two seats for the BJP in the Lok Sabha, Advani turned

Vajpayee's moderate Hindutva into a harder, more aggressive version. His 1990 *Rath Yatra* led to a resurgence of Hindu identity politics. It set into motion a sequence of events culminating in the demolition of the Babri Masjid in December 1992.

As Advani's hard Hindutva image solidified, Vajpayee gradually assumed the role of the consensual moderate. The combination worked to reassure voters that the BJP could be a responsible right-of-centre national alternative to the left-of-centre Congress. By 1998, re-engineering complete, the BJP formed the government as head of a 24-party NDA coalition. It was Vajpayee's mild-mannered charm that attracted parties like Omar Abdullah's National Conference and Mamata Banerjee's newly formed Trinamool Congress to join the NDA government. Both served as ministers in the Vajpayee cabinet.

With Vajpayee in retirement and Advani in the bad books of the RSS after calling Pakistan's founder Muhammad Ali Jinnah "secular" during a visit to Pakistan in 2005, the quiet ascension of Modi began. In May 2014, Modi became the most reviled Prime Minister India had elected, due largely to the allegation that he was complicit in the 2002 Gujarat riots on his watch as chief minister. A Special Investigation Team (SIT) report exonerated him in 2012 and the Supreme Court later endorsed the SIT report.

Modi has meanwhile shifted gears. After leading the BJP to a landslide victory in the 2019 Lok Sabha elections, Modi like Vajpayee of yore has become gentrified. He talks about inclusiveness, visits mosques, meets Pope Francis and plays the global leader at multiple G20 meets which he periodically chairs during India's presidency.

An excerpt from Modi's speech following the BJP's victory in 2019[10] could legitimately have been delivered by Vajpayee: "My beloved citizens of India, you have filled the bowl of this beggar with expectations, hopes and dreams. I understand the

---

[10] 16 February 2022.

gravity of this but I will tell the country that in 2014 you didn't know me much yet you trusted me. In 2019, after knowing me well you have given me more strength. This means that Indians have so much trust in us and as the trust increases, so does the responsibility. I might make mistakes but none of them would be with bad intentions. If I fall short of any expectations, then criticise me but the things I say publicly, I will try to live up to those expectations."

Home Minister Amit Shah is increasingly projected as the new hard Hindutva icon. He convinced Modi to invalidate key provisions in Article 370 and settle the J&K issue once and for all. He led the crackdown, along with National Security Advisor Ajit Doval, in September 2022 on the terror group Popular Front of India (PFI). Shah's performance in Parliament has taken on a new edge.

His hardline image has achieved the impossible: just as Advani made Vajpayee look statesmanlike, Shah is doing the same for Modi.

A spate of articles by Indian authors in the run-up to the country's 75th anniversary of Independence in August 2022 called India a failed state. This was part of an old Indian tradition that misses, often deliberately, the wood for the trees. So how has India done as an independent nation in the past 75-plus years?

In an op-ed in *Business Standard*[11], India's former foreign secretary Shyam Saran made several observations but arrived at erroneous conclusions.

Saran wrote: "Mahatma Gandhi was more than aware of the demons that lurked under the surface among India's incredibly diverse multitudes: of fires that could be ignited through the easy sale of hate. Which is why he was so passionate about Hindu-

[11]16 February 2022.

Muslim unity, the emancipation of the lowest, most oppressed castes and communities of India and the embrace of a more inclusive and egalitarian pattern of economic development."

The need for Muslim-Hindu unity was obviously uppermost in the minds of every Indian leader before independence: Lokmanya Tilak, Subhas Chandra Bose, Jawaharlal Nehru, C Rajagopalachari, Babasaheb Ambedkar and countless others. How could it not be in an undivided nation which in the mid-1920s had a population of 270 million, of which 180 million were Hindus and 65 million Muslims, the rest comprising Buddhists, Christians, Sikhs and others? The Ottoman Caliphate was abolished in 1924. Gandhi's full-throated support of the Khilafat movement was to assure Muslims that they would be safe in an independent Hindu-majority India.

Saran noted that Gandhi was "opposed to India's partition, which he saw as a vivisection of India, a mortal wound that would fester for years to come. And so it has."

Partition brought unimaginable suffering to Hindus, Muslims, Sikhs and others. But what was the alternative? An undivided India with a 35 per cent Muslim population at birth, including those in a putative West Pakistan and East Pakistan? Unending civil strife could have resulted. That could have been a mortal wound festering in a new nation.

Muslim League leaders, led by Muhammad Ali Jinnah, regarded the Islamic Republic of Pakistan as their territorial and religious birthright. They were not prepared to live in a Hindu-majority India where they would have no special rights. Under the Mughals, they were part of the ruling hierarchy. Under the British, they were a favoured martial race. They made up a large section of the British Indian army. The British had a particular affinity for Muslims. After all, Islam's armies had conquered large swathes of Europe and were stopped only at the gates of Vienna in 1683. Spain was under Muslim rule for over 700 years, right until the decisive battle that liberated Granada in 1492.

As Anglo-Saxons, with genetic roots in Germany, the British

too, like Muslims, are a martial race. Post-Roman England had been settled by three German tribes—Angles, Saxons and Jutes. The British Royal family's name was, for centuries, the Germanic "Saxe-Coburg-Gotha" before it was quietly changed to "Windsor" in 1917 amidst the First World War against Germany. After Independence, Britain leant towards Pakistan. London played a nefarious role in the United Nations during the first India-Pakistan war over Jammu and Kashmir in 1947–48.

Saran noted that Gandhi was an advocate of ecological sustainability. He wrote: "During the time Gandhi lived, climate change was not a matter of concern but it is now clear that climate change is really a symptom of the much larger ecological emergency that our world is confronting today. And Gandhi foresaw, with a prescience that is truly astonishing, the ecological crisis that is upon us."

What Saran did not note was that colonial Britain had been spewing millions of tonnes of carbon dioxide in the atmosphere since the Industrial Revolution in the 1760s. Today's climate change crisis is a result of industrialised countries amassing great wealth while colonising and polluting the world.

Saran went on to quote Gandhi: "It took Britain half the resources of the planet to achieve prosperity. How many planets will a country like India require?"

Saran seemed to suggest that Gandhi believed colonising other nations and stripping them off their natural resources was the only way to "achieve prosperity".

Gandhi, of course, was avowedly anti-industrialisation. India lives in its villages, was his stern reminder to Indian leaders. Gandhi said: "God forbid that India should ever take to industrialisation after the manner of the West. The economic imperialism of a single kingdom (Britain) is today keeping the world in chains. If an entire nation of 300 million took to similar exploitation, it would strip the world like locusts."

For good measure, Saran added: "Indian culture has always

looked upon nature as a Mother, a source of nurture, and you must not take from her more than what allows her to regenerate and renew herself. This is what Gandhi tries to put across to the people of India who were already bedazzled by the affluence of the West: 'We may utilise the gifts of Nature as we choose but in her books the debits are always equal to the credits'."

India obviously needs to focus on sustainable development. But the keyword is development. The world is urbanising. In India, however, nearly 70 per cent of the population still lives in villages. The proportion is set to gradually reduce to 50 per cent as urbanisation accelerates.

Britain was happy to keep India rooted to its villages. Gandhi supported that rural idyll. Development passed India by during British colonial occupation. The average per capita income of an Indian in 1700 was around $600 (in adjusted currency). In Britain, the Netherlands and France, per capita income in 1700 was around $750. The gap between average European and Indian living standards in 1700 was relatively small.

By 1947, India's per capita income had plunged to $100 (again in adjusted currency). In Britain, the United States and Western Europe per capita income had meanwhile risen to over $5,000. The prosperity gap between the West and India had widened from 1.2x in 1700 to 50x in 1947. Colonialism had left its mark.

More than 76 years after independence, India's per capita income has risen from $100 to $2,500. By purchasing power parity (PPP) it is $7,500. Average per capita income (PPP) in Western Europe and North America is $45,000. The gap has narrowed from 50x to 6x and is falling further. There obviously is a long way to go. Saran is right to stress inclusive growth. But he misses the larger point. Without growth, inclusivity would be much harder to achieve. If India can sustain economic growth at 8 per cent a year for the next decade, prosperity, stripped out of India in the 1700s, will gradually return. So will inclusivity.

∽

The divided Opposition meanwhile searches for convergence. On issues, there is some; on leadership there is none. But on the need to evict the BJP from office in May 2024 there is absolute consensus. Is West Bengal Chief Minister Mamata Banerjee one of the principal threats to the BJP in the 2024 Lok Sabha election? Can she stitch together a fractious Opposition with conflicting agendas?

With several of her party members facing serious charges of corruption, Banerjee has adopted a three-pronged approach. One, to attract MPs and MLAs from other parties to the Trinamool Congress. Many are discards from their original parties. Pavan Varma, a former general secretary of the JD(U) who was expelled from the party, is just one example. Others like Kirti Azad, formerly of the BJP and latterly of the Congress, had long been sidelined. Babul Supriyo is a better catch. It shows that the TMC is a party in ascendance.

The second approach is more grounded: arranging the defection of groups of MLAs from small states. Banerjee's coup in Meghalaya to draw 12 Congress MLAs, including former chief minister Mukul Sangma, made the TMC the BJP's principal Opposition in the state. Banerjee is targeting the Northeast to establish a foothold in a key regional vote catchment. In Tripura's 2022 civic body elections, the TMC drew a blank but still attracted a vote share of more than 20 per cent, again making it the main Opposition party in the state ahead of the 2023 assembly election.

The third TMC tactic is to cut the Congress down to size. By targeting Congress MLAs in Meghalaya and Goa, Banerjee sent Congress' UPA allies a terse message. She has often refused to meet Sonia Gandhi or Rahul Gandhi on her whistlestop trips to Delhi. But under a united Opposition, she could still ally with the Congress in 2024—on her terms.

Banerjee, if anything, is realistic. She knows that the BJP will emerge by far the largest single party in the 2024 Lok Sabha election. Her objective is to reduce the BJP's numbers and then inveigle allies. The Janata Dal's HD Deve Gowda became prime minister in 1996 by winning just 46 seats in the Lok Sabha election. He allied with 119 Left-leaning parties while the Congress' 140 MPs supported the United Front (UF) government from outside. Banerjee is following the same asset-light model.

This is how Mamata's asset-light model works: The TMC wins 30–35 seats in 2024 out of West Bengal's 42 Lok Sabha seats compared to 22 it won in 2019. It knows that it will pick up like-minded allies but very few seats in other states. The fly in the ointment? The litany of corruption charges against the TMC's former ministers, many of whom are in jail awaiting trial.

In contrast, the Congress, following Rahul's Bharat Jodo Yatra, the Haath Se Haath Jodo outreach and the installation of Kharge as Congress president, is likely to end up as the second-largest party after the BJP in 2024. It hopes to better its 2019 performance when it won 15 seats in Kerala and 8 seats in Tamil Nadu in a seat-sharing pact with the DMK. It is also likely to do relatively well in 2024 in Karnataka's 28 Lok Sabha seats and make further inroads in Chhattisgarh and Jharkhand.

The Congress faces an old problem in bigger states: strong regional alliance partners will not allocate a significant number of seats for it to contest. This applies particularly to Maharashtra and Tamil Nadu. The Congress is in direct fights with the BJP for Lok Sabha seats in several states like Rajasthan, Madhya Pradesh, Chhattisgarh, Uttarakhand, Himachal Pradesh and elsewhere. The TMC is not a serious contender in any of these states. That dilutes its chances of picking up enough seats to emerge as the second-largest national party ahead of the Congress. AAP's attempt to displace the Congress as the principal Opposition to the BJP in states like Gujarat and Himachal Pradesh is a work in progress. So far it has only helped the BJP in Gujarat by cannibalising Congress votes. But it is laying a foundation for the future despite its anarchist past and corruption charges that continue to haunt its senior leaders.

In the 2014 Lok Sabha poll, the TMC recorded a national vote share of 3.8 per cent compared to the Congress' 19.3 per cent. In the 2019 Lok Sabha election, the TMC increased its national vote share only fractionally to 4.1 per cent. Congress vote share rose to 19.5 per cent. With such a low national vote share in 2024, can Banerjee hope to be a serious Opposition-led prime ministerial candidate? Almost certainly not, though in politics certitude is often the first casualty.

West Bengal chief minister Jyoti Basu was a consensus choice as prime minister of the United Front government in 1996 before the Left's politburo shot the proposal down. Banerjee had followed that development closely. The playbook could come in handy in 2024 during coalition negotiations. Counterintuitively, Banerjee's "Jyoti Basu strategy" will gain traction if the Congress performs strongly in states where it is in direct contests with the BJP. That will cut the BJP's tally and increase the Congress-led UPA's seats. Then, like HK Deve Gowda did, Banerjee could strike a deal with the Congress-led UPA and regional satraps to support a TMC-led alliance in a bid to win power at the Centre. What are the chances of this happening? Obviously, much depends on the Congress' final tally and Rahul Gandhi's troubled relationship with Banerjee. The two have never got along. A TMC-UPA alliance could be an early casualty.

Mamata and Rahul have the same electoral target: Muslims. Without minority votes, Banerjee would not be chief minister of West Bengal and Gandhi would not be an MP from Wayanad, having lost family fief Amethi to Smriti Irani in 2019.

The BJP, however, shouldn't be complacent. Despite victories in important states like UP and Gujarat, it has lost some political capital. Targeted violence against BJP workers by TMC, DMK and AAP in West Bengal, Tamil Nadu and Punjab has affected cadre morale. The surrender on farm laws and earlier retreats on the land acquisition bill have dulled the government's reformist credentials. Petrol and diesel prices remain high; inflation is a worry; job growth continues to languish.

And yet Modi has a strong hand going into the 2024 Lok Sabha election. Welfare schemes are delivering results. Infrastructure projects are gaining critical mass; industrial growth is up; India has the world's fastest-growing GDP among major economies despite trade disruptions caused by the war in Ukraine; the G20 presidency has lifted India's profile.

✂

Dissent is the lifeblood of democracy. Incitement is its death knell. In India, however, dissent often crosses the red line into incitement. "Your freedom ends where my nose begins." That is what reasonable restrictions to free speech mean: say and do what you want as long as you don't break the law, incite violence, cause public disorder, or impinge on others' freedom.

Insurgent groups have many benefactors: Pakistan-sponsored terrorists, Maoists, Kashmiri militants and local mujahideen groups. They instigate dissent in the hope that it will morph into violence and anarchy. The key for any government is to differentiate between dissent and incitement.

Treating both with the same heavy hand plays into the narrative of those who want violence, not debate. The "anti-national" controversy is a red herring. Journalists opposed to the government are not anti-national. But some of the anarchic causes they espouse are. The relationship between journalists and politicians is, by definition, adversarial. The fourth estate must obviously be a watchdog, not a lapdog. In the debate over "anti-nationals", the real anti-nationals escape scrutiny. They are the hidden instigators and their reach is both wide and malignant.

Sedition is a serious matter. It should be invoked in the rarest of rare cases. A colonial-era law aimed at curtailing Indian freedom fighters against the British, it has no place in an independent country. Nationalism can't be forced-fed to citizens. It is voluntary. Much more important is national interest. That needs protection and constant vigilance. Confusing nationalism with national interest allows the enemies of India to hide behind a veil. Mahatma Gandhi was a nationalist. So were Jawaharlal Nehru and Sardar Vallabhbhai Patel. Why then has nationalism acquired such odium in recent years? The short answer: the meaning of nationalism has been subverted. This subversion leads even "public intellectuals"—a term that has fallen into some disrepute—to miss the finer nuances of nationalism.

Why do Indian Opposition leaders, historians and academics misinterpret the true meaning of nationalism? A part of the reason is ideological. They despise Modi and imbue him with their false interpretation of nationalism by prefixing it as hyper-nationalism or Hindu nationalism. Their prognostications for India are invariably grim. The "references" to Kashmir in the United Nations Human Rights Council (UNHRC) are played up by this lobby of India-denigrators. The references that international bodies make are merely proforma. They carry no weight. The denigrators know this, but wilfully subvert the narrative.

The government deserves criticism across a host of issues. But criticism—which should spare nobody, including Modi—loses credibility if it is built on prejudice. India doesn't suffer from too much nationalism. It suffers from too little.

At an event, sociologist Ashish Nandy told the audience[12]: "I've worked on nationalism, so I am telling you with some confidence. You read all the nationalist texts and you tell me if this nationalism is different from our nationalism, or that nationalism is distinct from other kinds of nationalism.

"You cannot find it, all nationalisms are the same, the texts are the same, only the names, only the minor, trivial details differ. There is no difference between nationalism anywhere. Psychologically speaking they are absolutely the same profile."

Thus, in Nandy's view, Mahatma Gandhi's nationalism in the 1930s was the same as Adolf Hitler's nationalism in the 1930s.

[12]6 September 2019.

Read the key part of Nandy's comment again: "All nationalisms are the same. There is no difference between nationalism anywhere."

But, of course there is a difference—in both historical and contemporary terms. The finer nuances of nationalism need to be understood. One reason why the Congress and the Left have a poor understanding of nationalism is that they use European reference points. It is fashionable in the West and among India's nouveau elite to say that patriots spread 'love' and nationalists spread 'hate'. But that is a Western postcolonial construct based on expansionary European nationalism that led to World War II.

Indian nationalism is very different. German nationalism in the 1930s, for example, sought to invade and conquer. Indian nationalism under Mahatma Gandhi, in sharp contrast, was non-violent and sought to free India from British colonial occupation which, like German 'nationalism', was invasive, violent and expansionary. German or British nationalism was not nationalism at all but jingoism. Employing a deliberate sleight of hand, the left attempts to discredit Indian nationalism by conflating it with aggressive European "nationalism".

In India, ideologues on the right too make a fatal error: they conflate nationalism with Hindu nationalism. It is not. In its truest form, nationalism is inclusive. To protect the national interest means protecting every Indian's national interest: Hindu, Muslim, Christian or Parsi, rich or poor, Brahmin or Dalit, Sunni or Shia, male, female or transgender. Nationalism seeks national advancement, but not at the cost of other nations, races or creeds. Real nationalism is fair, open and embraces diversity. It seeks to guard India from terror, promote the country's economic interests by globalising the Indian economy, and protect the rights of minorities by empowering them.

Meanwhile patriotism, we are told, is the antithesis of nationalism. Patriotism is selfless and good. Nationalism is selfish and bad. This is how Nandy frames it: "Old-fashioned patriotism was good enough for even Europe at one time, and in India today, it is by blurring old-style patriotism and love for the country—which is natural and biological—that we have tried to strengthen nationalism. Nationalism by itself does not make that much sense as old-fashioned patriotism. Every Indian, I should say, is patriotic by nature. You don't have to teach them to be patriotic, but nationalism is an ideology. Nationalism is not only defined by the love of the country territorially where you were born, nationalism is defined by specific enemies and specific allies. Nationalism is built on that; patriotism doesn't have that kind of responsibility, it doesn't define your enemies or friends."

To Nandy, therefore, "nationalism is defined by specific enemies" while "patriotism doesn't define enemies or friends".

Nandy makes the same classical mistake others of his ilk do, conflating nationalism with aggressive intent. Gandhiji, a consummate nationalist throughout his life, used *ahimsa*, non-violence, as his credo. The enemy was specific—British colonialism—but he advocated non-violent means to confront and defeat it. He was a patriot and a nationalist and showed how they were two sides of the same coin. Left-leaning historians and academics strive to drive an artificial wedge between nationalism and patriotism. There isn't one.

A BJP MLA once said, "Hindustan is for Hindus". This is deplorable and symptomatic of extreme right-wing jingoism. It represents a fringe view that undermines real nationalism. It damages the cause of Indian nationalism and does nothing to advance national interest. All Indians—Hindus, Muslims and Christians—are Hindustani civilisation ally, geographically and genetically. The right must understand this. Indian nationalism has only one national identity.

The Economist devoted several pages to an essay on nationalism and what it means to different nations and peoples at different times in their history: "Thinkers like George Orwell and Elie Kedourie have argued that patriotism—tolerant, welcoming and reasonable—really has nothing to do with nationalism. It is a comforting thought; it separates decent people from the bigots who cling blindly to their own nation's superiority. But one person's patriotism is another's prejudice. In 1917 the Indian writer Rabindranath Tagore lamented how 'the people which loves freedom (the British) perpetuates slavery in a large portion of the world with the comfortable feeling of pride in having done its duty.' Genial English patriots were blind to the harm they caused."

Colonial British "nationalism" was neither patriotic nor nationalistic. It was racist and bombastic. So was the fraudulent nationalism of Lenin, Stalin and Mao which India's Left unthinkingly embraces. Like secularism, India's definition of nationalism is shaped by history. During the freedom struggle, Gandhi's nationalism was noble. Today, Indian nationalism has fallen victim to chicanery. In order to rescue it from the subverted definitions it has attracted, focus on three non-negotiables. One, nationalism is plural, open and welcomes diversity. Two, it is non-aggressive and non-expansionary unlike European nationalism. And three, it protects India's national interest.

In a virtual address to BJP national office bearers in Jaipur on 20 May 2022, Modi spoke of *Bharatiyata* (Indianness) as the soul of India. That should be Modi's credo, in 2024 and beyond, as much as it should be the Opposition's if it wishes to regain the nation's trust.

Section Two

OPPOSITION

EIGHT

Waiting for Rahul

IN SAMUEL BECKETT'S 1953 PLAY *WAITING FOR GODOT*, VLADIMIR AND Estragon, the two scruffy principal characters, wait endlessly for Godot, unseen and unknown, to arrive. He never does.

Unlike Godot, Rahul Gandhi does arrive—in time occasionally to address a kisan rally or a party conclave. The Congress faithful have mixed feelings about The Family's prodigal son. Veterans of Sonia Gandhi's old guard believed that once an energised Rahul returned from his 3,570-km *Bharat Jodo Yatra* they would again be ignored. Rahul proved them wrong. The succession is set—a rejuvenated Rahul has taken charge of the party while the president, Mallikarjun Kharge, focuses on organisational nitty-gritty. Priyanka remains the second-in-command now that her children are grown. Sonia is withdrawing gradually into a mentor role while rallying the party on critical issues and keeping a watchful eye on the official party president.

Rahul's *Bharat Jodo Yatra*, which ended in Srinagar in January 2023, resurrected him as a serious national leader. The physically demanding walk over a period of nearly five months and over 3,500 km demonstrated that the Congress had the countrywide organisational skills and financial resources to stage a complex logistical exercise involving thousands of party workers and leaders.

An NDTV-CSDS opinion poll conducted from 10–17 May 2023 found that Rahul's popular support had increased from

19 per cent in the 2019 opinion poll to 27 per cent. Modi's support base had fallen marginally from 44 per cent in 2019 to 43 per cent, narrowing the gap between the two leaders from 25 per cent to 16 per cent.

Rahul's disqualification from Parliament by a Gujarat Court in March 2023 helped create a sympathy wave. But it was the big win in Karnataka in May 2023 that raised Rahul's political stature and the Congress' morale. It gave the double-engine of Modi-Shah pause for thought.

As I wrote[13] at the time: "The BJP erred by over-exposing Modi with more than 20 campaign rallies across the state during the last two weeks of electioneering. It revealed the weakness of the Modi-Shah strategy, especially in the selection of candidates and allowing rebellion among senior leaders to fester.

"Modi has successfully steered India through the Covid-19 pandemic and economic turbulence caused by the Russia-Ukraine war. He has built transformative schemes. The Gati Shakti National Master Plan is scaling up India's infrastructure. Digitisation has created one of the world's best financial transaction systems, Unified Payments Interface (UPI).

"Along with these are initiatives on tap water, last-mile electrification and near-universal health insurance. Despite expenditure on these and many other welfare schemes, the fiscal deficit has remained in check. Tax revenue, both personal and corporate, has risen steeply. So have collections under the Goods and Services Tax (GST). India remains on track to become the world's third largest economy by 2027. In 2014, it was the tenth largest."

"What Modi hasn't done well is build a second line of top leaders. Shah is his trusted second-in-command. Yogi Adityanath and Himanta Biswa Sarma have been given enhanced electoral responsibilities. But the BJP remains a one-man army. If it is

[13]*The Times of India*, 18 May 2023.

to win a third term in 2024, the BJP's high command needs to empower more leaders."

With four key assembly elections due by December 2023 – Rajasthan, Madhya Pradesh, Chhattisgarh and Telangana – the BJP will have to re-examine its electoral playbook. The defection of several senior leaders in Madhya Pradesh from the BJP to the Congress in May 2023 could be an ominous portend.

India Today reported[14]: "Senior BJP leader Deepak Joshi is not just a three-term MLA and minister, but no less than the son of late chief minister Kailash Joshi – with deep roots in the Jana Sangh and the BJP. On 6 May 2023 he joined the Congress in Bhopal in the presence of state Congress chief Kamal Nath. The day also saw another BJP leader, former BSP MLA Radhelal Baghel, changing sides.

"Amid Joshi's exit, BJP leader Kailash Vijayvargiya, who has been looking for a new role, also weighed in. 'There are issues within the BJP that are being addressed. The Congress doesn't have it in itself to defeat the BJP in Madhya Pradesh. But yes, if we don't address the issues in the organisation, the BJP will defeat the BJP'."

Rahul and Priyanka played a significant role in the Congress victory in Karnataka. Sonia, though unwell, addressed campaign rallies in the state. The Gandhis knew that Karnataka was a low-hanging fruit, waiting to be plucked, following the Bommai government's record of corruption and misgovernance.

The 2024 Lok Sabha election is obviously an entirely different matter. With a new Opposition coalition, it is a battle for the soul of India: its values, goals and character. India stands on the cusp of greatness – economic and geopolitical. The next five years will determine whether the tryst with destiny that Nehru promised in 1947 will finally be fulfilled. That is why the 2024 Lok Sabha poll will be historic in the direction it sets for the country.

---

[14] 22 May 2023.

Most Congressmen and women talk privately of three things that worry them about Rahul following his *Bharat Jodo Yatra*. One, that he is still not accessible. Two, that he disappears at key moments when his presence is most needed. And three, that he doesn't follow through on key issues.

The Congress, and specifically the Gandhi family, has not yet fully grasped how much India has changed in the past few years. The young have no time for dynasts whom they see as corrupt and entitled. When I began writing the biography of former Prime Minister Rajiv Gandhi, I was struck by two things: his innate decency; and his political innocence. The decency stayed till the end. The innocence didn't.

Is Rahul Gandhi more like his father or does he have the instincts of his mother Sonia? It is easy to dismiss Rahul as a political novice—not to be taken seriously. Many made that mistake about Indira Gandhi, writing her off as a *"gungi gudiya"*. She spent 16 years as prime minister proving her detractors wrong.

Rajiv too was written off as a "pilot-prime minister". In spite of the taint of Bofors and the 1984 anti-Sikh pogrom, history may record that had a Liberation Tigers of Tamil Eelam (LTTE) suicide bomber not killed him in May 1991 at the age of 46, Rajiv would have proved a better second-term prime minister.

Rahul has a mildly patronising attitude towards poverty: a sort of *noblesse oblige* commitment to protect the poor – not by freeing them from the yoke of poverty through job-creating, wealth-generating economic reforms but by anti-capitalist slogans and tokenism. A visit to a Dalit village today, another padyatra tomorrow, a temple visit the day after. In short, provide the poor with platitudes but follow policies that are pro-poverty rather than pro-poor.

Indira Gandhi, with her 1971 slogan *garibi hatao*, did the same. Rajiv tried to break the mould but succumbed eventually to Delhi's Byzantine politics. The poor seek jobs and growth. They want low, stable food prices. Their children need quality education and aspirational mobility. It is a delicate balance. The Modi government is still struggling to strike that balance. If newly energised Rahul wants to be a contender in 2024, he will have to show that he rejects grandmother Indira Gandhi's economic and governance legacy.

In a well-researched book, *Autumn of the Matriarch: Indira Gandhi's Final Term in Office*, reviewed perceptively by Zareer Masani in *India Today*, author Diego Maiorano says that many ills of India's political system can be traced back to Indira Gandhi's last term in office. Masani wrote in his review: "Like the Bourbon royal family in revolutionary France, the Gandhi dynasty in India learned nothing and forgot nothing from the Emergency. A quick return to power was the surest means of avoiding prosecution for the crimes of the Emergency; Maiorano's thesis is that most of the negative aspects of Indian politics can be traced back to the early 1980s, when Mrs Gandhi presided over a regime of almost unmitigated corruption and dynastic intrigue.

"Her final term was untramelled by the anti-poverty, socialist slogans of her earlier years and was motivated by a single-minded determination to establish herself and her sons in an unassailable position of power for at least a generation to come. Maiorano's exhaustively researched account of those years shows how she set out to achieve this by systematically undermining institutions such as the civil service, judiciary, parliament and even her own party. The aim was to fill all positions of power with sycophants and the result was to compromise the integrity and independence of the institutions on which a healthy democracy depends."

∽

A decades-long Nehruvian consensus was broken by Modi. The consensus had held firm for 67 years—from 1947 to 2014. What were its core principles? First, secularism. Second, socialism. Third, non-alignment. Fourth, dynasty. Indira Gandhi injected the words "secularism" and "socialism" into the Constitution, during – without a trace of irony – the Emergency.

Even through the six Vajpayee years, 1998–2004, the consensus held. Its long duration nurtured an ecosystem composed of a curious amalgam: Marxist historians, Macaulay's colonially seduced bureaucrats, faux secular intellectuals, compromised journalists, and sycophantic politicians worshipping at the altar of the Nehru-Gandhi dynasty. These common threads formed the architecture of a secular, socialist democracy. Muslims were appeased, not empowered. They were kept in secular ghettos, paraded out every five years to vote for the Congress and its fair-weather allies. Dalits were paid lip service. Like Muslims, they formed a rich vote catchment—however poverty-stricken they remained.

Poverty and socialism went hand-in-hand. While the GDP of countries in the rest of Asia—from Malaysia to Thailand—grew at over 7 per cent a year through the 1960s and 1970s, India crawled at the Nehruvian growth rate (wrongly dubbed the "Hindu growth rate") of under 3 per cent a year. Had India's GDP growth matched that of other Asian countries in that 20-year period, India's economy would today be double its size at $7.5 trillion, not $3.75 trillion. Per capita income would be nearer $5,000 than $2,500 and poverty levels below 5 per cent, not today's 10 per cent. In short, 150 million more Indians would have been lifted out of the poverty they live in today.

The Nehruvian consensus was suffused with good intent: Nehru himself was an honourable man, if mistaken in the way he tackled Pakistan and China. He was colony's child and allowed himself to be swayed more often than was good for India by the Anglo-German charms of Lord Mountbatten (whose original family name was Battenberg: "berg" is German for "mount", hence the Anglicised surname).

Though he was an excellent first prime minister of India and responsible for building a strong institutional architecture for a newly independent country, Nehru's heirs in the Congress began distorting his legacy right from 1966 when daughter Indira became prime minister. Dynastic politics spread like a virus through the body politic. It infected Indian governance with cronyism, feudalism and sycophancy.

India's intellectual elite, which often fell in line with the British during the Empire, dutifully fell in line with the Empire's heirs. The Nehruvian consensus was blessed at birth by the British who had ensured India's economy grew at less than 0.5 per cent a year during 190 years of British colonial rule.

The Nehruvian rate of growth between 1947 and 1991, though slow, was higher than during the previous 190 colonial years. Indians, always easily satisfied, were content. Through this period, socialism and secularism took firm political root. Muslims remained disempowered. Their poverty and backwardness endured. It eventually led to resentment and Islamic radicalisation. A bankrupt treasury in 1991 forced Prime Minister Narasimha Rao and his finance minister, Manmohan Singh, under intense IMF pressure, to wring economic reforms out of a calcified system devoted to povertarianism.

During the 2014 Lok Sabha campaign, Modi attacked Nehruvian politics. Dynasty was dissected. Left-leaning povertarian economics was exposed. Communalism dressed up as secularism was disrobed. The Lutyens' ecosystem of corruption, sycophancy and dynasty stood exposed. Public anger catapulted Modi to power. That is when the problems began. Seizing power is easier than exercising it. In the first days of his prime ministership, Modi made a fatal error: he assumed that the Nehruvian ecosystem could be shamed into introspective retreat.

The Nehruvian consensus, led by the crafty and the wealthy, regrouped. Gradually, it struck back. US President Barack Obama's visit to India on Republic Day in 2015 was followed by insinuations that "church attacks" were orchestrated by right-wing extremists. Modi's ministers, meanwhile, scored own goals with intemperate statements. Award wapsi and the intolerance debate cast Modi as a dictatorial prime minister who had spawned an atmosphere of fear in minorities, who was callous about Dalits, and who had damaged India's secular image globally.

The Modi government made things worse for itself by cloaking itself in silence. Half-truths and disinformation were allowed to become the gospel truth. Clarifications came too late. Truth needs speed and clarity to survive, while lies thrive in an information vacuum. It is a lesson the Modi government's ponderous communications system still hasn't quite learnt.

✎

Those who defend dynastic politics in India employ two spurious arguments. The first: even a democracy like the United States has political dynasts. The Bushes, Clintons and Kennedys are offered as clinching evidence. The second: just as lawyers' children become lawyers, doctors' children become doctors, and actors' children become actors, so politicians' children also become politicians.

But professionals in medicine and law earn their degrees. Businessmen owe their position to specific financial shareholding. Actors are made and unmade every Friday. In contrast, the purpose of democracy is to widen voter choice—not narrow it. By choosing dynasts over merit, political parties limit the choice voters have and lower the overall level of competence in Parliament.

The first president of the United States, George Washington, took office in 1789. Since then, in 234 years and through 46 US presidents only thrice has a single family produced more than one US president: John Adams (1797–1801) and his son John Quincy Adams (1825–1829); William Harrison (who died in office after serving for just a month in 1841) and his grandson Benjamin Harrison (1889–1893); and more recently the two George Bushes—exceptions that prove the centuries-old rule in American politics: dynasties don't work. Presidents Theodore Roosevelt and Franklin Roosevelt are often cited as examples of successful US dynasts in the 20th century—but they were only fifth cousins.

In Britain, less than 10 per cent of the House of Commons has previously had a family member in politics. There is no Churchill dynasty. In France, there is no de Gaulle dynasty. In Germany, there is no Adenauer dynasty. The Kennedys are a storied example of dynasty's fading appeal. There has been no Kennedy president after JFK. Ted Kennedy made one presidential attempt in the 1980 election—but lost to Jimmy Carter in the Democratic primaries. In the Republican primaries in 2016, George W. Bush's brother Jeb Bush was forced to withdraw after a disappointing debating performance with his rivals, including Donald Trump.

Anti-dynasty sentiment in the US is so strong that President John Kennedy's daughter Caroline was denied a bid for a New York senate seat by the Democrats. That's akin to Priyanka Gandhi-Vadra being denied a Congress ticket in future from Rae Bareli.

Researchers at the Asian Institute of Management (AIM) Policy Centre in Manila tested the causal relationship between dynastic politics and poverty in the Philippines. Their findings were significant. The AIM Policy Centre found that constituencies in the Philippines with dynastic candidates were 26 per cent poorer than those with non-dynastic candidates. Nearly 68 per cent of legislators in the Philippines parliament are dynasts. In sharp contrast, only 6 per cent of senators in the United States Congress are dynasts. The per capita income of the Philippines (a former US colony) and the US are respectively $3,500 and $70,000.

The Congress pioneered dynastic politics in India. The die was cast when Jawaharlal Nehru, an unflinching democrat in public, appeared to be a closet dynast in private. He appointed his 42-year-old daughter Indira president of the Congress in 1959. The transformation of the Congress from a party of freedom fighters into a family owned enterprise began barely a decade after the Mahatma said it should be disbanded after Independence and remoulded into a party relevant in a democratic India, not a British colony. While Nehru, a refined and sensitive man, took the first hesitant steps to introduce dynasty in India, Indira Gandhi cast it in stone.

Long compared to grandmother Indira for political nous, Priyanka Gandhi-Vadra has been politically active since 1991 when she was just 19 years old. Throughout the 1991 Lok Sabha election, Priyanka campaigned tirelessly for her father Rajiv Gandhi. Rajiv was still hurting from his defeat in the 1989 General Election. The Congress had plummeted from over 400 Lok Sabha seats in 1984 to less than 200 seats in 1989. The extent of that fall would be exceeded only 25 years later, when the Congress plunged from 206 seats in 2009 to 44 seats in 2014.

It was 19-year-old Priyanka (brother Rahul, then 20, was away in the United States) who flew to Chennai in the early hours of 22 May 1991, along with mother Sonia, to bring back her father's body to Delhi in a special aircraft from Sriperumbudur, the temple town 42 km from Chennai where Rajiv was assassinated. She showed steel then, comforting her mother, standing by her brother when he flew back from the US, and appearing composed during the funeral.

When the Congress was routed in the Lok Sabha election in 2014, a photograph of Priyanka walking back home with a protective arm around an emotional Rahul's shoulder after he had addressed an impromptu press conference, captured her role as the family's quiet, behind-the-scenes support system, absorbing everything, awaiting the right moment to emerge from the shadows. Mother Sonia's poor health prompted Priyanka to take on a more proactive role after the 2019 General Election.

But even during her earlier quiet phase, Priyanka's writ ran large over the Congress. The decades-old clamour from Congress loyalists for her to enter politics never died down. In the 2017 Uttar Pradesh assembly election, Priyanka played a key but behind-the-scenes role in selecting candidates. Loyalists shielded her, as they did Rahul and Sonia, from criticism following the Congress' humiliating defeat in UP as the BJP coasted to a landslide victory. The 2022 UP assembly poll was Priyanka's litmus test. She failed it, with Congress vote share dropping from 6.25 per cent in the 2017 election to just over 2 per cent in 2022. Once again, the party faithful protected her, deflecting the blame to a weak ground-level organisation.

Behind Priyanka's easy demeanour lies a shrewd mind. Her marriage in 1997 to Robert Vadra, then a small-time businessman, surprised many in her closed circle. Within a decade, Vadra had transformed himself into a real-estate mini-tycoon, cutting deals, sculpting himself at gyms, and gate-crashing Delhi's *nouveau riche* Page 3 circuit. It was evident even back then, over a decade ago, that Vadra would pose a risk to Priyanka's political career.

Having inherited her mother Sonia's restrained canniness, Priyanka cultivated an image of the stoic victim standing by her persecuted husband, forgiving her father's killers, and subtly playing up her likeness to grandmother Indira Gandhi. Like Rahul, Priyanka has never held a real job—apart from voluntary NGO work. She remains Rahul's key confidante, bypassing Congress leaders decades older.

The spectacle of Congress leaders pleading with Rahul Gandhi to stay on as party president after the party's defeat in the 2019 General Election, prostrating themselves outside his residence, and resigning *en masse* from party posts demonstrated what ails India's feudal political families. It took Gandhi's open letter attached to a tweet to finally convince the Congress that he meant what he had been saying for months: he wanted power without responsibility.

Three years later, in October 2022, the Congress finally held an election to choose a non-Gandhi party president. After a "friendly" contest, 80-year-old loyalist Mallikarjun Kharge defeated 66-year-old Shashi Tharoor to become the first non-Gandhi Congress president since 1998. For the Gandhis, though, it was business as usual. Kharge provided the perfect foil to deflect criticism of dynasty. In practice, he played his anointed role: a family appointed CEO who sought the Gandhis' "guidance" for every policy decision.

∽

Family run political parties have lowered the standard of public life. In the Congress, the Gandhi family's writ continues to run large despite the installation of Kharge as party president. The party faithful fear that self-destructive competing factions will spring up if the Gandhis retreat too much into the background. Sonia Gandhi is unwell and unwilling to take charge. Priyanka has flattered to deceive. The new "reborn" Rahul remains an enigma. Much will depend on how he conducts himself as the 2024 Lok Sabha election nears.

The BJP's own troubles should ideally energise the Congress. The Modi government's surrender to farmers in 2021 over reformist agriculture legislation was an opportunity for Congress to regroup. The UP assembly election in 2022 was another missed opportunity. Neither strengthened the Congress ahead of 2024. Other Opposition parties that emulated the Congress' feudal-family business model have suffered too. In the 2019 Lok Sabha election, most dynastic parties were punished by voters—Lalu Yadav's RJD (zero seats), Akhilesh Yadav's SP (five seats), Chandrababu Naidu's TDP (three seats), Sharad Pawar's NCP (four seats), HD Kumaraswamy's JDS (one seat) and Mehbooba Mufti's PDP (zero seats).

The writing was on the wall. Not many feudal Opposition politicians though read it. BSP's Mayawati appointed a brother (Anand Kumar) and a nephew (Aakash Anand) as national vice-president and national coordinator respectively. Mamata Banerjee's nephew Abhishek moved smoothly into his role as the Trinamool Congress' heir apparent.

Whenever nepotism raises its feudal head, electoral consequences follow with a time lag. The BJP was once proud to be non-dynastic. Atal Bihari Vajpayee's foster family and LK Advani's son Jayant and daughter Pratibha scrupulously kept themselves out of electoral politics. But the virus is beginning to spread. There obviously will never be a Narendra Modi dynasty. His brothers lead quiet, middle-class lives in Gujarat. But there should never be an Amit Shah political dynasty either, nor a Rajnath Singh dynasty. But signs elsewhere in the party are ominous.

Minister of state for Information and Broadcasting Anurag Thakur, son of the former chief minister of Himachal Pradesh, Prem Kumar Dhumal, is just one example. His younger brother Arun Dhumal was treasurer of the BCCI and now heads the cash-rich Indian Premier League (IPL). But of the BJP's 302 current Lok Sabha MPs, comparatively few are dynasts. That should be no reason for self-congratulation. Dynasts are rising through the ranks of the BJP at the state level. That must stop.

At lower levels too, in the states and legislative councils, the BJP must be unyielding in its effort to promote merit and not fall prey to nepotism. Let the sons and daughters, nephews and nieces, brothers and sisters, find their own professions and shine in them. The door on their lateral entry into politics should be kept tightly shut. The ecosystem of entitlement that dynasty builds around itself acts as an iron wall. It's tough for talented outsiders to break through. But once you do get in, you become beholden to the privilege and pelf inside. As an outsider, Modi was aware of this iron wall within Lutyens' Delhi.

There are some in the BJP who have grown to enjoy the ecosystem of entitlement. The prime minister must beware of these elements. They may not be dynasts themselves but their sympathies lie with those who are. The Lutyens' ecosystem, like reinforced concrete, is difficult to crack open. Outsiders either get converted or stay out. Can Modi break this iron wall of privilege? If he doesn't, it could eventually co-opt the BJP.

Empirical studies have confirmed that political dynasties beget poverty. The most successful countries in the world are those that have long rejected dynastic politics. One of the ways political dynasts hold sway over a poor, feudal electorate is by appeasing it with subsidies. A study by India's former chief economic advisor Krishnamurthy Subramanian (currently representing India as director at the International Monetary Fund) and economist Abhishek Bharadwaj found dynasty damages democracy subtly but cruelly. "It's a legacy of retaining power through reckless populism," they wrote. "The numbers depict a key narrative: Building a mountain of subsidies without worrying about its disastrous economic consequences."

Unless the Congress undergoes an internal catharsis, it will remain a feudal family fief. The outcome is bad governance, nepotism and incompetence. Following in the Congress' malign footsteps, several political families in states across India established the lucrative business of regional dynastic political parties in the 1980s and 1990s. All without exception have spawned corruption, misgovernance and nepotism.

When dynasty takes precedence over merit, the quality of governance suffers. Globally, the evidence is as damning as it is in India. The late Robert Mugabe, who was president of Zimbabwe for 37 consecutive years during which he devastated the country's economy, wanted his wife Grace, accused of corruption and despotism, to succeed him as president days before he was removed from office in a choreographed army coup. In Cuba, Fidel Castro's brother Raul tried, with limited success before he died, to reverse the ruinous socialism that has impoverished his island country.

North Korea, Pakistan and the sheikhdoms of the Middle East are other examples of how political families in various countries have curtailed their citizens' freedoms, supported extremism and imposed medieval laws to safeguard their dynastic cabals.

In India, dynastic politics has spawned mediocrity. The global investor and author Ruchir Sharma wrote in his book, *Democracy On the Road: A 25-year Journey Through India,* about a two-hour meeting his travelling group had with Rahul Gandhi in 2007: "Rahul spoke for one hour 59 minutes over a two-hour dinner."

There's a lesson in that for Rahul on how he could spend the next few months leading up to the 2024 Lok Sabha election: listening.

∞

NINE

Role of the Gandhi Dynasty

THE BJP'S CLEAN SWEEP IN FIVE OUT OF THE SEVEN STATES THAT WENT to the polls in 2022 placed the party in a strong position for the 2024 Lok Sabha poll. Defeat in Punjab and Himachal Pradesh was expected but wins in Uttar Pradesh, Uttarakhand, Goa, Manipur and Gujarat underlined Modi's connect with voters. The victory in Uttar Pradesh in February-March 2022, however, combined Modi's vote-pulling charisma with Chief Minister Yogi Adityanath's mass popularity. Yogi emerged as the single biggest long-term political beneficiary of the 2022 UP assembly election.

For the Congress, the message from the seven assembly elections in 2022 was grim. The party responded in early 2023 with its Haath Se Haath Jodo outreach campaign aimed at energising its ground game across six lakh villages. The Congress' defeat in Uttarakhand, Gujarat and Goa, where it was in a direct contest with the BJP, with AAP playing spoiler, was a warning sign ahead of 2024. Key state assembly elections are due later in 2023. Following Congress' win in the Karnataka poll in May 2023, the most closely states watched will be Rajasthan, Madhya Pradesh, Telangana and Chhattisgarh in November-December 2023. They will offer clues ahead of the 2024 Lok Sabha poll.

Rahul and Priyanka meanwhile have to take important decisions to rebuild the Congress from ground up. A non-Gandhi party president like Mallikarjun Kharge is only the first step in the overhaul the party needs. This goes against the very feudal grain of the Congress, embedded in 1969 when Indira Gandhi split the party into two, converting it into a family run enterprise. But unless the Congress transforms itself into a modern political party, it will continue to lose elections and steadily atrophy. After losing Punjab to AAP, the Congress now governs just two large states in India – Rajasthan and Karnataka. Chhattisgarh and Himachal are scarce compensation. In Jharkhand the Congress plays second fiddle to regional ally Jharkhand Mukti Morcha (JMM). In Tamil Nadu, it is a fringe ally of the ruling DMK.

AAP's landslide win in Punjab had echoes of its earlier sweeps in Delhi. AAP made gains in Goa and Gujarat as well. It targeted Himachal with mixed results. Will this be enough to elevate AAP leader Arvind Kejriwal to the status of a credible challenger to Modi in 2024? Unlikely. The reason: quite apart from Rahul Gandhi, powerful regional satraps like Mamata Banerjee stand in his way.

Banerjee's landslide victory in May 2021 in West Bengal – a bigger state than Punjab with 42 Lok Sabha MPs to Punjab's 13 MPs – was as impressive as Kejriwal's win in Punjab. The Trinamool Congress, despite its flop show in Goa, will emerge as the second biggest Opposition party in the 2024 Lok Sabha by dint of its stranglehold on West Bengal. That will place it behind only the Congress which benefits from its national electoral legacy in a smattering of states like Kerala, Karnataka, Tamil Nadu, Madhya Pradesh, Chhattisgarh, Telangana, Jharkhand and Rajasthan.

With several claimants from the Opposition for prime ministership in 2024, Modi will seek to remain above the fray, watching Opposition leaders undermine one another. Sharad Pawar, Uddhav Thackeray and MK Stalin had made it clear that there could be no combined Opposition front without the Congress. But can Kejriwal and Rahul Gandhi work together in INDIA? Can Mamata and Rahul, who till recently could barely stand the sight of each other, bury their differences to challenge Modi's BJP?

Uttar Pradesh showed that in a binary contest against the BJP, an Opposition party like SP along with its small alliance partners can nearly triple its seats from 47 to 125. But that outcome needed the BSP's Mayawati to in effect withdraw from the contest. It's unlikely that any Opposition leader will be as self-sacrificial in 2024. That remains Modi's trump card.

Kejriwal meanwhile is an enigma. He began his career as an executive in Tata Steel but soon joined the Indian Revenue Service (IRS) before leaving to become an activist. The Anna Hazare movement in 2011–12 elevated his profile. The newly formed Aam Aadmi Party won landslides under Kejriwal's leadership in the Delhi state assembly election in 2015 with 67 out of 70 seats and in 2020 with 62 seats.

Can AAP eventually fill the national opposition space that the shrivelled Congress once occupied? Most powerful regional opposition satraps are handicapped by strong identification with their states. Mamata Banerjee's appeal doesn't travel well outside West Bengal as the results of the 2022 Goa Assembly polls underscored. The Trinamool Congress won just 5.2 per cent vote share, and no seats. The same parochial regionalism afflicts other prime ministerial challengers: K Chandrashekar Rao (Telangana), Nitish Kumar (JDU) and Naveen Patnaik (Odisha)—though Patnaik prefers total power in Bhubaneswar to shared power in Delhi).

Kejriwal stands out because he's not tied down to a region. Hence the belief among those disappointed by Congress' inconsistent challenge, despite Rahul's refurbished avatar, that Kejriwal's AAP is the natural successor to the Gandhis' Congress as a national alternative to BJP. But there is a difference between promise and delivery. Kejriwal has morphed from an anarchist to a politician only in the past three years. In his anarchist days, he called Prime Minister Narendra Modi a psychopath and abused the late Arun Jaitley. He was forced to apologise to Jaitley in court to end a criminal defamation case. As Delhi chief minister, he slept in a dharna for days in the waiting room of the lieutenant-governor's office.

AAP is a tightly run ship. Most of its co-founders have left or been thrown out, including Yogendra Yadav, Prashant Bhushan, Kumar Vishwas and several others. Punjab Chief Minister Bhagwant Singh Mann, a former comedian, is a lightweight politician with the strings pulled in Delhi by Kejriwal. Raghav Chadha, a chartered accountant, is AAP's professional face. He ran the party's successful Punjab election campaign in 2022. But the corruption charges against Manish Sisodia and Satyendra Jain, who spent months in prison, have tarnished AAP's image.

Kejriwal though is a long-term player. He is targeting the next round of assembly elections after the 2024 Lok Sabha poll leading up to the 2029 General Election to capture the Congress space nationally. But with strong regional leaders in most Opposition-ruled states unlikely to give Kejriwal room for manoeuvre, AAP will be left fighting in Congress and BJP states. That poses a problem for AAP. Significant Congress-ruled states like Rajasthan and Chhattisgarh are not amenable to AAP's style of politics. In the far more compact Himachal Pradesh, AAP drew a blank in December 2022 with 1.10 per cent vote share and zero seats.

BJP-ruled and NDA states are even tougher to break into as the examples of Uttar Pradesh and Uttarakhand have shown. Without BJP's Hindi heartland states and without Opposition-ruled states in the south and the east, AAP could run into an electoral wall. Kejriwal knows this. After having experimented with Gujarat and Himachal in 2022, he will now focus on Haryana (his home state) where BJP's leadership has been lacklustre. Assembly elections are due there in October 2024.

Kejriwal is trying hard meanwhile to avoid Rahul Gandhi's mistake of openly appeasing a Left-Islamist vote bank. He has positioned himself as a good Hindu but not necessarily a votary of aggressive Hindutva. It is precisely Kejriwal's shifting ideological positions, however, that have drawn the sharpest criticism:

his lack of principles. Delivering education and healthcare to a resource-rich city-state like Delhi and winning an emotive election in Punjab are not enough to dispel perceptions of AAP's alleged dalliance with Khalistani separatists and ambivalence on Pakistan-sponsored terrorism. By questioning the Uri surgical strike in 2016 and the Balakot air attack deep into Pakistan in 2019, Kejriwal revealed a side of his personality that he today increasingly downplays.

✆

The Opposition must fulfil three criteria. One, it should be constructively adversarial to the government, not merely disruptive. Two, it must articulate cogent alternative polices to those the government is currently pursuing. And three, it must have the numbers to present voters with a real alternative at the next general election.

The Congress has not articulated coherent policies except to excoriate the BJP – which as the principal Opposition it is fully entitled to do. But neither Sonia Gandhi nor Rahul Gandhi has proposed specific, constructive policies on economic, tax and labour reforms, tackling China's bellicosity, neutralising Pakistan's proxy terror war, fighting Maoism, and improving law and order. The Congress should have instituted a shadow cabinet immediately after the May 2019 general election. Every shadow minister – from home and defence to external affairs and environment – should be proposing domain-specific policies on a regular basis.

The only concrete policy suggestion that has emerged from the Congress is the uniform income scheme. As the Congress' data analytics chief Praveen Chakravarty put it: "We have all heard of the fable where a person was searching for his keys under a streetlight, not because he lost them there but because that is where the light was. This 'streetlight effect' is recognised as an observational bias in social science. The government's economic team seems to suffer chronically from such a bias. Apparently, it is time to flash the 'V' sign for victory and to reflect the shape of the economic recovery."

Why has the electorate turned against the Congress over the years? Under the leadership of the Gandhi family the party has developed into a feudal force in Indian politics. Indira Gandhi's 1975–77 Emergency, during which more than 1,00,000 journalists, Opposition leaders and civil society activists were jailed (including LK Advani, Atal Bihari Vajpayee and the late Arun Jaitley), revealed an autocratic reflex in the Congress. Indians' fundamental rights were suspended for nearly two years. The Constitution was subverted. The Supreme Court was subordinated.

In 1986, Rajiv Gandhi—whose career was impaled by bad advisors—planted the seed of communalism in mainstream politics by overturning through parliamentary legislation a 1985 Supreme Court order that had granted maintenance to an elderly divorced Muslim woman Shah Bano. But it wasn't till 1998, when Sonia Gandhi took over the presidency of the Congress, that the authoritarianism of the party became evident. The crude, thoughtless overnight eviction of then Congress president Sitaram Kesri was an early sign.

When the Congress assumed power at the Centre in 2004 after a hiatus of eight years, it showed its feudal instinct. While Prime Minister Manmohan Singh was the gentle, erudite face of the Congress-led UPA government for ten years, the Gandhis called the shots behind the scenes.

TEN

Heralding Corruption

AS YOU DRIVE DOWN BAHADUR SHAH ZAFAR MARG IN NEW DELHI, a row of buildings appears to the right. They house some of India's oldest newspaper organisations—*The Times of India*, *The Indian Express* and *National Herald*.

Dubbed India's Fleet Street (before Britain's newspapers moved out to cheaper London real estate), the road is named after India's last Mughal emperor Mirza Abu Zafar Sirajuddin Muhammad Bahadur Shah Zafar. Modern printing presses hum in these buildings, spewing out lakhs of newspapers every day for distribution across the city. Editors and correspondents work late into the night to report the stories we read the next morning.

One building on this busy row though falls silent at night. Unlike the others, it has neither a printing press, nor a daily printed newspaper. The story of *National Herald* lies at the centre of a Delhi court case in which Congress leader Rahul Gandhi and UPA chairperson Sonia Gandhi are on bail. The Congress has called the trial of the Gandhis a "witch hunt". There are, in fact, two issues being contested.

One, a case filed by former Rajya Sabha member Subramanian Swamy against the Gandhis and others for alleged misappropriation of *National Herald's* assets.

Two, the income tax department's charge that a private company, owned by the Gandhis, Young Indian Pvt Ltd, concealed income of ₹154 crore, leading to the imposition of tax and penalty of ₹249 crore. Both charges have been denied by the Gandhis, whose counsel include P Chidambaram and Abhishek Manu Singhvi, both Congress loyalists.

Associated Journals Ltd was incorporated in 1937. It began to publish *National Herald* in September 1938. Founded by Jawaharlal Nehru, Associated Journals had over 1,000 shareholders, mostly Congress leaders. By 2008, *National Herald,* operating from its seven-storied building Herald House on Bahadur Shah Zafar Marg, had recorded losses of ₹90 crore. Staff was retrenched. The newspaper ceased operations in 2008.

On closure of *National Herald,* Associated Journals Ltd carried a debt of ₹90 crore on its books. The money had reportedly been lent to it by the Congress from public funds. Under the Representation of the People Act, 1950, political parties are not allowed to give loans.

Two years after shutting *National Herald,* the Gandhis in 2010 incorporated Young Indian Pvt Ltd, a not-for-profit Section 25 company with a paid-up capital of ₹5 lakh. The shareholding pattern of Young Indian Pvt Ltd is interesting: 76 per cent of its equity is owned by Rahul and Sonia Gandhi (38 per cent each); the balance 24 per cent was owned by the late Congress treasurer Motilal Vora and other Congress loyalists.

Rahul and Sonia's newly formed Young Indian Pvt Ltd meanwhile decided to buy out the equity of Associated Journals Ltd and settle its ₹90 crore debt. To raise funds to buy Associated Journals, Young Indian found a generous firm in Kolkata which lent it ₹50 lakh interest free. Young Indian duly paid ₹50 lakh to acquire Associated Journals' entire shareholding. At the same time, the Congress wrote off Associated Journals' ₹90 crore debt.

The chairman of Associated Journals at the time? Motilal Vora.

The treasurer of the Congress at the time? Motilal Vora.

Vora died in 2020. The case lingers in court. It is unlikely to reach a conclusion in the near future.

Young Indian Pvt Ltd, by paying ₹50 lakh borrowed interest-free from a Kolkata company, had by 2012 acquired not only the entire equity of debt-free Associated Journals Ltd and its defunct newspaper *National Herald,* but also its prime properties spread across India – including the seven-storied Herald House in New Delhi. The conservative value of these properties? Upward of ₹2,000 crore.

In 2014, Subramanian Swamy smelt a rat in the deal. Undeterred by India's tortuously slow judicial system, he filed a case in a Delhi court against what he alleged was misappropriation of *National Herald's* valuable assets by the Gandhis and others at a negligible cost.

As *The Indian Express* reported[15]: "A number of shareholders of Associated Journals Ltd (AJL) have claimed that the company's chairman, Motilal Vora, and its directors did not inform them or obtain their approval while deciding to transfer its entire equity to Young Indian Pvt. Ltd. (YIL) in December 2010. At least 10 shareholders that the *Indian Express* spoke to said their approval had not been sought by the management."

An analysis of AJL's balance sheet reveals that its fortunes soared after the Gandhis closed the *National Herald* in 2008 and rented out its properties once AJL became a subsidiary of YIL. In 2008–09, AJL made a loss of ₹33.78 crore. In 2013–14, it made a net profit of ₹7.95 crore. Its rental income in that year stood at ₹9.40 crore. Current balance sheets remain opaque.

Assuming only 20 per cent of AJL's property across India is currently rented out (there are several unoccupied buildings) and further assuming that rental yields are on average 4 per cent per year, the value of AJL's properties can be easily computed: ₹15 crore (estimated rental income in 2022–23) x 5 (20 per cent of space rented out) x 25 (4 per cent rental yield) = ₹1,875 crore. This is roughly in line with the ₹2,000 crore estimated

[15]14 July 2016.

valuation of Herald House and other AJL properties—although their current valuation could be significantly higher.

A FAQ statement issued by the Congress claimed that Rahul and Sonia haven't gained from YIL. The statement asks rhetorically: "Does YIL today own the property owned by AJL? No, both YIL and AJL are separate entities. All assets and properties of AJL continue to remain with AJL."

This is of course disingenuous. AJL is a wholly owned subsidiary of YIL. Thus the total rental income and assets on AJL's balance sheet must form part of the consolidated accounts of YIL. Subramanian Swamy told the *Indian Express*: "Now the government should move forward and immediately attach the National Herald building (in New Delhi). The building was built with help from the then government, which gave land, almost for free, to National Herald. Young Indian Pvt Ltd had no business, as a charitable company under Section 25, to acquire controlling shares of the commercial company. They should reverse the deal."

The income-tax department, meanwhile, filing its own charges, has demanded ₹249 crore from Young Indian Pvt Ltd in taxes and penalties for concealing income of ₹154 core in assessment year 2011–12. The key obviously lies in the court examining all the balance sheets of Young Indian Pvt Ltd from 2012 to the present. They will reveal the income and expenditure from renting various floors of Herald House for commercial gain. Those defending the Gandhis believe they have a compelling argument: a not-for-profit Section 25 company can't withdraw profit. Its directors, Rahul and Sonia Gandhi, cannot therefore benefit.

They can, however, debit all manner of expenses – from chartering private aircraft to paying for travel, hotels, medical care, overheads, staff salaries and myriad other items. The properties of Associated Journals Ltd belong to the government. They were given virtually free on lease by the government to select media houses decades ago for the sole purpose of publishing newspapers.

Stung by the court case in which Sonia, Rahul and others

remain out on bail, the Congress launched *National Herald* as a weekly Sunday newspaper with an active website. This, it believes, will be a winning argument in court when the case comes to trial. If *National Herald* no longer publishes a daily printed newspaper but just a website and a weekly newspaper out of Bengaluru, should its properties be returned to the government? The question too is this: why would a not-for-profit Section 25 charitable company like Young Indian Pvt Ltd want to take over property valued at ₹2,000 crore without paying for it?

The Modi government has shown scant interest in pursuing the case in the trial court. Dr Swamy's attention, immersed in myriad other issues, too seems to have drifted. In India, corruption is bipartisan. *The National Herald* case has, for all practical purposes, been buried. It will be exhumed at a convenient moment by the Modi government.

ECONOMY

ELEVEN

Bouncing Back After a Global Crisis

FOLLOWING THE GLOBAL FINANCIAL MELTDOWN IN SEPTEMBER 2008, many ambitious projects in India turned sour. When the global economy seizes up, high-interest debts become difficult to service. That was the genesis of the Indian bank NPA crisis. What did the Reserve Bank of India (RBI) do? Instead of lowering interest rates (as the United States Federal Reserve did) to reduce the cost to industry of servicing debt, it raised interest rates. That's like sprinkling water on a drowning man.

Raghuram Rajan was chief economic advisor to the ministry of finance in the Congress-led UPA 2 government in 2012–13. On being appointed RBI governor in September 2013, Rajan controversially continued raising interest rates, increasing the corporate sector's cost of borrowing and squeezing growth.

Over the past decade, every RBI governor (including Rajan) had based monetary policy on keeping inflation low. Caught in a pincer between a global economic slowdown and high interest rates at home, bank loans had begun to turn bad after 2008. Large corporates found themselves in a classic debt trap: huge borrowings at high interest rates amidst an economic downturn. Rajan had a bird's-eye view of the growing bank NPA crisis before being appointed RBI governor.

P Chidambaram was finance minister in 2013–14 and also during 2006–08 when the bulk of today's NPAs were created. Now the story becomes murkier. Though bank loans made to

several large corporates in 2006–08 had turned bad by 2013, the
balance sheets of those banks did not classify them as NPAs.
Rajan concedes that there was "evergreening"—banks rolling over
bad loans and accumulated interest in the hope that industrial
projects would be revived, corporate growth restored and bad
loans paid back.

What did the RBI under its new governor Rajan do? By
September 2013, Indian economic growth had slowed to below 5
per cent. Corporates were crying hoarse over high interest rates.
And yet Rajan kept interest rates high, citing inflation as the
main enemy that must be slayed. Despite the red flags, the RBI
did not crack the whip on banks to classify bad debts as NPAs.
Evergreening continued. Loans continued to be rolled over along
with interest. Bank balance sheets remained artificially clean.

In May 2014, the BJP-led NDA took charge of an economy
run into the ground. Inflation was still high despite the RBI's
misguided effort to control it with steep interest rates. GDP
growth had plummeted. Banks had stopped lending to corporates
sagging under the weight of high-cost debt. On taking office,
Modi erred by not publishing a white paper on this appalling
state of affairs. He conceded that he did not do so to avoid
the risk of global investors fleeing India. With hindsight though,
transparency in 2014 would have added to India's credibility,
not led to capital flight.

Rajan says he informed the new Modi-led PMO – though he
doesn't say when – of the looming (but as yet hidden) bank
NPA crisis which had led to a steep fall in private investment.
The Modi government asked the RBI in 2015 to tighten rules
to classify bad debts as NPAs within a set time frame. No more
evergreening was to be permitted. In 2016, the Modi government
legislated the Insolvency and Bankruptcy Code (IBC). Under
the IBC, promoters for the first time fear they could lose their
companies. Many have. Most are now serious about repaying
their bank loans. The new NPA classification rules led to an

explosion of hidden bad debts, now recognised in bank balance sheets as NPAs. As a result, banks recorded huge quarterly losses. They wrote off NPAs from their books that for years lay hidden under the "current loans" classification.

Rajan's successor as RBI governor, Urjit Patel, reduced interest rates in 2016 and 2017 to help corporates lower their borrowing costs and revive private investment. New RBI classification norms for NPAs and the IBC have ensured that bank NPAs have peaked and are now declining. By 31 March 2023, NPAs had been significantly pared. Banks are now in the pink of health. After the 2023–24 Union Budget in February 2023, the accent has shifted on increasing both government and private investment in capital expenditure. Banks are willing to lend, pushing for public deposits at higher rates as credit demand from industry and retail surges.

Despite trade disruptions caused by the Ukraine conflict and Western sanctions on Russia, India's economy has weathered the storm. It is now the world's fastest growing large economy. A study[16] by Harvard University's Centre for International Development concluded that India will continue to be the world's fastest-growing economy over the next ten years. This is what the Harvard study said: "India has the potential to be the fastest growing economy over the coming decade, according to new growth projections presented by researchers at the Center for International Development (CID) at Harvard University.

"The researchers used their newly updated measure of economic complexity, which captures the diversity and sophistication of productive capabilities embedded in a country's exports, to generate the growth projections. The global landscape for economic growth shows greatest potential for rapid growth in South Asia and East Africa. Conversely, oil economies and other commodity-driven economies face the slowest growth outlook.

---

[16]July 2017.

India tops the global list for predicted annual growth rate for the coming decade at 7 per cent."

In 2022, India displaced Britain to become the world's fifth largest economy. It is set to overtake Germany in 2025 and Japan in 2027 to emerge as the third largest global economy behind the United States and China. As Modi, busy in his role as leader of the G20 during India's year-long presidency, prepares to fight the 2024 Lok Sabha election, a revival of economic growth, following the pandemic and the Russia-Ukraine war, is crucial. The last thing he would want, after spending ten tortuous years lifting a keeling boat out of the water and steering it in the right economic direction, is to hand over its stewardship to those who nearly sank it ten years ago.

⁄⁄

In the spring of 1964, shortly before his death, Nehru was asked in private by his closest colleagues what he regarded as his greatest failure as India's first Prime Minister. Nehru replied: "I could not change the administration. It is still a colonial administration and one of the main causes of India's inability to solve the problem of poverty."

When Modi became prime minister, he took two immediate key decisions. One, he disbanded the Groups of Ministers (GoMs) that had mushroomed to more than 20 during the UPA government. Two, he called a meeting of more than 75 senior bureaucrats cutting across ministries.

The message: you now have direct access to me. Work hard and work fast. The intent: replace India's notorious red tape with a red carpet—a Modi campaign promise. The outcome: the babus worked hard and fast for several months. Without tedious, interminable and often infructuous GoM meetings, the bureaucracy became energised.

It didn't last. The Indian bureaucracy is a unique animal. Created as the Indian Civil Service (ICS) by the British, it formed what Jawaharlal Nehru called India's "steel grid". The ICS morphed after Independence into the IAS but the single alphabetical change hid the fact that real changes did not occur. The ICS had served an exploitative empire. The nomenclature of its officers gave the game away: for example, District Collectors were principally tasked to collect taxes from the districts.

After Independence, the IAS should have changed not only such honorifics but also its mission: to serve, not rule. The steel grid of the civil service has long rusted. Worse, it has been co-opted by politicians. Bureaucrats, of course, aren't all inert. Some have been agents of transformation. Many young IAS officers, posted in Maoist-infested areas, are brave, committed and selfless. The problem arises when Central postings beckon. The lure of the entrenched political-bureaucratic nexus with easy pickings can tempt the best. IAS reforms are essential. Modi's attempts have been focused and patient but borne limited results. More drastic reforms must now be his priority in the remaining months of his second term.

The appointment of an IAS officer Ashwini Vaishnaw as minister of information technology and railways underscores how talented civil servants can be policy gamechangers. Former foreign secretary S. Jaishankar, a former IFS officer and now India's much praised external affairs minister, is a particularly evocative example of a bureaucrat making an outstanding minister.

Apart from remoulding the bureaucracy, among the most urgent governance tasks is reforming the criminal justice system. In September 2006, the distinguished former director-general of police (DGP) Prakash Singh wrung a landmark order from the Supreme Court on sweeping police reforms. The SC order followed Singh's petition aimed at reforming India's corrupt and dysfunctional police which lies at the heart of virtually every law and order problem.

Shockingly but not surprisingly, the Supreme Court's seven-point directive on police reforms has been subverted by almost every government – central and state. The vicious cycle of bad policing and a broken criminal justice system are closely interlinked. Singh's petition sought to attack the root of the problem. The Supreme Court delivered one of its most enlightened orders but then failed in its duty to enforce that order.

Here's what its seven-point judgment ordered:

1. Constitute a State Security Commission (SSC) to:
   (i) Ensure that the state government does not exercise unwarranted influence or pressure on the police; (ii) Lay down broad policy guidelines and; (iii) Evaluate the performance of the state police.
2. Ensure that the DGP is appointed through a merit-based transparent process and has a secured minimum tenure of two years.
3. Ensure that other police officers on operational duties (including superintendents of police in-charge of a district and station house officers in-charge of a police station) are also provided a minimum tenure of two years.
4. Separate the investigation and law and order functions of the police.
5. Set up a Police Establishment Board (PEB) to decide transfers, postings, promotions and other service related matters of police officers of and below the rank of deputy superintendent of police and make recommendations on postings and transfers above the rank of deputy superintendent of police.
6. Set up a Police Complaints Authority (PCA) at state level to inquire into public complaints against police officers of and above the rank of deputy superintendent of police in cases of serious misconduct, including custodial death, grievous hurt, or rape in police custody and at district levels to inquire into public complaints against police personnel below the rank of deputy superintendent of police in cases of serious misconduct.
7. Set up a National Security Commission (NSC) at the union

level to prepare a panel for selection and placement of Chiefs of the Central Police Organisations (CPO) with a minimum tenure of two years.

Had these seven Supreme Court directives been implemented, acts of criminal violence would not have disappeared but they would certainly have been mitigated. When the police conspire with—or are seen to conspire with—criminals, public faith in the law and order machinery is rapidly eroded. Events in Maharashtra, West Bengal, Punjab, Uttar Pradesh and the northeast involving rogue policemen and subversive police action underscore the serious nature of the problem.

Political parties in states like Kerala and West Bengal routinely use police laxity or complicity to kill political opponents. Common criminals are emboldened to rape and murder, knowing that the dysfunctional criminal justice system will shield, not punish, them.

For this outrageous state of affairs, the courts and the government must share equal blame. An especially shocking outcome of their lethargy is jails that are overcrowded with undertrials. Many prisoners have already spent more time in jail than the maximum sentence they would have served had they been convicted. The Modi government has shown as little intent to implement police reforms, even in states where it is in power, as past governments. The catch-all excuse that policing is a state subject doesn't hold up to scrutiny.

Governments use the police to guard their interests, not the public's. As Maja Daruwala, director of the Commonwealth Human Rights Initiative, observed[17]:

"States have chosen four approaches: Actively resist the Supreme Court's order; lie doggo and do nothing; do something but do it wrong; and finally, get out from under the Supreme Court's orders by passing laws which not only do not conform to the court's orders but actually give statutory sanction to bad

---

[17] 22 September 2016.

practices. For instance, in the majority of the 17 Police Acts passed since 2006, state governments have given themselves the sole discretion to appoint police chiefs instead of choosing from a panel recommended by the UPSC. In many of the nine operational Police Complaints Authorities currently in place, their design has been subverted by appointing serving police officers as judges in their own cause. Elsewhere, their functioning has been hobbled by the lack of independent investigators."

The Supreme Court has been quick to haul up minor offenders for contempt. It must now hold state governments and the Centre to the same standard for being in contempt of one of the most important reforms in Indian law enforcement.

Like a compromised law and order machinery, poor healthcare infrastructure can have negative consequences on economic productivity. The years-long Covid-19 pandemic served to underscore the lack of health facilities in especially rural areas as well as in tier-2 and tier-3 towns. In cities, private hospitals overcharge patients at will. In villages, healthcare amenities are rudimentary. In towns, government hospitals provide appalling patient care: unsanitary operating theatres (OTs), poorly trained staff and crumbling infrastructure. The centre spends just 0.9 per cent of GDP on healthcare – a figure though set to multiply following the ravages of Covid-19.

In contrast, in Britain, for example, the budget of the National Health Service (NHS) is ring-fenced from cuts. At over £200 billion (₹20 lakh crore) it is 7 per cent of Britain's GDP. In the United States though, the Affordable Care Act (popularly known as Obamacare) fell apart at the seams. Despite the Biden administration's best efforts, a suitable alternative is yet to emerge, leaving millions of poor Americans (mostly blacks and Hispanics) without access to affordable medical insurance.

According to Dr Devi Shetty, founder of the large hospital

chain Narayana Health, "There are three main problems with Indian public health, and none of them have to do with lack of money. The problems are: (i) acute shortage of medical specialists; (ii) lack of career progression for nurses; and (iii) accountability. Shortage of medical specialists is evident even in a state like Karnataka which has the largest number of medical colleges. Yet there are over 1,200 vacancies for specialists in government hospitals. Unlike in the past, an MBBS doctor with adequate training but without a postgraduate degree is legally barred today from performing a caesarean section, an anaesthetic procedure, an ultrasound or interpreting a chest X-ray.

"The top 10 causes of death in India cannot be treated by an MBBS doctor. In simple terms, even a brilliant MBBS doctor cannot do anything more legally than what a housewife is permitted to do. These rigid regulations were created by the Medical Council and upheld by the Supreme Court for patient safety. Unfortunately, we also have an acute shortage of postgraduate seats needed to convert the existing two lakh MBBS doctors into specialists. Because of the shortage of specialists, Indian maternal and infant mortality rates are worse than some sub-Saharan African countries. Ten years ago, maternal mortality rate (MMR) of Maharashtra was as bad as in the rest of the (otherwise) prosperous south Indian states.

"In 2009, Maharashtra's health ministry recognised diplomas from the then 96-year-old College of Physicians and Surgeons (CPS) to convert MBBS doctors into specialists. Today, nearly a thousand specialist medical officers working for the Maharashtra health service are not MD or MS but diploma holders from CPS. By 2013, these diploma holders had produced a Maharashtra miracle: they dramatically reduced its MMR from 144 to 68, half of Karnataka's MMR. Very soon, Maharashtra will be challenging Kerala for the number one spot.

"Fortunately, the Union health ministry is considering recognising CPS diplomas across India. The National Board of Examinations is also converting large government hospitals as teaching institutes to train medical specialists. With trained and certified gynaecologists, paediatricians, anaesthetists and radiologists, community health centres and taluka and district hospitals will become the most vibrant hospitals."

India clearly has many advantages in terms of innovation, generic formulations and talented doctors, as Dr Shetty points out. But unless healthcare receives a greater allocation of resources from the government and investment from the private sector, Indian patients, rich and poor, urban and rural, will remain victims of a broken system. A once-in-a-century pandemic, Covid-19, has awoken governments at the Centre and in the states to the danger of neglecting and under-funding healthcare.

☙

Despite the successful Goods and Services Tax (GST), India remains under-taxed. Farmers, for example, even those whose earnings after all expenses exceed ₹1 crore a year, pay no income-tax. The ministry of finance has over several Union Budgets consistently disappointed middle-class salaried employees by keeping personal taxes relatively high. Acutely aware of the anger building in the BJP's trader vote catchment, Modi has advocated a taxpayer-friendly system. However, frequent and often arbitrary regulatory changes have dismayed both middle-class Indian taxpayers and foreign investors.

Throughout twelve-and-a-half years as chief minister of Gujarat, Modi was an unapologetic capitalist. Always a relatively prosperous state, growth in Gujarat accelerated under Modi. The state attracted global investment and the 'Gujarat model' of economic development became a byword. There were holes in this story but it was still largely true that Modi had acquired the reputation of an economic reformer. It was the promise of transferring the Gujarat economic model to the slowing Indian economy in 2012–13 that made Modi a serious prime ministerial candidate. His muscular version of nationalism helped—but economic hope bedrocked his candidacy.

P. Chidambaram had failed to revive the economy when he returned as finance minister in July 2013. Ten months later he handed to the incoming NDA government a distressed economy after ten roller-coaster UPA years—high inflation, a large fiscal deficit, and low GDP growth since 2011.

India needs sustained real annual GDP growth of 8 per cent to lift out of marginal poverty over 300 million Indians who still lead lives below acceptable standards. Only consistently high economic growth can do this—creating well-paid rural and urban jobs and relieving rural distress. Modi's most successful innovations have been to heal historical infirmities—sanitation, health insurance, financial inclusion, last-mile electrification, tap water, subsidised housing, and digitised delivery of food and fertiliser subsidies to cut out middlemen.

Like a good doctor, Modi has tried to cure a patient with multiple, pre-existing diseases—and succeeded to a large extent. But in going about the task of curing a 76-year-old atrophied system, he has failed to execute economic reforms in agriculture and land. In 1991, Narasimha Rao and Manmohan Singh were forced by the International Monetary Fund (IMF) to liberalise the Indian economy which for 44 years had limped along at an average annual growth rate of 3 per cent. To achieve consistent annual GDP growth above 7 per cent, Modi must sharpen his focus on economic reforms as sweeping as those Rao and Singh delivered a generation ago. That is the direction Modi's policies are now taking with the focus on digitalisation and infrastructure under the PM Gati Shakti Master Plan.

∽

JRD Tata famously said population was one of India's biggest liabilities. Ironically, it may turn out to be one of India's biggest assets. The demographic dividend is already upon us. The dividend kicks in when the total number of Indians in the "productive" age group of 15–65 years surpasses the number of Indians above the age of 65 and below the age of 15. India entered this zone in 2018. The productivity dividend is estimated to last till 2055 when the population of over-65s and under-15s will once again overtake the total number of working-age Indians between 15 and 65. The window of India's demographic dividend will thus remain open for another 30-plus years.

On 1 January 2016, China officially ended its one-child policy. China's fertility rate is now below replacement levels. According to the United Nations, the country's population will plateau at around 1.45 billion and then start dropping. Beijing's parks are already packed with retired folk, many in their 70s and 80s. The greying of China, as the median age rises, is the opposite of India's youthful demographic dividend. While India needs to find jobs for its growing population, China needs to reverse its population decline.

This is a social time bomb. As a country ages and its population declines, the ratio of elderly pensioners to young wage earners rises. This puts a huge strain on government finances. Taxes inevitably rise to pay for welfare, healthcare and pensions of those above 60. The young, in poorly paid jobs or without jobs at all, end up paying for their parents' and grandparents' social security. It is not a recipe for social harmony. The Chinese know this. While rebalancing their economy they are encouraging young couples to have more children. They serve as the country's future insurance policy. Significantly, countries where populations are rising have the world's fastest-growing economies.

In 1700, China was the world's most populous nation with 152 million people. Along with India it was one of world's two largest economies. Together the two Asian giants produced nearly 50 per cent of global economic output. The yet-to-be United States in 1700 was still a smattering of thirteen British colonies. Britain had a population of 5.2 million at the time and produced a mere 3 per cent of the world's economic output.

Colonisation and the Industrial Revolution changed the world dramatically over the next 200 years. By 1870, the average Briton was six times richer than the average Chinese. Beyond the numbers, however, lies the emerging story. For the first time since the West became the world's dominant geopolitical, military and economic force, the tide has turned decisively. The rise of China and India, and the relative decline of the West will establish a new world order. No one is more aware of this than President Xi Jinping, in his third term as China's most powerful leader since Mao Zedong.

The United Nations Population Fund (UNFPA), formerly known as the United Nations Fund for Population Activities, says economic growth peaks during the period when a country's working-age population of 15–65 is greater than the very old and the very young. Japan's demographic dividend began in 1964, leading to 25 years of high economic growth and the "Japanese miracle". Though it technically lasted till 2004, Japan's growth petered out from the 1990s. China's own demographic dividend began in 1996, coinciding with its surging economy and double-digit annual GDP growth, but is expected to last for an even shorter period than Japan's demographic dividend. The key reason is Beijing's one-child policy that 50 years later has progressively reduced the number of young Chinese as a ratio of the country's total population.

The "greying" of China is one of the causes of Beijing's economic slowdown. Its demographic dividend has run its course and wound down. While the trade war with the United States and the Covid crisis have contributed to a dip in China's economic growth, the steep fall in the productive population aged 15–65 constitutes a long-term structural economic weakness for China. A young, productive workforce spurs economic growth. But as a country becomes wealthier, women tend to have fewer children. Lower fertility rates lead to a gradual shift towards an ageing population. Moreover, as people grow richer, they live longer, increasing the ratio of over-65s relative to those in the working-age group of 15–65.

India's female fertility rate has fallen dramatically since Independence. It was 5.9 children per woman in 1950, 3.8 in 1994, 2.2 in 2018 and 2.1 in 2022. The replacement rate or Total Fertility Rate (TFR), when births and deaths are roughly equal, is around 2.1. Thus India's population will likely plateau at over 1.50 billion. It overtook China's population in mid-2023.

The other key metric is the dependency ratio—the percentage of the very old and very young who are supported by those in the productive 15–65 age group of the population. For India, this dependency ratio was as high as 81.5 per cent in 1966. It fell to 60 per cent in 2005 and to 49.8 per cent in 2018 when India formally entered its accelerated demographic dividend zone. Thus for the first time since Independence, India today has fewer dependents than workers. A further fall is the dependency ratio is likely by the end of this decade.

India's demographic dividend though comes with a warning: it can quite easily be squandered if education, health and skill development don't keep pace. Pessimists speak ominously of a "demographic disaster" if young workers in the productive age group are not given the skill sets needed in a rapidly changing economy. Poverty is a big handicap. Malnutrition is another. When nearly a quarter of the working-age population lacks education, healthcare and skills, the demographic dividend can be wasted. It is therefore critical to get India's health and education parameters up to scratch. The Covid-19 pandemic only underscored the urgency of reform in these critical sectors.

Modi is right to focus on delivering welfare benefits to the poorest Indians. But the focus on skill development and vocational training is crucial too. Such micro measures need to be supplemented with macro-economic initiatives. Unless the economy returns to a consistent 7–8 per cent growth trajectory, thereby providing jobs and investment opportunities, India might miss the demographic dividend bus. The window is narrow. Of the 30-odd years India has left, the first 20 years, from now till the early 2040s, are critical. As China and Japan witnessed, the effects of the demographic dividend begin to taper off, after an initial burst, as populations age.

∾

No country in the world has converted a straightforward annual statement of government accounts into televised theatre as India does every February. In the United States, the annual budget passes without a ripple. It is discussed threadbare in the Senate and in House committees but it is not an annual make-or-break fiscal event. Britain, from whom India picked up this bad habit, does attach some importance to the Chancellor of the Exchequer's annual March budget. But even in Britain the focus is increasingly on year-round economic reforms and periodic mini-Budgets rather than an annual fiscal smorgasbord.

In the grand tradition of Indian Union Budgets, finance ministers tinker with taxes: an increase of ₹25,000 in exemptions here, a 5 per cent cut in excise duty there, a tweak in personal income-tax slabs everywhere. And then follows an hour of small changes in duties across a laundry list of items: jewellery, tobacco, automotive, machine tools, consumer goods and so on and so forth. An annual Budget should in fact focus on one big idea.

Modi was right when he said[18] that the period between 2014–29 was "very important" for the Indian economy. The period, he declared, covers three Lok Sabhas – 2014–19, 2019–24 and 2024–29. It was lost on no one that the 15-year period Modi referred to was a statement of intent: he would fight to win the 2024 Lok Sabha poll but after 2029, having spent 15 years as prime minister, he might consider stepping aside.

---

[18]23 November 2022.

What are Modi's economic prescriptions? For decades India shunned foreign investment. Scarred by colonialism, prime minister after prime minister blocked a significant Western role in the economy. Jawaharlal Nehru recognised at Independence that Britain had left India with inadequate infrastructure, a rudimentary industrial base, low literacy and high levels of poverty. The nation had an economic mountain to climb. Nehru's solution was to follow the Soviet model of a centrally planned economy.

Some of this was justified. Few in the private sector, bar the Tatas and Birlas, had the capacity at Independence to build large industrial plants. Hence Nehru's relentless focus on the public sector – SAIL, BHEL, HAL – as well as on publicly funded IITs and IIMs. For two centuries the British used Indian money and labour for British benefit. Nehru was right in initially following a public sector model to build India's economy, denuded by decades of rapacious foreign exploitation. But his successors, especially Indira Gandhi, did great economic damage by not liberalising the economy in 1966 when she took office. Prime Minister P V Narasimha Rao and Finance Minister Manmohan Singh eventually did so in 1991. The lost 25 years are a burden India still carries.

However, with India emerging as the world's fastest-growing large economy, it is an opportune moment for policymakers to change their mindset and use foreign funds for India's benefit just as the reverse occurred during British colonial rule. Foreign direct investment (FDI) in infrastructure is especially vital: roads, railways, bridges, waterways, airports, factories, sea terminals, and housing. The Modi government must let foreign money pour in, whether through debt or equity, in established legacy firms like Tata and Reliance or in innovative startups and standalone greenfield ventures.

India's leaders let the poor down for decades. They must finally recognise that only when the economic pie grows bigger can it be distributed more widely and fairly to reduce inequality.

To achieve that the prime minister has little time left in his second term to recharge the economy before the full rigours of campaigning for 2024 set in.

✍

As the after-effects of the Covid pandemic on the economy and trade disruptions waned, India emerged as one of the world's most attractive investment destinations. Several factors came together to create a sweet spot for the country. The first was China's slowing economy. Highly leveraged Chinese firms were a heartbeat away from a debt trap. Real estate prices plunged. GDP growth fell to below 3 per cent. Covid remained a threat.

Ruchir Sharma had written presciently in his 2016 book, *The Rise and Fall of Nations*: "It will be difficult for any country to grow as rapidly as 6 per cent, and all but impossible for China. Nevertheless, in an effort to exceed that target, Beijing is pumping debt into wasteful projects, and digging itself into a hole. The economy is now slowing and will decelerate further when the country is forced to reduce its debt burden, as inevitably it will be. The next step could be a deeper slowdown or even a financial crisis, which will have global repercussions because seven years of heavy stimulus have turned the world's second largest economy into a bloated giant."

Sharma's analysis in 2016 of China's economic slowdown appeared prophetic in 2023. India's uptick in reforms meanwhile helped drive growth. Foreign direct investment (FDI) has been liberalised across sectors. Red tape may not have quite been transformed as yet into the red carpet Modi promised in his 2014 Lok Sabha election campaign. But the ease of doing business in India has steadily improved.

Global investors are noticing. As Dominic Barton, then CEO of McKinsey, said[19]: "People had given up on India. They felt

---

[19]26 November 2014.

India is too complicated and it was difficult to get anything done. It had dropped in the last five years on people's priority (list). I think it has gone right back up, people are interested, obviously people are going to want to see action but I think the feeling is they will, because this government seems serious. I was advising clients not to come to India two years ago because it was complicated…and companies and clients were deeply frustrated with the bureaucracy, no decisions were getting made. Companies were saying…let us go to Africa, let us go to Nigeria, let us go to Indonesia, let us just go to the US, but that has changed. I think because if you look at the trends that are going on in the world, India is right in the centre."

And yet India is far from being a perfect marketplace. There are two principal shortcomings that need to be fixed. First, the legal and judicial system. Commercial disputes take far too long to resolve. Second, certainty of the tax regime. The retrospective tax introduced by then finance minister Pranab Mukerjee in 2012—and inexplicably not repealed by the late finance minister Arun Jaitley—was finally scrapped under international legal pressure in 2021. It did more harm to India's business credibility than any other single piece of legislation.

Investors, domestic and foreign, want certitude of tax laws. But India's tax system still carries detritus of the past. Foreign investors increasingly see India as the last big market opportunity to extract the high returns that are no longer possible in Europe, North America and Japan. China's self-imposed economic wounds have led to foreign firms diversifying some of their supply chains out of the country. India obviously can't afford to be complacent as the "China plus one" momentum picks up. Africa, with roughly the same population of 1.40 billion as India, but spread over 55 sovereign nations, increasingly beckons. Despite endemic corruption and civil wars it will almost certainly emerge as the next big investment destination. Chinese, European, American and

Indian companies (like Bharti Airtel and Vedanta) are already in Africa. More will follow.

The Covid-19 pandemic irrevocably changed the way the world lives and works. Businesses have struggled to keep up. Ajit Balakrishnan, co-founder of the advertising agency Rediffusion, explained[20]: "People working under one roof dates back only to the Industrial Revolution in England in the late 18th century. Richard Arkwright—the inventor of 'water frame', a large cotton spinning machine powered by a water-wheel—found his machine too large to fit into a single house. So he assembled all the people working under one roof in a centralised location in Derbyshire, England, and called it Cromford Mill, the 'factory'. Till then, all weaving of cloth had been done throughout the world by craftsmen working from home. Just as Arkwright's water frame drove the creation and spread of the 'factory', it was the parallel growth of industries like banking, rail, insurance and telegraphy that created the need for a large number of clerks to handle order processing, accounting, and document filing, which created the 'office'.

"It is widely believed that the East India Company's location in Leaden Hall Street, London, in 1729 from where an army of bureaucrats managed their colonial possessions was the first large 'office' in the world. Are we therefore simply returning to the old normal that we today call the new normal? Work from home (wfh), work from anywhere (wfa) and a hybrid mix of using a centralised open-plan office for weekly or bi-weekly meetings rather than a structured 9–5 office is now normal practice. Technology is the enabler. Gen Z—those born after 1996—have embraced the hybrid model. They will drive change in corporate culture as they assume power and responsibility this decade."

But the future of work has dimensions beyond workplaces. Gen-Zers are far more likely to take on gig jobs, sacrificing

---

[20]*Business Standard*, 17 August 2020.

the comfort and security of a fixed corporate tenure. For them, work-life balance is a priority. Twenty-somethings in their first jobs are as much at home on Twitch, Wickr and Reddit as they are on LinkedIn, Facebook, Twitter or Instagram. Changing social media habits are a signpost of the corporate future. These aren't just future CEOs. They are today's consumers.

Even communications have changed. A likely casualty will be email as people increasingly communicate on P2P (peer to peer) platforms. Only when you want to send a "Dear All" communication will email be used. For the rest it will be P2P. Mark Zuckerberg was quick to spot the trend. Meta is an attempt to stay relevant and draw millennials and Gen-Zers back to Facebook and its metaverse. ChatGPT with its Al-driven technology is a decade-defining innovation.

Technology is a double-edged sword. It has levelled the playing field, giving women new opportunities. Technology and wfa/wfh have cut down commuting. That suits women. They can multitask more seamlessly with family and work. There are obviously infrastructure constraints in many smaller homes with joint families that make wfh a challenge, but the benefits of hybrid working outweigh the constraints. Besides, a lot of work from home (or anywhere) can be done in a small corner with a laptop or smartphone.

Indians have one more advantage in the new work matrix: natural empathy. A reason why Indian-origin CEOs like Sundar Pichai (Google), Satya Nadella (Microsoft), Arvind Krishna (IBM) and Shantanu Narayen (Adobe) score over US CEOs is the calm and empathy they bring to the table. As Silicon Valley investor Vivek Wadhwa noted in an op-ed in *Hindustan Times*[21]: "Indians learn to be resilient, battle endless obstacles, and make the most of what they have. Entrepreneurship, along with the creativity and resourcefulness required to deal with all the obstacles, is part

---

[21] 6 December 2021.

of life. These are all traits that any board would recognise—and value—especially when the alternatives are arrogant company founders who believe they are entitled to their jobs. This is what I believe has given Indian CEOs that real advantage.

"When Satya Nadella took over as CEO of Microsoft in February 2014, he inherited a toxic culture in a company considered a tech dinosaur. Bill Gates, its founder, had been known for berating employees, and Steve Ballmer, who succeeded Gates, continued the hardball business tactics that partners loathed. Sundar Pichai, too, inherited a company with cultural problems. Google was known for having a permissive workplace culture, where sexual relationships between top executives and employees generated internal tensions. He created a culture with better values."

Empathy and calm are qualities that will increasingly define corporate culture in 2024 and beyond.

TWELVE

Smart Cities and Climate Change

WAY BACK IN THE 1980s, MJ AKBAR, FOUNDING-EDITOR OF *The Telegraph*, said only half in jest that Indians might soon need a visa to travel to Bombay (as it was then known). Akbar was briefly minister of state for external affairs in the Modi government and Bombay is now Mumbai. But the sentiment he expressed then still holds: Mumbai contributes around 30 per cent of total tax revenue to the Indian treasury but gets a fraction of it in return to develop the city's infrastructure.

Most cities across India suffer from poor infrastructure though not on the same scale as Mumbai. Delhi is fortunate in having a city government with a large budget. An elected chief minister like Arvind Kejriwal, however unpopular he may be with the Modi government, ensures a modicum of accountability. The late Sheila Dikshit during her 15-year tenure as chief minister vastly improved Delhi's infrastructure, including giving the city its metro network. Under Kejriwal, health care and education have been a key priority even as his government is enmeshed in serious allegations of corruption.

Every major city in the world has an elected mayor who functions as a chief executive. With him or her vests both power and accountability in the city's daily management. It took tough-as-nails Rudy Giuliani, New York's former mayor, to clean up a city that had fallen victim to crime, drugs and sleaze. Another mayor Michael Bloomberg, who served three terms from 2002 to 2013, restored New York's reputation as the world's financial centre after the 9/11 terror attack.

In London, former mayor Boris Johnson, later Britain's ousted prime minister, backed the congestion charge introduced by his predecessor Ken Livingstone in 2003 to decongest traffic in central London. His successor Sadiq Khan, London's first Asian-origin mayor now serving his second term, is proactive in the city's fight against incidents of Islamist terrorism. Both London and New York have benefitted from having directly elected, accountable mayors.

In sharp contrast, Mumbai's mayor is a figurehead. The mayor has no powers, no accountability and no visibility. It is time urban centres across India are run by elected officials voted directly to office, as the London and New York mayors are, with both power and accountability. An elected, empowered mayor will mitigate corruption and run the city with a degree of professionalism. The Maharashtra government wants to compress Mumbai's several planning authorities into one planning authority under an empowered and accountable mayor.

One of Modi's key schemes is Smart Cities. While communications, Wi-Fi technology, water management and sanitation are part of the scheme, it ignores governance of India's cities. No amount of high-tech embellishments will make 'smart' cities livable urban centres unless they are accompanied by governance reforms.

Consider how the government defines a smart city: "A smart city is an urban region that is highly advanced in terms of overall infrastructure, sustainable real estate, communications and market viability. It is a city where information technology is the principal infrastructure and the basis for providing essential services to residents. There are many technological platforms involved, including but not limited to automated sensor networks and data centres. In a smart city, economic development and activity is sustainable and rationally incremental by virtue of being based on success-oriented market drivers such as supply and demand. They benefit everybody, including citizens, businesses, the government and the environment. Many of these cities will include special investment regions or special economic zones with modified regulations and tax structures to make them attractive for foreign investment. This is essential because much of the funding for these projects will have to come from private developers and from abroad."

Smart cities need smart governance. That implies a mayor directly elected by citizens and answerable to them. It is an urban reform across Indian cities the prime minister should place at the top of his priorities.

∽

The promise of renewables – especially solar power – as a source of clean and plentiful energy is a driving force in the Modi government. Other Modi schemes may receive more media acreage but solar power is what populates Modi's vision. Solar will be one of the biggest—and among the cheapest—sources of energy in the future. India is well equipped to take advantage of this shift.

Wind power is another source of clean energy India is increasingly tapping. Windy Europe is doing this successfully though costs are still high. Nonetheless, Bloomberg projects that wind power will account for 13 per cent of total global installed capacity by 2040. Altogether, clean and renewable energy sources will contribute nearly 50 per cent to global power capacity by 2040 compared to just 16 per cent today. Coal, gas and hydro will fall collectively from 75 per cent to 43 per cent.

For India, achieving a fine balance between industrial development and clean energy can help it meet the carbon emission targets formulated at the COP26 and COP27 climate change summits in Glasgow in November 2021 and in Sharm el-Sheikh in November 2022. Solar is the key that could unlock India's future under the sun.

Before the Industrial Revolution began in Britain in 1760, carbon dioxide (CO_2) emissions were negligible. For the next 200 years, Britain, the rest of Europe and the United States industrialised rapidly. In the process, they polluted the atmosphere and built their wealth. Factories in Manchester spewed smoke; coal was mined in Newcastle; African slaves worked as bonded labour on cotton plantations as America's industrialisation gathered pace. Carbon emissions rose exponentially.

Having created modern, prosperous, industrialised societies, the West finally woke up to the problem of global warming in the 1970s. The first quasi-climate summit was held in Stockholm in 1972. Known as the First Earth Summit, it focused on the environment. But the real impact of global warming hadn't quite sunk in. It was only in 1987 that the UN General Assembly adopted what it termed the Environmental Perspective to the Year 2000. Since then climate change has increasingly become a hot-button global issue.

Since 1751, over 1.7 trillion tonnes of CO_2 have been emitted. Which countries are the principal polluters? The United States has emitted more than 400 billion tonnes of CO_2, a quarter of the cumulative global total, since 1751. Next comes China with 200 billion tonnes of CO_2, though much of that has been emitted in the last 40 years.

But the biggest historical polluter as a continent is Europe. It has spewed over 525 billion tonnes of CO_2 into the atmosphere since 1751 while building industrialised and prosperous societies. India, targeted by the rich world to cut its carbon emissions, has emitted just over 40 billion tonnes of CO_2 since 1751—a minuscule 2.5 per cent of the cumulative global total.

The statistics also reveal how industrialisation in India was retarded by nearly 200 years of colonialism. Britain deliberately suppressed the growth of Indian industry. Indian raw material was bought with Indian tax money, shipped to Britain, manufactured in the carbon-polluting factories of Manchester, and shipped back to

India to be sold at exorbitant prices. Wealth flowed from India to Britain as Britain industrialised at India's expense and began the process of global warming that is today a climate change crisis.

Average temperatures have already risen by 1.10 degrees Celsius over the pre-industrial average. The key issue is who should bear the principal burden of cutting carbon emissions? Historical polluters like the US and Europe? Or rising polluters like China and India? Modi has long argued that India's industrial development cannot be held hostage to unreasonable cuts in its carbon emissions.

Modi is, in fact, a climate change evangelist. He wrote a book, *Convenient Action: Gujarat's Response to Challenges of Climate Change*, published by Macmillan in 2011 when he was still chief minister of Gujarat, suggesting how the threat of global warming can be countered by a balanced reduction in carbon emissions without harming economic growth. This was before climate change had become an emotive global concern.

Two issues arise. The first is the $100 billion annual funding that developed countries—the world's historical polluters—pledged to provide to developing countries to mitigate the developmental impact of meeting global warming goals. That money has not materialised. The rich world says it will start paying up only after 2023. Meanwhile it continues to prevaricate over contributors and recipients in the "loss and damage fund" mandated under the COP27 agreement at Sharm el-Sheikh in November 2022.

The second issue is India's industrial development. India missed the bus to create an industrialised and wealthy nation during two centuries under British colonial rule. India's real industrial growth began only after Independence. The momentum cannot be allowed to be slowed just as it is reaching an inflection point. That would have serious ramifications on reducing poverty, hunger and malnutrition. "Net zero" or carbon neutrality as a target is ambitious but achievable for some nations. Around 50 countries—mostly from the rich, industrialised world which created the climate crisis in the first place—have pledged carbon neutrality by 2050.

Already industrialised, most are now service economies. Britain, for example, closed one of its last coal mines, *The Bradley Mine* in Durham, in August 2020. Services now account for 80 per cent of British GDP. Wealth already built, Britain can afford to achieve net zero.

Can India? Modi has argued strongly for climate justice. In essence, it means India will work towards reducing carbon emissions—which obviously is in India's environmental interests—while keeping its development goals firmly in mind. India does not have the luxury of Europe or America to de-industrialise when it is still industrialising. Nonetheless, Modi has pledged that India will achieve net-zero by 2070.

China is today the world's biggest carbon emitter, followed by the US and India. In per capita terms, however, the US has the worst record, emitting 16.1 tonnes of CO_2 per American. China emits 7.1 tonnes per person and India just 1.9 tonnes per person. India has set a goal of generating 450 GW of clean renewable energy by 2030 along with several other measures, including its ambitious hydrogen mission, to move towards net-zero emissions in a calibrated manner that does not hamper economic growth.

The Industrial Revolution that helped the rich world acquire wealth would not have been remotely as successful without European colonialism of Asia and Africa and black slavery in America. Action on global warming is critical but nations that have polluted the world for centuries must now pay the price.

∽

India's first prime minister Jawaharlal Nehru and legendary industrialist JRD Tata, both acknowledged as architects of modern India, had a close but at times frosty relationship. Nehru was a Fabian socialist, Tata an unabashed capitalist.

A conversation between them, published in Gita Piramal's book *Business Maharajas*, reveals Nehru's mindset and why India spent 44 post-Independent years till 1991 pursuing socialist economic policies. Piramal wrote: "JRD remembered one particularly sharp exchange of words. Nehru told me, 'I hate the mention of the very word profit.' I replied, 'Jawaharlal, I am talking about the need of the public sector making a profit!' Jawaharlal came back: 'Never talk to me about the word profit, it is a dirty word'."

If Nehru considered "profit" a dirty word, daughter Indira Gandhi took the prejudice further. She nationalised banks, raised the income-tax rate in the highest income bracket to 97 per cent and established the Licence Raj. Crony capitalism grew deep roots. To his credit, son Rajiv Gandhi did try to prise the economy from the grip of crony capitalists whose success lay more in their proximity to the corridors of power in Delhi than on merit. Most of Rajiv's early "A" team was made up of private sector executives like Arun Nehru and Arun Singh. They were soon swept away by the old ecosystem that lived on patronage and favours.

Rahul Gandhi seemed to understand his father's unfulfilled ambition to create a merit-based system, shorn of cronyism and nepotism. He briefly ran an infotech company called Backops with its headquarters in Mumbai, far from the labyrinthic machinations of Delhi. But he was quickly co-opted by dynastic politics. Less than 20 years after he "inherited" the Amethi parliamentary constituency from his father in 2004, Rahul has regressed all the way back to grandmother Indira Gandhi's politics of povertarianism.

The symbolism of povertarian politics remains strong in India more than 76 years after Independence. By calling the Modi government a "suit-boot sarkar", Rahul changed the economic narrative. Unlike Rahul, Modi grew up in relative poverty. He knows how the poor live, their hopes, needs and dreams. Aspiration is the bedrock of the poor. Every parent wants his or her child to have a better life, better education, and better opportunities.

For Rahul the kurta-pyjama is a form of inverted snobbery. He can afford Savile Row suits. Aspiration drives those who can't. When Nehru told JRD Tata that profit was a dirty word, more than 60 per cent of Indians lived in dehumanising poverty. For them profit was not a dirty word. It was an escape from poverty and the route to a better life for themselves and their families.

Modi, despite his political shrewdness, initially fell into Rahul's trap. For two years after the suit-boot sarkar taunt, he embraced Nehruvian povertarianism. It was only deep into his second term that he publicly praised industrialists as creators of wealth for middle-class shareholders and of jobs for millions across socio-economic demographics.

The economist Swaminathan S Anklesaria Aiyar wrote cuttingly in *The Times of India* in 2021: "The Left – including Rahul Gandhi – may pretend that the source of all corruption is the suited-booted businessman. Yet the thrashing of Rajiv Gandhi in the 1989 election and of Sonia in 2014 flowed from voter conviction that the biggest crooks were those in khadi and Gandhi caps. The second term of the UPA government from 2009 to 2014 was marked by scams galore, and a massive anti-corruption agitation led by Anna Hazare that finally cooked Congress' goose. In (this) era, which Congress still extols as the great socialist legacy of Jawaharlal Nehru and Indira Gandhi, free business decisions and competition did not exist. Every industrial licence was a favour bestowed through political discretion, and not competitive rules. Every import licence, every foreign exchange allocation, every clearance and permit was a favour."

Modi's rediscovery of India's wealth-creators is notable. And yet it should not blind him to the remnants of cronyism that still exist in the system. The Licence Raj is gone. Businessmen and their proxies no longer prowl the corridors of North Block. Industrialists don't need to meet the prime minister. He actively discourages such meetings. But the bureaucracy, used to decades of cronyism, remains hidebound. Decisions still take far too long. Many procedures, despite Modi's efforts to introduce technology and transparency into processes, still remain discretionary and arbitrary.

Change though is in the air. The emergence of a new generation of startup entrepreneurs has turbocharged the economy with innovation, creating new opportunities and levelling the playing field. Young men and women are moving into the middle-class faster than they could have imagined a decade ago. Meanwhile, technology-based online education, finance and health care have created new avenues for many women, making them economically independent. No longer are they tied to the tradition of an early arranged marriage. No longer too are daughters always considered a burden on a family. To many, they are today a boon and a source of pride.

During the initial years of UPA 1, India's GDP growth soared. Between 2004 and 2008, the economy grew at an average real annual rate of over 7.5 per cent. The aviation sector was a collateral beneficiary. Airlines like Jet Airways made full use of a booming economy. One airline though was about to face headwinds: Air India.

Praful Patel, then a senior member of the Nationalist Congress Party (NCP), was minister of state (MoS) for civil aviation between 2004 and 2011. There was no union minister of civil aviation. Patel was the boss. In 2006, I interviewed Patel at his residence in Mumbai which he would visit frequently though he was at the time based in Delhi. Patel is an affable man. He spoke enthusiastically about Indian aviation and the great plans he had to make it world class.

Privatisation of India's shambolic metropolitan airports had begun. Mumbai, Delhi, Hyderabad and other cities soon had gleaming new modern airports run by private sector infrastructure companies like the Adani Group and GMR with the Airports Authority of India (AAI) retaining a minority stake in a private-public-partnership (PPP) model.

Plans were also drawn up to merge Air India with domestic carrier Indian Airlines. The logic was superficially seductive: economies of scale, higher profitability, integration of engineering and pilot resources, and route rationalisation. Not everyone was convinced that the AI-IA merger, approved by an empowered group of ministers in February 2007, was a good idea. But with India fast becoming a large aviation market, "route rationalisation" took on a new meaning.

Gulf-based carriers like Emirates and Qatar Airways were keen to increase flying rights from India to the Gulf. Over three million Indians live and work in the UAE alone. The India-UAE, India-Qatar and other Gulf routes were Air India's bread and butter. Indian Airlines too had profitable flying rights on several Gulf routes.

Following the AI-IA merger those lucrative flying rights should have all gone to the merged entity. Instead, most were allocated to Emirates and other Gulf carriers in an extraordinary act of generosity by India's civil aviation ministry. The AI-IA merger was already attracting severe criticism. Now the giveaway of profitable Gulf flying rights to foreign airlines in 2008 drew even sharper criticism.

The Comptroller and Auditor General (CAG) reported in 2011 that the civil aviation ministry's decision to massively expand bilateral entitlements hampered Air India. The report added: "As an illustrative case of the liberalisation of bilateral entitlements, the sequence of events relating to the Dubai sector, covering the period from May 2007 to March 5, 2010 [when the seat capacity was increased from 18,400 seats/week to 54,200 seats/week and points of call in India were increased from 10 to 14], clearly demonstrates the one-sided nature of benefits to Emirates/Dubai through enhancement of entitlements and additional points of call in India."

Meanwhile, the global economy was tanking. Lehman Brothers collapsed on 15 September 2008. The financial meltdown spread across the United States and Europe. India's relatively closed economy was insulated from the worldwide recession in 2008. But for the AI-IA merger, badly implemented in fits and starts, the downturn couldn't have come at a worse time. Not only had AI-IA lost many of their profitable Gulf flying rights, the recession had hit overall profitability. Air India's problems had begun to mount. After the merger, things became rapidly worse for AI. Debt spiralled. Service suffered. The airline, long used for free junkets by bureaucrats and their families, began the slow slide to the bottom even as allegations of corruption swirled.

According to a report on 31 March 2019 in the *Hindustan Times*, "Investigative agencies are actively looking into the roles of some ministers of the United Progressive Alliance (UPA) in awarding favourable air traffic rights to some West Asian airlines in 2008–09 that damaged the interests of the state-run Air India, government officials said, echoing a statement issued by the Enforcement Directorate (ED). Agencies, including the ED, the Central Bureau of Investigation (CBI) and the income-tax department, are processing vital clues in this regard, provided by lobbyist Deepak Talwar, currently in judicial custody, the officials added, requesting anonymity. It has been revealed that accused Deepak Talwar illegally engaged in liaisoning/lobbying with politicians, ministers, other public servants and officials of the Ministry of Civil Aviation for airlines such as Emirates, Air Arabia and Qatar Airways for securing undue benefits for them. He illegally managed to secure favourable traffic rights for these airlines during 2008–09 at the cost of the national carrier, Air India, ED said in a statement on Saturday."

On the same Saturday, 30 March 2019, the ED filed a prosecution complaint against Talwar for "causing a huge loss to

Air India by favouring the foreign airlines." The ED's allegations are serious. It told the court that the Gulf carriers paid middleman Deepak Talwar ₹272 crore "in lieu of securing favourable traffic rights." It provisionally attached the hotel Holiday Inn in Delhi's Aerocity, alleging that the hotel was built with a portion of the "proceeds of crime" that can be traced back to Talwar.

If a middleman like Talwar received a bribe of ₹272 crore from foreign carriers as the ED alleges, the amount received by those who engineered the deal in the civil aviation ministry would be many multiple times higher. But the case had – not surprisingly – been weakened, as the defence lawyer pointed out, by the fact that the ED has not questioned any serving or former officials from the civil aviation ministry, nor any current or former civil aviation minister: Praful Patel (2004–11), K. Vyalar Ravi (January 2011–December 2011), Ajit Singh (2011–2014), Ashok Gajapathi Raju (2014–18), Suresh Prabhu (2018–19), Hardeep Singh Puri (2019–2021) and Jyotiraditya Scindia (2021 onwards). It was only in July 2022 that Praful Patel's property was attached for an entirely different case related to land dealings with the late fugitive Iqbal Mirchi.

The integration of Air India and Indian Airlines, far from saving overall costs through synergies, made the merged AI a white elephant with unserviceable debt. Air India, crippled by design, flew on, overstaffed and weighed down by huge debt till it was acquired by the Tata Group in a successful privatisation in 2022. The revival of Air India under the Tatas could transform the dynamic of the country's aviation sector.

∽

Employment data from the National Sample Survey Office (NSSO) and the Centre for Monitoring Indian Economy (CMIE) does not fully capture the hottest trend in jobs: the gig economy. Worldwide more and more millennials in a post-pandemic world are opting for project-based work that give them freedom, space and challenges. Automation and artificial intelligence are shrinking traditional industrial jobs, quickening the trend towards assignment-based work. With work-from-anywhere being the new normal, gigs are catching on.

In India, jobs data captures less than 50 per cent of all jobs. Most jobs tracked are in the formal economy but it's in the informal economy where many new-economy jobs are being created. The next time Swiggy delivers your dinner at home or you ride an Ola cab to office, you are supporting the informal economy. Mall workers, healthcare startups, interior designers, web coders and food caterers form a layer of gig jobbers who make India's informal economy far larger than is generally believed. The downside obviously is low pay and lack of job security. But as India's new-economy and startup ecosystems mature, both wages and job tenure will rise. That has been the trend in the United States and Europe where the gig economy is rapidly gaining traction with rising wages and clear job contracts.

TeamLease Services, a professional human resources company, estimates that 56 per cent of new jobs in India are being generated by the sharing/gig economy "across the blue-collar and white-collar workforce." If indeed such a large proportion of new jobs are being created in the informal economy, NSSO and CMIE employment data would be inadequate to judge the growth of jobs in India as the economic recovery gathers steam. Moreover, Mudra loans to self-employed small entrepreneurs, ranging from ₹50,000 to ₹10 lakh, have spawned millions of small businesses. These range from food stalls with just two employees to mobile health clinics with several employees. Again, these are jobs in the expanding informal economy not captured by NSSO or CMIE data.

Nowhere are more informal jobs being created than in e-commerce. Amazon, Jio, Flipkart and a host of "social commerce" and food delivery sites are on a hiring spree. They are also turbocharging "knock-on" industries: logistics, transport, software, payment gateways, artificial intelligence, warehousing and packaging. Every time you buy a product on Amazon, work is instantly parcelled out to a chain of suppliers – from the retail store stocking that product to the courier delivering it to your doorstep

The Open Network for Digital Commerce (ONDC) has meanwhile been a game changer in India's bustling e-commerce ecosystem. It has democratised online commerce and is widely hailed as e-commerce's UPI moment. The Unified Payments Interface has become a symbol of India's ability to roll out world-class solutions in digital technology.

How will ONDC impact e-commerce giants Amazon and Walmart-Flipkart? Shreya Nandi decoded ONDC's unique digital architecture in *Business Standard*[22] shortly after its soft launch in April 2022: "ONDC works on the principle of an open network where a buyer and a seller don't have to be on the same platform to conduct business with each other. Rather, the network enables them to be digitally visible and transact no matter what platform or application they use. Imagine ONDC as a common catalogue or a registry where the seller doesn't need to follow a separate set of compliances for different marketplaces. Similarly, consumers are able to see sellers from all marketplaces such as Amazon and Flipkart, and even their neighbourhood kirana stores.

"The aim is to enable large-scale democratisation of digital commerce by providing a level playing field to both large and small merchants in the country. The network enables buyers and sellers registered with it to be visible and discoverable by adopting the ONDC architecture. Over a period of time, the hope is that this will result in rapid digitalisation of small businesses and consumers. The open network concept is not restricted to

---

[22]30 April 2022.

the retail sector but extends to mobility, food delivery, and travel among others."

Small traders and retailers complain that Amazon and Walmart-Flipkart don't give them priority in search results. Discounts on the two e-commerce sites have driven large numbers of kirana stores out of business. They can't afford to sell goods at below cost price which e-commerce sites can in order to build a large GMV (gross merchandise volume) which boosts their valuation. For example, Walmart bought Flipkart for $16 billion in 2018. The company has spun off its subsidiary PhonePe, which came along with the Flipkart acquisition, and plans to go public in 2023–24. In a testament to ONDC's prowess, Amazon, Walmart-Flipkart and Jio Platforms have onboarded the new open architecture. All three say they are committed to working closely with ONDC as it scales up.

India's $1 trillion retail market is growing exponentially, propelled by two drivers. One, an upwardly mobile middle-class; and two, rising purchasing power. For the Modi government, ONDC serves a purpose beyond democratising e-commerce. The BJP has a large vote bank among kirana shop owners. Small traders have long been fighting against the predatory pricing and monopoly of e-commerce giants like Amazon and Walmart-Flikart. ONDC could be one of the BJP's silver bullets in the 2024 Lok Sabha election.

India has over 12 million kiranas. To protect them foreign direct investment (FDI) in inventory-based multi-brand online retail is prohibited. Amazon and Walmart-Flipkart have had to resort to convoluted arrangements with designated sellers to circumvent FDI rules. Its platform-agnostic model enables ONDC to function as a neutral discovery interface for buyers across multiple e-commerce sites. Just as UPI has helped boost the business transactions of payment companies like PhonePe, Paytm and GooglePay, ONDC is functioning similarly as a catalyst and facilitator in the digital e-commerce ecosystem.

E-commerce is revolutionising not only the jobs market but consumer habits. As Joydeep Bhattacharya and Sanjay Wali reported in *Mint*[23]: "A homemaker in Coimbatore who used to buy groceries from the neighbourhood store now simply orders online what she needs the night before, to be delivered at 7.00 am. It arrives on time, just after her morning puja, every day and she pays her bill at the end of the month using her mobile wallet. The e-store that delivers her groceries customises reminders and options, almost seeming to know what she will need before she realises it. This is the contemporary scenario of grocery retail, and it is an exciting time to be a retailer and a consumer in India. The overall Indian grocery market is set to grow from about $550 billion to nearly $1 trillion in five years. The addressable market for FMCG players is about $250 billion today and is estimated to double in the next five years, according to Bain & Co."

This presages an excellent future for job creation but raises hackles among kirana stores. Will such seamless e-commerce drive kiranas into oblivion? Is that why the Modi government has barred FDI in multi-brand retail, since traders form its core constituency? The fears are unfounded. As with all innovations, there is a period of disruption before equilibrium is restored. After several years of Flipkart, Amazon and Jiomart operations, kirana stores remain resilient. Many have become an integral part of the e-commerce ecosystem. Their sales volumes have risen. Those that remain outside the ecosystem, selling directly to local customers, have the advantage of customer loyalty.

Four conclusions are therefore clear. First, NSSO and CMIE data captures jobs principally in the formal economy where employment is structured and measurable. Second, the informal economy, which is unstructured, comprises a significant slice of the overall Indian economy. Third, the sharing and gig economy

---

[23]1 March 2019.

has expanded the size of the informal economy and is adding an estimated three million jobs a year – which traditional jobs data doesn't fully capture. Fourth, Mudra loan-financed micro-entrepreneurs are moving away from low-paid blue-collar jobs to self-employment and generating jobs for others in their tiny enterprises.

The quality of jobs, rather than merely their quantity, should now be the principal concern for the Modi government. It should publish NSSO data along with a white paper on the exciting dynamic of new-economy jobs in India. That will ensure economists analysing jobs data don't miss the wood for the trees.

THIRTEEN

India, the Startup Hub

INDIA'S STARTUP ECOSYSTEM IS THE WORLD'S THIRD LARGEST AFTER the United States and China. Bengaluru, Gurugram, Noida, Mumbai and Hyderabad are buzzing with new startups in fields as diverse as artificial intelligence, big data, space technology, electric vehicles, logistics, deep machine learning, social commerce, payment gateways, green energy, drones, fintech, edtech, food delivery, gaming and regional language video streaming. Despite a funding winter, India has over 120 unicorns (companies valued at over $1 billion), the third highest globally.

But in spite of the Indian government's efforts to ease the process of registering a company, startups still face a mountain of bureaucratic hurdles. In Singapore it takes 30 minutes to set up a company. Several Indian startup entrepreneurs are choosing to register their businesses in countries like Singapore or the United States.

Consider the story of Navin Suri. Rachel Chitra, writing in *The Sunday Times of India*[24]: "For Navin Suri, who was heading Bank of New York Mellon's asset management business in Hong Kong, Singapore was the obvious choice when it came to setting up. He said he had always heard about the 'ease of doing business' in Singapore but even he was taken aback when it took him less than 30 minutes to set up his data technology company. From getting his registration number to signed MoUs, it all got

---

[24]14 April 2019.

done between 10.40 and 11.10 SGT. 'I even got a prompt from the government with the suggestions as to how I could set up a website', says Suri, co-founder of Percipient."

While it recently made a few missteps, Singapore has achieved a fine balance between strict regulation and fast delivery. The corruption-free environment and tough, transparent and quick audits help startups establish credibility with customers and potential investors. Other countries in East Asia are emulating the Singapore model and attracting droves of Indian startup entrepreneurs.

Rachel Chitra added: "Governments in Southeast Asia are now offering a range of mentorship, seed funding, introduction to investors, faster regulatory clearances and a hands-on approach to solve any and all problems. From funding their laptops (if they are a small startup to providing salary subsidies for experienced hires (aged 60 and above), the business-friendly atmosphere is omnipresent. Industry sources say one in seven startups in Southeast Asia are started by Indians or Indian-origin CEOs. 'In our Singapore Fintech Association, three of ten board members are Indians, the others are Chinese or Malays,' says Varun Mittal, board member, Singapore Fintech Association and founder of HelloPay, which was sold to Alibaba Financial. 'Seeing the exponential growth of our cluster of 350 startups, the Monetary Authority of Singapore actually organised an event in Mumbai and Delhi to further highlight opportunities for those who want to set up base here'."

Over-regulation in India kills silently. It affords discretionary power to authorities. Corruption and "settlement", in time-honoured Indian fashion, are the inevitable result – a throwback to an era India should have left behind in 1991. Change though is underway. In late 2022, in a sign of the times, Flipkart-Walmart's industry-leading payment gateway PhonePe relocated its headquarters from Singapore to India as it separated from its parent in preparation for an Indian IPO.

First term: Narendra Modi takes charge of the Prime
Minister's office on 26 May 2014.

PM Modi addressing dignitaries at the inaugural ceremony
of the new Parliament building on 28 May 2023.

PM Modi addressing a joint session of the
US Congress, Washington DC, on 22 June 2023.

PM Modi greeting Vice President Kamala Harris
at the joint session of the US Congress.

PM Modi arrives at the White House for a State Banquet Dinner hosted by President Joe Biden on 22 June 2023.

PM Modi meeting the PM of Egypt, Mostafa Madbouly, in Cairo, Egypt, on 24 June 2023.

PM Modi with VP Kamala Harris at a State Department
Luncheon at the White House on 23 June 2023.

PM Modi in a bilateral
meeting with US President
Joe Biden at the White
House on 22 June 2023.

PM Modi with a Pakistani delegation led by Nawaz Sharif following the PM's inauguration on 26 May 2014.

First day first show: Pakistani PM Nawaz Sharif at PM Modi's inauguration on 26 May 2014.

PM Modi with British PM Rishi Sunak.

Franco-China entente? Emmanuel Macron and Xi Jinping.

External Affairs Minister S. Jaishankar at the G20 meet.

Congress leader Rahul Gandhi addresses a public rally in Shillong, Meghalaya, on 22 February 2023 soon after completing the Bharat Jodo Yatra.

Priyanka Gandhi walks with Rahul Gandhi in the Bharat Jodo Yatra, 24 November 2022.

AICC General Secretary Priyanka Gandhi in Raipur, Chhattisgarh, for the Congress Plenary Session on 25 February 2023.

West Bengal CM Mamata Banerjee at the 46th International
Book Fair in Kolkata on 30 January 2023.

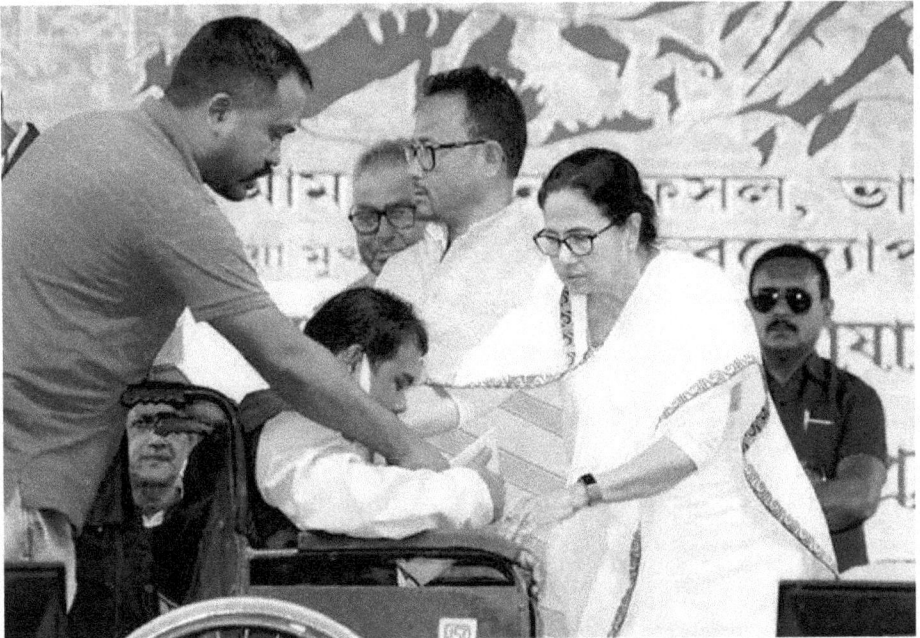
West Bengal CM Mamata Banerjee at
Kanchenjunga Stadium in Siliguri.

PM Modi greets Japanese PM Fumio Kishida at Hyderabad House.

PM Modi greets Italian PM Georgia Meloni.

PM Modi celebrates Diwali with soldiers near the LOC.

Congress leader Rahul Gandhi celebrates the party's
Karnataka assembly victory in May 2023 with Siddaramaiah
and DK Shivakumar.

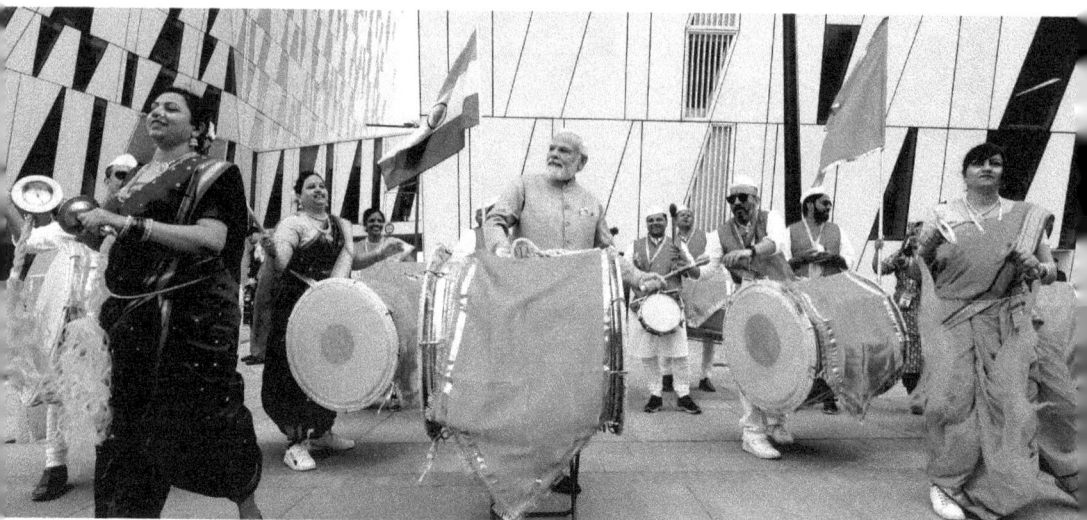
PM Modi at a Community Reception in Copenhagen,
Denmark, on 3 May 2022.

Interacting with school students and staff aboard the Vande Bharat
Express in Tamil Nadu on 8 April 2023.

PM Modi at the Global Buddhist Summit 2023 in New Delhi on 20 April 2023.

PM Modi meets spiritual leaders from the Christian community on Easter at Delhi's Sacred Heart Cathedral Catholic Church on 9 April 2023.

Union Minister of Finance and Corporate Affairs Nirmala Sitharaman meets former president of World Bank Group David Malpass in New Delhi on 22 February 2023.

Apple CEO Tim Cook greets PM Modi in New Delhi on 19 April 2023.

The Indian and Ukrainian delegations in Hiroshima.

PM Modi holds a bilateral meeting with Ukraine President
Volodymyr Zelensky in Hiroshima, Japan, on the sidelines
of the G7 summit on 20 May 2023.

PM Modi arrives at Port Moresby in Papua New Guinea
on 21 May 2023 and is greeted by PM James Marape.

Quad Leaders' Summit in Hirosima on 20 May 2023.
L to R: US President Joe Biden, Australian PM Anthony Albanese,
Japanese PM Fumio Kishida and PM Narendra Modi.

Largely resistant to new technology, Indian agriculture has grown tortoise-like over decades. There is no reason, however, to believe that the agricultural sector should forever be consigned to low growth rates. Doubling the annual agricultural growth rate from 3 to 6 per cent will, despite its low weight age of 14 per cent in the overall GDP pie, add a crucial 0.5 per cent to overall economic growth, taking India nearer to 8 per cent GDP growth levels. For this to happen, agriculture needs deep reforms to boost productivity per acre by reprioritising crops sown, creating a new technological ecosystem, and revamping market distribution.

In a well-researched article in the *Hindustan Times*[25], Nachiket Mor, national director of the Bill and Melinda Gates Foundation, developed the argument for increasing agricultural productivity by citing China's success: "In March 2018, *Nature* magazine published a ground-breaking 10-year study by China Agriculture University involving millions of small holder farmers adopting enhanced practices. Through a scaled, countrywide effort, farm productivity rose by 11 per cent while the use of nitrogen fertilisers – critical to increasing crop productivity, but also harmful to the environment when overused – declined by 14–18 per cent. The profitability of the intervention, even before monetising the positive environmental impacts, was $12.2 billion.

"The programme was an impressive marriage of knowledge workers, researchers, farmers, new technology, and businesses – all supported by a committed government that stayed the course. The result stunned the scientific community for its scale, success and impact. Between 2005 and 2015, China Agricultural University led a nationally coordinated initiative for 20.9 million smallholder farmers in wheat, rice and maize to promote adoption of enhanced management technologies for greater yields and reduced environmental pollution. The project began by conducting

[25]12 March 2019.

over 13,000 field studies across all agro-ecological zones, from the subtropical south to the frigid north. Based on the trials, over 1,152 agricultural scientists from 33 agricultural universities collaborated with local farmers and experts to develop packages of recommended practices tailored to local conditions."

This level of collaboration between government, scientists, NGOs and farmers is lacking in India. Vested interests continue to oppose genetically modified (GM) crops which could significantly boost per-acre profitability. Enhanced Chinese agricultural productivity helps the country produce over 600 million tonnes of food grains annually. India, with roughly the same population as China but larger fertile farm acreage, has struggled to produce 300 million tonnes of food grains per year.

It is only through innovation that Indian agriculture can climb out of its decades-long rut of low growth. When over 50 per cent of a country's population lives off agriculture but the sector contributes only 14 per cent to GDP, farmer distress is the inevitable consequence. Crucially too, boosting farmers' incomes will drive rural consumption. Over 65 per cent of India's population lives in rural areas. A rise in their purchasing power, directly or indirectly through the farm sector, will deliver a powerful boost to the overall economy. Agricultural reforms, implemented well, have the potential to relieve farmers' distress and return the economy to a higher sustainable trajectory of growth.

However, when more than half the country's population involved directly or indirectly in agriculture is exempt from paying tax, the government will always be burdened with a large fiscal deficit. That in turn compels it to moderate the defence budget, keep allocation on healthcare below 1.5 per cent of GDP, curtail spending on education, and cut subsidies across sectors.

Most Indians employed in agriculture own small land holdings and eke out marginal livelihoods. Around 10,000 farmers die by suicide every year. Many are heavily indebted to money lenders who charge usurious interest rates. Farm labour is equally destitute.

Workers on farms own no land and depend on seasonal MNREGA work or employment at low contract wages on big farms.

But there is a third category involved in the agricultural sector: wealthy landholders who make large profits from farming. They too pay no tax. Should they? The answer to that question has political and economic consequences. Many rich farmers with large annual incomes are politically powerful. Indeed, a few of the wealthiest 'farmers' are politicians themselves. They form a close-knit lobby which has long opposed taxing agricultural income on the grounds that most farmers are very poor.

They are right about that. What they don't say, however, is that a creamy layer of over 5 per cent of those involved in the agricultural sector are rich. They can afford to pay tax. Fewer than 70 million assesses currently file tax returns. This would go up significantly if wealthy farmers came under the ambit of personal income tax. It could lift tax revenue substantially, possibly by a fifth over targeted personal tax revenue. The wealthiest 5 per cent of India's agriculturists each own dozens of acres of land and employ poor labourers to work on them. Many launder their cash income, fearing no income tax raids since they don't have to file returns.

India's tax-GDP ratio has stagnated at around 12 per cent. If wealthy "farmers" contribute to the tax pie, India's tax-GDP ratio will begin to rise. The average international tax-GDP ratio is 20 per cent. The tax-GDP ratio in industrialised countries like France and Britain is, respectively, 24.6 per cent and 24.9 per cent even though agriculture forms a small part of total GDP in both countries.

Politicians across parties will fiercely resist agricultural tax reform. Rich farmers and their *arhityas* (middlemen) in Punjab and Haryana, who led the farmers' protest against three progressive farm laws in 2021, were terrified of one particular clause in the aborted farm legislation: mandatory submission of their Permanent Account Number (PAN). That would have revealed whether or not they possessed a PAN and, if they did, the details of their bank transactions.

Wealthy land owners who have net annual incomes in excess of ₹1 crore regarded the PAN clause as the thin edge of the wedge if the government decides to tax farm income over a specific annual threshold. It explained the ferocity of the farmers' 13-month-long protest led by wealthy famers and their commission agents in Punjab and Haryana while landless labourers from Uttar Pradesh and Bihar continued to work unprotestingly on their large farms.

What should the annual tax threshold for farmers be? A starting point could be a net income of over ₹10 lakh a year after deducting all expenses (fertilisers, tractors, power, seeds, loans, labour). This should attract a flat concessional tax rate of 10 per cent. Net incomes above ₹20 lakh would be taxed at 20 per cent and net incomes above ₹50 lakh at 30 per cent. Since over 95 per cent of farmers would fall outside these income thresholds, they would remain tax-exempt.

As Ashok Gulati, one of India's most respected voices on the agricultural sector and currently Infosys Chair professor for agriculture at ICRIER, wrote in *The Indian Express* on 31 January 2022: "If the Union government wants the biggest bang for its buck, the right approach is to double or even triple the amount on agri-R&D, especially in the emerging areas of high-value agriculture (horticulture, medicinal plants, livestock, fishery, etc). This is not just to raise their productivity but also build efficient value chains to supply these to lucrative markets, so that farmers' incomes can be significantly augmented."

Modi is aware of how enhancing technological solutions can improve farm productivity. Speaking in January 2022 at the golden jubilee celebrations of the International Crops Research Institute for the Semi-Arid Tropics (ICRISAT) in Hyderabad, the prime minister said: "To save our farmers from climate challenges, our focus is on the fusion of both 'back to basics' and 'march to future'. Our focus is on more than 80 per cent of small farmers of the country who need us the most. One important aspect is digital agriculture. The 2022–23 Union Budget is focused on natural farming and digital agriculture. We are working towards higher agricultural growth, inclusive growth and conserving natural resources. Digital agriculture is gaining popularity and this is something we will also have to adopt."

Modi's focus on agri-tech is welcome. But bolder reforms are necessary. The government was forced to backtrack on the farm laws. Will it have the courage to institute even more far-reaching reforms? It would appear not. But taxing wealthy farmers is a bullet India will, sooner or later, have to bite.

Modi's decision in November 2021 to repeal the three farm laws was seized upon by the Opposition as a sign of Modi's political vulnerability to concerted pressure. The farmers' agitation was of course never aimed at repealing the farm laws alone. The subterranean objective was weakening Modi ahead of the spate of assembly elections and the Lok Sabha poll in 2024. In the end, the crushing BJP victory in Uttar Pradesh in March 2022 exposed the claims of widespread support against the farm laws. A member of the Supreme Court-appointed panel set up to assess the opinion of farmers revealed that their report showed 86 per cent of all farmers surveyed actually favoured the repealed farm laws.

Parallels were drawn between the Congress-led UPA 2 government's abject surrender to anti-corruption activist Anna Hazare in 2011 in its eighth year in office and the BJP-led NDA government's capitulation to the farmers' agitation in its own eighth year in power in 2021–2022. The end result for the Congress a decade ago was a collapse in credibility and a rout in the 2014 Lok Sabha elections. The parallel, however, needs a caveat. The UPA government was immersed in alleged corruption scandals. With or without the anti-corruption crusade of Anna Hazare, it was heading towards defeat. The Modi government is electorally in a stronger position. But warning lights are flashing.

The retreat on the farm laws strengthened the nagging perception that the Modi government will put bad politics ahead of good economics. The three farm laws were beneficial for the majority of India's farmers. Repealing them sets back agricultural reform by years. Wealthy farmer-politician leaders could in future twist the knife in. Having bludgeoned the government, they have demanded Parliament pass an MSP law. When a government resorts to a policy of appeasement, it surrenders more than just its credibility. It surrenders its political options.

∽

Modi is a loner. He often dines alone at his sprawling three-bungalow residence, briefed daily by a close group of advisors, some drawn from his days as Gujarat chief minister. Modi has spent his second term resetting India's foreign policy. He has strengthened defence and strategic cooperation with the United States-led West, befriended the Arab world as well as Israel, used surgical strikes to increase the cost to Pakistan of terrorism and built close ties with the United States, Europe, Australia, Japan, South Korea and the littoral states in the South China Sea as both an instrument of geopolitics policy and a lever against an increasingly bellicose China.

Modi is set to spend the final months of his second term—and make no mistake, he does not wish to be merely a two-term Prime Minister—on economic policy and, as president of the G20, placing India at the heart of the unfolding new world order before he hits the campaign trial for the 2024 Lok Sabha election.

CHINA

FOURTEEN

A Historical Turning Point

THE 20TH NATIONAL PARTY CONGRESS OF THE CHINESE COMMUNIST Party (CCP) in October 2022 endorsed an unprecedented third five-year term for Xi Jinping as general secretary of the CCP. Months later, Xi was named president of the People's Republic of China (PRC) for a norm-breaking third successive five-year term. The 19th National Congress in 2017 had enshrined the "Xi Jinping Thought" in the Constitution at the end of a week-long conclave. "Mao Thought" and "Deng Theory" are the only two such previous enshrinements.

There were few dissenting voices against Xi's elevation. Rivals were cut down to size. Xi's loyalist and allies now occupy key positions in the CCP, Politburo and the powerful military commission. Xi will have to tread carefully though. He has alienated many powerful people. Opinions, while heavily censored in China, were polarised following Xi's endorsement of Russia's invasion of Ukraine and his zero-Covid policy that locked down parts of the country, including Shanghai, for months before it was disbanded in the face of unprecedented public protests. The subsequent surge in Covid cases and deaths, the slowing economy and the collapse of the real estate sector caused distress among ordinary Chinese.

In his first five-year term, from 2012–17, Xi purged or jailed nearly one million officials on charges of corruption. Several senior army generals were sacked. China's armed forces were now firmly under Xi's command. In his second term, 2017–22,

Xi adopted a belligerent stance in the South China Sea and on Tibet, Taiwan, the Line of Actual Control (LAC) and Xinjiang. His tacit support of Pakistani terrorism made him a disruptive challenge for Indian policymakers. Xi's third term, as general secretary of the CCP and president of China, which runs till the end of 2027, could be the most challenging yet with a military invasion of Taiwan not ruled out.

The Russia-Ukraine conflict marked an historical turning point in the balance of global power. The rift between Russia and the rest of Europe has widened more than at any time since the Cold War. The China-Russia axis has meanwhile developed into a long-term geopolitical threat to the West: China is an economic superpower, Russia a failing but disruptive military power. The alliance is a direct challenge to the global supremacy of the US-led West. The Russia-Ukraine conflict accelerated the change in the world's geopolitical architecture. The West enabled China for 30 years to gain technological parity on the assumption it would be a counterweight to Russia. The opposite has happened, driving Russia into China's arms.

℗

When the Soviet Union collapsed in 1991, Vladimir Putin was a 38-year-old KGB colonel in Leningrad. Within nine years, in 2000, he was president of Russia. For several years during the early 2000s, Putin deliberated on the idea of aligning Russia—territorially emasculated and economically weakened after nearly a decade of Boris Yeltsin's corrupt presidency—with Western Europe. He even considered, briefly, applying for membership of the European Union.

In return, Europe gave him the cold shoulder. The US had become the sole superpower after the dissolution of the Soviet Union. NATO began to expand eastwards. Several East European countries lined up to join: Poland, Hungary and the Czech Republic in 1999, followed by Bulgaria, Romania, Slovakia and Slovenia.

Three key former Soviet states—Estonia, Latvia and Lithuania—which share a border with Russia were also made NATO members in 2004. After 2009, Croatia, Albania, Montenegro and North Macedonia were eased into NATO. In two decades, NATO had expanded from 16 to 30 countries.

For over 40 years during the Cold War, the Soviet-led Warsaw Pact powers in eastern Europe had served as a military counterweight to NATO. In 1991, the balance of power shifted decisively. Following the collapse of the Soviet Union, the Warsaw Pact was dismantled; its seven founding members—ranging from Poland to Romania—are all today members of NATO. Sweden and Finland's membership application was fast-tracked following the Russia-Ukraine war.

For a while, recognising Russia's economic and military potential, the G7 in 1997 admitted Moscow to a newly minted G8. The idea was an old one: keep your enemies close. In 2014, following Russia's annexation of Crimea, Russia was "expelled" (the euphemism used was "removed") from the G8, which reverted to its old G7 format comprising the US, Canada, Britain, France, Germany, Italy and Japan. The irony escaped no one. All G7 members were active combatants in World War II; the first four were the victorious Allies, the latter three, the defeated Axis powers. Now, all seven had common cause and a common enemy: Russia. But by the time it was expelled from the G7 in 2014, Russia had become economically far stronger than it had been when the Soviet Union collapsed in 1991.

The annexation of Crimea in 2014 sent a message to the West: Russia was challenging the old world order. Washington, however, was now increasingly preoccupied with the rise of China. It believed that Russia was a European power, not a global threat to the US-led world order. Russia's invasion of Ukraine turned that theory on its head.

The Modi government's nuanced stand on the Russia-Ukraine war took into account a new multipolar world of autonomous alliances. For years, Europe looked at India with cultivated indifference. China was the flavour of the season. Trade between the European Union (EU) and China surged. Meanwhile, India-EU trade limped along. Three factors have cooled ties between the EU and China.

First, Covid-19 dealt a blow to China's infrastructure projects ranged across Europe. Work on the Belt and Road Initiative (BRI), designed to create a new Silk Route from China to Western Europe through Central Asia, stalled. Second, Beijing's aggressive militarisation in the South China Sea raised red flags in Brussels. China reacted by insisting on strict European adherence to the "One China" policy. When EU member-state Lithuania allowed Taiwan to open a representative office in its capital Vilnius in November 2021, Beijing reacted with fury. It snapped diplomatic ties with the Baltic nation and expelled the Lithuanian ambassador from Beijing.

The third factor affecting Europe-China ties had the most significant long-term implications: China's quiet support for Russia's invasion of Ukraine. The EU reacted angrily. Several European companies in China moved some supply lines to Vietnam, the Philippines and India.

Western Europe has spent 78 years after the end of the Second World War, which killed over 50 million Europeans, to build a peaceful, prosperous Europe. The Balkan wars in the 1990s which dismembered Yugoslavia were confined to Eastern Europe. Russia's invasion of Ukraine brought the spectre of war back to the heart of Europe.

West European politicians remain fearful of the long-term economic costs and security threats of Russia's aggression. They had become gentrified after 78 years of peace. They willingly participated in airstrikes on Syria, Iraq and Yemen. Their armies fought the Taliban in Afghanistan for two decades as part of NATO. But a land or air war in Europe was hitherto unthinkable.

China is meanwhile positioning itself as the world's leading superpower by 2049, the 100th anniversary of the founding of the People's Republic of China. Its economy may or may not match America's over the next decade depending on whether its economic slowdown persists. Its military will take far longer to catch up with America's formidable armed forces. But an authoritarian China under Xi clearly poses a greater threat to the Western world order than the Soviet Union did.

As *The Economist* wrote[26] of Xi: "His personal powers reflect his exalted sense of mission. He is president, head of the party and 'supreme commander', a title last conferred on Deng. He bestrides the bureaucracy like a colossus, having swept away and replaced almost all the party leaders and local governors in China's 31 provinces, as well as much of the top brass of the People's Liberation Army (PLA)."

India is building a coherent long-term strategy to counter China's aggression and Xi's growing hegemonistic ambitions. The Ladakh standoff underscored two truths. One, that China is territorial by instinct. It will continue its creeping acquisition of other countries' sovereign territory—on land or at sea—as long as it can get away with it. Two, when confronted, China can be made to back down.

Beijing remains especially sensitive over the Dalai Lama. It used the 2017 Communist Party's Congress to warn world leaders not to meet the Dalai Lama, saying it would constitute a "major offence". Zhang Yijiong, then head of the Communist Party's Tibet working group, told reporters on the sidelines of the party Congress: "Any country, or any organisation, accepting to meet the Dalai Lama, in our view, is a major offence to the sentiment of the Chinese people."

Zhang, then also an executive vice-minister of the United Front Working Department of the Communist Party, was harsh in his criticism of the Dalai Lama: "After fleeing China in 1959

---

[26]14 October 2017.

the Dalai Lama established a so-called government-in-exile (in India) whose goal and core agenda is the independence of Tibet and to separate it (from) China..."

Since the disastrous 1962 war, India has had a negative reflex action on matters regarding Tibet and China. In this context it is important to note the views of Prasenjit K Basu, a Singapore-based economist whose book, *Asia Reborn: A Continent Rises from the Ravages of Colonialism and War to a New Dynamism,* has key insights on Asia's past, present and future.

In an interview with senior journalist Aditi Phadnis in *Business Standard*[27], Basu criticised India's Tibet policy: "Nehru was a brilliant historian: his *Glimpses of World History* is a masterpiece. But his naiveté on statecraft was astounding, as if his knowledge of history was somehow utterly separated from his approach to governance and foreign policy. Sardar Patel saw clearly that India's traditional role as Tibet's main ally (and the only country with four consulates in Tibet while China had no representation in 1950) was essential to India's security, (but) Nehru allowed China to invade and occupy Tibet – while doing nothing militarily or diplomatically to thwart this thrust from a rogue Communist regime that most of the world didn't recognise as legitimate at the time."

Such historical errors of judgement have allowed Beijing to control the India-China narrative for decades. That is beginning to change under the Modi government. The confrontation in Ladakh was the first sign of a more robust policy to counter Chinese aggression.

∞

China is a totalitarian and oppressive state. It blocks Facebook, Twitter, Google and other internet sites. Its citizens have few freedoms. Its economy is slowing, its population ageing. Many

---

[27] 21 October 2017.

"wonder towns" built during the boom years are ghost cities with empty buildings and empty roads. In the northwest province of Xinjiang, China has ruthlessly changed the region's Muslim-majority demographics over the years by resettling ethnic Hans there. As a result, Islamist terror attacks—many ironically originating in Pakistan-occupied Kashmir (PoK)—have risen. The Chinese media blocks such news. The government disallows foreign journalists from independent visits to Xinjiang.

A Reuters report[28] drew a grim picture of ethnic tension in Xinjiang and Beijing's nervous, heavy-handed response: "China says it faces a serious threat from Islamist extremists in Xinjiang. Beijing accuses separatists among the Muslim Uighur ethnic minority there of stirring up tensions with the ethnic Han Chinese majority and plotting attacks elsewhere in China. A Chinese security source, speaking on condition of anonymity, said the new security measures in Xinjiang were not politically motivated, but based on fresh developments and intelligence. The Communist Party has vowed to continue what it terms a 'war on terror' against spreading Islamist extremism. In Xinjiang, this can also be seen at weekly flag-raising ceremonies that Uighurs, a Turkic-speaking people who once formed the majority in Xinjiang, are required to attend to denounce religious extremism and pledge fealty under the Chinese flag."

Will India's stand on Tibet aggravate matters? When China illegally builds infrastructure in PoK and Gilgit-Baltistan for the China-Pakistan Economic Corridor (CPEC) despite Indian protests, New Delhi should not worry unduly about upsetting Beijing over Tibet. The Chinese government has the mindset of a hegemon: stand up to it and it will stand down. Appease it and it will be emboldened.

Modi has crafted a calibrated policy on China. It is time to expand on it. The Dalai Lama's future visits to Tawang in

---

[28]10 August 2018.

Arunachal Pradesh should be encouraged. Free Tibet activists should be allowed to voice their protests around the country in greater numbers even as trade and diplomatic channels with China remain open and robust.

India has good trading links with Taiwan as well. They need to grow. Bilateral India-Taiwan trade is expanding rapidly. More diplomatic engagement by India with Taiwan's first woman prime minister, Tsai ing-Wen, is not untenable despite the lack of official diplomatic relations. Closer links with Vietnam, the Philippines and South Korea, all of whom have territorial disputes with Beijing, should form part of India's new China strategy.

Well-known academic Kanti Bajpai's book *India Versus China: Why They Are Not Friends,* shows how critical it is for India to construct a new China doctrine. Bajpai, a former headmaster of Doon School, like most members of the old, entitled elite, views India through a fog-encrusted prism.

In an article in *The Indian Express*[29], Bajpai wrote with a funereal air: "In no conversation about international affairs, regional geopolitics, global and Asian economy and technology, and even contemporary culture (art, music, literature, fashion) is China absent. The same cannot be said for India. You can't have soft power if you're not even in the conversation. China evokes awe; India evokes silence, a polite shake of the head, or exasperation. Classical India may stand head-to-head with classical China in the regard it garners, but contemporary India has been left a distance behind. Until we recognise that, we can't do much about it."

That encapsulates how outdated some Indian strategic thinkers are about India-China relations. Typically, the flood of articles in the Indian media "celebrating" the 100th anniversary of the Chinese Communist Party on 1 July 2021 glossed over the CCP's toxic record of human rights abuse and extra-territorial aggression.

---

[29]24 June 2021.

Indian policymakers have long followed a timid approach to international affairs. That is changing under External Affairs Minister Jaishankar. After India's successful presidency of the G20 concludes on 30 November 2023, Indian leaders should increasingly prepare for a future G3 world order of the three largest global economies in the late 2020s: the United States, China and India. While China seeks a G2 power structure with the US, both Beijing and Washington know that India's growing economic and military power, along with a potential marketplace of 1 billion consumers, makes it an indispensable future ally— and an intransigent adversary.

Beijing has employed threat, coercion and occasional diplomacy to keep India out of America's geopolitical orbit. That plan unravelled in eastern Ladakh. The US and a coalition of western and eastern democracies see India as an essential part of a global security mechanism to counter China's belligerence. India lies at a strategic point in the arc between the Indian Ocean and the South China Sea. As a balancing pivot between the US and China, India holds a geostrategic advantage it has so far not fully leveraged. It has important economic, military and financial strengths that policymakers had not deployed till it took charge of the G20.

India's messaging though still remains rudimentary. China continues to control the narrative. Indian journalists have in the past been taken on choreographed tours of China and asked to write complimentary articles on Beijing's technological accoutrements, ignoring its atrocities in Xinjiang and the clampdown on dissent in Hong Kong and Tibet. While building a strong China-Pakistan strategic doctrine, India's policymakers must now communicate like a rising power: proactively, not reactively. China has financed Western media outlets and policy think tanks to promote Beijing's distorted narrative. Confucian Institutes dot the US, Middle East and Europe, functioning as instruments of Chinese soft power. The Biden administration's tough curbs on the Chinese semiconductor industry presage a growing confrontation between the world's two largest economies. For its part, as a rising power, India must act, and speak, like one. It holds, through 2023, the presidency of both the G20 and the Shanghai Cooperation Organisation (SCO). That gives India two powerful global platforms to sharpen its geopolitical voice.

∽

Can a major country's economy grow at 24 per cent a year? The answer: no—not if it's a normal country. But China isn't a normal country so in the five years between 2006 and 2011 its GDP grew at an astonishing average of 24 per cent a year.

In 2006, China's GDP was $2.75 trillion. In 2011, it had miraculously nearly tripled to $7.55 trillion within five years. Working the math backwards, that's equivalent to an average nominal GDP (real plus inflation) growth rate of just over 24 per cent a year.

This was the take-off point for China's economy. It catapulted from the fourth largest economy in the world in 2006, behind the United States, Japan and Germany, to the second largest in five years. In 2006, the GDP of the United States was $13.81 trillion, five times China's. By 2011, US GDP had risen to $15.54 trillion, just twice China's.

Thus, between 2006 and 2011, China's economy had grown from being one-fifth ($2.75 trillion) of America's ($13.81 trillion) to half ($7.55 trillion) of America's ($15.54 trillion). The reason for this economic version of Mao Zedong's Great Leap Forward is difficult to pin down. China had never grown for five continuous years at an average of 24 per cent a year before 2006 and hasn't done so after 2011. Indeed, the rise over the past decade in China's GDP from $7.55 trillion in 2011 to $16 trillion in 2021 reflects an average annual growth rate of a more normal 7.5 per cent. It therefore took China ten years to double its GDP between 2011 and 2021. But it took just five years to nearly triple GDP between 2006 and 2011.

Look for clues to explain this anomaly at the yuan-dollar rate. In 2021, it averaged 6.46 yuan to the dollar. The exchange rate ten years ago in 2011, remarkably, was exactly the same: 6.46 yuan to the dollar. Through the decade, the rate fluctuated very little. But rewind to 2005–06. The yuan-dollar rate was over 8.1 yuan to the dollar. Thus between 2006 and 2011, the Chinese currency had strengthened against the US dollar by up to 25 per cent.

Since GDP is measured in US dollars, the appreciating yuan helped bump up China's economy by at least 25 per cent. Had the yuan remained steady during 2006–11, China's GDP in 2011 would have been nearer $6 trillion instead of $7.55 trillion. That would have reduced the average annual growth rate of the Chinese economy in 2006–11 from a miraculous 24 per cent to a more credible 14 per cent. Without fudging, the annual growth figure would have been even lower.

In stark contrast, the Indian rupee over the same period weakened significantly. In 2011, the exchange rate was ₹45 to a dollar. In 2021 it was ₹75 and in 2023 over ₹80. If like the yuan, the rupee had remained steady through 2011–21 at 45 to the dollar, India's GDP in 2023, measured in dollars, would be over $6 trillion, elevating it immediately from the world's fifth largest economy to the third largest, ahead of Japan and Germany and behind only the US and China.

India has an ecosystem that constantly seeks a weak rupee. The export lobby is for obvious reasons a fierce votary of a weak rupee. India's merchandise trade deficit and an inflation differential with the US were key reasons why the rupee has historically depreciated at an average of 3 per cent a year. Exports, despite a constantly weakening rupee over the past ten years, have risen only in the past two years after a long period of stagnation. That belies the argument that a weak rupee is essential for export growth. Quality of merchandise, cost of logistics and timely shipping are equally important. India needs to improve on these instead of focusing only on a weak rupee to boost exports.

According to V Anantha Nageswaran[30], India's chief economic advisor (CEA), "Of all the economic fundamentals that influence exchange rates, the one enduring factor is the inflation differential. In other words, relative purchasing power parity (PPP) holds over long horizons. Nearly a decade ago, in their annual investment returns yearbook for Credit Suisse, financial historians Elroy Dimson, Paul Marsh and Mike Staunton noted that the pound sterling had depreciated by about 1 per cent on average per annum between 1904 and 2004. The annual inflation differential between the UK and the US was also around 1 per cent. So, assuming that inflation differentials will do a better job of explaining the dollar-rupee exchange rate over a five-year horizon is not an unrealistic assumption.

"But even the US Federal Reserve concedes that the high inflation rate in America that was considered transient is now deemed more permanent. Consumer-price inflation rate has been stubbornly at or above 5 per cent for the last five months. So, for any USD-INR forecast, higher inflation rates in India over the US that have been the default factor for the past few decades cannot form the basis (of depreciation any longer)."

A more accurate comparison between major economies is to examine GDP as measured by purchasing power parity (PPP). When economies are quantified at current exchange rates tied to the US dollar, the local value of goods and services in developing, low-cost countries is skewed. PPP calculations equalise these cost differentials. They also give a correct sense of relative living standards, factoring in costs and wages.

According to the IMF, China's and India's GDPs (PPP) in 2024 are estimated to be, respectively, $32 trillion and $12.5 trillion.

[30]*Mint,* 8 November 2021.

The GDP gap of 2.5x is half the 5x differential suggested by comparisons using nominal GDP based on current exchange rates. Similarly, if by current exchange rate calculations, China's per capita income of $12,500 is five times larger than India's ($2,500), the gap in PPP-based per capita income between the two countries ($23,000 vs. $9,000) is again 2.5x, not 5x, providing a more accurate picture of their citizens' respective living standards.

With India entering a decade of high economic growth and China's economy slowing to around 3 per cent a year, the gulf in per capita income is set to narrow further by 2030. To achieve consistent real (excluding inflation) annual GDP growth above 7 per cent, India needs to continue with strong structural reforms. That should be the Modi government's overriding priority.

FIFTEEN

1979: The Defining Year

WHEN THE HISTORY OF THE 20TH CENTURY IS WRITTEN, 1979 WILL count as one of its most defining years. The Iranian revolution overthrew the US-backed Shah of Iran in 1979 and changed the complexion of Middle East politics. Ayatollah Khomeini usurped power and set off a decades-long confrontation with the West. In 1979, at the height of the Cold War, the Soviet Union made the fatal mistake of invading Afghanistan. The United States, Saudi Arabia and Pakistan collaborated to create an army of jihadis to fight the Soviets who, defeated finally after a decade, retreated in 1989.

Afghanistan was left with the detritus of trained terrorists with no one to fight. They drifted to Pakistan-occupied Kashmir (PoK) and, under the watchful eyes of the Pakistani army's Inter-Services Intelligence (ISI), were unleashed on the Kashmir Valley. In the 34 years since that sponsored insurgency began in J&K, Pakistan-abetted terrorism has metastasised into a malignant, but unsuccessful, strategy to bleed India by a thousand cuts.

In 1979 another seminal event took place that few at the time paid much attention to: Chinese leader Deng Xiaoping introduced a series of economic reforms that would catapult China from an impoverished country with a per capita income lower than India's to the world's second-largest economy with a per capita income of a high middle-income country.

India began its economic reforms 12 years after China, in

1991, but liberalisation has been halting and beset with political and bureaucratic roadblocks. As a noisy, multi-party democracy with plural ethnicities, India was always likely to implement economic reforms in fits and starts. China had no such qualms. The Communist Party's word is law. Dissenters are jailed or killed. Foreign competition is controlled by state fiat. Global news sites and social media platforms remain blocked in China.

Since 1991, liberalisation has helped the Indian economy more than double its average annual growth rate to 7 per cent from the 1960s–1970s growth rate of 3 per cent. But liberalisation has also spawned crony capitalism and corruption. This spurted during the freewheeling decade of UPA1 and UPA2 between 2004–2014. Bank loans were often granted on the basis of a phone call from the ministry of finance to the chairman of a public sector bank (PSB). That was the genesis of the NPA virus which laid low many banks and which the Insolvency and Bankruptcy Code (IBC) was designed to remedy.

China's single-minded determination to focus on growth, infrastructure and education has paid dividends. Cities like Shanghai and Beijing now have per capita incomes of over $50,000, rivalling income levels in Europe and the United States. While vast swathes of the countryside are still poor, China's average per capita income of $12,500 at current exchange rates places its living standards in the range of a Latin American country. According to Hyde Chen, an equity analyst with UBS AG in Hong Kong, "Historical experiences from mature economies suggest that household incomes of wealthy and poor areas in China will likely converge over time. In China, the income convergence is taking place at a fast pace, with the household per-capita income gap between lower-tier cities and tier-1 cities narrowing."

Prosperity is beginning to change the character and lifestyles of ordinary Chinese. In the 1980s, very few Chinese, estimated at less than 50,000, travelled abroad. The number of annual foreign trips made by Chinese in a non-Covid year is over

130 million—a moving mass of people equal to the combined population of Britain and France.

China is urbanising rapidly as well. Its urban-rural ratio has risen to 70 per cent compared to 82 per cent in the US. India lags behind at 34 per cent while middle-income Thailand is at 50 per cent. India's democracy represents a short-term impediment to growth. But in the long run, freedom will prove a significant asset. China could discover that the cost of dictatorship can be a heavy social burden. After attaining a basic level of prosperity, history tells us that societies demand freedoms—of choice, dissent, liberty and electoral franchise. Without these, no amount of gleaming office blocks, automated homes and superhighways can serve as compensation.

What can India do to catch up with China on the key parameter of education? In 1998, China began a campaign to create world-class universities. Within 20 years, several Chinese universities climbed into the top 200 rankings of global educational institutions. Since university rankings are skewed towards research paper citations in peer-reviewed academic journals, apart from the quality of faculty and infrastructure, Indian universities have lagged far behind. Democracy, while priceless, carries a cost. India has paid that price. It must implement the New Education Policy, in letter and spirit, to reap its benefits.

✠

Chinese President Xi Jinping is a princeling: his father Xi Zhongxum was a senior political leader in the People's Republic of China. Modi comes from a humbler background. But the two men have one quality in common: ruthlessness. Xi knows that by the late 2020s the world's three largest economies will be the United States, China and India. In this geopolitical triangle, China and the US will form the two largest angles and India the smallest. India though will be a vital cog between two superpowers.

As this century unfolds, India will increasingly play in this new Great Power rivalry the role Britain played during the 20th century. With Britain today an emasculated power and continental Europe facing a hostile Russia, India is the only regional power with a large economic and military presence that the US can rely on to counter China. Modi has changed the grammar of India's China policy.

India must now deploy the four important levers it possesses. It must use each with calibrated robustness. Tibet, Taiwan, Xinjiang and demography provide India the means to keep China off-balance in the same way Beijing has kept India off-balance for years. The crackdown on dissent by Beijing too affords the Modi government significant opportunities to place global pressure on China's rogue behaviour across the LAC. China exploits the weak but respects the strong. As head of the SCO in 2023, Modi must jettison decades of India's appease-China diplomacy. It hasn't paid dividends in the past and it is unlikely to do so in the future.

Mao Zedong, founder of the Peoples Republic of China, said in 1954 that Tibet was China's "right hand palm" and Ladakh, Nepal, Bhutan, Sikkim and the area known today as Arunachal Pradesh were the palm's "five fingers". Mao believed it was the duty of the Chinese Communist Party (CCP) to "liberate" the territories India had "occupied" (Ladakh, Sikkim and Arunachal Pradesh) as well as the independent nations of Bhutan and Nepal.

Why does Tibet continue to both obsess and terrify Beijing? Without sovereignty over Tibet, its outlandish claim on the five fingers – never proclaimed as official policy by the PRC – becomes void. China's Tibet paranoia has a long history. Tibet was intermittently an independent country for centuries. It came under the rule of China's Qing dynasty in 1720 but won back independence in 1912 when the Qing dynasty fell. Tibet's independence was short lived. China invaded Tibet in 1950, annexing it forcibly in 1951.

India suddenly found itself sharing a land border with China. Through most of history, Tibet and the Himalayas served as a buffer between India and China. Without Tibet, there would be no Line of Actual Control between India and China. China is an expansionist power. It continues to test India's will across the LAC. Though the People's Liberation Army is not geared for winter warfare in mountainous terrain, Beijing hopes to wear India down with endless talks between military commanders and diplomats.

China's paranoia over growing unrest among Tibet's seven million people has meanwhile led it to employ the same oppressive methods on the local population as it did with restive Uighur Muslims in Xinjiang. Tibet and Xinjiang are China's two largest provinces. Without them, the total land area of the PRC would shrink by over 30 per cent. Rural workers in Tibet have been pushed into labour camps. These resemble military-style barracks similar to those in Western Xinjiang.

An investigation by Cate Cadell of Reuters revealed several facts that have not received wide international attention because the CCP has subverted key global media and academic organisations to downplay the draconian human rights abuses in Tibet and Xinjiang. In her report, Cadel quoted[31] Adrian Zenz, a Tibet and Xinjiang researcher: "This is now, in my opinion, the strongest, most clear and targeted attack on traditional Tibetan livelihoods that we have seen almost since the Cultural Revolution of 1966 to 1976."

A large number of Tibetans regard China as a brutal occupying power. They draw sustenance from – and declare loyalty to – Tenzin Gyatso, the current Dalai Lama. At 88, the Dalai Lama knows China is simply running the clock down on him. It will, on his demise, appoint its chosen Panchen Lama as the Dalai Lama's successor. That would effectively end the centuries-old institution of the Dalai Lama.

Beijing views the Dalai Lama's visits to Tawang in Arunachal

---

[31] 22 September 2020.

as subversive. China calls the state South Tibet and has publicly declared its claim on it. Less well known is that the Dalai Lama fled to India via Tawang to set up the Tibetan government-in-exile in Dharamsala. As Dipanjan Roy Chaudhary wrote in *The Economic Times*[32]: "The Tawang monastery, known as the Galden Namgey Lhatse Monastery in Tibet, was founded by Lama Lodre Gyatso in 1680–81 according to the wishes of the fifth Dalai Lama, Ngawang Lobsang Gyatso. It is also the seat of the Karma-Kargyu sect. The Chinese Communist Party has been of the opinion that without controlling Tawang it cannot have legitimacy over Tibet."

For India, the Dalai Lama's occasional visits to Tawang present an opportunity to re-evaluate the relationship with China. An agitated Beijing continues to issue periodic statements opposing the visits. "China and India are two major developing countries and we are close neighbours," the Chinese foreign ministry said. "It is very important for the two peoples to maintain sound and steady China-India relations. But such a relationship has to be built on certain foundations. Such visits will have deep damage on China-India relations. We have asked India to stick to its political pledges and not to hurt China-India relations. It'll come down to India to make a choice."

In the past India has made that choice: sit on the fence. But the policy of placating China ended after the Ladakh incursion by Chinese troops and the Indian Army's success in thwarting the PLA's attempt in December 2022 to occupy the Yangtze heights. Modi has reset India's China policy at a time when Beijing is plagued by a revival of Islamist threats in Xinjiang, disputes with the West following the Russia-Ukraine conflict, an economy hit by a real estate crisis, periodic unrest in Tibet and rising tensions over Taiwan.

∽

[32] 5 April 2017.

Beyond the Ladakh standoff lie larger geopolitical questions. What were China's real intentions behind the sudden aggression at five points across the LAC in 2020? Doklam was relatively easier to decode; after 73 days the Chinese withdrew with minor face-saving concessions from both sides. The Ladakh entanglement arose from more complex geopolitical concerns in Beijing. India's growing strategic ties with the US worried it. New Delhi, it decided, needed to be taught a lesson.

India had angered China during the Covid crisis by making it mandatory for Chinese companies to seek government approval before investing in India. Chinese companies were previously allowed to use the automatic route. Beijing was further needled when two BJP MPs, including the feisty Meenakshi Lekhi, attended the swearing-in of Taiwan's anti-China president Tsai Ing-wen in 2020 through video conferencing. To rub it in the MPs conveyed fulsome congratulations to the president for winning a second successive term.

Beijing views India as both a regional rival and a future global adversary allied with the United States-led West and a coalition of Indo-Pacific "middle" powers like Japan, Australia and South Korea. India is a crucial cog in this anti-China alliance. It has a large and expanding military. India's geography places it in command of the vital Indian Ocean Region (IOR). Its youthful demography contrasts sharply with ageing China.

Xi is the principal culprit in China's aggression. He has made China a more authoritarian state at home and a more expansionary one overseas. He has protected Pakistan, a state sponsor of terrorism, at every global forum while blocking India's entry into the Nuclear Suppliers Group (NSG).

Whenever Beijing feels pressured, it lashes out. The last British governor of Hong Kong, Chris Patten, called China's crackdown on Hong Kong in 2019–20 a "breach of the 1984 Sino-British agreement" that returned Hong Kong to China in 1997 but safeguarded all its liberties till 2047. Following Patten's criticism,

China warned Britain that interfering in "China's internal affairs would backfire", hinting that a trade deal between post-Brexit Britain and China would be a casualty. Sino-UK relations slid further after the launch in 2021 of the AUKUS alliance between the US, Britain and Australia which China believes is aimed squarely against it.

In 2049 the People's Republic of China will mark the centenary of its founding. Xi has set that as the milestone when China overtakes the United States as the world's principal superpower. All of China's actions must be viewed through this geopolitical prism: the transgressions in eastern Ladakh, the militarisation of islands in the South China Sea, the national security law in Hong Kong, the aggressive air sorties around Taiwan, the clampdown on Uighurs in Xinjiang, the diplomatic confrontation with the West over Ukraine and Russia, the subversion of scientists in the United States, the theft of Western intellectual property, and the coordinated cyberattacks on foreign government assets.

This presents the Modi government with its most intractable foreign policy challenge in the build-up to 2024. It is no secret that Xi would prefer a China-friendly Congress-led Opposition to prevail in the next Lok Sabha election. In 1980, when its economy was the same size as India's, China bided its time and focused on growth at all costs. Beijing is not lulled by India's stop-start economic growth, noisy democracy and slow decision-making. It recognises that India will be a formidable economic power in less than a decade. On a historical time scale, that's the blink of an eye.

China also knows that India's armed forces, currently under-funded but undergoing rapid indigenisation, are expanding. It realises that with a middle-class consumer market of 500 million, a world-class software sector and the third largest startup universe globally, India will be a force to reckon with in the near future.

That complicates Xi Jinping's third-term blueprint. The prospect of an alliance between the US-led West and India is a major concern for Beijing, whether in the form of the Quad or its security linkages with AUKUS.

Beijing uses Pakistan-sponsored terrorism to pin India's security forces to the Line of Control (LoC). It blocks India's efforts to become a permanent veto-carrying member of the United Nations Security Council (UNSC). In Beijing's long view, there can be only two superpowers by 2049: the US and China. Xi went through the charade of the Wuhan and Mahabalipuram informal summits with Modi, in 2018 and 2019 respectively, to keep India in good humour and in the hope of keeping it equidistant from the US and China. The ploy failed. The battle lines are now immutable.

China's miscalculation in Ladakh will extract a geopolitical cost for Beijing. It could also give Modi important foreign policy leverage ahead of the 2024 general election.

SIXTEEN

The Untold Covid Story of Wuhan

ON A COLD WINTRY DAY IN JANUARY 2020, HARVARD UNIVERSITY HAD unusual visitors. Agents from the Federal Bureau of Investigation (FBI) arrested 60-year-old Professor Charles Lieber, a renowned expert in nano science and head of Harvard's chemistry and chemical biology departments.

As *The New York Times* reported on January 28, shortly after his arrest: "By afternoon, one of Harvard's scientific luminaries was in handcuffs, charged with making a false statement to federal authorities about his financial relationship with the Chinese government. His arrest sent shock waves through research circles. Dr Lieber was one of three scientists to be charged with crimes. Zaosong Zheng, a Harvard-affiliated cancer researcher, was caught leaving the country with 21 vials of cells stolen from a laboratory at Beth Israel Deaconess Hospital in Boston, according to the authorities. The third was Yanqing Ye. Prosecutors said she hid the fact that she was a lieutenant in the People's Liberation Army, and continued to carry out assignments from Chinese military officers while at Boston University. Ms Yanqing was charged with visa fraud, making false statements, acting as an agent of a foreign government and conspiracy. She was in China and was not arrested."

What did Lieber's arrest have to do with the global spread of the Covid-19 pandemic? Joining the dots pointed to a secretive nexus between US scientists and China's state authorities in their bid to access highly classified US research, especially in biotechnology. The Hong Kong-based *South China Morning Post* reported in March 2020 that "patient zero"—the first carrier of the coronavirus—was a 55-year-old man from Hubei province, detected as far back as 17 November 2019. However, it was only on 31 December 2019—by when the virus had already had nearly two months to infect unprotected people—that the Chinese government released initial information on the new virus.

It was too late. Contacts between millions of Chinese during the lunar new year festival, when many travel to and from mainland China, had proceeded unhindered. The virus spread rapidly across the world from its epicenter in Wuhan, the capital of Hubei and a city of 11 million people. By locking down Hubei for several months in 2020, the Chinese Communist government ensured the infection was controlled largely within the province.

Other countries were not as successful. Planeloads of Chinese workers fly between Wuhan and Milan where hundreds of Chinese-owned factories churn out designer leather bags and other products. That explains why Italy, especially the northern Lombardy region, was so severely affected by the virus in the spring of 2020. From Italy, part of the European Union's Schengen borderless visa region, the virus spread quickly during the two-month unprotected window to Germany, France, Spain and, with a time lag, Britain.

Wuhan is one of China's most important high-tech hubs. Like Harvard Professor Charles Lieber's contractual work with the Wuhan University of Technology, a large number of US scientists worked on assignments with Chinese universities. Lieber's arrest had a chilling effect on the American scientific community.

Wuhan itself is a city of many parts. It hosted the "Wuhan Spirit" informal summit between Prime Minister Narendra Modi and President Xi Jinping in 2018. But Wuhan has much more to commend itself. The city has attracted investors from 80 countries. It hosts over 6,000 foreign-owned companies. *Fortune*

500 firms have a large presence in Hubei—85 have investments in the province. Wuhan has a large bio-industry. Located in a picturesque area dubbed "Biolake"—known officially as the Wuhan National Bio-Industry Base—the complex has six centres: biology innovation, biomedicine, bio farming, medical devices, medical health and bioenergy. The Wuhan University of Technology which, according to the FBI, paid Harvard Professor Lieber $50,000 per month and a lump sum of $1.50 million – all of which Lieber concealed from both Harvard and the US government – has 27 innovative research centres and several laboratories.

The coronavirus was not the first time a deadly infection has travelled to Europe from China. In 1347, the Plague, also called the Black Death, killed millions in Europe. The source was traced back to rodent carriers on a Chinese trading ship which berthed at various European ports. The source of Covid-19 remains a matter of investigation – an investigation that has been repeatedly stalled by China.

For two years China evaded Covid-19. In 2022, however, mutated variants spread through several Chinese regions including Shanghai, the country's economic hub. Xi's zero-Covid policy extracted a heavy economic and social price with a series of regional city lockdowns worsening the economic slowdown. The abrupt withdrawal of the zero-Covid policy in December 2022, however, led to a surge in infections among an inadequately vaccinated Chinese population.

∽

As they sat side-by-side on a swing near Ahmedabad's Sabarmati riverfront in September 2014, Modi and Xi seemed set to open a new chapter in the complex Sino-Indian bilateral relationship. The relationship today is in disarray. The signs were ominous at that September meeting itself: soldiers from the PLA intruded into Indian territory at the Arunachal Pradesh border even as Modi and Xi, accompanied by his glamorous singer-wife Peng

Liyuan, appeared to have established a close rapport. It took a firmly worded request by Modi for Xi to order Chinese troops back to their territory.

Over the next several years China turned increasingly hostile towards India. Beijing meanwhile built economic and diplomatic bridges with Nepal, Bhutan and Sri Lanka in an attempt to surround India with a string of thistles in South Asia. Why does India worry China so much? Border disputes between the two countries are hardly new.

China knows that the India-US axis is a powerful force for the future. It could severely dent China's hegemonic ambitions in the parabola curving upwards from the South China Sea through the Indian Ocean, rising across the Middle East to Africa and Europe. Beijing's Belt and Road Initiative (BRI) has been disrupted by India's strong, unyielding opposition. India and Bhutan, significantly, are the only two South Asian countries which have rejected the BRI. India has meanwhile created an alternative north-south corridor through Iran, central Asia and Russia. The Chabahar port in Iran provides direct access to land-locked Afghanistan, bypassing Pakistan.

In a one-party Communist dictatorship like China, there's no bureaucracy to delay weapons purchases, no consensus needed to cut bank interest rates, no Opposition to satisfy on foreign policy and no electorate to be held accountable to. Since 1979, when Deng Xiaoping initiated economic reforms, China has transformed itself. It now leads the world in artificial intelligence, machine learning, data analytics, robotics, electric vehicles, supercomputing and the Internet of Things (IoT). The Biden government's ban on China's chip-making ecosystem was triggered by Beijing's rapid advance in manufacturing wafer-thin chips.

Kenneth Rogoff, professor of economics and public policy at Harvard University, predicted in 2018: "Many economists worry that robots and artificial intelligence (AI) will eventually take away most jobs, leaving most humans to while away their time engaged in leisure activities. As the rising importance of robotics and AI blunts China's manufacturing edge, the ability to lead in technology will become more important. Here, the current trend towards higher concentration of power and control in the central government, as opposed to the private sector, could hamstring China as the global economy reaches higher stages of development."

India had long been wary of China. Nehru did not trust the Chinese "one bit", according to a book by G. Parthasarthy (GP) who in 1958, a year before the Dalai Lama fled to India, was sent by Nehru as ambassador to China. GP's son Ashok Parthasarthy (who was science and technology advisor to Indira Gandhi) quotes from his father's book using notes GP had made of a conversation in which Nehru said: "So GP, what has the Foreign Office told you? Hindi-Chini Bhai-Bhai? Don't you believe it. I don't trust the Chinese one bit. They are an arrogant, untrustworthy, devious and hegemonistic lot. Your watchword should be eternal vigilance. On important matters, you should send your telegrams only to me. You must ensure that Krishna (Menon) does not come to know of these policy guidelines of mine to you. Krishna believes that no socialist country (read China) would ever attack a non-aligned country (read India)."

Not much has changed since Nehru's unflattering assessment of China except that Beijing is now a global technological, economic and military power. It is in the realm of new technologies and geo-economics that future battles will be won or lost. The Russian-made S-400, for example, is a formidable air defence system. Deployed as a deterrent against China along the LAC and against Pakistan on the LOC, an array of S-400s, in place by 2024, will recalibrate the balance of power between Beijing and New Delhi. Washington deliberately did not use its 2017 legislation, Countering America's Adversaries Through Sanctions Act (CAATSA), against India in response to New Delhi's acquisition of S-400s. The White House did not even object to India renewing a military-technical agreement with Russia right through 2021–31. The US needs India to help police the Indo-Pacific theatre.

Washington continues, however, to complain about inter-operability problems with India's Russian-made defence equipment and classified US military technology. It worries that these will be leaked to the Russians when both US and Russian weaponry are used in Indian war drills. The bigger irritant in India-US ties is India's policy of strategic self-interest. The US itself has followed this policy with ruthless efficiency since the end of World War II. It paid not the slightest attention to strictures by the United Nations Security Council (UNSC) on conducting an illegal war on Iraq in 2003 for non-existent weapons of mass destruction (WMDs). It continues to mollycoddle Pakistan over terrorism against India. It backs tabbed a close NATO ally, France, over AUKUS.

Strategic self-interest means playing to your strengths and exploiting weaknesses in others. The key is to spot these vulnerabilities and leverage them to your benefit. Washington was blindsided for decades into helping China's economic surge. The wooing of China by Nixon and Kissinger persuaded the US, fixated on the Cold War with the Soviet-led Warsaw Pact powers, to let Beijing access its technology.

China and Pakistan—one a protector of terrorists, the other a sponsor of terrorism—are not pleased with India's new geopolitical assertiveness, amplified by its presidency of the G20. China's vulnerabilities over Taiwan, Tibet and Xinjiang now receive greater attention from New Delhi. Deferring to China has not paid since the 1950s. It did not pay in Ahmedabad, Wuhan or Mahabalipuram. A more robust, clinically assertive policy better serves India's national interest in a rapidly evolving world order.

∽

When the pioneering universities of Europe – Oxford, Cambridge, Bologna, Heidelberg and the Sorbonne – were founded around the 1200s, their mission was ecclesiastical. Religious teaching dominated learning. Science had little place in their curricula. In England, Oxford initially taught courses in Latin. English hadn't developed as a coherent separate language. Over the next three centuries, English grew out of Latin and French but at heart remained Germanic. Chaucer's *The Canterbury Tales*, written during 1387–1400, is in barely recognisable "Middle English". Nearly two centuries later, in the 1500s, when William Shakespeare began writing plays, English had finally acquired form and content, still replete though with words from Middle English.

The scientific revolution in the 1600s laid the foundation for the Industrial Revolution a century later. For the next 250 years, the West dominated science and industry, helped by rapacious colonialism and the lucrative slave trade from Africa to the new American colonies. The tide began to turn in the 2000s. China, South Korea and Japan led a wave of Asian nations using technology to leapfrog over several eras of the Industrial Revolution and create modern, technology-driven societies.

The key to China's emergence as the world's second largest economy lay in its relentless focus on science and innovation. *The Economist* explained[33]: "The huge hopes China has for science have promoted huge expenditure. Chinese spending on R&D grew tenfold between 2000 and 2016. The spree is reminiscent of the golden years of 'big science' in post-war America. Between the International Geo-physical Year of 1957 and the cancellation of the Super conducting Super Collider (SSC) in 1993, America's government unfailingly invested ever more resources of an ever more powerful economy into the things which the leaders of its scientific community most wanted. From the creation of quarks to the cloning of genes to the netting of Nobel prizes, American science came to dominate the world.

---

[33]12 January 2019.

"Measured against that boom – one of the most impressive periods of scientific achievement in human history – China's new hardware, grand as it often is, falls a bit short. It has been catching up, not forging ahead. It has not been a beacon for scientists elsewhere. And far from benefiting from a culture of inquiry, Chinese science takes place under the beady eyes of a Communist Party and government which want the fruits of science but are not always comfortable about the untramelled flow of information and the spirit of doubt and critical scepticism from which they normally grow."

Despite this criticism, and Beijing's brazen theft of intellectual property rights, China's scientific revolution should encourage the Indian government to change the way it handles innovation. But far from instilling a scientific temper in the country, there has been an ill-advised effort to use India's "Vedic" science as proof that an alternative science can be created in India. It can't.

In January 2019, the Indian Science Congress (ISC) in Jalandhar was rocked by presentations that bore little reality to modern science. In a strong indictment of the "pseudo-science" that was allowed free play at the ISC, Dinesh C. Sharma, managing editor of *India Science Wire*, wrote: "The just-concluded Indian Science Congress (ISC) session in Jalandhar attracted widespread attention, though for the wrong reasons. Like its previous sessions, this one too had a fair share of absurd claims – falling in the realm of pseudo-science and mythology. Some such anti-science talks were delivered by those who occupy high academic positions. Even this is not surprising because, in the past, ministers have made comments mixing mythology with modern science."

Pseudo-science has powerful adherents in India. For example, the book *Bharatiya Vidya Saar* published by Bharatiya Vidya Bhavan made several outlandish claims. Among them: Rishi Agastya invented the electro-voltaic cell; Rishi Bharadwaj wrote Vaimanika Shastra 5,000 years ago on the construction of aircraft;

and the Rig Veda mentions the speed of light and the theory of gravitation.

Such claims do nothing for the credibility of Indian science. The Indian Space Research Organisation (ISRO) has put India on the global space exploration map while the Tata Institute of Fundamental Research (TIFR), the Indian Institute of Science (IISc) and the Bhabha Atomic Research Centre (BARC) have for decades been respected globally. Instead of building on these centres of scientific excellence, the Modi government has not fully leveraged the brand equity of even the IITs which have produced some of the finest tech entrepreneurs in Silicon Valley.

Science is the building block of technology. Most innovations over the past 20 years have emerged from Silicon Valley and sprouting tech hubs in China. Indian tech companies like Infosys, Wipro and TCS had till recently focused on low-hanging fruits: outsourcing services and back-end technology management. The post-pandemic digital and cloud economy has given new wind in their sails. The interface between the IITs and the corporate sector though needs to be deepened so that innovation has the funding to flourish. The success of Indian space technology startups is a sign that young entrepreneurs are changing this dynamic and catching up with China.

The scale of China's assault on America's intellectual property (IP) assets was highlighted by Federal Bureau of Investigation (FBI) director Christopher Wray. He said at a security conference in April 2020: "The FBI has about a thousand investigations involving China's attempted theft of US-based technology in all 56 of our sealed offices and spanning just about every industry and sector. They are willing to steal their way up the economic ladder at America's expense. They are not just targeting defence-sector companies. The Chinese have targeted companies producing everything from proprietary rice and corn seeds to software wind turbines to high-end medical devices. And they are not just targeting innovations and R&D. They are going after cost and pricing data, internal strategy documents, really just about anything that can give them a competitive advantage.

"They are also targeting cutting-edge research at our universities. China is using a wide range of methods and techniques. And I'm talking about everything from cyber intrusions to corrupting trusted insiders. They've even engaged in outright physical theft. They've pioneered an expansive approach to stealing innovation through a wide range of actors, including not just Chinese intelligence services but state-owned enterprises, ostensibly private companies, certain kinds of graduate students and researchers, and a whole variety of other actors all working on their behalf."

China little cares about international opinion. But the media exposé of the horrific treatment of over one million Chinese Uighur Muslims kept in prison-like detention camps in Xinjiang continues to create global outrage despite the CCP funding friendly Western politicians, journalists and lobbyists. China has vowed to integrate Taiwan into the mainland, using military force if necessary. The sale of US military weaponry to Taipei is seen by Beijing as deliberate aggravation. Equally worrying to Beijing is that, despite a crackdown on dissidents in Hong Kong, there could be a resurgence of unrest there in future.

When the former British colony was handed back to China in 1997, Hong Kong's economy was nearly 20 per cent the size of China's. Today it is a mere 2 per cent. But Hong Kong's value to Beijing goes beyond the size of its economy. It is home to over one hundred global banks and has a vibrant stock market. It attracts Chinese companies to list there rather than on the New York Stock Exchange, giving China access to an alternative source of global finance at its doorstep, along with Shanghai, as relations with Washington deteriorate and important Chinese companies delist from Wall Street.

"Hong Kong is China's conduit," *The Economist* observed[34]. "It

---

[34] 6 June 2020.

accounts for nearly 60 per cent of direct investment both into and out of China. It has a mighty share of offshore yuan-denominated payments. Western firms put money and headquarters there because it is seen as part of the Western system. Its currency is tied to the American dollar. It ranks third in the world as a financial centre; its banking assets are worth a whopping 851 per cent of GDP.

"For many global firms, Hong Kong is both a gateway to the Chinese market and central to the Asian continent – more than 1,300 of them have their regional headquarters there. If Hong Kong came to be seen as just another Chinese city, Hong Kongers would not be the only ones to suffer. The threat is real. Since he took over as China's leader, Xi Jinping has been making it clearer than ever that the legal system should be under the party's thumb. China must 'absolutely not follow the Western road of judicial independence,' he said in one speech."

A paranoid China has warned the US against sending any "misleading signals" to "ultra-radicals" in Hong Kong many of whom had gone underground after protests were crushed in 2020–21 and dissidents arrested. Hong Kong's China-friendly bureaucrats have constantly angered Hong Kongers by lavishing praise on the stringent national security law. As a Special Administrative Region (SAR) of China till 2047, Hong Kong has less than a generation left to come to terms with a transition from a freewheeling capitalist city to being part of totalitarian Communist China. It is not a prospect anyone in Hong Kong relishes.

∽

President Xi Jinping continues to receive sharp international criticism for modifying China's Constitution to abolish the two-term limit for president. There is bottled-up anger too within the Chinese Communist Party at the "speed, stealth and guile" with which Xi bulldozed the Constitutional change in 2018 and went on to win an unprecedented third term as the CCP's general secretary at the 20th National Congress in October 2022.

The New York Times revealed the extent of the stealth: "Some 200 Chinese Communist Party officials gathered behind closed doors in January 2018 to take a momentous political decision: whether to abolish presidential term limits and enable Xi Jinping to lead China for a generation. In a two-day session in Beijing, they bowed to Xi's wish to hold on to power indefinitely. But a bland communiqué issued afterward made no mention of the weighty decision, which the authorities then kept under wraps for more than five weeks. The decision was abruptly announced only last week, days before the annual session of China's legislature, the National People's Congress. The delay was apparently an effort to prevent opposition from coalescing before formal approval of the change."

The decision was endorsed by the CCP in November 2021 and formalised just before the end of Xi's second five-year tenure in October 2022. Xi's power grab could, however, backfire in the long term. Analysts are calling it a blunder that will constrain China's rise as a superpower. Xi's crackdown on tech companies has alarmed both domestic and foreign investors. Dissent could in future lead to civil protests though the government periodically puts down any challenge to its authority.

Nitin Pai, founder-director of Takshashila Foundation, wrote[35] insightfully on how social tensions in China could impact Beijing's foreign policy: "The beginning of the end of China's rise is not necessarily the beginning of China's fall. Even if the spiralling doesn't go all the way down, it is almost certain that the favourable external environment—where the powerful West invested in China's rise in the hope that this would bring the country into the international community—will no longer obtain. US trade tariffs and the increasing regional

---

[35]*Business Standard,* 9 March 2018.

enthusiasm for political and security frameworks to balance China's dominance will increasingly constrain Beijing's policy space. Meanwhile, the domestic and social consequences of slower growth among manufacturing, construction, real estate and infrastructure industries will start kicking in."

SEVENTEEN

Nehru's China Blunder

DID INDIA'S FIRST PRIME MINISTER, JAWAHARLAL NEHRU, COMMIT A historic blunder by turning down an offer made, first, by the United States in 1950 and then, in 1955, by the Soviet Union to become a permanent member of the United Nations Security Council (UNSC)? Were these offers made at all? And if so, were they merely feelers, not a serious reflection of intent by the two superpowers at the beginning of the Cold War?

Two schools of thought have emerged. The first holds that the US and the Soviet Union merely broached the subject of a permanent UNSC seat for India. The offer was a feeler. Nehru's sister Vijaya Lakshmi Pandit, then India's representative at the UN, was firmly against India "usurping" China's claim to a permanent seat. Nehru agreed with her assessment. China, he wrote to her, is a great nation and deserves permanent membership of the UNSC.

Both he and his sister, highly influential in the US and at the UN, felt that India must be a neutral party in the Cold War. By accepting the offer of a permanent seat in the UNSC, however informal the offer was, the two Nehru siblings felt India would need to take sides in international crises like the Korean War. That would compromise India's position as a founder of the non-aligned movement (NAM).

The second school of thought holds a diametrically opposite point of view. India misread the situation. It dismissed Washington's overtures in 1950 when the US wanted to contain the influence of the People's Republic of China which had in 1949 won a civil war against Chiang Kai-Shek's nationalists who fled to Taiwan. As the Republic of China (ROC), it represented the PRC at the UN from 1949 to 1971. The Soviet Union in 1955 too wanted India as a permanent member of the UNSC but Nehru again brushed off the offer as not being a serious one. This, the second school of thought holds, amounted to compounding the earlier historic error of rejecting Washington's offer of a UNSC seat in 1950 for which India, over 70 years later, is paying a heavy price.

Which of the two schools of thought has greater merit? For the answer, turn to original sources. In painstaking research, Anton Harder, a PhD scholar specialising in Sino-India relations, wrote in 2015: "The issue of India's right to a seat on the UNSC has centered on Nehru not seizing several alleged opportunities for India to join the UNSC as a permanent member in the 1950s. The question, however, goes beyond Nehru's reputation, as it provides rare insights into India's relations with the United States and the People's Republic of China at the beginning of the Cold War.

"The 1955 offer from the Soviets is well-documented, although perhaps not widely known. The 1955 incident was publicly discussed in 2002 in print by AG Noorani, a major scholar of modern Indian history and politics. However, new evidence of an even earlier offer—by the US in August 1950—to assist India in assuming a permanent seat at the UNSC has recently emerged, adding substantially to what Noorani earlier wrote. Nehru's rejection of the US offer underlined the consistency of his conviction that the PRC's legitimate interests must be acknowledged in order to reduce international tensions. Integrating the PRC into the international community by conceding its right to the Chinese seat at the Security Council was, in fact, a central pillar of Nehru's foreign policy.

"The documents critical to answering these questions are

stowed away in the Vijaya Lakshmi Pandit papers held at the Nehru Memorial Museum and Library (NMML). The importance of Pandit's papers lies in her relationship with her brother Jawaharlal Nehru. The Pandit papers have not been deployed thus far in studies focused on India's relationship with China. In late August 1950, Pandit wrote to her brother from Washington, DC, where she was then posted as India's ambassador to the United States: 'One matter that is being cooked up in the State Department should be known to you. This is the unseating of China as a Permanent Member in the Security Council and of India being put in her place.'

"Nehru's response within the week was unequivocal: 'In your letter, you mention that the State Department is trying to unseat China as a Permanent Member of the Security Council and to put India in her place. So far as we are concerned, we are not going to countenance it. That would be bad from every point of view. It would be a clear affront to China and it would mean some kind of a break between us and China.'"

Anton Harder did his dissertation on Sino-Indian relations for the period between 1949 and 1962. Writing for the (Woodrow) Wilson Centre (in 2015), he added more detail to his earlier analysis:

> The issue of India's right to a seat on the United Nations Security Council (UNSC) is a controversial one in India today, but it is not new. The historical controversy has centered on the culpability of independent India's first Prime Minister, Jawaharlal Nehru, in not seizing several alleged opportunities for India to join the UNSC as a permanent member in the 1950s. Nehru's critics, then and now, accuse him of sacrificing India's national interest on dubious grounds of international morality. The question, however, goes beyond Nehru's reputation, as it provides rare insights into India's relations with the United States and the People's Republic

of China (PRC) at the beginning of the Cold War.

New evidence of an offer by the US in August 1950 to assist India in assuming a permanent seat at the UNSC has recently emerged. Nehru's rejection of the US offer underlined the consistency of his conviction that China's legitimate interests must be acknowledged in order to reduce international tensions. Integrating China into the international community by conceding its right to the Chinese seat at the Security Council was in fact a central pillar of Nehru's foreign policy. Nehru's scepticism about accepting this offer, and thereby disrupting the dynamics of the UN, revealed the reverence he had for the international organisation, despite its flaws. Nehru's sense that India deserved recognition as a great country was made plain, although this was qualified by his refusal to compromise core principles to gain such recognition.

What was the context of the US offer for India to join the UN Security Council? Nehru's reference to the US's offer is frustratingly vague with no hint of the circumstances or timing in which it was made. However, research done in the correspondence of Mrs. Vijaya Lakshmi Pandit, Nehru's sister, and holder of various major diplomatic positions in the late 1940s and early 1950s, illuminates the subject. In late August 1950, Pandit wrote to her brother from Washington, DC, where she was then posted as India's Ambassador to the United States:

'One matter that is being cooked up in the State Department should be known to you. This is the unseating of China as a Permanent Member in the Security Council and of India being put in her place. I have just seen Reuter's report of your answer to the same question. Last week I had interviews with [John Foster] Dulles and [Philip] Jessup, reports of which I have sent to Bajpai. Both brought up this question and Dulles seemed particularly anxious that a move in this

*direction should be started. Last night I heard from Marquis
Childs, an influential columnist of Washington, that Dulles
has asked him on behalf of the State Department to build
up public opinion along these lines. I told him our attitude
and advised him to go slow in the matter as it would not
be received with any warmth in India.'*

Nehru's response within the week was unequivocal:

*'In your letter you mention that the State Department is
trying to unseat China as a Permanent Member of the
Security Council and to put India in her place. So far as
we are concerned, we are not going to countenance it.
That would be bad from every point of view. It would be a
clear affront to China and it would mean some kind of a
break between us and China. I suppose the state department
would not like that, but we have no intention of following
that course. We shall go on pressing for China's admission
in the UN and the Security Council. I suppose that a crisis
will come during the next sessions of the General Assembly
of the UN on this issue. The people's government of China
is sending a full delegation there. If they fail to get in there
will be trouble which might even result in the USSR and
some other countries finally quitting the UN. That may please
the State Department, but it would mean the end of the UN
as we have known it. That would also mean a further drift
towards war. India, because of many factors, is certainly
entitled to a permanent seat in the Security Council. But
we are not going in at the cost of China.'*

Harder concluded in his research paper: "Nehru's determined
rejection of the US plan to place India in China's seat at the UN
Security Council reflected the particular reverence and centrality
placed on the UN by what one might call a 'Nehruvian' foreign
policy. The UN was important to Nehru because he regarded it

as the venue for the resolution of international conflict on the basis of sustained dialogue and attempts at internationalism; to keep this effort up was to forestall war."

Nehru's generosity to China in 1950 did not forestall war 12 years later. While the geopolitical imperatives of the 1950s cannot be viewed entirely through a contemporary prism, Nehru's decision to cede veto-carrying membership of the UNSC to China has led, decades later, to increasingly aggressive Chinese behaviour.

∽

Former foreign secretary Maharaj Krishna Rasgotra's book *A Life in Diplomacy* deserves more attention that it has received. Rasgotra served as foreign secretary in Prime Minister Rajiv Gandhi's administration. Rasgotra had a bird's eye view of not only India's diplomacy in the Indira Gandhi and Rajiv Gandhi years but also during Jawaharlal Nehru's prime ministership when he was a rising IFS officer.

I met Rasgotra in his compact home in a quiet, leafy area of Delhi when I was researching my biography of Rajiv Gandhi. "In the three months I worked with Rajiv Gandhi as his foreign secretary," Rasgotra told me, "I did not have to wait for a decision longer than was necessary. There was never any piling up of my ministry's papers in the PM's office. The prime minister was learning fast: he would consult a variety of opinions and on difficult issues he would float one of his own, sometimes a decoy, to invite the opposite view so that he could weigh its merits and demerits more exhaustively."

But it is Rasgotra's views on Jawaharlal Nehru in his book that stirred debate and shed more light on events during Nehru's prime ministership. Two specific questions need corroborative answers: One, did Washington offer India a United Nations Security Council (UNSC) seat in 1950 by unseating Communist China – an offer Nehru reportedly declined? Two, did US President John F Kennedy in 1961 offer India nuclear weapons technology which would have made India a nuclear power before China exploded its first nuclear device in 1964 – again an offer Nehru turned down?

Rasgotra wrote in his book: "United States President John F Kennedy made an extraordinary gesture towards India. American intelligence had learnt that China's nuclear programme was progressing towards a weapons' detonation in 1963. Kennedy, who was an admirer of India's democracy and held its leader Jawaharlal Nehru in very high esteem, felt that democratic India, not communist China, should be the first Asian country to conduct a nuclear test. So, it is said, that the President sent a letter, written in his own hand, to Nehru offering help to India to conduct a nuclear test, and that accompanying the Kennedy letter was a technical note from the chairman of the US Atomic Energy Commission setting out the assistance his organisation would provide to Indian nuclear scientists to detonate an American device from a top of a tower in the Rajasthan desert.

"A detailed paper on this subject was circulated at a meeting which I chaired in 2014 to honour G Parthasarathy on his 100th birth anniversary by his son, Ashok Parthasarathy. According to Ashok, Nehru shared the letter with only two persons, G Parthasarathy (GP), who had returned from China on completion of his tenure as India's ambassador on the very day Ambassador Galbraith had personally handed Kennedy's letter to Nehru, and Dr Homi Bhabha, whom Nehru had urgently summoned from Bombay to discuss Kennedy's offer. In his letter Kennedy had said that he and the American establishment were aware of Nehru's strong views against nuclear tests and nuclear weapons, but emphasized the political and security threat China's test would spell for Nehru's government and India's security. 'Nothing,' Kennedy's letter emphasised, 'is more important than national security.'

"Ashok's paper also stated that Bhabha was for immediate acceptance of Kennedy's offer, and Nehru himself was not disinclined to it; for he promptly instructed Bhabha to 'work out a plan of action on a most urgent basis, should we finally accept Kennedy's offer'. GP, on the other hand, wanted a couple of days to mull over all the various implications of the offer, and he utilised the time for long talks with Galbraith and BM Mullick, India's pretentious intelligence chief, but ignored their advice favouring acceptance of the offer. In the end what he told Nehru was in line with Nehru's own convictions and perhaps also what Nehru wanted to hear. So, Kennedy's well-meaning offer of a lifetime was gently and thankfully turned down.

"Of course, all this is hindsight wisdom, but one thing is certain: India's acceptance of Kennedy's offer would have deterred China from launching its war of 1962 and even imparted a note of caution to Field Marshal Ayub Khan's plans for war in 1965. Nothing deters an aggressor more than a couple of big bombs in the armoury of the target of his hostility."

There is a twist in this story. Ashok Parthasarthy, GP Parthasarthy's son and a former scientific advisor to Indira Gandhi, told *The Hindu*[36] that Rasgotra accessed the information on Kennedy's offer to Nehru from what was "part of a committee to bring out a centenary volume on Mr Parthasarathy's father." He added: "No one else apart from me knew about President Kennedy's offer to Pandit Nehru which was narrated to me by my father. Mr Rasgotra took this information which was shared with him exclusively for the purpose of the book which I am editing and will be published soon."

According to *The Hindu*[37] report, "Mr Rasgotra however narrated in the 'Notes' section of the book that he had personally seen 'no evidence' of the Kennedy offer and he read the paper by Prof (Ashok) Parthasarathy which he accessed while chairing a committee which planned the centenary celebration for GP. He had demanded to see the letter from Ashok Parthasarathy who

[36]22 June 2016.
[37]22 June 2016.

owns all the papers related to G Parthasarathi. However, Ashok Parthasarathi had told him that the Kennedy letter was lost."

Nehru was a man of talent, vision and patriotism. But the path to perdition, to amend an old metaphor, is paved with good intentions. Rasgotra's measured analysis needs wider debate – of Nehru, the UNSC seat and Kennedy's offer to help India become a nuclear power ahead of China. That would have made India one of the founders of the Nuclear Suppliers Group (NSG) rather than the supplicant it is today.

ॐ

On 30 June 2022, India officially became the world's fifth largest economy, overtaking Britain. Germany (no.4) and Japan (no.3) are within striking distance. Several questions arise. What does this mean for the new world order that is taking shape after the Russia-Ukraine war? Will India's rise allow it to claim its rightful place in global affairs? The old world order is on life support. Six members of the G7—Britain, France, Italy, Germany, Canada and Japan—no longer merit a place at the high table. The seventh, the United States, will be a white-minority country by 2040. The balance of global power is shifting rapidly from west to east. Three of the four largest economies in 2030 will be Asian: China, India and Japan.

The histories of the four are starkly different. The United States is a European colonial settlement. Millions of slaves were shipped to it from Africa. The African-American descendants of those slaves today comprise 12.5 per cent of the US population. In the mid-19th century, the newly independent United States invaded Mexico. A large swathe of today's southern US is former Mexican territory, including Texas, California, Arizona, Nevada, Utah, Colorado and New Mexico.

Hispanic Americans are the fastest growing demographic in the US. Most of California is bilingual, with sign ages in English and Spanish. Ironically, what the US seized by military force from Spanish-speaking Mexico is coming back across the border through reverse cultural colonisation by migrants.

White Anglo-Saxon Protestants (WASPs) still control the levers of economic and political power in the US. But that too is changing. The shift is most pronounced with young politicians like Ron DeSantis, who is of Italian origin, and Ted Cruz and Marco Rubio (both of Cuban origin) growing in influence. Joe Biden himself is only the second Catholic, non-WASP US president in US history. John F. Kennedy in 1960 was the first. Of Irish descent, Biden knows his ancestors' history: Ireland was Britain's first colony. Few in Ireland have forgotten the great potato famine of the 1840s inflicted upon it by Britain.

Gavin Sheridan, writing in *The New Statesman,* describes Britain's "dark history" with Ireland that resonates to this day with Irish-Americans: "The famine—perhaps more so than any other event in Irish history—shapes Irish perceptions of its relationship with Britain. It is worth recalling the *laissez faire* nature of London's response, which largely involved a policy of letting Irish people starve, either because it was claimed that it was their own fault and they deserved it or because ideologically, you could not give something to someone for nothing.

"Or, as the assistant secretary to Her (now His) Majesty's Treasury, Sir Charles Trevelyan, wrote, the famine was an 'effective mechanism for reducing surplus population'. He continued: 'Judgment of God sent the calamity to teach the Irish a lesson, that calamity must not be too much mitigated... The real evil with which we have to contend is not the physical evil of the Famine, but the moral evil of the selfish, perverse and turbulent character of the [Irish] people'."

⁓

Beijing meanwhile knows that it has only a short window of opportunity to intimidate India into accepting China's regional hegemony before that window slams shut. But the clock is already running down on China: it may already be too late as India's resolute stand in Ladakh has shown. By 2030, India will be too strong economically and militarily for China to coerce territorially—a fact Beijing understands.

President Biden has assembled the largest team of Indian-origin cabinet members and advisors of any US President, including his personal pick of Vice-President Kamala Harris. None of this means that US policy on India would undergo a dramatic shift in the short term. But a new direction has been set. Washington recognises that India is now an indispensable global ally against China.

While post-Brexit Britain is a diminished power, the US-UK real-time intelligence sharing alliance remains strong. Along with the other Anglosphere nations—Canada, Australia and New Zealand—the "Five Eyes" intelligence network is a crucial element in Washington's global security doctrine. But the old "special relationship" with Britain has frayed.

From Jawaharlal Nehru to Atal Bihari Vajpayee, the dictum in Indian foreign policy has been: softly, softly. The West prefers a rising power like India that doesn't rock the geostrategic boat. India in the past dutifully complied. It used various stratagems to justify this passivity. Non-alignment ensured Indian neutrality at the United Nations. Then came the 21st century embrace of "strategic autonomy". This simply meant that India would abstain on controversial resolutions and keep an arm's length from military alliances. The Ukraine-Russia conflict, with India abstaining from several UN resolutions condemning Russia, underscored this.

In his first term, Modi followed the Nehru-Vajpayee doctrine: woo old friends (the United States) and appease old enemies (China). By the end of his first term, Modi realised it wasn't working. China saw India's silence on the Dalai Lama and Taiwan as a weakness. Doklam and eastern Ladakh followed. The old belief of keeping your friends close and your enemies closer no longer applied to China.

In his second term, Modi shifted gears. China's border aggression was militarily challenged. Pakistan was punished with both ground and air strikes. A further shift in gear is now needed. A more muscular Quad is one arrow in India's geopolitical quiver. Those who believe that the Quad has been diluted by the AUKUS alliance between the United States, Britain and Australia miss the point. Two of AUKUS's three members (Australia and the US) are India's partners in the Quad. The two alliances are complementary.

Apart from giving Australia nuclear-powered (but not nuclear-armed) submarine technology, AUKUS has one striking element. It places Britain and Australia firmly against China. Till four years ago, before China brutally put down the pro-democracy protests in Hong Kong, both Australia and Britain were wooing China on trade and technology. That flirtation is over.

Equally important is India's deepening alliance with France. India must explore opportunities in the Francophone universe of former French colonies in North Africa and elsewhere. France can prove a stable partner and provide India military, economic and technological options outside the Anglosphere of the US, Canada, Britain and Australia. This is an era of multiple alliances and groupings: the G20, Quad, SCO, BRICS, RIC, and BIMSTEC all have intrinsic logic.

France is the only nuclear power on the European continent bar Russia. The Rafale deal has led to deeper engagement between the two countries through two separate trilaterals with Japan and the UAE. This will serve as additional firepower in India's security arsenal against China and Pakistan.

GEOPOLITICS

EIGHTEEN

Unwrapping the Middle East Puzzle

FROM 2015, SAUDI ARABIA AND THE UNITED ARAB EMIRATES, ARMED WITH the most advanced weaponry from Western countries inflicted a devastating conflict on the Houthi rebels in Yemen. Though a ceasefire prevails, tens of thousands of Yemenis, including countless women and children, have perished in Arab-Western coalition air strikes.

The powerful Western media has tried to airbrush the genocide which could not have taken place without lethal Western arms and logistical support. The Yemen genocide is now widely accepted as a war crime. The West's role in the genocide, especially that of the US and Britain, has been malign. Britain publicly disparaged indiscriminate airstrikes on Yemeni targets. Privately, it sold billions of dollars' worth of advanced weaponry to Saudi Arabia and the UAE. British and American military advisors sat in Saudi war rooms to help target attacks in Yemen and offer logistical and intelligence support.

The Yemen war was essentially a proxy battle between Shia Iran and Sunni Saudi Arabia before the entente cordiale between Tehran and Riyadh. The Houthi rebels were backed and armed by Iran. With Arab troops faring badly against the Houthis, Riyadh hired former Pakistani Army Chief Raheel Sharif in 2016 to lead the coalition's stuttering effort.

The *Strategic Culture Foundation,* an online journal, wrote on June 19, 2018, at the height of the conflict: "The Saudi coalition, which includes Emirati forces and foreign mercenaries, is fully backed by the US, Britain and France. This coalition says that by taking the port of Hodeidah it will hasten the defeat of Houthi rebels. But to use the cutting off of food and other vital aid to civilian populations as a weapon is a blatant war crime.

"As the horror of Hodeidah unfolds, Western media has confined its focus narrowly on the humanitarian plight of Hodeidah's inhabitants and the wider Yemeni population. But British and US journalists have been careful to omit the relevant context, which is that the offensive on Hodeidah would not be possible without the crucial military support of Western governments. The BBC, France 24, CNN, Deutsche Welle, *The New York Times* and *The Washington Post* are among media outlets spreading misinformation on Yemen. For example, in its report, *The Washington Post* did not mention the fact that airstrikes by Saudi and Emirati forces are carried out with American F-15 fighter jets, British Typhoons and French Dassault warplanes."

When confronted with evidence of guilt, Britain was quick to resort to glib non-sequiturs. Alistair Burt, the UK's Middle East minister at the time, said without a trace of embarrassment: "I think that the hand of the United Kingdom can be seen in the work that we have done with the (Saudi) coalition over time in order to ensure that should things go wrong, there is proper accountability."

Proper accountability is unlikely to be upheld in the Yemen genocide. The Saudi-Western strategy was historically to neutralise Iranian influence in the Middle East on the pretext that it foments terrorism even though it was the Saudis who initially funded and armed al-Qaeda and the Islamic State (IS). Iran's influence in the Middle East has meanwhile grown. It extends to Syria, Iraq, Lebanon, Qatar, Afghanistan, Turkey and Yemen. Iraq is Shia-majority. Syria's ruling Alawite sect is Shia-affiliated. Shias are a majority in Bahrain, though its rulers are Sunnis. Lebanon's powerful militia Hezbollah is Shia.

The rapprochement between the principal powers of the Middle East – Saudi Arabia, Iran and Syria – along with China's increasing economic and military presence in the region will reduce US influence in a volatile geography where Israel's conflicts with Palestine and Iran remain unresolved.

The US and British governments have come under increasing pressure to end arms sales to Saudi Arabia and the UAE. They are reluctant to do so despite the UN castigating their role in the Yemen genocide. For a declining power like post-Brexit Britain in particular, weapons sales to Saudi Arabia are both a source of revenue and a means of shoring up its waning influence in the Middle East.

Modi has invested significant personal capital in improving ties with Saudi Arabia and the UAE. As the Gulf Arab states mend relations with Israel, Modi's Middle East policy must balance competing interests in the region, given India's longstanding commercial and civilisational relationship with Iran. Tehran's doctrinaire Islamism, however, makes Iran a difficult country to deal with.

For Modi, the Middle East has been a fulcrum of his evolving geopolitical strategy. He is a keen student of history and knows the region is at an important crossroads – economically and politically. The Middle East began to unravel in 1918. Fresh from victory in the First World War, the US, Britain and France carved out the region among themselves using a combination of military force, deceit and co-option. As dozens of world leaders gathered amidst a drizzle in Paris on Sunday, 11 November 2018 to commemorate the end of World War I, the events of a century ago must have rekindled historical memories.

For example, Iraq (the former Mesopotamia), Palestine and Transjordan were occupied by Britain under a mandate after the First World War. Syria and Lebanon went to France, also under a mandate. Much of the rest would soon be subsumed by Saudi Arabia. The al-Saud family had captured large areas of the

Ottoman empire, defeated in the First World War. In 1932, the al-Sauds named the new country the Kingdom of Saudi Arabia.

The Second World War further altered the geography of the Middle East. But it did not loosen the West's control. Oil had been struck. The deserts of Saudi Arabia and the former Persian Empire (Iran) as well as Iraq promised an oil and gas bonanza. America's grip now tightened. Imperial Britain and France, weakened by WW2, began a gradual political withdrawal from the Middle East but not from its oil wells. Their petroleum companies ran the region's new oil fields.

The bargain was simple: Western military protection in exchange for oil and geostrategic assets as the Cold War with the Soviet Union loomed in the late-1940s. Iran and Iraq presented a particularly difficult problem for Washington. The Shah of Iran, Mohammad Reza Pahlavi, had succeeded his father Reza Shah Pahlavi, founder of the Pahlavi dynasty, in 1941. Reza Shah Pahlavi had been forced to abdicate following the Anglo-Soviet invasion of Imperial Iran.

Young Mohammad Shah Pahlavi (he was 22 when he took over as monarch during WW2) would soon become Washington's puppet. Iran was America's most favoured nation in the Middle East—till 1979. Ayatollah Khomeini's revolution that year changed the political dynamic in the Middle East more than any other single event. Overnight, Iran became America's most reviled enemy, a status that, more than four decades later, remains unchanged.

Meanwhile, America's relationship with its other puppet regime of the time, Iraq, was being handled more covertly. Saddam Hussein, under the watchful gaze of the Central Intelligence Agency (CIA), had played a leading role in toppling the Iraqi government in a coup in 1968, bringing the Ba'ath party back to power. He was initially as much America's asset in the Middle East as the Shah of Iran had been till he was overthrown by Ayatollah Khomeini.

In 1979, Iraq was still a secular country. Women walked

to work in skirts. Saddam, a Sunni, ruled his 60 per cent Shia majority nation with an iron fist but allowed Shias reasonable opportunities to participate in government and the bureaucracy. To its east though, Iran was in ferment under the Ayatollahs. Iran's descent into Islamic fundamentalism, the US feared, could spread like a virus across the Middle East. The Shah had meanwhile fled to Egypt after the Iranian revolution. He died there, aged 60, in 1980.

In 1980 too, as if on cue, the US instigated a devastating eight-year war between Iraq and Iran. The CIA covertly ran the war. Over 5,00,000 Iraqi and Iranian soldiers died in a battle of attrition that ended in stalemate in 1988. America's objective was to use Saddam's regime to overthrow Ayatollah Khomeini in Iran. Two great civilisations, Mesopotamian and Persian, were thus made to fight each other in a brutal war that left half-a-million Arabs and Persians dead.

Saddam, frustrated by the war and increasingly unhappy at America's interference in Iraq, made a fatal mistake in 1990 by invading Kuwait, another oil-rich American protectorate, on the grounds that it had historically been part of Iraq and would on amalgamation give Iraq access to the waters of the Persian Gulf. Overnight, Saddam became America's enemy. Iraq was invaded, Kuwait "liberated" in the Gulf war in 1991 and debilitating decade-long sanctions imposed on Iraq. No-fly zones over Iraq prevented vital medicines and food reaching Iraq. Thousands of Iraqi children died as a result. In 2003, Iraq was again invaded by the US and its allies on the fabricated charge that it possessed weapons of mass destruction (WMDs). Saddam himself was hunted down and killed in 2006.

According to Brown University's Watson Institute[38], "No one knows with certainty how many people have been killed and wounded in Iraq since the 2003 US invasion. However, we

---

[38]December 2022.

know that between 184,382 and 207,156 civilians have died
from direct war related violence caused by the US, its allies, the
Iraqi military and police, and opposition forces from the time
of the invasion through October 2019. The violent deaths of
Iraqi civilians have occurred through aerial bombing, shelling,
gunshots, suicide attacks, and fires started by bombing. Many
civilians have also been injured.

"Because not all war-related deaths have been recorded
accurately by the Iraqi government and the US-led coalition,
the numbers are likely much higher. Several estimates based
on randomly selected household surveys place the total death
count among Iraqis in the hundreds of thousands. Several times
as many Iraqi civilians may have died as an indirect result of
the war, due to damage to the systems that provide food, health
care and clean drinking water, and as a result, illness, infectious
diseases and malnutrition that could otherwise have been avoided
or treated. The war compounded the ill effects of decades of
harmful US policy actions towards Iraq since the 1960s, including
economic sanctions in the 1990s that were devastating for Iraqis."

For Modi, ever the pragmatist, the "new" Middle East presents
an opportunity. Warm ties with the Saudis and Emiratis have
coincided with tensions in relations between Pakistan and the
two dominant power centres in the Middle East. Saudi Arabia
and the UAE have been angered by Pakistan's dalliance with
Turkey and Iran, both non-Arab Muslim states. For India, the
Middle East increasingly presents commercial and geostrategic
opportunities. The high-profile visit of Chinese President Xi
Jinping to Saudi Arabia in December 2022 when he met with a
galaxy of the region's monarchs and presidents has lent India's
diplomatic strategy in the region greater urgency.

༄

In the lives of nations, as in the lives of men, come points of
inflection. India is on the cusp of one such transformation. When

the British left India in 1947 the country had few industries, rudimentary infrastructure and a miniscule GDP. Today India is the world's fifth largest economy and on target to be the third largest, according to the IMF, by 2028.

Nehru was a conscientious parliamentarian, encouraged robust debate in the Lok Sabha (even with his estranged son-in-law Feroze Gandhi) and was widely respected in India and abroad. His daughter Indira was the opposite. During the 1975–77 Emergency, she subverted the judiciary, the press and the Constitution. As India turned 76 in August 2023, building trust in institutions of governance has become ever-more critical.

To strengthen India's plural social texture, Modi must now urgently help build institutions of good governance at every level—from panchayat to parliament. Historians will come to see the 2019 General Election as a pit stop for Modi. He was always looking at victory in 2024 to complete his ambitious structural, social, economic and foreign policy goals. The BJP meanwhile needs to build a second line of leadership. Mentoring new leaders, however, must start now. Modi's Union Cabinet has hard-working ministers but more domain experts need to be inducted. There are precedents: Nehru's first Cabinet had several technocrats, including the economist John Mathai, who served as India's first railway minister and later as finance minister.

Modi has made it a point to use Republic Day to underpin a specific foreign policy initiative. In January 2015, Barack Obama became the first United States president to be chief guest at India's Republic Day. The move signalled Modi's desire to forge a closer strategic partnership with the US. In 2016, French President François Hollande was chief guest as India focused on building deeper economic ties with the European Union (EU). The chief guest at the Republic Day parade in 2017 was Abu Dhabi's Crown Prince Mohammed bin Zayed Al Nahyan. Modi had made the Middle East a focal point for his foreign policy by nuancing the outreach to Israel (a significant defence partner) as well as to the Gulf kingdoms (where several million Indians work).

Modi continued the practice of inviting global leaders on Republic Day (except in 2021 and 2022 during the Covid-19 pandemic) who fitted in with India's geo-economic and geopolitical strategy. Egyptian President Abdel Fattah el-Sisi was chief guest on 26 January 2023, signifying Modi's continuing outreach to the Arab world, given China's growing influence in the region. The most intriguing was the 2018 invitation to ten ASEAN leaders. It carried several messages with nuanced subtexts. First, it was an extension of India's Act East policy. For decades, India has followed a Look East policy. ASEAN, one of the world's most powerful trading blocs, had in the past shown scant interest in India's foreign policy vision which emphasised strategic priorities to its west rather than to its east.

Modi changed that perception. He has invested considerable political time and capital on boosting ties with East Asian countries. By inviting ASEAN's ten leaders Modi also sent a powerful message to China which has disputes with several ASEAN member-nations, including the Philippines, Indonesia, Malaysia, Thailand, Brunei and Vietnam. ASEAN countries like Singapore and Malaysia have large ethnic Indian populations, especially from Tamil Nadu. Many have strong cultural links with Indian Buddhism. All this gives Indian soft power an edge in an Asia increasingly dominated by China's hegemonic ambitions.

India's decision in November 2020 to stay out of the 15-member Regional Comprehensive Economic Partnership (RCEP), which includes the 10 ASEAN members, China, Japan, South Korea, Australia and New Zealand, does not preclude entry at a later date. Besides, India has bilateral FTAs with several RCEP members on more favourable trade terms than RCEP currently mandates.

India needs to play its geopolitical cards astutely in South Asia as well. China has already replaced India as Nepal's largest investor. And yet the Chinese haven't won hearts and minds in Kathmandu. Nepalese shopkeepers complain about wealthy Chinese tourists driving up real estate prices, edging locals out of the market. India clearly must react to China's growing influence in India's backyard – from Bangladesh to Sri Lanka – with its own alliances among the littoral states of the South China Sea in order to protect maritime trade and safeguard regional security. This resonates well with the pragmatic, mercantile members of ASEAN.

NINETEEN

Russia-Ukraine and the Saxon-Slav Conflict

THE "WAR INDUSTRY" IS A VITAL COG IN THE US ECONOMY. THE RUSSIA-Ukraine conflict handed Washington two geopolitical gifts: one, a post-pandemic boost to its military-industrial complex; and two, critical real-time intelligence on Russia's military tactics, weapons and battlefield weaknesses. The war has diminished Russia, perhaps terminally, and made Europe increasingly dependent on the US.

The United States was born out of invasion, so invasion of other countries is second nature to it. Early English colonists settled North America in the 1600s. They drove indigenous Indians off the land they and their ancestors had lived. The annexation was done with ruthless precision. Sioux tribes who resisted the invading Englishmen were killed. Those who survived died of smallpox and other European diseases that were unknown in North America. Native Indians had no immunity to them.

Empirical evidence bears out the clinical cruelty with which the colonial invasion of America unfolded between the 1600s and 1700s. The population of indigenous Indians in North America before the English colonists arrived in the early 1600s was estimated at around 18 million. By the late 1700s, when the United States became an independent nation, the population of indigenous Indians had plunged to six million.

Meanwhile, a new country had been formed on the other side of the Atlantic: Britain. Till 1707, Britain didn't exist. It was only after the kingdoms of England and Scotland merged through the 1707 Acts of Union to form the "United Kingdom of Great Britain" that the UK as a sovereign entity came into existence.

As Britain lost its colonies in the newly formed United States during the 1776–83 war of independence, it cast its eye eastwards: India would replace America as Britain's principal colony overseas. There was a difference though. America had been an invasive Anglo-Saxon colonial settlement. India, from the beginning, was an ancient land to be plundered, not settled.

When the British occupation began in 1757 through the East India Company, the population of the subcontinent was 182 million. At the peak of British colonial rule in India, the total number of white British citizens—from administrators to soldiers—was 1,25,945, according to the 1861 Census. For everyone Briton there were thus 1,500 Indians.

Back in the United States, British colonial settlers, who now called themselves Americans, had become restless. They wanted more land. Mexico had won independence from Spain in 1821. The Britons-turned-Americans seized the opportunity and invaded Mexico. The American-Mexican war took place in 1846–48. Using superior weapons and tactics, the Americans annexed large swathes of Mexican sovereign territory—from Texas to California. Under the 1848 treaty of Guadalupe Hidalgo, Mexico ceded 2.4 million sq. km of its territory to the US.

What does all this have to do with Russia's invasion of Ukraine? It re-emphasises that it is wrong to invade another country, whether it is Ukraine, Taiwan, Mexico or India. The Eurasian Ottomans invaded copiously and cruelly. Britain, France, Spain and Portugal built empires by invading Asia, Africa and Latin America. But Europeans weren't satisfied with usurping other peoples' land: they wanted free labour.

The centuries-long transatlantic African slave trade ranks as among the most inhumane extraterritorial crimes in history. In the 1600s, Liverpool was a tiny impoverished hamlet. By the 1800s, it had become a prosperous town on the back of the lucrative African slave trade. Liverpool's leading businessmen had made vast fortunes shipping Africans to Britain's North American colonies.

The Africans were captured from the Ivory Coast, Ghana and other west African coastal countries, manacled in chains and shipped to Britain's American and Caribbean colonies where they were sold to wealthy Americans to a life of bonded slavery. After Britain abolished the transatlantic slave trade in the 1830s – due more to mercantile than humanitarian compulsions – indentured labour replaced slavery. Poor Indians and Africans were shipped to British colonies to work in sugar plantations as bonded servants with virtually no human rights. The Nobel prize-winning author VS Naipaul's ancestors were among those shipped by the British to colonial Guyana as indentured labourers.

⁓

Hitler was contemptuous of Russians and Ukrainians who are Slavs. At a critical point in World War II in June 1941, he dropped plans to invade fellow-Saxon Britain and invaded Slav Soviet Union instead. That error cost Germany WWII four years later.

The Saxon-Slav proxy conflict erupted again in the decade-long Balkans war in the 1990s that dismembered the former Slav nation Yugoslavia following carpet bombing by US and British warplanes. The Russia-Ukraine war too was an intra-Slav conflict but remote-controlled by Saxons in Washington and London. Their capacity to wage destructive proxy wars remains as unparalleled in the modern world as it was through history.

After World War II, the US propped up dictators and puppet-monarchs in Latin America and the Middle East. It made a pact with the sheikhs of the post-Ottoman Middle-East to deny Arab citizens voting rights in return for US military protection, ostensibly against Israel but in reality against popular democratic movements in their own countries.

With such a past, it is not surprising that the US continues to follow a foreign policy of unapologetic self-interest in Asia to secure its geopolitical objectives. But the US has an Achilles' heel. By the 2040s, it will for the first time in its history become a non-white-majority country. African-Americans, Latinos and Asians comprise nearly 30 per cent of America's population today. By 2045, that figure will rise to 51 per cent. The implications of this demographic shift will resonate across social, ethnic, economic and cultural faultlines.

Russia's invasion of Ukraine created three collateral outcomes. One, it terminally diminished Russia as a Great Power. This poses a challenge to India, forcing it to reconfigure its deeply entwined economic, trade and military ties with Moscow. Two, China is now America's principal rival. It poses a bigger threat to Washington that the Soviet Union did during the 40-year Cold War. The geopolitical balance of power will turn on how Beijing and Washington compete and collaborate. Three, India stands in the middle of the unfolding contest between two axes: the US-led alliance and Greater China, including Hong Kong and, in future, Taiwan. New Delhi will forge a third axes of neutral nations across Asia, Africa and Latin America aligned to the US-led coalition of democracies but with strongly independent foreign, security and economic policies.

∾

President Biden's diverse administration is praised for the number of men and women in key leadership positions. But gender equality in the developed world has a mixed history. If you were a woman and lived in France in 1944, you wouldn't have been allowed to vote. France, the land of Voltaire and liberté, egalité and fraternité, was among the last European countries to give women the right to vote. Britain wasn't much better: British women got the full vote only in 1928. South America was worse. Women in Chile were not allowed to vote till 1961.

Over 50 countries today have elected women heads of government (not counting women monarchs). Since British women won the right to vote, the country has elected three women as prime minister—Margaret Thatcher in 1979, Theresa May in 2016 and Liz Truss in 2022 (though May and Truss were elected through internal Conservative party polls).

At first glance, South Asia seems a feminist haven: every major country in the region has had an elected woman head of government: Sirimavo Bandaranaike, Indira Gandhi, Benazir Bhutto and, in Bangladesh, both Sheikh Hasina and Begum Khaleda Zia. Sri Lanka in fact holds the distinction of being the first country in the world to elect a woman leader—Sirimavo Bandarnaike—in 1960. The progressive impulse is illusory. All four South Asian women leaders inherited their position from their father or husband, albeit through democratic elections. The winner here is feudalism not feminism.

To rise to its full potential, India must not only boost its economy and military but strengthen its social fabric and gender equality. As India's demographic dividend unfolds, New Delhi's bargaining power with a declining US and a totalitarian China sitting on a tinderbox of suppressed freedoms will grow—if South Block gets its strategy right. The most productive way to deal with the US – in areas ranging from security and trade to climate change and technology – is to demonstrate clinical self-interest. The first Indian prime minister to do this was Indira Gandhi in the Bangladesh war in 1971. It earned her the wrath of US President Richard Nixon and Secretary of State Henry Kissinger.

Modi has studied the US closely. He first went there more than 25 years ago and visited it several times before becoming chief minister of Gujarat in October 2001. The cornerstone of Washington's foreign policy is to preserve its superpower hegemony for as long as possible. On its geopolitical chessboard are three key pieces: China, Russia and Iran. Consider each:

1) An economically powerful China needs to be contained. Washington wants India to play a pivotal regional role in this. Hence Biden's overtures to Modi.

2) Iran's nuclear ambitions threaten US interests in the Middle East. Hence the unrelenting US-led sanctions that have sought to cripple Iran's economy.

3) Russia is a disruptive threat to the West, having occupied Crimea and eastern Ukraine. US-led sanctions have shackled Russia's economy but the growing China-Russia axis has upset the balance of global power.

Since it is inevitable that the US, China and India will be the world's three leading economic powers by the end of this decade, Indian policymakers, for their part, must learn to think like a chess grandmaster in an endgame with three key pieces left on the geopolitical chess board as the centenary of the country's Independence in 2047 nears: China, India and coloured-majority America.

✺

A trio of powerful nations has historically fashioned the warp and weft of geopolitics. In the late 19th century, the three great powers were imperial Britain, the United States and a rising Germany. In the mid-20th century, the US, Britain and the Soviet Union formed the dominant troika.

Like water, geopolitics finds its own level. Centuries of European domination are clearly over. They began with the transatlantic slave trade and colonialism. These were followed by the creation of Western-dominated institutions like the United Nations, World Bank and IMF. When gunships were no longer viable, these institutions projected Western power through global finance and UNSC vetoes. The G7 was an outcome of this world order. The grouping comprised the world's most industrialised economies after the Second World War: the US, Britain, Canada, France, Germany, Japan and Italy.

Of these only the US will count as a global power in 2030. The G7 will no longer be a powerful global entity. China and the US have diametrically opposed political, social and economic concerns. As an increasingly heterogeneous society, the US contrasts sharply with homogenous Han-ethnic Communist China. America teems with religious and ethnic diversity, a free and fierce media, a checks-and-balances democracy though riven by social disparities, and accountable government. China has none of these.

A putative member of the emerging G3 in the next decade, India has an historic opportunity to influence the ebb and flow of world events. But to do that, Indian policymakers will have to achieve three objectives over the next several crucial years.

First, education. India is creating millions of graduates every year. Many are unemployable because they have been taught to learn by rote, never question, and always be obedient. To create an ecosystem of innovation as the US and China have done, Indian education must be reformed from the bottom up as the NEP aims to do. Primary school infrastructure needs to be modernised, teachers better paid and exams restructured to measure creative, questioning minds rather than those who memorise learning by rote.

Second, India's diplomatic outreach needs a larger foreign office presence. For a country that will inevitably be a part of a future G3, Indian diplomatic strength globally is inadequate. China has 4,500 diplomats working abroad. The US has over 20,000. India has just 2,700, of whom less than 900 are IFS officers. That is one reason why India still punches below its geopolitical weight. Lateral appointments of talented professionals to the diplomatic corps from outside the IFS cadre are urgently required.

Third, governance. The strength of America lies in its institutions—an independent judiciary, a powerful legislature, strong law enforcement and ombudsmen at every level of government.

Corruption exists despite this in the US. The difference with India is swift justice. To shape a new G3, India has to grow economically, mitigate poverty, reform education, strengthen diplomacy and focus unsparingly on good governance. If it does not, the G3 too, like the G7, will have a short lifespan.

Both the G7 and the permanent members (P5) of the UNSC reflect a tainted world order. Consider, for example, the record of the seven nations that comprise the G7. The US built its prosperity on 250 years of African slavery and the usurpation of indigenous peoples' land in North America. It practised legal racial segregation till as recently as the mid-1960s. Blacks in the US had few human rights and little democracy.

Turn to Britain. It ran 55 per cent of the European transatlantic slave trade to North America. Large fortunes were made in the bustling slave ports of Liverpool, Bristol and Southampton. The human rights of Asians and Africans in British colonies were violated daily. In the former British penal colony of Australia, 311 cases of massacres of Aborigines by British settlers, several in the 20th century, have been officially documented.

France, the world's seventh largest economy, behind India and Britain, fought brutal colonial wars in Algeria and Indo-China well into the 1950s. Canada, for all its inclusive rhetoric, is essentially a breakaway ex-colony of British loyalists who refused to join American revolutionaries in their war of independence, but was an active partner with the newly formed US in evicting indigenous Indians from vast tracts of land they had lived on for centuries.

Germany and Italy's fascist track record in World War II does not bear retelling. The seventh member of the G7, Japan, is the token non-white inclusion in this hoary club on account of its large economy, not its ruthless assault on Southeast Asia as an ally of Germany in World War II.

India presents an awkward problem for the West. Rising China can be excoriated for its totalitarianism. But India, a diverse, noisy, still-poor democracy, is different from everything the West has encountered since it constructed the current world order. The post-pandemic growth trajectory of India is irreversible, whichever political coalition is in office. Western leaders have always been wary of a rising India: Asian, democratic and diverse. Its rise, without resorting to colonial plunder, centuries-long African slavery and genocide of indigenous people in other lands, unsettles them.

After spending seven decades fighting the paranoia of a potential domino effect of Soviet communism spreading in Indo-China and elsewhere, the West is now confronted with the prospect of Communist China dominating global economic, technological and – over time – military power. The West used to look at India as an unreliable, Nehruvian, nose-in-the-air, non-aligned, left-leaning nation after Independence. It gravitated towards Pakistan, the geostrategic gun-on-hire.

The rise of China poured cold water over Western heads. The West needs Indian maritime resources in the Indo-Pacific. It grudgingly accepts that India's consumer market will be the largest in the world in the next decade, ahead of even China, whose population has begun shrinking and greying. The Quad is a continuation of the West's geopolitical pivot towards India that began with the India-US civil nuclear deal in 2005-08 That pivot has brought the two countries closer together as strategic partners than at any time since India's independence.

In a provocative article published in 2019, Jim O'Neill, the former chairman of Goldman Sachs Asset Management who first coined the acronym BRIC, wrote it's "time up" for the G7 group of nations. Replace this old world order, he said, with a new G7 comprising the US, the European Union (as a bloc), Japan and the four BRIC nations, Brazil, Russia, India and China.

Out go post-Brexit Britain and Canada from the old G7.

France, Germany and Italy stay on only as part of the collective EU. As a former UK treasury minister and former chair of British think tank Chatham House, O'Neill's proposition was taken seriously—for exactly 10 seconds.

The old world order, represented by the current G7, has no intention of giving up its global clout, however much that clout has shrunk in recent years. O'Neill himself wrote with a nudge and a wink that nothing of the kind he was proposing was likely to happen. "While Canada and post-Brexit Britain would lose some of their current influence," he said, "they would have no less of it than similarly situated countries such as Australia. At any rate, they need not worry. There is no reason to expect a diplomatic overhaul of this scale anytime soon."

The West uses the global levers of security, finance and politics and its dominance of the UNSC, IMF and World Bank to impose economic sanctions, invade sovereign nations, wage extraterritorial wars, and control global finance. Media is a key instrument to mould global opinion. Western media is careful not to use Western reporters to distort facts. It recruits Indian or other Asian journalists in order to innoculate itself from the charge of racism.

European nationalism brought war and misery to the world throughout the first half of the 20th century. For the previous 200 years, from the 1750s to the 1950s, Europe and its invasive Anglo-Saxon settlements in America and Australasia, the African slave trade to the Americas, and the colonisation of Asia and Africa, lifted Western societies to great wealth and global influence. The post-1945 world order was designed to preserve that wealth and influence. The order has reached its expiry date.

Section Six

SECULARISM

TWENTY

Fear of the "Other"

WHEN THE NARENDRA MODI GOVERNMENT TOOK OFFICE IN MAY 2014, dire warnings were issued. There will be communal riots, predicted one newspaper. The Samajwadi Party (SP), the Left and the Congress joined the chorus. *The Economist*, analysing Modi's first year, wrote: "This newspaper chose not to back Mr Modi in last year's elections because of his record on handling religious strife ... We are happy that our fears of grave communal violence have so far not been realised."

Keki Daruwala, a former member of the National Commission for Minorities, challenged that view in *The Economic Times* in an article on 30 May 2015, provocatively titled: *So What If There's Been No Riots?*

Daruwala wrote: "There has been no sectarian riot worth the name since the NDA government came to power in May 2014. But is this the measure of the well-being of minorities? No houses burnt, no Muslims or Christians stabbed, so all is hunky-dory? Rajeshwar Singh of the Dharam Jagran Samiti, the man reportedly behind the RSS' ghar wapsi programmes, states in Etah, UP, that 'India, will be made free of Muslims and Christians. India is the country of Hindus alone'."

Have Daruwala's fears been proved right eight years after he wrote this provocative article in May 2015?

India is secular not because Indira Gandhi inserted the word into the Constitution during the Emergency in 1976 but because

Hindus are innately secular. Of the world's major religions, Hinduism is the only faith without a prophet. No one founded Hinduism—unlike Christ, Mohammad, Zoroaster, Abraham, Confucius, Mahavira, Buddha and Guru Nanak.

Hinduism, or Sanatana Dharma, evolved organically. The Vedas (circa 1800 BC) predate the second oldest religious text, Judaism's Torah (circa 1300 BC), by several hundred years. Sanatana Dharma is the world's oldest organised religious philosophy. It was followed by Judaism, Zoroastrianism and then in quick order by Jainism, Buddhism, Confucianism and Christianity. Islam is a relatively young religion as is Sikhism. Of these nine major faiths, four were founded in South Asia (Hinduism, Buddhism, Jainism and Sikhism), four in West Asia (Judaism, Zoroastrianism, Christianity and Islam), and one in North Asia (Confucianism).

Thus every major religion is of Asian origin. Europe appropriated Christianity through the Roman Empire. Jesus Christ was a brown-skinned, dark-haired Semitic Jew born in Bethlehem. His ancestry was Middle Eastern. Later depictions of him in popular culture (movies, plays, photographs, media) showed him as Caucasian with European features and fair hair. The myth endures.

India, the birthplace of nearly half the world's nine major religions, has long been a haven for the other half. The first Jews arrived in India on Kerala's Malabar coast in 542 BC and form one of the world's oldest and most peaceful Jewish communities. India, unlike Europe, has never seen anti-Semitic persecution.

The first Christians came to India, again in Kerala, in 52 AD, before Christianity had even encountered Europe. Zoroastrians fled Islamic persecution in Persia (today's Iran) and found refuge in Gujarat in 720 AD, becoming one of India's most successful communities (Parsis). Muslims from Arabia came to India in the 7th century to trade. The markets of Basra in Iraq bustled with buyers of Indian spices and condiments.

Sword-wielding Islam, meanwhile, was conquering large swathes across Europe. After centuries of conquests, Islam's armies reached the gates of Vienna before being defeated in battle in 1529. Islam now turned its full attention to India. The Mughals were Chaghtai Turkish warlords from Central Asia. Unlike Christians, Jews and Parsis before them, they came to India to conquer, not seek refuge.

The final systematic European invasion of the subcontinent was by the British, following the Battle of Palashee (Plassey) in 1757. The British were shrewder than earlier invaders. They sensed that religious conversions would complicate their main objective for conquering India: to profiteer. They usurped Indian raw materials to fuel the industrial revolution back home and expanded the British Empire through trade backed by guns and warships. The British had lost their American empire in 1776 just as they were building a new one in India. Without India, there would have been no British Empire.

Britain, a Protestant nation, rarely converted Indians during its 190-year occupation of the subcontinent. That is why there are relatively few Protestant Christians in India: the bulk of Indian Christians are Catholics, converted by Portuguese and Spanish Jesuits who both preceded and followed the British into India (Bombay, Goa, Puducherry, Kerala, the Deccan and elsewhere). Their focus, unlike the Protestant British, was not trade but proselytisation. The conversions of Dalits and other disenfranchised Hindus to Christianity over several centuries, however, led to just 2 per cent of India's population eventually being converted to Catholicism by the time European colonisation of India ended.

Islam followed a different route. The Mughals converted Hindus by sword or inducement, using two devices: one, exemption from paying the *jizya* tax imposed on Hindus; and two, escape from the dehumanising caste system into a more egalitarian if harsh, didactic Islam.

This historical background is necessary to put in perspective the debate over "the safety" of Christians and Muslims in India. Over 250 million Muslims and Christians live in India. The vast majority are not discriminated against. Jews and Parsis have lived trouble-free, prosperous lives in India for centuries. In Pakistan, minorities (Hindus, Christians and others) have been virtually exterminated. In parts of the Middle East, minorities (including Hindus) don't have basic civil rights. In Europe, minorities (Muslims) live under strictures (no hijabs in public places in France and Belgium, no new minarets on mosques in Switzerland). In the US, cartoons of the Prophet are drawn in defiance of Islam's tenets and copies of the Quran burnt. India meanwhile remains, for all communities, the secular haven it has been for centuries.

✍

Islam was civilisationally advanced. But just when medieval Christianity in Europe was reforming itself by setting up universities like Oxford, Cambridge, Heidelberg and the Sorbonne in the 13th and 14th centuries, Islam took the wrong turn in the road. For the next several hundred years it brandished the sword, not the pen. Early Islamic advances in science and medicine were lost.

Islam swept through south-eastern Europe, southern Spain, Portugal and the central Asian republics. The Indian subcontinent was an afterthought, invaded first by various Muslim warlords and then the Mughals led by the failed Turkic-Mongol Babur. Global Islam suffered a setback in 1918 when it was defeated by the Allies in World War I. Its lands were confiscated. Pliable Arab dictators, remote-controlled by the United States, Britain and France, were installed. The centuries-old Ottoman caliphate was dissolved on 3 March 1924.

America's invasion of Iraq in 2003, the thousands of innocent civilians killed in US air strikes and the millennium-old Sunni-Shia conflict form a combustible mix. From it emerged, first, al-Qaeda and then the Islamic State (IS). Radical Islam continues to pose a global threat. It is fungible and exportable. Pakistan is its epicentre, abetting terrorism against India and helping to install the Taliban in Afghanistan.

India must obviously remain the plural, tolerant and diverse society it is and has historically been. Creating false equivalences, however, is a thriving Indian cottage industry. It is important, therefore to define "Islamist" ideology. Islamic and Islamist may appear to differ only alphabetically, but they are worlds apart. Islamists are violent: the Taliban, Islamic State-Khorasan (IS-K), Lashkar-e-Taiba (LeT), Jaish-e-Mohammed (JeM) and Tehreek-i-Labbaik Pakistan (TLP) are Islamists. Terrorism is their Islamist calling card. No country, not even Talibanised Afghanistan or radicalised Pakistan, would call themselves an Islamist Emirate or an Islamist Republic. They are careful to name themselves, respectively, the Islamic Emirate of Afghanistan and the Islamic Republic of Pakistan. Even those with extremist views know better than to employ the word Islamist to describe their country's ideology.

There is, of course, a purpose to the creation of false equivalences. It goes back to root causes. Under Mughal rule, Hindus were treated as second-class citizens. *Jizya* was collected only from non-Muslims. Hindu resentment bubbled, but under the surface. It found no outlet. During British rule, Hindus again were treated badly, often brutally. Hindu resentment drove the freedom movement and led eventually to the eviction of the British from India. But the British weren't quite done with India. During their 190-year indirect and direct rule, they had, with callous deliberation, deepened cleavages between Hindus and Muslims. The British co-opted Muslims whom they regarded as a martial race—like the Anglo-Saxon British themselves. Hindus were interested in profit, Muslims in war, the British believed. As Winston Churchill said during a speech at Royal Albert Hall on 18 March 1931: "While the Hindu elaborates his argument, the Moslem sharpens his sword."

The Anglo-Muslim nexus continued after 1947. It was British

diplomatic skullduggery at the UN in 1948 that stopped India from capturing large swathes of Pakistan-occupied Kashmir (PoK). India's first Prime Minister Jawaharlal Nehru fell into the British-Pakistan trap, ordering Indian troops to halt their assault.

The British left India, keeping their Indian political clones behind. They continued to appease minorities, refusing among other concessions to codify Muslim personal law. Hindus, their resentment choked for centuries, finally rebelled. It is the single biggest reason for the rise to power of the BJP and, specifically, of Modi. If the Congress and other political parties had practised even-handedness on matters of faith, the BJP's raison de'être would have eroded.

Trinamool Congress (TMC) leader Mamata Banerjee was right when she said that "Congress has made Modi strong". But she misstated the reason. Modi didn't become strong because the Congress "isn't serious about politics", as Banerjee theorised. It is strong because the Congress with its dishonest secularism alienated enough Hindus to allow Modi to tap into Hindu angst. That angst had simmered for generations. It boiled over in May 2014 and again in May 2019. Will it cool sufficiently by May 2024 to give the Opposition an opportunity to prise open the gates to power at the Centre?

The BJP needs to be careful not to overplay the religious card for electoral gain. Hinduism, despite its evolved philosophy, needs to reform too. It has too many superstitions. The caste system is cruel. It must go. And the ethos of Hindu fatalism must be set aside. But in the end, every Indian – Hindu, Muslim, Christian or Jew – is, first, a Hindustani civilisationally and everything else second. That, not majoritarianism, should be the guiding principle of India.

~

There are three categories of influential Muslim leaders: political, religious and societal. All three have betrayed young Muslims.

Politicians have a vested interest in keeping Muslims backward. Since 1947, they have employed a fraudulent version of secularism. Hindu personal law was codified in the mid-1950s. Muslim personal law remains based on Sharia. Elements of the law as practised in India are more regressive than even those in Islamic countries like Saudi Arabia.

The Shah Bano case in 1985 revealed the true nature of Muslim personal law. A destitute Muslim widow was given a monthly maintenance allowance of ₹500 by the Supreme Court. The Rajiv Gandhi government used its 414-seat majority in the Lok Sabha to overturn the Supreme Court's verdict in 1986. Appeasement politics now became mainstream. Other parties followed the Congress. Indian secularism was defined as Muslim-first secularism. Dr Manmohan Singh sanctified this by saying, early in his prime ministership, that minorities had first right to India's resources.

Rahul Gandhi has accelerated the Congress' Muslim-first policy. It is no accident that he chose Wayanad in Kerala as his second constituency in the 2019 Lok Sabha election. Rahul lost Amethi to Smriti Irani but won comfortably in Wayanad where Muslims from 28.65 per cent and Christians 21.34 per cent of the population.[39]

Religious leaders have added a second layer of toxicity to the secularism practised by political parties like the Congress, SP, RJD and others. They constantly seek emotive issues to mislead their flock. They have used tropes over *ghar wapsi,* love jihad and hijab to distract young Muslims from becoming an integrated part of Indian society. Instead of encouraging Muslim students to focus on the technology-led knowledge economy, they are kept engaged in destructive arguments over issues like the hijab. The result: as both the Sachar Committee and the Ranganath Misra Commission reports showed, and new NSSO statistics have

---

[39]2011 Census.

underscored, Muslims are the most backward and impoverished community in India – more so than even Dalits.

Societal leaders in the Muslim community meanwhile feed on its sense of grievance. Muslims are constantly told that under the Modi government they are treated as second-class citizens. The opposite is actually true. Muslims have been allowed to retain their personal laws. They pray on public land. They use loudspeakers for *azaans* at 5 am even though courts have forbidden it at that hour. Their Waqf Boards sit unhindered on land valued at several thousand crore rupees. Mosques are well protected. They rarely suffer from vandalism by Hindus. Moreover, "liberal" journalists, lawyers, activists and NGOs rally instantly to minority causes.

What then really bothers Indian Muslims? For centuries, their ancestors ruled over Hindus. Most Indian Muslims are former Hindus, converted to Islam by either force or inducement. That has created subconscious angst which often finds an outlet in aggression. The British co-opted Muslims, pitting them against Hindus. Winston Churchill had withering contempt for the "soft" Hindu and admiration for the "martial" Muslim.

After Independence, Jawaharlal Nehru continued the Muslim-first policy, dressed up as "secularism". Real secularism favours none, empowers everyone. Nehruvian secularism failed that test. Muslims, used to 400 years of being pampered, first as rulers, then as a co-opted community by the British, and finally as a favoured vote bank by the Congress, were dismayed by the BJP's victory in 2014. Modi ended the Muslim-first policy minorities had taken for granted for decades, indeed centuries. That era is over. Muslims must now be empowered in order to integrate them into a modern, technology-driven India.

The online conference "Dismantling Global Hindutva" in September 2021 would have deserved little or no attention but for its attempt to mainstream Hinduphobia. Had Ivy League universities in the US allowed their forums to be used to advocate "dismantling" Islam or Christianity through such a conference, it would have been shut down. The same abuse directed at Jews or Muslims would be termed unacceptably anti-Semitic or Islamophobic, punishable by applicable local laws. Civil society, academia, political leaders and media across the world would have condemned it. Apart from facing legal and punitive action, those who engaged in such abuse would be ostracised and declared persona non grata.

Some argue that Hindutva is not Hinduism. The 2021 conference attacked only Hindutva, not Hinduism. Therefore, they say, this is as acceptable as attacking radical Islam, not Islam itself. One preaches violence, the other peace. The analogy obviously is false. Hindutva has its unsavoury elements such as the Bajrang Dal, but the fount of Hindutva ideology, the RSS, does not pose a threat to India or the world. Radical Islam does.

This is how a Supreme Court bench defined Hindutva in an historic three-bench judgment led by the late Justice JS Verma in December 1995. While a larger bench may be constituted to re-examine the judgment at a future date, the apex court's definition stands as of today: "No precise meaning can be ascribed to the terms 'Hindutva'; and no meaning in the abstract can confine it to the narrow limits of religion alone, excluding the content of Indian culture and heritage. It is difficult to appreciate how in the face of these decisions, the term 'Hindutva' per se, in the abstract, can be assumed to mean and be equated with narrow fundamentalist Hindu religious bigotry. The term 'Hindutva' is related more to the way of life of the people in the subcontinent. It is difficult to appreciate how the terms 'Hindutva' or 'Hinduism' per se, in the abstract, can be assumed to mean and be equated with narrow, fundamentalist Hindu religious bigotry, or be construed to fall within the prohibition in Sub-sections (3) and/ or (3A) of Section 123."

Is Hindutva under a BJP government more sinister than the Supreme Court believed it was in 1995 when it delivered the above judgment? The PV Narasimha Rao-led Congress government was in power. The fear among India's minorities today is that a more muscular version of Hindutva under Modi has led to a majoritarian Hindu Rashtra.

India has over 1 billion Hindus. At the height of his power, when he led the BJP to victory in 303 seats in the 2019 Lok Sabha election, Modi could muster less than half the 80 per cent Hindu vote. If India was a majoritarian country, the BJP would have won a far greater vote share than 37 per cent in the 2019 general election. India's diversity – across religion, caste, language and region – ensures that majoritarianism remains unattainable under even a "Hindu" government like the BJP.

What then drives Hinduphobia? The answer: a combination of domestic politics and a Left-Islamist global ecosystem. Since Modi took office in May 2014, this ecosystem has linked up seamlessly with Opposition parties in India. NGOs, activists, journalists, retired army officers and former bureaucrats have been deployed to use media and the courts to construct a narrative of how India is sinking into an abyss of Hindu majoritarianism.

Most news portals that have sprung up after 2014 offer a smorgasbord of motivated reportage. With Modi winning two successive Lok Sabha elections and having weathered the economic crises caused by the Covid-19 pandemic and the Russia-Ukraine war, the NGO-led global ecosystem and sections of the Indian Opposition continue to attack the core ideological base of the Modi-led BJP.

The logic is seductive: the prime minister may have a coat of Teflon that makes him impervious to public criticism despite missteps. But if Hindutva can be demonised globally, Modi may feel the pressure. This ecosystem knows how keen Modi is on protecting his global reputation. The new line of attack targets this supposed Achilles heel.

The strategy could backfire. The more you attack Hindutva and by corollary Hinduism, the more, ironically, you strengthen Modi's "Hindu" credentials. Over the past few years, Modi has been under fierce attack by a section of the Sangh Parivar faithful for not being "Hindu" enough and embracing "soft" secularism in the Atal Bihari Vajpayee mould to attract global praise.

An escalating attack on Hindutva by "secular" parties draws the hard right back towards Modi rather than further away from him. If Modi is being attacked by Western NGOs, Leftists and Islamists for being too "Hindu", the hard right may believe he must be doing something right after all.

⚮

When Uttar Pradesh Chief Minister Yogi Adityanath spoke of making India a Hindu Rashtra, he touched a raw nerve. The "idea of India" is religion-neutral. Secularism is central to this idea. The problem of course lies with the definition of secularism.

The classical idea of secularism (empower all, appease none) is not Sitaram Yechury's or Rahul Gandhi's idea of secularism (empower none, appease some). The problem with Hindu Rashtra, however, is not its underlying concept of national unity within religious diversity, which has been India's civilisational ethos for centuries, but the way the word Hindu is misinterpreted. A Hindu Rashtra does not mean, and certainly should not mean, a Hindu-centric Rashtra where Muslims, Christians, Parsis and Jews are treated as second-class citizens. It simply means an all-encompassing civilisational unity that transcends religion.

There is a civilisational Hindu in every Indian – whatever his or her private faith. That kernel of Hinduism is not religious but civilisational. A Tamil Hindu, for example, has more in common culturally with a Tamil Muslim than with a Punjabi Hindu. Similarly, a Maharashtrian Muslim often has greater kinship with a Maharashtrian Hindu than with an Assamese Muslim.

In India's complex geography and a history dotted with

invasions by Christians from Britain, Spain and Portugal and Muslims from Central Asia, religion became a lightning rod for politicians who use their counterfeit versions of secularism to divide, not unite. The problem is exacerbated by two other factors. First, India is one of the most religious countries in the world. Research has shown that well over 90 per cent of Indians of all faiths believe in God and pray regularly. In Britain, in contrast, regular Church-goers have dropped by nearly 50 per cent over the past 20 years. The second complicating factor is that India's Muslims are civilisationally and culturally more "Hindu" than they care to admit. This causes several dichotomies.

The call, for example, by the Dewan of the Ajmer Dargah, Syed Zainul Abedin, to support a ban on eating beef underscores the growing divisions within the Muslim community. Shias, Sufis, Memons and Bohras are more akin to India's civilisational ethos than Sunnis. It is the formers' syncretic Muslim culture rather than the Wahhabi-influenced Sunni fundamentalism that Indian secularism needs.

Despite the efforts of Pakistan to radicalise India's Muslims, they remain largely immune to the currents of Islamist fundamentalism sweeping other parts of the world. If that had not been the case, over 210 million Muslims could easily have converted India into the world's suicide bomb capital. Even in Jammu & Kashmir, where Pakistan has tried since 1989 to Islamise the Valley, Kashmiri Muslims, used stones, not suicide bombs, as their weapon of choice during previous insurgencies, demonstrating the residual influence of Sufism in Kashmir's plural history.

So is Adityanath wrong about Hindu Rashtra? Should he not instead have said Bharat Rashtra? It is much the same argument as the one between Hindutva and Bharatiyata. India is a nation of plural and parallel identities: within its fold lie all religions – equal, separate, but bound by a common thread of Bharatiyata. So why not call Hindutva, Bharatiyata? Atal Bihari Vajpayee famously did just that, saying the terms were interchangeable:

Hindutva is Bharatiyata, he said, and Bharatiyata is Hindutva. Modi agrees with this in principle but not necessarily always in practice – or in public.

Just as Hindus must accept Bharatiyata's plural embrace, Adityanath should regard a plural Bharat Rashtra as his guiding force. Invoking religion may draw votes but development needs all Indians to rise above their faith.

TWENTY-ONE

Hinduism Needs Reform Too

LIKE ALL THINGS ANCIENT, HINDUISM NEEDS CONSTANT CARE OR ITS wisdom can turn into dogma. The Abrahamic religions suffer from this malady. Islam is tethered to the Quran written over 1,300 years ago. Rather than interpret its verses in modern, socially liberal terms, Islamic clerics have frozen them in time. That has led to appalling gender injustice. It has also sanctioned a violent interpretation of jihad which the Quran in its verses defines as self-defence, not conquest, but with enough semantic ambiguity to justify violence against infidels.

Christianity is similarly didactic. The Catholic Church, despite some recent efforts at reform, does not ordain women priests as a matter of "divine law". It regards homosexuality as a "moral evil". And it encourages belief in miracles. The break in the 16th century between the Catholic and Anglican Churches led to the formation of Protestant majorities in Anglo-Saxon countries like post-Reformation Britain.

Islam and Christianity have fought each other over territory and faith for more than a thousand years. Hinduism, passive and inward-looking, has meanwhile absorbed invasion, subjugation, tyranny and plunder. It gave rise to Buddhism and Jainism, both older than Christianity and Islam. Neither though could replace Hinduism in its birthplace.

But this shouldn't blind Hindus to the need for reform. Modi is certainly aware of this. Hinduism is amorphous, organic and shapes itself into whatever form its practitioner wants. You can pray at a temple or at home or not at all and yet be a good Hindu. You can be agnostic or atheist and still be a good Hindu. But Hinduism's formlessness and sponge-like absorptive capacity can be a double-edged sword. Lack of discipline breeds disorder and division. Caste looms large as one of its biggest dangers.

It is argued that the caste system in Hinduism helped India escape the fate of other countries whose native religions succumbed to mass conversions to Islam or Christianity. The caste system has two concepts: varna and jati. Varna in Vedic India was linked to the profession one followed based on aptitude, skill and interest. It was flexible and allowed social and occupational mobility. Jati, in contrast, was defined by birth. You couldn't escape the jati you were born into.

Defending caste, Rajeev Srinivasan, an IIT and Stanford alumnus, wrote in *Swarajya* magazine[40]: "To consider resilience, think of the fact that of all the civilisations that the Muslims encountered when they swept out of Arabia, Hindu civilisation is the only one that did not get wiped out. Great, established cultures such as Egypt and Persia and all the Buddhist cultures of Central Asia were completely erased in a very short time. In the case of Hinduism, the jati served as the node.

If your allegiance was to a particular jati, in essence, the destruction of other jatis had little effect on you.

"In one sense this is bad because of the lack of unity of purpose, but on the other hand, the system is resilient. I think this baffled Muslim invaders. Initially, they thought the centre of Hinduism was Somnath, so they sacked it, and nothing happened. Then they thought the centre was Benares, and they sacked it; again Hinduism did not vanish.

"Humans have an innate need to belong. Jati is an innovation that uses this drive for many positive (but alas, also negative)

---

[40] 19 December 2015.

things. A flexible system of jatis where occupational value
determines its market price was a good idea. An ossified system
still seems to function pretty well, and I am not sure that jati
will disappear with urbanisation."

Beyond such historical justifications of caste lies today's reality.
The riots that took place in Pune and Mumbai on 1 January 2018
during the celebration of the 200th anniversary of the British-Dalit
victory over the Peshwa-Brahmin-Marathas in Bhima-Koregaon show
how caste remains a dagger aimed at the heart of Hindu society.

Whatever the justifications of "distributed systems" of jati and
their historical role in protecting Hinduism from invading Islamic
and Christian armies, the argument does little credit to Hinduism.
If a religion needs a caste-based distributed system – and the
cruel injustices that go with it – to merely survive onslaughts from
outside, it speaks poorly of its inherent strength. There must be
a higher ambition than mere survival. Caste allowed Hinduism
to survive but not to thrive. That is the defeatist thought process
that continues to burden Hinduism.

Indeed, Hinduism fell into such deep decay that it needed
Christian invaders to, first, subdue it and then bring modern
education to the subcontinent, sparking its renaissance. Economist
Angus Maddison theorised that India accounted for nearly 24 per
cent of global GDP before the British colonised the country and
systematically destroyed its industries, trade and crafts. But that
was an India of 650 princely kingdoms, united by geography
and culture but divided by religion, language, region – and caste.

Caste is today a potent electoral weapon. To be a great
religious philosophy, and not be held hostage to cynical electoral
politics, Hinduism must shed old shibboleths and embrace reform.
Dalits must be allowed entry into every Hindu temple. So must
women. There can be no exceptions and no excuses. This too
should form part of Modi's 2024 election manifesto.

Few want to meet the fate of the journalists and cartoonists of *Charlie Hebdo*, murdered by Islamist terrorists. Islamophobia is rightly condemned. Hinduphobia though is acceptable in living rooms across upper middle-class urban India. The pathology of this curious phenomenon needs examination but consider first *The Economist*'s story on Muslims in India whom it calls "An Uncertain Community". The magazine grudgingly concedes that "India's Muslims have not, it is true, been officially persecuted, hounded into exile or systematically targeted by terrorists, as have minorities in other parts of the subcontinent, such as the Ahmadi sect in Pakistan."

The Economist adopts a patronising, all-knowing tone towards India's secular ethos that echoes India's homegrown Hinduphobes. Most Indian Hinduphobes are, strangely, Hindus. They call themselves secular, but are often not. Secularism requires religion-neutrality. They lack that. Bias colours their views. They organise global conferences to "dismantle Hindutva". So why are sophisticated, educated Hindus, who aspire to secularism so Hinduphobic? Because they misread completely what real secularism means.

As I wrote in my 2014 book *The New Clash of Civilizations: How The Contest Between America, China, India and Islam Will Shape Our Century*:

> Influential sections of especially the electronic media, suffused with hearts bleeding from the wrong ventricle, are part of this great fraud played on India's poverty-stricken Muslims—communalism with an engaging secular mask. The token Muslim—from business to literature—is lionised but the common Muslim languishes in his ghetto. It is from such ghettos that raw recruits to the banned Students Islamic Movement of India (SIMI) and the Indian Mujaheedin (IM) were most easily found. India's religious diversity though is deeply embedded.

Six of India's highest constitutional functionaries have been Sikh (prime minister), Christian (UPA chairperson), Muslim (chief election commissioner), Parsi (chief justice of India), Dalit (speaker of the Lok Sabha) and Hindu (president). There is no other country in the world with such breathtaking plurality at the highest level of leadership.

Consider Britain: only Protestant (not Catholic) Christians can be monarch. In Saudi Arabia and Pakistan, minorities have severely restricted rights. Unlike burqa-banning Western democracies such as France and Belgium, Indian secularism does not separate church from state. It allows them to swim together in a common, if sometimes, chaotic pool.

Communal polarisation suits the BJP. The organic rise of majoritarianism underpinned its success in the 2014 and 2019 Lok Sabha elections. The question is: can it work in 2024? Or will a united, resurgent Opposition spring a surprise?

Modi hasn't spelt out in clear terms what he believes differentiates Hindutva from Hinduism. Hindutva in its early formulation was a response to the muscularity of Islam and Christianity in colonial India. Both were invasive. Both proselytised—by force or allurement. But as India and Hinduism regain their civilisational self-confidence after centuries of subjugation, Hindutva must now reshape itself into an inclusive philosophy based on Hinduism's own highly evolved precepts.

Former Union Culture Minister Mahesh Sharma violated the first principle of inclusive Hinduism when he called Dr APJ Abdul Kalam a "nationalist despite being a Muslim". In Bharatiyata, you are Indian first. Religious identification is unnecessary. It was disappointing too to hear Omar Abdullah tell a packed Lok Sabha during the July 2008 trust vote on the India-US civil nuclear deal that he was "a proud Muslim and a proud Indian." A truly secular Indian would have reversed that order and said he was a proud Indian first and also a proud

Muslim (or, as the case may be, a proud Hindu, Christian, Sikh, Parsi or Jew). Your national identity supersedes your religious identity.

Anirban Ganguly in a blog[41], weeks before Modi became prime minister, wrote this about the inclusive nature of Hinduism: "When Mirra Alfassa (The Mother) of Pondicherry (now Puducherry) declared that India was her 'true country, the country of my soul and spirit' and that though she was French 'by birth and early education' she was 'Indian by choice and predilection', the Mother was essentially speaking from a conviction that came from a deep and unconditional immersion into the essence of Bharatiyata. (And) when Sister Nivedita, wrote that it was 'by a gradual and loving study of how she [India] came to be, can we grow to understand what the country actually is, what the intention of her evolution and what her sleeping potentiality may be', she was essentially pointing at the practice of evolving or enhancing this sense of Bharatiyata, a sense that she had herself marvellously imbibed from her Master.

"It is in Nivedita's words that one finds the best description of the essential Bharatiyata that Swami Vivekananda's personality radiated. Describing the Swami's personality and how it held within its cradle the essence of Indianness, Nivedita movingly wrote, 'He had learnt, not only the hopes and ideals of every sect and group of the Indian people, but their memories also. The songs of Guru Nanak alternated with those of Mirabai and Tansen on his lips. Stories of Prithvi Raj and Delhi jostled against those of Chitore and Pratap Singh, Shiva and Uma, Radha, Krishna, Sita-Ram and Buddha...His whole heart and soul was a burning epic of the country, touched to an overflowing of mystic passion by her very name'."

All this of course does not mean that inclusive Hinduism endorses a return to a distorted version of secularism which

---

[41] 28 April 2014.

appeases rather than empowers minorities. True secularism treats all religions equally. It favours none.

✌

The 2024 Lok Sabha election, following close on the heels of the emotive inauguration of the Ram Mandir, will be a test for Modi's version of Hindutva. It will also be a test for the Opposition. Around mid-2017, buffeted by a series of state assembly defeats, Rahul Gandhi had an epiphany: playing the Hindu Brahmin card. Why hadn't we thought of it earlier, he apocryphally asked his advisors. The Congress, he reckoned, had damaged itself electorally by being seen as a "Muslim party". Hindus, even moderate, long-time Congress supporters, were deserting the Congress.

The saffronisation of the Congress began haltingly. First came Rahul's widely publicised visit to the Kedarnath temple in Uttarakhand. The December 2017 Gujarat Assembly election was a key test. If the Congress' new-found Hindu-centricism found resonance on Modi's home turf, long a polarised Hindutva stronghold, it could succeed in other states as well.

In certain state assembly elections, the Congress went saffron with a vengeance. For example, the Congress promised the Madhya Pradesh electorate before the November-December 2018 assembly election that it will build *gaushalas* in every panchayat. It pledged to develop Rath Path Gaman, the route Lord Ram took during his exile. The Congress manifesto went on, unblinkingly, to say that it will begin commercial production of *gau mutra* (cow urine). To emphasise its new saffron credentials, in case there was any lingering doubt, the Congress promised that, if elected, it would establish a "spiritual" department in its state government though it didn't say whether sadhus or sants would head it.

The Congress won Madhya Pradesh in December 2018 only to lose it in within a year to defections and subsequent bypolls in

2020. Rahul Gandhi experimented with a "saffron-lite" strategy at both the national and state level. But a *gaushala*-friendly policy has not worked for the Congress in states like Uttar Pradesh where the percentage of Muslims is higher than in Madhya Pradesh.

For a while in 2017, during the Gujarat Assembly elections, a temple-hopping Rahul played cat and mouse with soft Hindutva. After the 2019 Lok Sabha drubbing Congress suffered, Rahul changed tactics. His decision to contest the 2019 Lok Sabha polls from two constituencies, Amethi and Wayanad, was widely mocked. Amethi had been a Gandhi pocket borough for decades, nurtured with benign neglect by Rahul since his entry into electoral politics in 2004.

By choosing Wayanad in Kerala as his second seat in the 2019 Lok Sabha election, Rahul unwittingly telegraphed two messages: one, that he feared losing to the BJP's feisty Smriti Irani in Amethi; and two, that a safe second seat had to have a large minority electorate. Rahul duly lost in Amethi and won in Wayanad. It was the first time a Gandhi dynast had been defeated in a family fief since Indira Gandhi's post-Emergency loss in Rae Bareli (to bête noire Raj Narain) in the 1977 Lok Sabha poll.

Will Rahul's hard Left turn and embrace of minority fundamentalist parties harm or help Congress in the 2024 General Election? Clearly, a strategy that aims at targeting a 15 per cent Muslim electorate nationally along with a small, Left-leaning Hindu demographic slice risks alienating moderate Hindus who till recently had looked askance at what they perceived as the BJP's majoritarianism.

⸎

Bill Clinton famously declared, "It's the economy, stupid", during his presidential campaign against George H Bush in 1992. It usually is in a national election, though not necessarily so in India. The Kargil war, not the economy, won Atal Bihari Vajpayee the September 1999 General Election. The exploding refugee crisis in East Pakistan ahead of the Bangladesh liberation war won Indira Gandhi the March 1971 Lok Sabha poll even though the economy was lumbering along at a growth rate of 3 per cent a year. Rajiv Gandhi's tragic assassination allowed the Congress to form a minority government led by P V Narasimha Rao in the May–June 1991 General Election despite a bankrupt national treasury.

Will the inauguration of the Ram Mandir electrify Modi's vote base, especially in Uttar Pradesh, in 2024 despite inflation and unemployment? Modi is India's canniest politician. He knows that the BJP has lost some amount of goodwill among the middle-class due to inflation, fuel prices and cumbersome taxation compliances. The rural poor have been hit particularly hard by the paucity of jobs.

A refurbished Rahul Gandhi, following his 3,570-km Bharat Jodo Yatra, believes he can still stitch together a viable UPA coalition. A repeat of 2004 is not impossible. Could Modi lose the 2024 Lok Sabha election? Rahul may be mocked by BJP supporters but it would be unwise to underestimate either him or the pull of dynasty in feudal India. And yet, Rahul remains Modi's most effective vote-getter and hapless punching bag despite his nearly five-month-long *yatra*. Why do Rahul's personal attacks against Modi backfire?

Modi shot into national prominence after winning his second successive assembly election in Gujarat in 2007. By 2012, the BJP's leadership duopoly of Vajpayee-Advani had turned from a double engine into a triple engine of Vajpayee-Advani-Modi. Ahead of the 2024 Lok Sabha election, does UP Chief Minister Yogi Adityanath have enough support to turn the BJP's double engine of Modi-Shah into a triple engine of Modi-Shah-Yogi? The evolution of a potential Modi-Shah-Yogi troika has three significant differences from the past troika of Vajpayee-Advani-Modi.

First, Modi is no Vajpayee. He is fit and still has fire in his belly. *Second,* Amit Shah is no Advani. At 58, he is nearly 30 years younger than Advani was in 2013. Shah will remain Modi's heir unless circumstances change dramatically—poor health or a series of big election defeats on his watch. *Third,* Yogi is no Modi. At 51, however, he has age on his side. As a six-term Lok Sabha MP and second-term chief minister of India's biggest state with a population almost as large as Pakistan's, he has a wealth of administrative experience.

In May 2015, as I said earlier in this book, the Mumbai Press Club invited senior journalist Rajdeep Sardesai and I to debate the first year of Modi's prime ministership in front of an audience of over 100 editors and reporters. At the debate I likened the economy Modi had inherited to a truck with a broken engine, its chassis lying upside down. Even Sardesai, a visceral Modi critic, sitting on the dais beside me, couldn't help but agree.

As I said at the event, Modi came to power on the slogan *sabka saath, sabka vikas.* But the overwhelming accent on winning elections at any cost has led the BJP to increasingly use caste and religion in electioneering. That has deeply polarised sections of society. Modi has declined to hold a single press conference during his tenure as prime minister. In the absence of information, disinformation prospers. One-way communications through *maan ki baat,* tweets and occasional one-on-one interviews with carefully selected journalists are not substitutes in a democracy for regular, robust unscripted press conferences.

When I first met Modi, it was clear that he was a man of few words. I let my work speak for itself, he said with a smile. But in a complex, rapidly changing world, silence on key public issues is no longer an option. It can be mistaken for indecisiveness or indifference. Modi's silence on the horrific post-poll violence in West Bengal on BJP workers by Trinamool Congress cadre in May 2021 still rankles with the BJP's rank and file. The steady drip-drip departure of BJP leaders to the TMC underlines the political cost of both silence and inaction.

From Modi's perspective, winning elections remains the priority. That is as it should be for any politician. But not speaking, and not acting, when both are needed, can carry an unexpected electoral cost.

The Congress, meanwhile, is repeating the mistakes that have haunted it for years: not trusting younger non-Gandhi Congress leaders enough to give them key positions in the party. In 2014, it appointed the nondescript Mallikarjun Kharge as leader of the party in the Lok Sabha. He posed no future threat to the Gandhis and owed his position to that singular quality of facelessness. The Congress' choice of Adhir Ranjan Chowdhury as its leader in the 2019 Lok Sabha followed the same pattern: promote a leader who poses no danger to the party's Gandhi dynasty. When Congress in October 2022 held its first inner-party election in 24 years for president, Kharge was chosen to be the titular but self-effacing head, quietly obedient to the Gandhis.

Modi though has other things to worry about than the dysfunctional Congress. The economy needs revival, jobs need to be created, over-regulation must be curbed, security challenges met and, above all, inflation controlled. A key task for Modi will be to rebuild trust in institutions and make good his pledge of minimum government, maximum governance. Ministers must be encouraged to speak up on the progress of their departments. The impression that this is a two-man Modi-Shah government is unhealthy for democracy.

Modi has himself often declared that India needs a strong Opposition. Without it, democracy atrophies. And that poses a challenge for all, including the BJP. Anti-incumbency in 2024 will be stronger than most imagine. The idea that Modi will be prime minister for 15 years or more can actually do Modi more harm than good. In politics, goodwill is a priceless commodity. But like all commodities, its value can fall as rapidly as it rises. That is a lesson a teenage Modi absorbed while wandering in the Himalayas. It is unlikely he has forgotten it.

On the global stage, Modi has long shed his reticence. At international summits, Modi is everywhere at once. He often completes over 20 bilateral meetings with world leaders in 48 hours apart from delivering key speeches. At Quad, BRICS, SCO and G20 meetings, Modi often has the first and last word. He convinced the United States to join his long-cherished project – the International Solar Alliance (ISA) – and launched the One Sun One World One Grid (OSOWOG) transnational initiative. He was the voice of reason in the Russia-Ukraine war, famously telling Russian President Vladimir Putin that "today's era is not of war".

As president of the G20, Modi strides the global stage with confidence. India's position as a "swing" power, sought by both the US-led West and the Russia-China axis, gives Modi opportunities to leverage India's global profile ahead of the national electoral challenge of 2024.

TWENTY-TWO

Adityanath's 80:20 Formula

IN 1893, AT THE WORLD PARLIAMENT OF RELIGIONS IN CHICAGO, SWAMI Vivekananda said: "I am proud to belong to a religion which has taught the world both tolerance and universal acceptance. We believe not only in universal toleration, but we accept all religions as true. I am proud to belong to a nation which has sheltered the persecuted and the refugees of all religions and all nations of the earth. I am proud to tell you that we have gathered in our bosom the purest remnant of the Israelites, who came to Southern India and took refuge with us in the very year in which their holy temple was shattered to pieces by Roman tyranny. I am proud to belong to the religion which has sheltered and is still fostering the remnant of the Zoroastrian nation."

As the global audience of senior clerics listened, Vivekananda continued: "If the Parliament of Religions has shown anything to the world it is this: it has proved to the world that holiness, purity and charity are not the exclusive possessions of any church in the world, and that every system has produced men and women of the most exalted character. In the face of this evidence, if anybody dreams of the exclusive survival of his own religion and the destruction of the others, I pity him from the bottom of my heart."

Indians of all faiths should absorb the wisdom of those words. Politicians use religion to divide. So was Yogi Adityanath being communal when he said, while campaigning for the 2022 UP assembly election, that the polls would be decided on an 80:20 basis? Most believed he was referring to UP's near-20 per cent Muslim population voting in a bloc against the BJP. But what Yogi obviously meant was that there exists an 80:20 division among Indians on specific issues. In UP, Yogi knew as well as anybody else that the BJP's vote share would not exceed 45 per cent in the assembly election. It didn't. It increased to 41 per cent, just 2 per cent more than the party's 39 per cent vote share in the 2017 assembly poll. Yogi knows that Hindus are divided when it comes to elections. If all of India's Hindus – 80 per cent of the population – voted for the BJP, it would win landslides in every assembly and Lok Sabha election.

Unlike Muslims who vote in one bloc, Hindus are divided by caste, region, language and ideology. So what does the 80:20 division really signify? It reflects the thin slice of self-appointed Hindu "liberals" who consistently support issues that are against India's national interest.

Nearly all Muslims (15 per cent) support, for example, Muslim girls' right to wear the hijab in an educational institution even if that institution has a specific dress code for students which disallows any clothing identified with a religion. Turbans are excluded because they form an essential part of Sikhism. But would Sikhs be allowed to carry kirpans into school? Would Hindus be allowed to wear saffron robes (of the kind Yogi wears) in a school classroom with a specific dress code?

The right to wear the *hijab* even in institutions where clothing with a religious identity is specifically disallowed – like Hindu saffron scarves – is supported by that thin slice, perhaps 5 per cent, of Hindus who believe they are liberals. They are not. True liberalism is progressive and tolerant. The liberalism of the 20 (15 + 5 per cent) is neither. It encourages a regressive, patriarchal practice that submerges a Muslim girl's identity and makes her subservient to Muslim men. The 5 per cent slice of "liberal" Hindus is small but influential.

The success of *The Kashmir Files,* a 2022 film on the forced exodus of Kashmiri Hindu Pandits from the Valley, again divided India into a broadly 80:20 dichotomy. The majority empathised deeply with the gentle, scholarly, peace-loving Pandits who were driven out of their homeland by Pakistan-backed Islamist terrorists. But the 20 (15+5) argued that the film was not factual. Minorities often identify themselves not with the victims but the perpetrators. But what of the influential 5 per cent? Do these self-appointed liberal Hindus have neither the wisdom nor the moral acuity to distinguish between good and evil? The ethnic cleansing of four lakh Pandits from the Kashmir Valley was a great evil.

The fact that mainstream Bollywood actors, directors and producers remained silent on why none of them had made an honest film on the Kashmiri Pandits for 30 years shamed them into that silence. But for the 5 per cent slice, the shame rarely lasts long.

The recurring *hijab* controversy is a proxy battle between reformers and anti-reformers who want to transport Muslim girls back to the medieval ages. By arguing that the *hijab* is obligatory under Islam and protected by Article 25 of the Constitution which guarantees freedom of religion, those who oppose reforms deliberately misinterpret Article 25.

It's important to read Article 25 in conjunction with Article 21 and Article 14. As Abhishek Mishra of ABP explained[42]: "Freedom of religion is part of the Indian Constitution. Nevertheless, it is the weakest fundamental right of all the available fundamental rights in Part III. The Supreme Court has laid down that what is guaranteed under freedom of religion is core of religious belief and anything which is not core has no protection under Article 25. In the Quranic injunction, the word *hijab* is not mentioned at all. What is mentioned is 'wrap their head-cover over their

---

[42]12 February 2022.

chest'. The *hijab* should therefore be understood as a piece of cloth to cover the head and chest (not face) of women."

Freedom of religion is not absolute. It is subject to reasonable restrictions. This is similar to freedom of speech guaranteed under Article 19(1)(a). This again is subject to specific conditions—that it does not cause public disorder, incite an offence, compromise security of the state, violate public decency, and so on. Indeed, Article 25(i) specifies that freedom of religion is subject to the maintenance of "public order and morality". If the basic premise of pro-*hijab* votaries is accepted, it will create a divide not only between Muslims and non-Muslims but among Muslim men and Muslim women—and, worst of all, between two classes of Muslim women.

Muslim men with a regressive mindset would be emboldened to compel their wives and daughters, who do not currently wear a *hijab*, to henceforth wear one. The rift within families would widen. Those who wear a *hijab* would embrace court judgments in favour of petitioners as a vindication. Those who do not war a *hijab* would regard those judgments as an illiberal imposition.

Pro-*hijab* petitioners insist that wearing a *hijab* is "obligatory" under Islam but "not mandatory". Ignore that semantic contradiction for a moment. "Not mandatory" means that those who don't want to wear a *hijab* need not. But when you defy what's obligatory in your religion, you risk ostracism from the wider community.

The gulf between two classes of Muslim women—*hijabis* and non-*hijabis*—will thus deepen, causing social tension. Is this what the Muslim community wants?

Pratap Bhanu Mehta, writing in *The Indian Express*[43], thundered: "The court will make the same mistake when it adjudicates the matter under the essential practices test that most of us have been saying is an insidious piece of judicial chicanery. This is religion by fiat, not by the freely defined subjectivity of its

---

[43]23 February 2022.

adherents. The court can decide what compelling state interest might be under Article 14 or Article 21. But it should leave the interpretation of religion alone."

What Mehta in essence was telling courts is this: The *hijab* matter is none of your business. Leave the interpretation of religion to the clerics. So in Mehta's view, the courts are subordinate to *mullahs* and priests—Muslim, Hindu or Christian—when it comes to interpreting religious practice, however backward, regressive and oppressive that practice is. It would be difficult to find a more reprehensible view on how constitutionality should be interpreted: by clerics, not courts.

Mehta and many others like him are well-intentioned. They truly want to help Muslims. And how do they do this? By encouraging Muslim women to exercise their "free choice" – even if that choice isn't entirely free – to be covered from head to toe as they are in Saudi Arabia, Iran and (increasingly in) Pakistan. Indian Muslims are already the most impoverished and backward community in India. Why might this be so? Because political parties like the Congress, CPM, NCP, SP, RJD, NC and AIMIM have treated Muslims as an electoral prize. They are paraded every five years to vote and then returned to their ghettos.

India is never going to be a "Hindu Pakistan" as some warn darkly. But in order to be truly secular, India needs to stop segregating Muslims and treating them as mere minorities. The more we segregate minorities, the more we make them feel cut off from the mainstream. Despite India being a Hindu-majority country, Muslims have occupied virtually every constitutional post: president, vice-president, speaker and governor. Except one: prime minister.

The Congress was in office for 55 years: 1947–77, 1980–89, 1991–96 and 2004–14. It reserved largely ceremonial posts (president, vice-president and governor) for Muslims and the really important post of prime minister for the Nehru-Gandhis (Jawaharlal, Indira and Rajiv) and their co-opted loyalists

(Narasimha Rao and Manmohan Singh). Rao turned mildly rogue only when safely out of power and was duly punished with posthumous ostracism by the Gandhis for his temerity.

⁓

Modi says he has a single-minded vision for India: no Indian should go to sleep hungry; there must be equality of opportunity; technology can enable India to become a middle-income country in a decade. Modi's single-mindedness has two separate compartments: development and elections. His incremental economic reforms fall into the first silo. For Modi winning a third term is crucial. He found a hollowed-out economy when he took office in 2014. The bureaucratic ennui, the old power brokers in Delhi, the media's entrenched vested interests—all had to be overcome.

Ahead of 2024, only half the job is done. To win the 2024 General Election, Modi needs to relentlessly build on the BJP's national vote share. That is why, to him, the means often justify the end. If Modi wins the 2024 Lok Sabha election, he will by 2029 have been prime minister for 15 years. That's longer than every Indian prime minister except Jawaharlal Nehru (16 years, 9 months) and Indira Gandhi (16 years). Will Modi want to carry on and contest the May 2029 General Election? Modi will be 78; Shah, 65; Yogi, 56.

In the Opposition, Sonia Gandhi will be 82; Rahul, 59; Priyanka, 57. India in 2029 will also be a very different country. Other leaders may have emerged. But the man the Congress-Left opposition fears most is Adityanath.

Adityanath has been criticised for introducing "Hindutva-plus" in Uttar Pradesh. Contrary to the popular impression that he spends more time on the affairs of his Gorakhnath *math* than on governing the state, the second-term chief minister is a hard taskmaster. He begins meetings with bureaucrats at 6 am. The sessions last for several hours. The meetings reconvene at 6 pm and go on till midnight. Bureaucrats unlucky enough to be part of both the early morning and late-night meetings are sleep-deprived. Adityanath's second term (2022–27) as chief minister of India's largest state will determine the role he plays nationally after the 2024 Lok Sabha election.

TWENTY-THREE

Why Indian Secularism is Different from Western Secularism

SWORN IN AS PRIME MINISTER FOR A SECOND SUCCESSIVE TERM IN MAY 2019, Modi remarked that minorities have been "deceived" by a false narrative of secularism. Was he right? Classical secularism separates state from church. That is the Anglo-Saxon Protestant definition. The United States, increasingly Catholic and evangelical, and much of continental Europe see it differently. By banning burqas from public spaces, for example, France and Belgium are allowing the state to intervene proactively in matters of faith.

In India, secularism carries an entirely different meaning. It is a cynical political tool. For centuries, Indians took secularism for granted. Parsis fleeing persecution in Iran, Jewish refugees and Christian migrants made India their home. In a seeming contradiction, India has also been a crucible of communalism for centuries. Hindu-Muslim riots were endemic. But secularism as an antonym for communalism entered the political lexicon only after Indira Gandhi inserted it into the Constitution in 1976 during the Emergency. Since then it has become a political device to create, and secure, vote catchments.

Well before the BJP came to power in 2014, I defined secularism thus: "Jawaharlal Nehru was a secular man. He would have been mortified at what passes off as secularism in modern India. In its purest sense, secularism requires treating religion as a private matter. It must not enter the public domain. Pray in public or pray in private. But keep your faith at home. Influential sections of especially the electronic media, suffused with hearts bleeding from the wrong ventricle, are part of a great fraud played on India's poor Muslims: communalism dressed up as secularism. The token Muslim is lionised—from Azim Premji to Aamir Khan—but the common Muslim languishes in his ghetto."

Since losing power in 2014, the Congress and its allies in the UPA have used Muslims as cannon fodder. The politicians don't particularly care about Muslim welfare. If they did, Muslims wouldn't be the country's most impoverished community after over 55 years of Congress governments. In clash after communal clash, Muslims end up suffering in the service of their masters. For over 75 years, those masters gave them no education. Young Muslims remain food delivery boys and car mechanics. Not startup founders. They are not empowered. And yet they continue to troop out every five years to vote for the parties that gave them nothing but instilled in them a fear of the "other".

～

To key to retaking electoral power, the Opposition believes, lies in damaging India's global reputation. India must be portrayed as an unsuccessful country. To bring Modi down, India must first be brought down. Academics and journalists have been commandeered. Their job is to amplify the message: BJP is unfit to govern; India's social fabric is torn. Congress leader Rahul Gandhi had led the attack from the front in the run-up to the 2019 Lok Sabha election. His *chowkidar chor hai* taunt was meant to damage Modi sufficiently to give the Congress-led UPA a fighting chance to form a minority government in 2019 with support from regional parties.

The Congress' in-house data analytics team had told Gandhi with a confidence bred on the campuses of American Ivy League universities that the UPA would win 170–190 seats in 2019 and the BJP could be kept down to 150 seats. A repeat of 2004 –

when the Congress stitched together a Left-supported government with just 145 seats against the BJP's 138 seats – was, the party analytics team said, plausible. It was "game on".

It wasn't. To the Congress' dismay, the BJP won 303 seats in May 2019. Its own tally crawled from 44 seats in 2014 to 52. The data analysts who had briefed Gandhi on the likelihood of the Congress winning 170–190 seats in 2019, fell silent, emerging only later to write hand-wringing op-eds in newspapers.

The 2019 Lok Sabha defeat further enraged the Congress and its allies. The plotting resumed. The party though had by now realised that personal attacks targeting Modi on, for example, corruption in the Rafale deal were backfiring. The Covid-19 pandemic came as a Godsend. The Congress-led Opposition now turned to foreign media like *The New York Times* and *The Washington Post* to question the government's handling of the first wave of the pandemic in the summer of 2020. The collateral damage done to India's global reputation, despite supplying Covid vaccines to developing countries, was deliberate. To bring the BJP down and regain power, the Opposition was perfectly willing to damage India.

In the lethal second wave that struck India a year in the summer of 2021, bodies floating on the Ganga became the scimitar-of-choice to cut the BJP government down to size. Stories extracted from the foreign media were highlighted. Surely, the Opposition ecosystem thought, Modi can't recover from this. The general election was still three years away but the Left-Congress ecosystem in mid-2021 thought they finally had their man.

The government's new centralised vaccination drive that began in June 2021 upended the narrative once again. By December 2021, India had vaccinated a significant majority of its adult population. The third wave—Omicron—gave rise to hope briefly in the ecosystem. The hope waned with the third wave. It subsided in 2022. By 2023, Covid-19, despite the pandemic's surge in China, was no longer a key issue in the run-up to the 2024 Lok Sabha election.

In February 2020, Delhi was convulsed by riots on the day former United States President Donald Trump and his family arrived in Delhi with a large group of foreign journalists. The riots subsided soon after Trump left. The job was over. India's secular credentials had been suitably tarnished by a feral foreign press.

Empirical evidence shows that most communal riots in India are triggered by radicalised Muslims. In a horrific 1969 riot in Gujarat, a group of Muslims attacked a temple and Hindu sadhus, sparking a two-month-long riot. In 2002, Ganchi Muslims burnt 59 Ramsevaks to death in Godhra, leading to horrific riots.

Some in the BJP saw the 2019 Lok Sabha landslide as an affirmation of majoritarianism. It wasn't. It was a rejection of minorityism. Secularism, practised inclusively as it should be practised, ought to be the holy grail of the Modi government if it returns to power in 2024. Secularism is a noble calling. But political charlatans have practised the precise opposite since 1947.

Former Chief Justice of the Delhi High Court, AP Shah, in an op-ed in *The Hindu* on 28 December 2018, wrote: "Even those governments that proudly flaunt the label of secularism have subjected us to their non-secular realpolitik. Take the politics of Rajiv Gandhi, for instance, often touted as a 'secular' Prime Minister: his government not only overturned the Shah Bano judgment, but also banned Salman Rushdie's *The Satanic Verses* and had the locks of the Babri mosque in Ayodhya opened to Hindus."

By appeasing, but not empowering Muslims, Indian politicians have consigned two generations of Indian Muslims to poverty, joblessness and radicalism. The Modi government has long advocated its support for a ban on triple talaq and the implementation of a uniform civil code (UCC). The former is now law; the latter remains moribund in the BJP's manifesto.

When I was conducting townhalls with politicians, we invited Rahul Gandhi to one of the townhalls. I spoke to his then-assistant Kanishka Singh to formally invite Rahul. Kanishka was enthusiastic. He was particularly excited when I told him the audience would be young and comprise many minorities. "That's exactly the demographic we want!" he said animatedly.

In the end, Rahul never came. He was still finding his feet in politics in UPA 2. But the Congress' reflexive bias in favour of minorities was clearly evident in the conversations I had with Kanishka. That is a good thing—but it is a good thing only if your interest in Muslims is to empower them, not coddle them for votes. An educated, empowered Muslim would ask uncomfortable questions about what Congress politicians have done for the community since 1947.

Real secularism empowers. Fraudulent secularism disempowers. Mainstream Indian politicians have preached real secularism but practised the fraudulent version. The victim of this fraud: the ordinary Indian Muslim.

Over several years, a myth was carefully manufactured that "Hindu terror" poses an existential threat to Indian Muslims, Christians and other minorities. During the Congress-led UPA 1 and UPA 2 governments, this myth was given a label – "saffron terror". The crafting was meticulous. The Lashkar-e-Taiba (LeT) terrorist Ishrat Jahan, killed by the Gujarat police, became a secular *cause célèbre.* Websites sprang up describing her as an innocent college girl, murdered allegedly on the orders of then Gujarat Chief Minister Narendra Modi and state Home Minister Amit Shah. In Parliament, Union Home Minister Shivraj Patil spoke darkly of "Hindutva terrorism".

P Chidambaram, then finance minister, warned of the dangers of saffron terror. Terrorism, he said, had no religion—but it had a colour. Rahul Gandhi told a visiting American envoy, in a conversation leaked by Wikileaks, that right-wing terror was more dangerous to India's integrity than Islamist terrorism. Soon after, in November 2008—as if to cruelly mock that assertion— Laskhar-e-Taiba terrorists killed 166 people in two Mumbai luxury hotels, a Mumbai-based Jewish centre and Mumbai's largest railway station over three-and-a-half days of rampaging terror.

More than a decade later, Sam Pitroda, one of Rahul's senior advisors, seemingly questioned the Jaish-e-Mohammed's role in the 2019 Pulwama terror attack and the efficacy of the IAF's retaliatory Balakot air strikes. A cottage industry promoted the bizarre theory that "saffron terror" posed a danger to Indian democracy.

Rahul's attempted transformation into an observant Hindu, praying at temples, paying homage to the holy Ganga and visiting sadhus, was meanwhile met with an understanding wink from the Congress' faithful Muslim vote bank. Muslims knew which side Rahul was really on. His temple-love, they nudged each other, was only to win elections.

The foreign media was puzzled by all this chicanery. *The Economist* noted dolefully that the Congress is no longer "secular". In a March 2019 cover story on Prime Minister Narendra Modi, it wrote: "The BJP's main opponent, the Congress party, has largely dropped talk of secularism. Since winning the state of Madhya Pradesh in December, Congress has outdone the BJP on cow protection, budgeting millions to build shelters for retired cattle. Its national leader, Rahul Gandhi, now punctiliously visits temples."

It added: "The rival visions confronting India's 900 million voters have rarely been so sharply defined. Hindu nationalists regard India as a nation defined by its majority faith, much like Israel or indeed Pakistan. On the other side stand those who see India's extraordinary diversity as a source of strength. For most of the country's seven decades, multicoloured secular vision has prevailed. But the orange-clad Hindutva strain has grown even bolder. Under Mr Modi, the project to convert India into a fully fledged Hindu nation has moved ahead smartly."

The Economist's understanding of India's complexity is not sophisticated. Modi has, in fact, done less to drive the Hindutva agenda than both his detractors and benefactors expected. That Modi hasn't turned out to be quite the Hindutva icon people had hoped shouldn't surprise anyone with, unlike *The Economist,* a passing knowledge of Indian politics. During his tenure of over 12 years as chief minister of Gujarat, Modi ran the Vishva Hindu Parishad (VHP) out of the state, demolished Hindu temples that encroached on public spaces, and sent the VHP's fire-breathing president Praveen Togadia into near-oblivion.

Hinduism has more than 1.2 billion adherents worldwide. The other two major religions—Christianity and Islam—have respectively 2 billion and 1.6 billion followers globally. Uniquely though, the overwhelmingly majority of Hindus live in one country, India. By contrast, Christians and Muslims are widely dispersed across the world. The reason, of course, is the sword and the gun. Christianity proselytised with guns, Islam with swords. And Hinduism? It rarely proselytised. Its monks went to China, Cambodia, Indonesia and further east to share knowledge—not to convert. The great temples of Cambodia and Indonesia are testament to the benign influence of Hinduism. The challenge for India's over 1 billion Hindus now is to embrace modernity, rise above caste that holds so many back, and make Hinduism the all-embracing mother religion it was always conceived to be.

∽

The men and women who wrote our Constitution had a clearer idea of secularism than most political leaders do today. To them, secularism meant equal treatment for all religions, preferential treatment for none. Separate personal religious laws violate this definition of secularism. Dr Babasaheb Ambedkar said as far back as March 1947, when the Constituent Assembly had begun a preliminary drafting of the Constitution, that all citizens should have the right "to claim full and equal benefit of all laws and proceedings for the security of persons and property as is enjoyed by other subjects regardless of any usage or custom based on religion and be subject to like punishment, pains and penalties and to none other."

In short, Ambedkar believed that all personal laws—Hindu, Muslim, Christian, Sikh and others—must be codified under a uniform national law. The argument for 'one nation, one law' dates back to several months before Independence. As the Constituent Assembly began deliberating on this contentious issue, the Fundamental Rights Committee made a strong pitch for superseding archaic personal laws, some based on the Sharia, others on antiquated Hindu practices.

Ambedkar and his colleagues in the drafting committee received immediate opposition from Muslims. Hindus and Parsis were more sanguine. The distinguished Parsi libertarian Minoo Masani, a member of the Fundamental Rights Committee, wrote that it was the State's duty to replace personal religious laws with a universal common code. His colleague on the committee, Kanhaiyalal Munshi, another distinguished lawyer and conservative Hindu leader (who today would be called a Hindutvawadi), was even more robust in advocating uniform personal laws for all religions, including Hinduism. He said: "No civil or criminal court shall, in adjudicating any matter or executing any order, recognise any custom or usage imposing any civil disability on any person on the ground of his caste, status, religion, race or language."

Muslim objections, led by Muhammad Ali Jinnah (a Shia Khoja who drank Scotch, ate pork, and never prayed), were endorsed by Jawaharlal Nehru who bought Jinnah's argument of 'the dangers of a Hindu Raj' if Muslim personal law was interfered with. As a result, Ambedkar, Masani and Munshi's draft on superseding personal religious laws was made voluntary and non-enforceable.

Secularism tasted its first defeat literally days after Independence on 25 August 1947, when the report making universal personal religious laws voluntary was submitted to the Constituent Assembly. Mahboob Ali Baig, a member of the assembly, warned: "This contract is enjoined on the Mussalmans by the Quran, and if it is not followed, a marriage is not legal at all. For 1,350 years this law has been practised by Muslims and recognised by all authorities in all states. If today some other method of proving marriage is going to be introduced, we refuse to abide by it because it is not according to our religion. It is not according to the code laid down for us for all times."

Nehru gave in quickly. Jinnah had undermined Nehru's confidence to such an extent that the prime minister did not heed Sardar Vallabhbhai Patel's advice to stay the course. In the 1950s, parts of Hindu personal law were eventually codified, modernised and gender discrimination removed. But Muslim personal law remains stuck in the medieval Middle East that Mahboob Ali Baig rigidly wanted Muslims to adhere to.

More than 76 years after Independence, the debate on a uniform civil code has reached a decisive moment. The Supreme Court's judgment outlawing instant triple talaq (talaq-e-bidat) is a small step towards reform in Muslim personal law. However, the then Chief Justice J S Khehar made an observation in his dissenting order, days before retiring, placing talaq-e-bidat outside the purview of fundamental rights guaranteed in Part III of the Constitution.

Justice Khehar's minority dissenting judgment argued, "Religion is a matter of faith, and not of logic. It is not open to a court to accept an egalitarian approach over a practice which constitutes an integral part of religion. We cannot accept the petitioners' claim, because the challenge raised is in respect of an issue of 'personal law' which has constitutional protection."

This was triumphantly seized upon by the All India Muslim Personal Law Board (AIMPLB) to vindicate its medieval belief that Sharia supersedes the Indian Constitution on Muslim personal law. Nonetheless, the momentum for UCC is building. The Law Commission has speeded up compiling public opinion on a uniform civil code and submitting its report to the government for legislative action. A parliamentary standing committee has examined the matter. The AIMPLB will contest UCC fiercely. It has always opposed Muslim reform. Only by keeping their flock blind can the one-eyed continue to exercise power over their fiefdom.

TWENTY-FOUR

Behind Kashmir's Veil

VIVEK AGNIHOTRI'S FILM *THE KASHMIR FILES* UNPEELED MANY uncomfortable truths. A generation has grown up since the exodus of Hindus from the Valley began in 1989. Over 4,00,000 Kashmiri Hindus, threatened with violence by Pakistan-backed Islamist terrorists and radicalised local Kashmiri Muslims, left their ancestral homes.

Private satellite television did not exist at the time. Doordarshan ignored the Pandits' plight. More Indians tuned into CNN's coverage of the 1990–91 Gulf War prosecuted by the US-led coalition against Iraq than on the targeted communal violence against Hindus that was taking place in Kashmir. The Kashmir Valley was a favourite location among Indian filmmakers for its scenic beauty. But few filmmakers ventured to make significant movies on the ethnic cleansing of Pandits from the Valley. Instead, they made movies like *Haider* (2014), which gave a free pass to Islamist terrorism in Kashmir.

Bollywood's Khan triumvirate was part of the silence. Aamir Khan, a genuine seeker of the truth (*Satyamev Jayate*) with unlimited financial resources, could not bring himself to make a film on the plight of Kashmiri Pandits. Salman Khan, another actor with impeccable secular credentials who celebrates Diwali, Holi and Ganesh Chaturthi with the same passion he does Eid, shot many times in the Kashmir Valley, but never on the Pandits' ethnic cleansing. The Valley was increasingly under the influence of Wahhabi Islam in the 2000s, with the Hurriyat in charge of recruiting local militants and terrorism flourishing. Shah Rukh Khan, an actor who has reigned over popular Indian cinema for nearly three decades, gave the Kashmiri Pandit genocidal exile story a miss as well. For someone with cerebral aspirations, that was odd.

The rest of India's film industry fell into line. Even as stories of the horrific violence inflicted by Pakistan-backed Islamist terrorists and locals on peaceful, scholarly Pandits emerged in the media and literature, big film production houses turned away. As the wall of silence continued, several lakh exiled Pandits settled in Delhi, Jammu and elsewhere, started life afresh, often with just a trunk load of belongings they had managed to gather before fleeing the violence.

A new breed of television journalists had by now emerged. And yet the true story of the Kashmir exodus remained untold. Instead, the complicity of silence was broken by the complicity of engineered narratives. According to one particularly noxious version, the Pandits had only themselves to blame. They had 'monopolised' plum postings in Kashmir's bureaucracy, academia and the professions. The narrative was as dark as it was disingenuous. It harked back to labelling Jews in Germany in the 1930s. The Pandits, like the Jews, were an educated community. They were given responsibilities commensurate with their abilities. This isn't monopolisation; it's meritocracy.

Political power still lay in the hands of one family: the Abdullahs. That more appropriately fits the description of monopolisation of power. The Abdullahs' monopoly would be broken only several years later by the Muftis, creating a feudal duopoly in the Valley.

I travelled to Srinagar when Mufti Mohammad Sayeed was chief minister. Pakistan-sponsored terrorism had peaked. The Hurriyat separatists were spreading toxicity and violence across the Valley. During my interview with the chief minister, the

Mufti said his government was doing its best to bring a sense of normalcy back to the Valley. He died before he could. The biggest mistake the BJP made was forming an alliance government with Mufti's Peoples Democratic Party (PDP). The error still rankles. The Modi government has tried, but failed, to rehabilitate the vast numbers of exiled Kashmiri Pandits. Most have moved on and resettled in Jammu, Delhi and elsewhere.

Pakistan's malignant strategy has always been to make Kashmir a majoritarian Islamist state. It has achieved that demographically. But after the revocation of Article 370 and the conclusion of delimitation, the strategy has unravelled.

The Kashmir Files lifted the 30-year veil over the shame of the Valley. Pakistan's Islamist terrorists and radicalised Kashmiri Muslims threatened an entire community of peaceful Pandits for decades, driving them out of their homes into exile. Those who continue to propagate a fraudulent narrative of a community's ethnic cleansing are complicit in this evil. They decry Hindu majoritarianism in the rest of India but embrace Muslim majoritarianism in Kashmir. That is a betrayal of secularism.

Ensconced in Kailash Mansarovar, Rahul Gandhi continued to calibrate his own version of secularism. He tweeted in September 2018: "Shiva is the Universe." The tweet drove home two messages: One, that Rahul's discovery of his Hindu Brahmin roots was on track; and two, that if remote Kailash Mansarovar had Internet connectivity to enable tweeting, Modi's digital initiatives had borne fruit. The Kailash Mansarovar pilgrimage was part of the Congress' strategy to position Rahul as a liberal but devout Hindu who eschews hard Hindutva, but is willing to cohabit with its softer version.

Soft Hindutva is hard to define. Like Hinduism itself, it is elastic and can be moulded into any shape you want. One shape, pre-election, another post-election, and yet another when overseas. That is why soft Hindutva is Rahul's ideology of choice. It can be bent and shaped to appeal to a broad swathe of India's 80 per cent Hindu electorate. Muslims understand the electoral compulsions of Rahul's soft Hindutva. Christians too are sanguine. They've experienced the Congress' pro-Christian tilt over the years. They shrug away Rahul's dalliance with soft Hindutva. Sonia Gandhi, a staunch Catholic, remains a source of comfort. For the Congress, therefore, Rahul's soft Hindutva strategy is risk-free.

But is it? Not necessarily. Minority votes are fungible. Muslim women in particular may migrate to either the BJP over its strong stand on triple talaq or to parties like AIMIM or TMC or simply opt for NOTA.

In a Lok Sabha poll, four issues decide the outcome: caste, religion, jobs and development. By stressing his Brahmin caste credentials, Rahul could be skating on thin ice. The Brahmin vote pan-India is around 5 per cent. It can tip the balance in only a few constituencies. The Congress' public declaration that the party has "a Brahmin DNA" could prove counter-productive. OBCs and SC/STs may well move further away from the Congress. In Uttar Pradesh and Bihar, where caste plays a big electoral role, antagonising OBC, EBC and SC/ST voters could upset the Congress' mahagathbandhan partners. It also opens the door for Modi to replay his OBC card in rural India where the 2024 Lok Sabha election will be decided.

Despite being beset by corruption charges, West Bengal Chief Minister Mamata Banerjee remains one of the BJP's principal threats in the 2024 Lok Sabha election. Can she stitch together a fractious Opposition with conflicting agendas? Banerjee is realistic. Her objective is to reduce the BJP's numbers and then inveigle allies. The Janata Dal's HD Deve Gowda became prime minister in 1996 despite his party winning just 46 seats in the Lok Sabha election. He allied with 119 Left-leaning parties while the Congress' 140 MPs supported the United Front (UF) government from outside. Banerjee is following the same asset-light model.

Here's how the asset-light model works: the TMC wins 35-odd seats in 2024 out of West Bengal's 42 Lok Sabha seats compared to the 22 it won in 2019. It knows that it will pick up allies but very few seats in other states. In contrast, the Congress, despite its leadership problems and general ennui, is likely to end up as the second-largest party after the BJP in 2024. It hopes to emulate its 2019 performance when it won 15 seats in Kerala and 8 seats in Tamil Nadu in a seat-sharing pact with the DMK. It is also likely to do relatively better in 2024 in Karnataka (where it was wiped out in the 2019 Lok Sabha poll).

The TMC and Congress ironically face the same problem in bigger states: strong regional parties that will not give either Banerjee or Gandhi too many seats to contest. This applies to Maharashtra, Telangana, Andhra Pradesh, and Tamil Nadu. The Congress is in direct fights with the BJP in several states like Rajasthan, Madhya Pradesh, Chhattisgarh, Uttarakhand, Himachal Pradesh and elsewhere. The TMC is not a serious contender in any of these states. That dilutes its chances of picking up enough seats to emerge as the second-largest national party after the BJP.

In the 2014 Lok Sabha poll, the TMC recorded a national vote share of 3.8 per cent compared to the Congress' 19.3 per cent. In the 2019 Lok Sabha election, TMC increased its national vote share only fractionally to 4.1 per cent. Congress' vote share rose to 19.5 per cent. In 2024, both could rise – but again marginally.

Former West Bengal chief minister Jyoti Basu was a consensus choice as prime minister in the 1996 United Front government before the Left's politburo vetoed the proposal. Banerjee, then a young Congress politician, had followed that development closely. The playbook could come in handy in 2024 during coalition negotiations. Counterintuitively, Banerjee's "Jyoti Basu strategy" will gain traction if the Congress performs strongly in states where it is in direct contests with the BJP. That will cut the BJP's tally and increase the Congress-led UPA's seats. Then, like

Deve Gowda did, Banerjee will strike a deal with the Congress-led UPA and regional satraps to support a TMC-led alliance in a bid to win power at the Centre.

What are the chances of this happening? Much depends on the Congress' final tally and Rahul Gandhi's troubled chemistry with Banerjee. The two have never got along. Banerjee and Gandhi have the same target audience: Muslims. Without minority votes, Banerjee would not be chief minister of West Bengal and Gandhi would not be an MP from Wayanad. A "secular" alliance between the TMC, a Congress-led UPA and regional parties against the "communal" BJP is a theoretical possibility. In practice, it may fall apart before it even comes together.

✍

The advent of British rule in the 1750s gave rise to modern communalism. After a century of military warfare, the British had conquered various bits of India: from Bengal, Madras and Bombay to Sindh, Punjab and the Northeast. Following the First War of Independence in 1857 (wrongly termed Sepoy Mutiny by British historians), Indian sovereignty passed in 1858 from the East India Company to the British Crown.

One of the first things the British government did as sovereign ruler of India was to plant the poisonous seed of communalism. That seed has germinated over the last two centuries and grown into a forest teeming with mistrust between Hindus and Muslims, leading to Partition, rioting and suffering. How did the British set about their task? The army was the first target. Indians were strictly divided into regiments of Sikhs, Gurkhas, Pathans, Rajputs and Marathas. Meanwhile, the British 'government' in India removed all import duties on British-made cotton, destroying the industry in the subcontinent.

In January 1857, a Brahmin sepoy from a British regiment stationed in Dum Dum, five miles north of Calcutta, the capital of Britain's Indian empire, ran into a khalasi, a low-caste sepoy.

The khalasi asked the Brahmin for a drink of water from his lota. The Brahmin refused, saying: "I have scoured my lota, you will defile it with your touch."

Deeply affronted, the low-caste sepoy replied with some vengeful delight: "You think much of your caste, but wait a little, the sahib-log (Englishmen) will make you bite cartridges soaked in cow and pork fat and then where will your caste be?"

The Brahmin sepoy, reduced to smouldering silence, quickly carried the news to his comrades in the 34th NI British regiment. The rumour spread like wildfire. Both high-caste Hindus and Muslims were aghast. To touch by one's teeth the fat of the cow and the pig violated the most deeply held religious beliefs of the two communities. For Brahmins, the cow is sacred and biting gum cartridges greased with the lard of a cow or ox would be sacrilegious. It would also almost instantly cause them to be ostracised. The seeds of rebellion were sown.

Between January and May 1857, anger swelled. Brahmin sepoys began the revolt slowly. Those attached to the 34th NI stationed in Barrackpore refused on 26 February 1857 to receive their percussion caps for the rifle parade the next morning as they suspected that the cartridges were greased with cow and pork fat. Gradually, the revolt spread. At the 34th NI, where it had all started, the feelings were particularly intense. A sepoy named Mangal Pandey was the leader of the revolt. He called upon his fellow-soldiers to "join him to defend and die for their religion and caste".

Pandey of course was tried and executed. The 34th NI was disbanded. The British thought they had contained the revolt. They were wrong. The incidents of Barrackpore were repeated at Ambala towards the end of March 1857 and at Lakhanau (Lucknow) in May 1857 before the revolution was put down by a display of vengeful British brutality.

Nearly 170 years later, religion remains a potent weapon in the hands of the powerful to divide communities. The Protestant

British used religion with both finesse and force during their occupation of India. They ensured that divisions between religious groups deepened. It was an essential tool in the colonial strategy to stay in power in densely populated but divided India with its three tiers: villages, princely states and urban centres. Even sport was not spared. The British promoted the Pentangular cricket tournament, setting religious groups against one another—Hindus, Muslims, Parsis and Europeans—dismissing Mahatma Gandhi's objections at this attempt to create religion-based schisms in Indian society.

∽

After Independence, the communal virus that had infected society during colonial rule spread steadily. Most Indian Muslims continue to live in abject poverty. They remain under-represented in the IAS, in business, in startups, and in the professions: law, medicine, accountancy, management and engineering. Politicians give them sermons on secularism, not jobs.

To bring themselves into the mainstream, Muslims must regard themselves as Indians first. American Jews are an example. They are fiercely proud of their religion but they do not let their Jewishness supersede their Americanism. Muslims must not allow politicians to set a communal agenda, however secular its grammar. Some of the worst offenders are educated, influential "celebrity" Muslims who are complicit in keeping their vulnerable brethren in darkness.

As long as the Congress held a monopoly over political power, secularism was not part of the national narrative. Only after Jayaprakash Narayan's "total revolution" movement in 1974 did then Prime Minister Indira Gandhi search for a tool that could be a potent electoral asset. She found it in identity politics—identity based on faith. Rattled by JP's movement and aware that the *garibi hatao* slogan had delivered victory in March 1971 to the splintered Congress led by her, Gandhi chose socialism and secularism as the two pivots on which to consolidate political power. Recognising that minorities were an important vote catchment area, she used the Emergency in 1976 to rewrite the Preamble to the Constitution, adding the words "socialist" and "secular".

In themselves, the additions were harmless. They still are—except that they draw attention to two facts: one, that India is no longer the socialist nation it was under Indira Gandhi; and two; that India has always been steadfastly secular because, despite majoritarian impulses, the Hindu majority is by nature secular. That though has come under threat by deepening electoral polarisation as part of the BJP's Hindu-first nationalism and the Opposition's Muslim-first secularism.

Where does the liberal, secular Hindu figure in all this? Despite Modi's assertive Hindu religiosity, most Indians are secular in the truest sense of the word: religion to them is a private matter. It has no place in politics. But they are also swayed by the plight of fellow Indians who happen to be Muslims: impoverished, ghettoised and discriminated against. For every Azim Premji and Aamir Khan, there are millions of weavers in UP and spot boys in Mumbai who have no place in India's organised labour force.

Well-meaning, liberal Hindus ask: why? And the answer they come up with is: communalism. Yet the liberal Hindu doesn't dig deeper. The more politicians sequester Muslims into vote silos, the more the middle-class Hindu resents them. Discrimination, petty or large, mounts. Influential sections of the news media are part of this fraud played on India's Muslims: communalism with an engaging secular mask. The token Muslim is lionized—from business to literature—but the average Muslim languishes in his 76-year-old ghetto. It is from such ghettos that raw recruits to terrorist groups are most easily lured.

Islamist terrorism cannot be defeated by waging war on it. Radical Islam has to be defeated ideologically, its narrative reshaped. Obviously, the vast majority of the world's 1.6 billion

Muslims are peace loving. But it is within these moderate Muslims that the problem lies. Moderate Muslims do not accept that some of the edicts in the Quran preach violence. These edicts belong to the 7th century, not the 21st.

As Ali A Rizvi described it in an "Open Letter To Moderate Muslims" in the *Huffington Post*[44], there are many passages in the Quran and even Abrahamic texts of the Jews that should not be taken literally. The Jews have understood this; moderate Muslims have not. In his scathing open letter, Ali says Islam needs "reformers", not mere moderates.

The Open Letter goes on thus:

Finding consensus on ideology is impossible. The sectarian violence that continues to plague the Muslim world, and has killed more Muslims than any foreign army, is blatant evidence for this. But coming together on a sense of community is what moves any society forward. Look at other Abrahamic religions that underwent reformations. You know well that Judaism and Christianity had their own violence-ridden dark ages; you mention it every chance you get nowadays, and you're right. But how did they get past that?

Well, as much as the Pope opposes birth control, abortion and premarital sex, most Catholics today are openly pro-choice, practice birth control, and fornicate to their hearts' content. Most Jews are secular, and many even identify as atheists or agnostics while retaining the Jewish label. The dissidents and the heretics in these communities may get some flak here and there, but they aren't getting killed for dissenting.

This is in stark contrast to the Muslim world where, according to a worldwide 2013 Pew Research Study, a majority of people in large Muslim-majority countries believe that those who leave the faith must die. They constantly obsess

[44] 6 October 2014.

over who is a 'real' Muslim and who is not. They are quicker to defend their faith from cartoonists and filmmakers than they are to condemn those committing atrocities in its name.

Islam needs reformers, not moderates...The purpose of reform is to change things, fix the system, and move it in a new direction. And to fix something, you have to acknowledge that it's broken—not that it looks broken, or is being falsely portrayed as broken by the wrong people—but that it's broken.

That is your first step to reformation.

If this sounds too radical, think back to the Prophet Muhammad himself, who was chased out of Mecca for being a radical dissident fighting the Quraysh. Think of why Jesus Christ was crucified. These men didn't capitulate or shy away from challenging even the most sacred foundations of the status quo. These men certainly weren't 'moderates'. They were radicals. Rebels. Reformers. That's how change happens. All revolutions start out as rebellions. Islam itself started this way. Openly challenging problematic ideas isn't bigotry, and it isn't blasphemy. If anything, it's Sunnah.

Progressive Muslim voices echo those views. In an article[45] in *Foreign Policy* magazine, the activist Ayaan Hirsi Ali wrote why the Quran is interpreted so misleadingly by Muslim scholars and clerics: "To understand whether violence is inherent in the doctrine of Islam, it is important to look at the example of the founding father of Islam, Mohammed, and the passages in the Quran and Islamic jurisprudence used to justify the violence we currently see in so many parts of the Muslim world. In Mecca, Mohammed preached to his fellow tribesmen to abandon their gods and accept his. He preached about charity and the conditions of widows and orphans. (This method of proselytising or persuasion, called "dawa" in Arabic, remains an important

---

[45] 9 November 2015.

component of Islam to this day.) However, during his time in Mecca, Mohammed and his small band of believers had little success in converting others to this new religion. So, a decade after Mohammed first began preaching, he fled to Medina. Over time he cobbled together a militia and began to wage wars.

"Anyone seeking support for armed jihad in the name of Allah will find ample support in the passages in the Quran and Hadith that relate to Mohammed's Medina period.

"For example, Q4:95 states, 'Allah hath granted a grade higher to those who strive and fight with their goods and persons than to those who sit (at home).' Q8:60 advises Muslims 'to strike terror into (the hearts of) the enemies, of Allah and your enemies, and others besides, whom ye may not know, but whom Allah doth know.' Finally, Q9:29 instructs Muslims: 'Fight those who believe not in Allah nor the Last Day, nor hold that forbidden which hath been forbidden by Allah and His Messenger, nor acknowledge the religion of Truth (even if they are) of the People of the Book, until they pay the *Jizya* with willing submission, and feel themselves subdued.'

"Mainstream Islamic jurisprudence continues to maintain that the so-called 'sword verses' (9:5 and 9:29) have 'abrogated, cancelled, and replaced' those verses in the Quran that call for 'tolerance, compassion, and peace.' As for the example of Mohammed, Sahih Muslim, one of the six major authoritative Hadith collections, claims the Prophet Mohammed undertook no fewer than 19 military expeditions, personally fighting in eight of them. In the aftermath of the 627 Battle of the Trench, 'Mohammed felt free to deal harshly with the Banu Qurayza, executing their men and selling their women and children into slavery,' according to Yale Professor of Religious Studies Gerhard Bowering in his book *Islamic Political Thought*. As the Princeton scholar Michael Cook observed in his book, *Ancient Religions, Modern Politics*, 'the historical salience of warfare against unbelievers...was thus written into the foundational texts' of Islam.

"There lies the duality within Islam. It's possible to claim, following Mohammed's example in Mecca, that Islam is a religion of peace. But it's also possible to claim, as the Islamic State does, that a revelation was sent to Mohammed commanding Muslims to wage jihad until every human being on the planet accepts Islam or a state of subservience, on the basis of his legacy in Medina. The key question is not whether Islam is a religion of peace, but rather, whether Muslims follow the Mohammed of Medina, regardless of whether they are Sunni or Shiite."

TWENTY-FIVE

Come One, Come All

HINDUISM IS NOT A CODIFIED FAITH. LIKE A SPONGE, IT ABSORBS other faiths even when they come as conquerors, as Islam's armies did. The powerful Mughal Empire was so integrated into India's secular ethos that in the 17th century it cut its umbilical cord with the Ottoman Caliphate to which every other Islamic sultanate paid tribute. The British took India's innate secularism by the scruff of its neck and carved deep cleavages between Hindus and Muslims.

After Partition, Prime Minister Jawaharlal Nehru recognised that the knife the British had driven through Indian secularism, wounding it deeply, could only be healed by leaning the other way: giving Muslims who had chosen to stay on in India the confidence that they would be treated fairly. The intent was noble. In practice, it began India's journey down the slippery slope of faux secularism.

When you lean towards one faith, however pure your intent, you will lean away from another. For the next 50 years India practised secularism in name. A self-serving ecosystem soon sprung up. It had three principal actors: secular politicians, community leaders and liberal civil society. Politicians used secularism as a political weapon. Muslims were an attractive demographic: they lived in clusters and voted in clusters. Politicians exploited them systemically. They voted overwhelmingly for the Congress nationally. In the states, they voted for the Samajwadi Party,

Rashtriya Janata Dal, Nationalist Congress Party, Trinamool Congress and All India Majlis-E-Ittehadul Muslimeen.

The second element in the secular ecosystem was community leadership. It suited religious leaders to keep their flock in constant paranoia and under close watch. There was no attempt to empower or educate. The third element in the ecosystem – liberal Hindu civil society – gave enthusiastic support to the secular project. Activists, lawyers, journalists and academics did not realise that they were playing with political hypocrisy till it was too late.

An abiding weakness of Hinduism is internal fissures. Of India's 1.10 billion Hindus, a quarter are Dalits. For centuries they have been targets of a Brahmanical hierarchy. Together with a narrow slice of educated, liberal Hindus, Dalits form a third of the Hindu vote. That leaves the broad middle of the Hindu pyramid vulnerable to ministrations from an alternative political force. That force emerged in the shape of the BJP. It wove its way into the Indian mainstream in the 1990s and has since captured the expanding middle of the Hindu demographic pyramid.

The big electoral swing away from the Congress since 2014 has come from moderate Hindus disillusioned with the diet of compromised secularism they have been fed for decades. The biggest casualities in the secular project are Muslims, many intensely patriotic but now suspect in the eyes of even moderate Hindus. Instead of integrating Muslims into the mainstream of Indian life, the corrosive secular ecosystem has created a community that both the Sachar Committee and Misra Commission identified as economically more backward than Dalits.

India's 210 million Muslims could be an economic asset. They could also be a security asset. The vast majority of Indian Muslims have rejected the lure of Islamist terrorist groups. But fear and resentment built up over decades have kept Muslims from realising their full potential as Indian citizens. India needs a secular revolution that downsizes public displays of religiosity. The BJP was quick to exploit public anger against a false secular narrative. That allowed it to engage in an exaggerated and quite unnecessary exhibition of religiosity during, for example, events like the ground-breaking ceremony for the construction of the Ram Mandir in Ayodhya. A dishonest version of secularism has helped normalise exhibitions of Hindu and Muslim religiosity across faiths that in a truly secular country would be impermissible.

Why does the Modi government in the run-up to 2024 seem more vulnerable than it is? To be effective, power has to be projected. The Congress has plenty of experience in doing this. The BJP has relatively little. For the first time in 500 years, India is being governed by Bharat rather than by India. Bharat isn't used to exercising power. For centuries it has obeyed while others ruled. The Mughals were feudal. The British were feudal. The Congress is feudal.

The Mughals ruled India through an elaborate system of elite Indian durbaris. The British upgraded the system, making educated Indians their subaltern administrators and peasants their loyal sepoys. The structure, though, remained much the same as in the time of the Mughals: the narrow top of the pyramid comprised the British elite and its Indian retainers who commanded a broad base of the deprived, the poor and the dispossessed. India's 600-plus kingdoms were a part of this pyramid, their maharajas and nawabs independent only in name and loyal to the British who provided military protection in return for the kingdoms' tax revenue.

The Congress after Independence borrowed Britain's clothes. It did not change several colonial-era laws that had been designed to keep Indians under British subjugation. It did not reform the ICS. It did not democratise the party. Instead, it feudalised it further under one family.

Congressmen believed, as the British and Mughals had believed before them, that they were born to rule. The advent of new political combinations challenged this zamindari attitude in the 1970s. The first experiment under Morarji Desai's Janata government in 1977–79, following revocation of Indira Gandhi's Emergency, failed. The six Vajpayee years two decades later were relatively anodyne. Vajpayee was cut in a Nehruvian mould and loath to upset the old order.

The Congress, used to winning, not losing, elections, wasn't happy with the arrival of Modi in 2014. *Chaiwala, neech* and other epithets were showered on Modi to show their contempt for this usurper, the interloper who had dared to challenge their power. India was accustomed to being ruled by people who spoke good English, had nice table manners, and arrogated to themselves the permanent right to govern.

Discrediting Modi and eroding his credibility were put into operation as soon as the shock of the 2014 Congress defeat had faded. Modi meanwhile fell into a trap of his own making. He did not at first promote technocratic talent into his cabinet. External Affairs Minister S. Jaishankar and IT Minister Ashwini Vaishnaw remain exceptions in Modi's second term, though both are former bureaucrats. Modi has generally relied on IAS and IFS officers to implement his extensive welfare and infrastructure agenda.

In 2014, the question was: will Modi change the system or will the system change Modi? The prime minister did not answer that question in 2019. He will need to provide an answer before the 2024 General Election.

In an interview with *The Economic Times* in September 2019 Modi showed that he was aware of the problem. This is what he said: "Budgets are neither the beginning nor the end of our work in economic policy. My team and I are thinking about these issues all the time and acting on them. Ideas such as asset monetisation, asset recycling and a continued focus on strategic disinvestment

are aimed at raising funds for public capital expenditure. These
measures will boost growth and crowd-in private investment
soon. The issue is not merely about lowering of policy rates
by the monetary policy committee, but also about the cost of
availability of credit. We are working closely with the Reserve
Bank and the banking system to remove blockages in the flow
of credit, especially to small and medium enterprises. We are
also looking to remove all delays in government payments and
tax refunds so that cash flow in the economy revives."

✂

Amartya Sen, the former Master of Trinity College, Cambridge
University, makes no secret of his distaste for Modi's economic
and political governance. Sen (who lost his job as Chancellor of
Nalanda University in 2016 under controversial circumstances) says
dissent has been stifled, autonomy of universities compromised,
and institutions of governance subverted.

   Some of this is true. But Sen misses the bigger picture.
Universities in India have long been subjected to governmental
interference. The New Education Policy is the Modi government's
instrument to reform Indian education. When the Congress-led UPA
government was in office between 2004 and 2014, it passed the
Right to Education (RTE) legislation that did not help modernise
the Indian educational system. Its implementation was severely
criticised by educationists.

   It is important to criticise the Modi government. But one-
sided criticism traduces the critic, not the target of the criticism.
Dissent lies at the heart of democracy. Sen says little that is
original. But he erred when he called the Modi government a
"minority government". This is what Sen said: "Anti-national is
a peculiar term to come from a minority government. It shows
that there is a level of arrogance there. A 31 per cent vote share
(in 2014) certainly does not allow you to label the remaining
69 per cent to be anti-national."

Sen's comment is a misstatement of facts. Every government in India since Independence has been, by Sen's peculiar definition, a "minority government". Even in India's first general election in 1952, the near-monopolistic Congress led by Jawaharlal Nehru won a "minority" 45 per cent national vote share. In 1957 it won 47.7 per cent vote share. In the 1962 Lok Sabha elections, the Nehru-led Congress won 44.7 per cent vote share.

In her "landslide" 1971 Lok Sabha win, Indira Gandhi captured 43.6 per cent national vote share. As Indian politics became more fractured in the 1990s, vote shares declined. Narasimha Rao won 35.9 per cent in 1991. Manmohan Singh scraped home with 26.5 per cent national vote share in 2004 and 28.5 per cent in 2009. None of these governments would be branded "minority governments" by Sen. Selectivity does him no credit.

The NDA's vote share in the 2014 Lok Sabha election was nearly 40 per cent. In the 2019 Lok Sabha poll its vote share rose to 45 per cent, close to the scale of Nehru's victories (when the Congress had little or no national opposition). The NDA's 2019 vote share was higher than Indira Gandhi's in the 1971 general election which Sen would be mortified to describe as having led to the formation of a "minority Congress government".

Sen went on to tell *The Economic Times*[46]: "But I am also worried that people are feeling less free and less confident to express their points of view. That decline has been quite prominent in India."

That too flies in the face of facts. Ever since the Modi government took office, college campuses, TV panelists, newspaper op-eds, online news sites and opposition leaders have engaged in more dissent against this government and more criticism of its actions (as indeed in democracies they should) than the silent Manmohan Singh and stentorian Sonia Gandhi had to endure.

∽

---

[46]26 February 2017.

Modi has allowed the media to set the agenda without an effective information mechanism to counter it. And he has allowed elements in the Sangh Parivar to live up to the cardboard caricatures they are painted up as: illiberal, wild-eyed fanatics. In the end, if the old entitled elite has not yet been dismantled, the blame travels all the way to the top to Modi.

The BJP's inaction over violence targeting the party's workers in West Bengal and Kerala has alienated its core base. But for the lack of a strong united Opposition, the Modi government would have been staring at a difficult Lok Sabha election in 2024. The government's lack of "intellectual infrastructure" has made the task of the Opposition easier. In no other major democracy does a coalition of the defeated control the narrative as it does in India. And in no other major democracy does the government counter this narrative with such ineptitude. Modi has said his government must be open to criticism and learn from it. It is time to not only learn those lessons but to put them into practice. The perception battle, once lost, is rarely won back. The Opposition knows this. Hence the increasing intensity of its attacks as 2024 approaches.

Winning the 2024 Lok Sabha election will hinge on how quickly the prime minster recaptures the national narrative from those who distort it. Modi has cultivated a larger-than-life persona that places him above the fray. If things go wrong with the economy, Modi is given the benefit of the doubt by the average voter. This works well for Modi – for the moment. And the moment could last right up to 2024 when construction of the Ram Mandir in Ayodhya is expected to be completed. Unless there is a dramatic development that upends Modi's carefully choreographed Ayodhya moment, the BJP could well sweep the 2024 Lok Sabha election for an unprecedented third successive five-year term. Or might it not?

Rewind to Indira Gandhi. In 1972, shortly after the Bangladesh war, she appeared invincible. A cult developed around her. The

Congress had a 352-seat majority in the Lok Sabha. Mrs Gandhi's cabinet was filled with talented ministers but also many time-servers. Sycophancy was rampant. Congress president D K Barooah infamously declared, "India is Indira and Indira is India". Mrs Gandhi didn't bother to demur. She possibly believed him.

The similarity with Modi is uncanny. In his second term as prime minister, Modi has been deified. No newspaper op-ed, tweet or TV interview begins or ends without a minister referring to the "inspiring leadership of Modi ji".

Bad news awaited Indira Gandhi in her second term as prime minister. Jayaprakash Narayan launched a civil disobedience movement in 1974 against Mrs Gandhi's growing autocracy. A year later, Mrs Gandhi would make a fatal mistake. On 12 June 1975 the Allahabad High Court invalidated Mrs Gandhi's 1971 election victory from Rae Bareli. It debarred her from contesting elections for six years over a fairly minor electoral malpractice of using government machinery in the 1971 Lok Sabha poll against Raj Narain. Reacting imperiously, Mrs Gandhi imposed the Emergency 14 days later. When it was revoked in March 1977, the Congress was thrown out of power and Mrs Gandhi, after 11 years as prime minister – nine of them legitimately – barely escaped imprisonment.

The Congress is in decline today because it is no longer a cadre-based political party but a private family business. The Gandhis are the only shareholders. The others serve at their pleasure. Even thoughtful Congress leaders dare not defy the Gandhis. The BJP is dangerously close to emulating the Congress. Modi should receive honest advice, however unpalatable it is. By 1975, in her tenth year as prime minister, Indira Gandhi was receiving feedback from Siddhartha Shankar Ray, the former chief minister of West Bengal and Union cabinet minister, that was both inaccurate and self-serving. As his second five-year term draws to a close, Modi needs ministers who aren't afraid to disagree with him.

If Modi avoids the mistakes Indira Gandhi made deep into her second term, and focuses on bringing more independent-minded talent into his cabinet, victory in the 2024 Lok Sabha election is likely. That would make him the longest-serving prime minister since Jawaharlal Nehru and Indira Gandhi. But the culture of sycophancy within the BJP must end or history may be tempted to repeat itself.

∽

When he took office as prime minister in May 2014, Modi prostrated himself at the steps leading up to Parliament. Modi was in effect saying: I'm new to Delhi; I know the elite still think of me as a mere *chaiwala*; but with the Lok Sabha election over, we need to put aside our differences and cooperate with each other to create a new India.

The reaction was swift and dismissive. The old political elite, smarting from defeat in the 2014 Lok Sabha election, sneered at Modi's rustic ways. Modi 1.0 was still burdened with self-doubt. The old elite treated him with withering contempt. By 2018, it was clear that Modi had not changed Lutyens' Delhi even though his ministers now occupied large swathes of it. But Lutyens' Delhi was never about real estate as about a bent of mind.

Modi 2.0 emerged as a changed leader after winning a landslide in the May 2019 Lok Sabha election. Major Bills were tabled and passed in Parliament: the Jammu and Kashmir Reorganisation Act, 2019; the Citizenship (Amendment) Act, 2019; and the Muslim Women (Protection of Rights on Marriage) Act, 2019, criminalising triple *talaq*.

Modi 3.0's key task is the economy. Modi's instinct is to rely on bureaucrats in a PMO-centric government. Modi 1.0 and 2.0 focused on welfare and delivery: financial inclusion, health insurance, electricity, gas, water, roads, toilets, food, houses and digitisation. The production-linked incentive (PLI) scheme is possibly the government's most innovative economic initiative. It has the potential to transform India into an export manufacturing hub even as China's labour costs rise and draconian new rules drive foreign companies to diversify their production bases and supply chains out of China. The Unified Payments Interface (UPI) and Open Network for Digital Commerce (ONDC), both world-class digital services, are gaining global traction. The PM Gati Shakti Master Plan on infrastructure is transformative.

Members of the old Congress-led elite had humble origins. They climbed up the social, economic and political ladder till most had obliterated all evidence whence they had emerged. Sonia Gandhi, who lives in a taxpayer-owned Lutyens' bungalow valued at over ₹600 crore, was sent to England to study English 60 years ago, aged 16, by a family whose humble background mirrored Modi's own. I wrote in 2015, at the end of Modi's first year as prime minister: "Lutyens' Delhi is an idiom. Modi has tried to change that idiom of corrupt power brokers, complicit media and the beady-eyed politicians who preside over this toxic consensus. He hasn't succeeded—yet."

LIBERALISM

TWENTY-SIX

True-Blue Liberals

WHEN I WAS TEN YEARS OLD, RAJMOHAN GANDHI, THE MAHATMA'S grandson, visited our school. The Cathedral and John Connon School in Mumbai was unusual in that it wasn't a Catholic, Jesuit-run convent institution. Rather it was Anglo-Scottish with a Protestant ethic. The school has always had a diverse mix of students—from Salman Rushdie and Ratan Tata to those from humbler backgrounds. Hindus, Jews, Parsis, Bohras, Christians and Khojas formed a plural student body.

Rajmohan Gandhi had begun a movement called Moral Re-Armament (MRA). One of its programmes was *India Arise*. All us ten-year-olds were asked to be a part of it. Throughout the decade I spent in Cathedral, before being packed off at 16 to West Buckland School in Devon, England, not once did we encounter proselytisation. Religion was taboo. The fact that we were at a Protestant Christian school with a British headmaster (Reverend George Ridding) never once struck us. Cricket, tennis and our rock band, "The Bandits", where I played rhythm guitar, occupied most of our time apart from the occasional cramming before term exams.

Decades later, not much has changed at Cathedral School. After ex-Cathedralite Salman Rushdie won his first Booker Prize for *Midnight's Children*, he came to India at the invitation of my media company, Sterling Newspapers Pvt Ltd, to deliver two lectures on *Politics and the Novel*. The first talk, held to a packed ballroom at the Taj President in Mumbai, went off well. We then flew together to Delhi for Rushdie's second talk. The late Khushwant Singh presided over the event. Again, a large crowd attended.

As I wrote in a column later, "On the way to Delhi, Rushdie was immersed in a first proof copy of a book. Sitting next to him on the aisle seat (he had the window), I asked him whose book it was. 'Oh, it's the proof copy of Milan Kundera's *The Unbearable Lightness of Being*. Will be out soon'."

Rushdie has evolved over the years. Now 76, he revels in being an ageing but wise rebel. The vicious knife attack on him in 2022 at a literary event near New York City, though, left him severely injured. It showed that the threat to Rushdie's life due to his book *The Satanic Verses* remains ever-present.

Months before the knife attack, during a seminar in November 2021 at the Center for Contemporary South Asia at Brown University on *Politics, Religion and Culture: India and Pakistan*, Rushdie spoke of his childhood in Bombay (as it then was) and his current life and work in New York. Answering a question from Ashutosh Varshney, professor of International Studies at Brown University, on his book *Shame*, Rushdie said: "I should confess to a piece of family shame. I had an uncle by marriage who was the founder and the first head of the notorious ISI. My uncle was the basis for the character of General Zulfikar in *Midnight's Children*. Pakistan has played a dangerous game by giving safe haven to the Taliban. Everything in Pakistan is determined by its obsession with India. But Pakistan is what the Taliban would really like to capture. Afghanistan has colossal problems. Pakistan, a bigger country, is worth more to the Taliban."

That is the key insight from Rushdie: he believes the real target of the Taliban is Pakistan. Instead of Pakistan using its Taliban progeny to take over Afghanistan, the prize for the Taliban is the eventual ideological capture of Pakistan through Talibanisation.

Rushdie was on weaker ground when he answered a loaded question put to him by Varshney: "Is India going the Pakistani way?"

Rushdie knew it was a trick question but fell into the trap nonetheless. He tried initially to shrug away the "India is Hindu Pakistan" narrative popularised by Congress leaders like Shashi Tharoor. Said Rushdie dismissively: "[India] ain't quite there yet." But then he gave Varshney the answer he wanted: "The fact that Mr Narendra Modi has managed to sell to a lot of Indians the idea of Hindu majoritarian rule, which is anti-democratic, is truly tragic."

Out of touch with India, Rushdie can be forgiven for falling into Varshney's carefully laid trap. Those who mould the "India is Hindu Pakistan" narrative are responsible for selling a myth. If India was intrinsically communal, it would not have welcomed the early Jews, Parsis and Christians who came to the country seeking refuge and a new life. They lived in peace with local Hindu communities through the centuries. Hindu majoritarianism is a political narrative. The BJP uses it to polarise Hindu voters just as the Congress, Samajwadi Party and others use Muslim minoritism to polarise Muslim voters.

During the few days we hosted Rushdie in Mumbai and Delhi, it was clear he was an atheist. He wrote *The Satanic Verses* as a non-believer. In today's Pakistan, with its cruel blasphemy law, he would have met a fate worse than Ayatollah Khomeini's *fatwa* (decree). In India, *The Satanic Verses* agitated Muslims, forcing Prime Minister Rajiv Gandhi to ban it in 1988. But the protests died down and when Rushdie last visited India in 2013, he was made to feel welcome—except in Kolkata.

This is what Rushdie said at the time about Chief Minister Mamata Banerjee's ban on his visit to Kolkata: "The day before I was to travel to Kolkata, we were informed that the Kolkata Police would refuse to allow me to enter the city. If I flew there, I was told, I would be put on the next plane back. I was also told that this was at the request of the chief minister. I remember that after the Jaipur Literary Festival, Mamata Banerjee had said she would not allow me to enter Kolkata. She has made good that threat."

∽

Is liberalism then a lost quality in Indian politics and society? The core values of liberalism hardly need to be restated: plurality, openness, dissent, individual liberties, balance and fairness. The term "liberal right" is rarely used. The widely held belief is that liberalism is the preserve of the left. It obviously isn't. The liberal right welcomes foreign direct investment (FDI). In contrast, the liberal left has dog-eared ideas on economic reforms. It opposes FDI, privatisation and agricultural reforms. How then to construct a liberal right manifesto which is open, meritocratic, inclusive and tolerant?

The Economist marked its 175th anniversary in 2018 with an eight-page essay[47] spelling out a "manifesto for renewing liberalism for the 21st century". *The Economist* began publishing in 1843 as a small pamphlet. In an approximately 10,000-word essay in 2018, the magazine declared: "We were created 175 years ago to campaign for liberalism—not the leftish 'progressivism' of American university campuses or the rightish 'ultraliberalism' conjured up by the French commentariat, but a universal commitment to individual dignity, open markets, limited government and a faith in human progress brought about by debate and reform."

The Economist claimed in its essay that it was against colonialism (a distinctly non-liberal idea). It wrote: "*The Economist* was sceptical of imperialism, arguing in 1862 that colonies 'would be just as valuable to us…if they were independent'."

In the same breath, the magazine contradicted itself by republishing, in 2018, an excerpt of what its editors wrote in

---

[47]13 September 2018.

1862: "But 'uncivilised races' were owed 'guidance, guardianship and teaching'."

Note the words: "uncivilised races". Intellectual dishonesty survived in *The Economist's* editorial room between 1862, when its editors wrote that passage, and 2018, when its editors exhumed it.

But weren't the standards of 1862 different from the standards of 2018? Wasn't racism the "old normal", though oddly co-existing with the soaring ideals of 19th century Western liberalism?

Consider the era of the mid-1800s. The United States was in the throes of a civil war over, essentially, the continuation of black slavery. The shipping capitals of the transatlantic African slave trade to North America had for a century been Liverpool, Southampton and Bristol. The cities' businessmen and slave traders accounted for 55 per cent of the slave traffic shipped from Africa to North America.

During the same era, Britain committed several extra-territorial colonial atrocities but the centuries-long African slave trade was the most brutal. It was accompanied by colonial invasions in Asia and Africa and the genocide of Aborigines in Australia and indigenous Indians in North America. Apartheid in South Africa was a latter-day British-Dutch joint venture that lasted till 1990.

None of these "liberal" episodes find a mention in *The Economist's* manifesto to "renew traditional" British values of liberalism. The magazine did though make one domestic *mea culpa*: "Liberals were white men who considered themselves superior to the run of humanity. Though Bagehot (a former *Economist* editor), supported votes for women, for most of its early years *The Economist* did not. Bagehot feared that extending the franchise to all (British) men regardless of property would lead to 'the tyranny of the majority'."

Throughout the second half of the 20th century, liberal Western societies continued to engage in anti-liberal practices. Slavery was gone. Colonialism was over. Aborigines and 'Red' Indians had been exterminated or marginalised. Apartheid was on its last legs. And yet, the West found new ways to continue its liberal double standards. Institutions like the World Bank and the International Monetary Fund (IMF) kept a tight leash on global finance. By mandate, its heads were always, respectively, American and European. What gunships could no longer achieve, the dollar did.

The Economist wrote in its liberal manifesto without a trace of embarrassment: "21st-century liberals must remember two lessons from the 20th. The failure of the League of Nations between the (two) world wars showed that liberal ideals are worthless unless backed by the military power of determined nation states."

The period between the two world wars—the 1920s and 1930s—were in fact among the most illiberal in recent history: the rise of Hitler, the continuing British colonial occupation of India, and legally mandated racial segregation of African-Americans in the US.

The Economist ended its liberal manifesto with a waffle rather than a clear-cut doctrine:

> This essay has argued that liberalism needs an equally ambitious reinvention today. The social contract and geopolitical norms that underpin liberal democracies and the world order that sustains them were not built for this century.
>
> Geography and technology have produced new concentrations of economic power to tackle. The developed and the developing world alike need fresh ideas for the design of better welfare states and tax systems. The right of people to move from one country to another need to be redefined. American apathy and China's rise require a rethinking of the world order—not least because the huge gains that free trade has provided must be preserved.

So what is true liberalism in today's new world order? Freedom, equality, choice, dissent, tolerance, diversity and openness. Respect merit but provide equal opportunities to all. Enforce the rule of law firmly and fairly without which no liberal society can flourish.

India is a starkly unequal society. But within its diversity lie the molecular building blocks of liberalism. As India lurches, in its own chaotic civilisational way, towards a more equitable future, those building blocks can in time create a society based on fairness and tolerance—the markers of true liberalism.

∽

Liberals need to support issues, not ideologies based on false left and right paradigms. Here are two illustrative examples: on LGBTQIA+ rights, freedom of expression, diversity and gender equality, lean left. On free markets, an open economy and foreign investment, lean right. In short, don't be trapped in a left-wing or a right-wing bunker. Be a liberal on social policies and a liberal on economic policies.

What about religion and caste? India has unfortunately long been hostage to both. But in an evolved democracy, the only litmus test for liberalism is to be caste-agnostic and religion-agnostic. Condemn violence wherever it occurs, whoever be the victim and whoever the perpetrator. The two qualities that define the true liberal are fairness and balance.

Economic liberalism, meanwhile, demands free trade and free markets. An open economy encourages foreign investment, builds economic diversity and spurs competition, efficiency and prosperity. The most successful entities in the world are diverse, competitive and rules-based. What makes the US the world's economic superpower? An open economy, a meritocratic workforce, and rules-based governance.

Liberalism revolves around gender equality as well. No society can be successful if it does not give half its population the same rights and opportunities it gives the other half. Even historically regressive countries like Saudi Arabia are waking up to this reality. Mohammad bin Salman al Saud, Saudi Arabia's ruler, is easing the restrictions that imprison Saudi women in gender silos.

Liberalism requires acceptance too of sexual orientation. No modern nation can discriminate against a significant section of its citizens on the basis of sexual orientation. Globally the best estimate for the LGBT population as a ratio of the general population is between 7 and 10 per cent. In India that number would add up to around 70 million adult LGBT citizens. They must enjoy the same rights as the rest of their fellow citizens. It is the government's obligation to treat all citizens equally and fairly following the Supreme Court decriminalising same sex relationships.

There are thus five axioms of liberalism:

Axiom one: No religion is exempt from criticism: neither Islam, nor Hinduism, nor Christianity. Blasphemy is not taboo.

Axiom two: Shun violence. Argue with words, not guns. The answer to a book or a film is another book or film, not a fatwa.

Axiom three: Reject political dynasty. Feudalism and liberalism operate at opposite ends of the spectrum of a progressive, liberal democracy.

Axiom four: Don't divide people on the basis of religion or caste. Whether you are a Hindu or a Muslim, you are Indian first, Hindu or Muslim second. The idea of a Hindu Rashtra is illiberal. The idea of a Bharat Rashtra is liberal.

Axiom five: A liberal is tolerant. Even those on the hard right and the hard left must engage one another in civil debate. Words and reason, not abuse and invective, are the weapons of choice for real liberals.

"If you're not a liberal when you're 20, you have no heart. If you're not a conservative by the time you're 30, you have no brain."

Writing in *Bloomberg Businessweek*[48], Avi Tuschman added: "Variations of this saying have been attributed to Benjamin Disraeli, Otto von Bismarck, George Bernard Shaw, Woodrow Wilson, Theodore Roosevelt, Aristide Briand, and Winston Churchill. The thought first came, in fact, from a French statesman, François Guizot (1787–1874). Regardless of its origin, the adage raises a fascinating question: Do the young really lean Left because of passions and idealism? And as people age, do they incline toward the Right because they become more realistic or cynical?"

How do our politicians and opinion-makers fare when we apply these criteria? Most Indian left-leaners call themselves liberals. But the left is a didactic ideology. It resists change. It brooks no ideological dissent. India's left-leaning politicians still hanker after the Soviet economic model which has been discredited by every country except North Korea. Even China, the Indian left's old lodestar, embraced free markets in 1979 when Deng Xiaoping changed the course of Chinese economic history.

Liberal economic policies enlarge the economic pie. Leftist economic policies shrink the economic pie. What about equitable distribution? Here's the mistake political parties on the economic right like the BJP make: distribution of wealth is as important as creation. Just as liberal policies reward open, accountable market-led economies, social liberalism demands a specific set of values. Social liberalism accepts diversity in all its forms— gender, sexuality and community.

Colonial and Marxist ideologies have run their course worldwide. Those countries which are socially illiberal and politically feudal—North Korea, Iran and Pakistan, for example—will remain steeped in social and cultural backwardness. In India, the tussle

---

[48]18 April 2014.

between the left and right is largely a theoretical middle-class exercise. The poor are neither left nor right—just poor. To lift them out of debilitating poverty, progressive welfare distribution and social policies are the way forward.

Here's what Tuschman says about age, culture and ideology: "A 2004 study by psychologists Robert McCrae and Jüri Allik in the *Journal of Cross Cultural Psychology* of 36 cultures across Africa, Europe and Asia discovered that openness and conscientiousness differ between 18- to 22-year-olds and older adults. If an individual's political personality hasn't changed by the time of his or her 30th birthday, however, it's not likely to differ all that much at 40, 50, or 60.

"This isn't to say that all teenagers are liberal and all older people are conservative. In any age group, people are distributed along the left-right spectrum on a bell curve. The entire curve, however, moves somewhat to the right during the mid-20s. There is one life event, though, that greatly accelerates a person's shift to the right, and it often occurs in the 30s: parenthood. Its political impact is easy to see among a cohort of Canadian college students studied by psychologist Robert Altemeyer. Their scores on an ideology test at age 22 grew more conservative by an average of 5.4 per cent when they were retested at 30. But among those 30-year-olds who'd had children, conservatism increased by 9.4 per cent.

"Why did having kids push people to the right? Parents stay on the lookout for possible sources of danger that nonparents can ignore. This shift in perception is so strong it creates an illusory sense of risk; new parents tend to believe that crime rates have increased since they had children even when actual crime has dropped dramatically. Because 'dangerous world' thinking is associated with political conservatism, parenthood pushes people to the Right, and more so when they have daughters."

India needs a powerful new intellectual ecosystem that is not a colonial, Marxist or feudal derivative. *The Economist*, for example, says its journalism falls into the "radical centre". It explains its editorial policy thus:

> We like free enterprise and tend to favour deregulation and privatisation. But we also like gay marriage, want to legalise drugs and disapprove of monarchy. So is *The Economist* right-wing or left-wing? The answer: neither. *The Economist* was founded in 1843 by James Wilson, a British businessman who objected to heavy import duties on foreign corn. Mr Wilson and his friends in the Anti-Corn Law League were classical liberals in the tradition of Adam Smith and, later, John Stuart Mill and William Ewart Gladstone. This intellectual ancestry has guided the newspaper's instincts ever since: it opposes all undue curtailment of an individual's economic or personal freedom.
>
> But like its founders, it is not dogmatic. Where there is a liberal case for government to do something, *The Economist* will air it. Early in its life, its writers were keen supporters of the income tax, for example. Since then it has backed causes like universal health care and gun control. But its starting point is that government should only remove power and wealth from individuals when it has an excellent reason to do so.
>
> The concepts of right- and left-wing predate *The Economist*'s foundation by half a century. They first referred to seating arrangements in the National Assembly in Paris during the French Revolution. Monarchists sat on the right, revolutionaries on the left. To this day, the phrases distinguish conservatives from egalitarians. But they do a poor job of explaining *The Economist*'s liberalism, which reconciles the left's impatience at an unsatisfactory status quo with the right's scepticism about grandiose redistributive schemes. So although its credo and its history are as rich as that of any reactionary or revolutionary, *The Economist*

has no permanent address on the left-right scale.

In most countries, the political divide is conservative-egalitarian, not liberal-illiberal. So it has no party allegiance, either. When it covers elections, it gives its endorsement to the candidate or party most likely to pursue classically liberal policies. It has thrown its weight behind politicians on the right, like Margaret Thatcher, and on the left, like Barack Obama. It is often drawn to centrist politicians and parties who appear to combine the best of both sides, such as Tony Blair, whose combination of social and economic liberalism persuaded it to endorse him at the 2001 and the 2005 elections (though it criticised his government's infringements of civil liberties).

When *The Economist* opines on new ideas and policies, it does so on the basis of their merits, not of who supports or opposes them. Last October, for example, it outlined a programme of reforms to combat inequality. Some, like attacking monopolies and targeting public spending on the poor and the young, had a leftish hue. Others, like raising retirement ages and introducing more choice in education, were more rightish. The result, 'True Progressivism', was a blend of the two: neither right nor left, but all the better for it, and coming instead from what we like to call the radical centre.

The intellectual centre of gravity in India too is clearly shifting. A new generation of opinion-makers is emerging at the economic and socio-cultural centre. That is the liberal future—the liberal-centre. Modi and other politicians across the ideological spectrum should take note before 2024 envelops them.

❧

Canada's Prime Minister Justin Trudeau ticks all the right boxes of modern liberalism. He is determinedly plural. Half his cabinet comprises women. Several Sikhs head key ministries. He is gay-friendly, supports transgenders and doesn't have a racist bone in his body. He is the poster boy of the global left. And yet his tacit support of Canada-based Khalistani separatists – many with criminal backgrounds – reveals an unflattering side of Trudeau.

Liberal governance must encourage economic competition and set fair rules. The Narasimha Rao government worked towards these between 1991 and 1996. The Congress-led UPA in 2004–14 had good economic moments but was fatally compromised by corruption. The BJP-led NDA inherited an institutionally corrupt ecosystem in 2014.

To ensure good political and economic governance, the judicial system must be firm, fair and fast. As political theorist Francis Fukuyama wrote in *The End of History and the Last Man*, a successful country must satisfy three criteria: accountable governance, the rule of law, and transparent democracy. Neither Congress nor BJP governments have fully met these criteria.

A genuinely secular, plural society does not discriminate on the basis of caste, religion or gender, does not appease minorities, does not favour the majority, and keeps religion out of politics. The Congress has time and again failed these tests. The BJP has been brazen in using majoritarianism to win votes, taking the Congress' decades-long appeasement of Muslims to an entirely different level by institutionalising polarisation.

In a liberal society, ideology does not decide who leans right and who leans left. Issues decide where you stand on, for example, gender equality, freedom of speech, foreign investment, censorship, dissent, pluralism and national security. To be a true-blue liberal you should be equally comfortable with a Muslim man in a skull cap, a Muslim woman in a burqa, a Sikh with a kirpan and a Hindu with a trishul.

Real liberals reject prejudice, from wherever it comes. They welcome diversity. They support non-discriminatory civil common codes for Muslims and Parsis, for Hindus and Christians. They abhor appeasement and polarisation. They support rationalism and dismiss superstition. They are inclusive nationalists who put India first and their religious, caste, regional and linguistic identity second.

It is telling that the sharpest criticism of the 2017 Supreme Court order barring invocation of religion, caste, creed and language during electioneering came from "secular liberals". The order was in fact both intrinsically secular and liberal. Those who opposed it are neither. One of the arguments advanced against the Supreme Court order was that it was impractical to enforce. How, it was argued, can the Chief Election Commissioner (CEC) possibly monitor all the inflammatory speeches politicians make during election campaigns? In short, even though the Supreme Court was secular and progressive, self-declared secularists and progressives rejected it on the spurious ground of unenforceability.

This argument was given legs within 24 hours of the apex court's judgment by Mayawati asking Muslims not to "waste" their votes on the Samajwadi Party followed by the BJP's Sakshi Maharaj decrying Muslim women's propensity to have multiple children. Both denied they had invoked caste or religion. Nasim Zaidi, then CEC, busy with the Opposition's demand to delay the Union Budget, said nothing.

The argument on enforceability of court orders is flawed. Laws are made because they serve the public interest not because they are easily enforceable. The Supreme Court order barring politicians from using religion, caste, creed and language to influence votes was right in principle and, with effort, can be enforced and made to work in practice. The larger, subterranean, argument against the Supreme Court's secular verdict was that it wasn't actually secular at all.

Muslims believe they must retain their right to be swayed by religion-based sops during electioneering. The same argument is advanced for Dalits. Why bar the BSP from invoking Dalit pride by pointing to the grand statues built for Mayawati even while Dalits pine for social justice and upward economic mobility?

By using religion and caste in elections, political parties like the Congress, BJP, Samajwadi Party, BSP, RJD, Shiv Sena, NC, PDP, NC and AIMIM have divided Indians for years. That must stop. The Supreme Court's order represented only the first step. Strict enforcement by the Election Commission's large machinery is necessary in the 2024 Lok Sabha election. The court order backs the EC which can now disqualify a candidate for using religion, caste, creed or language to influence voters. The EC has been given legal teeth by the Supreme Court. It must use them in the forthcoming General Election.

The most unworthy argument against the Supreme Court's order was sub-textual: that the order somehow violated the freedom of politicians to campaign using all the polarising tools at their disposal—including religion and caste. This argument transported the issue from the sublime to the ridiculous. Opposing the Supreme Court order it cited the possibility of parties with a religion named within it (the All India Majlis-e-Ittehadul Muslimeen, for example) being potentially disqualified on account of the Supreme Court order.

This, of course, is untrue. The apex court order targeted—and rightly barred—the invocation of religion in electioneering. Parties with a religious or caste affiliation within their name, as long as they campaign without inflaming religious or caste passions, do not violate the Supreme Court order in letter or spirit.

The Supreme Court judgment sought to sever the umbilical cord between politics and religion in India. No amount of intellectual sophistry can discredit that objective or the legal means the court chose to achieve it. In the 2019 Lok Sabha election, however, the order was observed in the breach rather than in the observance. The same fate awaits it in 2024.

The Supreme Court is meanwhile wrestling with a slew of issues around the limits of free speech. If hate speech causes communal or caste enmity, it breaks the law. There are established provisions in the Criminal Procedure Code (CrPC) to deal with such breaches of law. There should be no ideological bias in judging these issues, just the sensible application of law.

Section Eight

BRITAIN

TWENTY-SEVEN

Disunited Kingdom

THE FULL ACCOUNT OF HOW 190 YEARS OF BRITISH COLONIAL OCCUPATION, from 1757 to 1947, impoverished India is one of the great untold stories of modern history. Congress member of Parliament and former junior external affairs minister Shashi Tharoor tried valiantly to tell the story in his 2017 book, *The Inglorious Empire: What the British Did to India,* but gaps remain. What, for example, was the quantum in inflation-adjusted wealth siphoned out of India by the colonial British? Should India seek reparations—and how might these be credibly computed?

While Tharoor's well-researched book deservedly received wide coverage in India and abroad, an excellent article on the subject by Venu Madhav Govindu in *The Wire*[49] passed relatively unnoticed. Govindu threw light on what Britain owed India from an accounting point of view. These are official empirical, figures. From here we can extrapolate Britain's colonial debt to India, an exercise I first did in an article in *The Illustrated Weekly of India* as far back as in the 1980s titled *Debt and Dishonour of the British Empire.*

But first, Govindu's arguments: "In 1931, the debt owed to Britain by India was said to be about ₹1,000 crore. At that time, the Indian National Congress argued that much of this amount was incurred by Britain in furthering its own interests. Based largely on the work of the Gandhian economic philosopher,

---

[49] 6 August, 2015.

JC Kumarappa, the Congress argued that the principle of natural justice would wipe out all of this debt and more. Therefore, it held that the future debt to be borne by a free India had to be subjected to the scrutiny of an impartial tribunal. The British political leadership and press roundly denounced this rather moderate position and treated it as a treacherous 'repudiation' of India's obligations.

"By the end of the Second World War in 1945, Britain had to finally reckon with the problem of its debt to India and other countries. Britain agreed to pay a debt of ₹1,600 crore but other calculations showed a rather different figure. In 1947, Kumarappa estimated that the Indian share of the costs of deployment of its soldiers was ₹1,300 crore. A similar amount of ₹1,200 crore was spent in expenses pertaining to the war. He argued that these and other costs ought to be borne by Britain, which led to a figure of ₹5,700 crore. This was many times larger than the British figure of ₹1,600 crore. Britain, Kumarappa asserted, should not be allowed to be the debtor as well as the judge and the jury of the debt. He lobbied for India to demand an impartial international tribunal on the matter. In the event, India failed to push for such an international settlement and the British view prevailed much to the detriment of independent India."

Let's take the ₹5,700 crore figure estimated by Kumarappa in 1947 as the starting point of what Britain owed India in purely commercial terms, not taking into account intangibles such as the economic cost of human life caused by British atrocities or the egregious strangulation of Indian economic activity and trade for nearly two centuries and extortionate taxation.

In 1947, the exchange rate was ₹13 to one British pound sterling. Thus ₹5,700 crore in 1947 was equivalent to £4.40 billion. What would that be in today's rupees/sterling?

The value of gold and real estate is an accurate indicator of how money appreciates over long periods of time spanning more than 76 years. In 1947, the price of 10 gms of gold was ₹80.

In 2023, the price of 10 gms of gold was around ₹50,000—an increase of over 600 times.

The rise in the price of a basket of real estate, commodities and household essentials over the past 76 years gives a similar cost-inflation index of between 500 and 600 times. The inflation-adjustment in British prices between 1947 and 2023 is around 200 times. An average home in Britain in 1947 sold for £1,000. Today it is £2,00,000. Since our calculations are in rupees and a depreciation of the rupee-sterling rate between 1947 and 2023 has been factored in, the multiplier of 600x for reparations holds.

Now to the math: according to Govindu, Britain's official debt to India in 1947 was ₹5,700 crore (£4.40 billion) at the prevailing exchange rate of ₹13 to one pound sterling. Multiply that by 600. At today's inflation and exchange rate-adjusted figure, the debt is therefore £2.70 trillion.

But this is just the tip of the reparations iceberg. We haven't yet computed the cost of India's near-zero rate of GDP growth during the 190-year British colonial occupation, nor the cost of lost economic value due to Britain's wilful destruction of Indian mercantile trade. If these are scientifically calculated, Britain's debt to India at today's prices would easily climb to Prof. Utsa Patnaik's computation of $45 trillion—15 times Britain's current GDP.

Tharoor says reparations aren't needed; an apology and a token payment of one pound sterling a year for 200 years will suffice. He is wrong. Reparations are needed. An apology and tokenism won't suffice. Tharoor wrote in the foreword to his 2017 book, *The Inglorious Empire*:

"India should be content with a symbolic reparation of one pound a year, payable for 200 years to atone for 200 years of imperial rule. I felt that atonement was the point—a simple 'sorry' would do as well—rather than cash. Indeed, the attempt by one Indian commentator, Minhaz Merchant, to compute what a fair

sum of reparations would amount to, came up with a figure so astronomical that no one could ever reasonably be expected to pay it."

For nearly 200 years Britain plundered India, committed brutal atrocities on Indian civilians and strangulated GDP growth. In the process, it financed its industrial revolution, its Napoleonic wars against France, its civil infrastructure and built the world's largest economy in the 1800s. That led to the creation of Britain's post-industrial leisure society and the soft power of music, film, literature, sport, media, television and culture that accompanied it: The Royal Family, The Beatles, James Bond, Sherlock Holmes and other symbols of Britishness.

What about Britain's contribution to India: railways, unification, the English language, the ICS/IAS, universities, the rule of law? Tharoor rightly sets each one in perspective. Consider, for lack of space, just one: the railways. "In this very conception and construction," Tharoor writes, "the Indian Railways was a big British colonial scam. Each mile of Indian Railway construction in the 1850s and 1860s cost (the Indian taxpayer) an average of £18,000, as against the dollar equivalent of £2,000 at the same time in the US."

In short, what Britain built in India with underpaid Indian labour and overtaxed Indian trade revenue was ruthlessly repatriated to pave the roads of London, finance British industries and subsidise Britain's imperial wars. India in effect ended up paying for its own colonisation. All the benefits accrued to Britain. All the costs were borne by India. It comes as no surprise that after 190 years of British colonial rule, India was in 1947 among the world's most impoverished, famine-wracked countries.

※

On 17 July 1917, an announcement from Britain's Royal Family appeared in *The Times,* London: "Whereas we, having taken into consideration the Name and Title of Our Royal House and Family, have determined that henceforth Our House and Family shall be styled and known as the House and Family of Windsor. And do hereby further declare and announce that We relinquish and enjoin the discontinuance of the use of the Degrees, Styles, Dignities, Titles and Honours of Dukes and Duchesses of Saxony and Princes and Princesses of Saxe-Coburg and Gotha, and all other German Degrees, Styles, Dignities. Titles, Honours and Appellations to Us or to them heretofore belonging or appertaining."

Why did the British Royals change their surname in 1917 from the German Saxe-Coburg-Gotha to Windsor? Few in Britain know about the British Royal Family's deep German roots. King Charles III's great-grandfather King George V spoke English with a German accent. He was fluent though in German. During World War I, the British government, which had kept the Royal Family's German ancestry well-hidden from the general British public, could no longer do so.

As a report[50] by Susan Flantzer put it: "By 1917, anti-German sentiment had reached a fevered pitch in the UK. The British Royal Family's dynastic name had gone from one German name to another, the House of Hanover to the decidedly more Germanic-sounding House of Saxe-Coburg-Gotha. Many British people felt that this implied a pro-German bias. Even Prime Minister David Lloyd George remarked as he was on his way to see King George V, 'I wonder what my little German friend has got to say.' Letters were pouring into the Prime Minister's office wondering how the British were going to win the war if the king was German."

As World War I raged, not only did the British Royals change their family name from Saxe-Coburg-Gotha to Windsor but they asked royal relatives to follow suit. First in line was the father of the last Viceroy of India, Lord Louis Mountbatten, a cousin

---

[50]unofficialroyalty. com

of the British Royals. The Mountbattens' family name was the Germanic Battenberg. The German word "berg", translated into English means mountain—hence the quick anglicisation of the Viceroy's name to Mountbatten. Had the family retained its original name, the last Viceroy of India would have been Lord Battenberg and the British monarch at Indian Independence would have been King George Saxe-Coburg-Gotha.

In an article in *Vanity Fair*, journalist Aatish Taseer, who had a three-year-long relationship with Princess Michael Kent's daughter – Lady Gabriella Windsor, exposed the petty racism that courses through the British bloodstream: "Princess Michael was famously scandal-prone. It was not that her father had allegedly been an SS officer, albeit a reluctant one; royals and Nazis go together like blini and caviar. It was that everyone above a certain age in Britain is at least a tiny bit racist. The colonial past made it almost second nature for Britons born at the tail end of the Raj to treat roughly a quarter of the planet as subject peoples. I was one of the first natives of that former empire to be dating a member of the royal family... (Princess Michael's) pair of black sheep in Gloucestershire were named Venus and Serena."

The racism drips down through the British establishment. Britain's former Home Secretary Amber Rudd was forced to resign following the Windrush scandal. Dating back to 1971, the Windrush affair was a British policy seeking "voluntary" deportation of black Commonwealth citizens who had arrived in Britain from 1948 to 1971 in response to Britain's call to ease its post-war labour shortage. Around 1,30,000 mainly Caribbean immigrants were targeted for deportation. Some were placed in detention centres. Rudd had made it obligatory for landlords, employers and healthcare service providers to list immigrants who didn't have paperwork when they arrived in Britain as children 60 years ago and faced deportation.

The racist impulse hasn't ebbed. Asylum seekers in Britain

were to be sent to Rwanda in December 2022 under a commercial arrangement with the African country till a legal challenge stalled the proposal. Indian-origin Prime Minister Rishi Sunak is not an enthusiastic supporter of the Rwanda proposal but hews robustly to the Tory party line on curtailing immigration.

As the Modi government constructs a new relationship with post-Brexit Britain, looking back is as important as looking forward. Those who don't learn from the mistakes of history are bound not only to repeat them but to compound them.

∞

When Robert Clive defeated the Nawab of Bengal, Siraj ud-Daulah, in 1757 in the battle of Palashee (Plassey) by bribing the Nawab's army commander, the traitorous Mir Jaffer, the real prize for the British was the right to collect tax from Bengali peasants, traders and farmers. The Nawab had levied a modest tax, allowing peasants a reasonable living. By 1765, within eight years of Clive's victory over the Nawab, all that changed. Taxes in Bengal were trebled. Unable to eke out a living, 10 million people out of Bengal's population of 30 million died of starvation in 1770.

Around 173 years later, in 1943, as the Second World War raged and the British Empire was on its last legs, Prime Minister Winston Churchill withheld vital food grains from Bengal, leading to the Great Bengal Famine in which over three million people died.

But back in the 1750s, the British were focused on making money. Britain was still a relatively poor country. The industrial revolution was some years away. The British were active in the transatlantic African slave trade to North America. Throughout much of the 1700s, Liverpool monopolised the brutal Atlantic slave traffic. The United States was a British colony till 1776. African slaves captured or bought from local middlemen by the British in Sierra Leone, Ghana and the Ivory Coast were shipped to North America in British vessels, commanded by British captains. Arms and legs chained in manacles, the slaves lay one above the other. Dozens died during the horrific 60-day transatlantic journey. Liverpool, a small hamlet in the 1600s, was transformed by the lucrative transatlantic slave trade into a thriving metropolis known more today as the home town of The Beatles than its cruel role in African slavery.

As Britain began to extort tax revenue from Indian peasants, the nascent Industrial Revolution took off in the late 1700s. It received a significant boost in the form of revenue and raw material from India. The British modus operandi was as simple as it was extortionate: it taxed Indian peasants three times what they had been taxed under the Mughals. That excess tax revenue collected was then used by the British to buy Indian goods – spices, textiles and gold – which were in great demand in Europe and North America.

Thus British tax collectors used Indian tax revenue to buy Indian merchandise, exported it and pocketed the profit – with zero investment. This system continued unimpeded virtually throughout the 190-year-long colonial period. In order to ensure that the peasants and traders from whom they extorted steep taxes to buy Indian goods for export did not realise they were being cheated, a ruse was employed. British tax collectors and British buyers of exportable Indian goods were deliberately employed as separate entities so that no connection could be made by traders and workers whose taxes were being used to drain the country's resources to enrich Britain.

Professor Utsa Patnaik, a leading economist, explains the scheme: "A large part of the producer's own tax payment simply got converted into export goods, so the East India Company got these goods completely free. The later mechanism, after the British Crown took over (in 1858), used bills of exchange. The only Indian beneficiaries of this clever, unfair system of linking trade with taxes were the intermediaries or *dalals*. Some of modern India's well-known business houses made their early profits doing *dalali* for the British."

In an op-ed for the *Hindustan Times* published on 30 October 2018, Professor Patnaik added context and detail to Britain's colonial rapacity: "How exactly did the British manage to diddle us and drain our wealth? That was the question that Basudev Chatterjee (later editor of a volume in the *Towards Freedom* project) had posed to me over 50 years ago when we were fellow students abroad. After decades of research I find that using India's commodity export surplus as the measure and applying an interest rate of 5 per cent, the total drain from 1765 to 1938, compounded up to 2016, comes to £9.2 trillion; since $4.86 exchanged for £1 those days, this sum equals about $45 trillion."

Professor Patnaik adds: "The exact mechanism of drain, or transfers from India to Britain, was quite simple. The key factor was Britain's control over our taxation revenues combined with control over India's financial gold and forex earnings from its booming commodity export surplus with the world. Simply put, Britain used locally raised rupee tax revenues to pay for its net imports of goods, a highly abnormal use of budgetary funds not seen in any sovereign country.

"The East India Company, from 1765 onwards, allocated every year up to one-third of Indian budgetary revenues, net of collection cost, to buy a large volume of goods for direct import into Britain, far in excess of that country's own needs. Since tropical goods were highly prized in other cold temperate countries which could never produce them, in effect these free goods represented international purchasing power for Britain which kept a part for its own use and re-exported the balance to other countries in Europe and North America against import of food grains, iron and other goods in which it was deficient.

"The British historians Phyllis Deane and W A Cole presented an incorrect estimate of Britain's 18th–19th century trade volume by leaving out re-exports completely. I found that by 1800 Britain's total trade was 62 per cent higher than their estimate, on applying the correct definition of trade including re-exports that is used by the United Nations and by all other international organisations. When the British Crown took over from the East India Company in 1858 a clever system was developed from 1861 under which all of India's financial gold and forex earnings from its fast-rising commodity export surplus with the world was intercepted and appropriated by Britain."

Professor Patnaik's work, published by Columbia University Press, has gained international traction. Jason Hickel, a columnist with *The Guardian*, wrote a piece for *Al Jazeera. com* on 14 December 2018, titled *How Britain stole $45 trillion from India: And lied about it.* The piece laid bare the deceit with which Britain accomplished its plunder of Indian wealth over nearly two centuries as well as the lack of acknowledgment in British society and among British historians of this egregious crime.

American historian and philosopher Will Durant toured India in 1930. This is what he wrote: "The British conquest of India was the invasion and destruction of a high civilisation, utterly without scruple or principle, careless of art and greedy of gain, overrunning with fire and sword a country temporarily disordered and helpless, bribing and murdering, annexing and stealing, and beginning that career of illegal and 'legal' plunder which now (1930) has gone on ruthlessly for 173 years."

Colonial reparations by Britain to India won't fully heal the wounds of India's 'high civilisation' that Durant wrote feelingly about. But they will be a step in the right direction to correct a historical wrong.

Were the British thus more rapacious than the Mughals? Unquestionably. They impoverished India in a way the Mughals did not. That does not absolve the Mughal Empire. It prosecuted wars of savagery against Indian kingdoms, destroyed thousands of temples, and converted millions of Hindus to Islam through the sword or financial inducement. The Mughals were a destructive, malignant force for over two centuries.

The British though exceeded them in the damage they did to India's economy. Why then is there relatively little anger against the British, while Muslim rule is rightly reviled? The reason is complex. Many Hindus in the 1700s despaired of the debauched Mughal Empire. They were relieved when the British defeated the Mughals. They regarded the Briton, who brought new weapons technology and avoided religious conversions, as the lesser evil than the Mughal. But between two evils, there is usually little to choose.

As Professor Patnaik points out: "Per capita annual foodgrains absorption in British India declined from 210 kg during 1904–09 to 157 kg during 1937–41, and to only 137 kg by 1946. If even a part of its enormous foreign earnings had been credited to it and not entirely siphoned off, India could have imported modern technology to build up an industrial structure as Japan did. Instead the masses suffered severe nutritional decline and independent India inherited a festering problem of unemployment and poverty."

⨏

In 1949, PM Jawaharlal Nehru faced a dilemma. Should newly independent India continue to remain in the British Commonwealth? Indian nationalists had through the 1930s and 1940s fought against India's future association with a body headed by an imperial power. Nehru himself declared that India would have nothing to do with the last vestige of British imperialism. "Under no circumstances," Nehru wrote, "is India going to remain in the British Commonwealth."

In 1949, circumstances changed and so did Nehru's mind. The British, impoverished by World War II and in heavy debt to the US over war funding, were desperate to cling to a semblance of global power. The British government hastily renamed the 'British

Commonwealth' the 'Commonwealth of Nations'. Republics—as India was shortly to be—could remain as members. Previously only British dominions could.

The move was widely criticised in India. Nehru's capitulation allowed Britain to extend the myth of its imperial power. Nehru agreed to sign the London Declaration on 28 April 1949 which in part stated: "The government of India has...declared and affirmed India's desire to continue her full membership of the Commonwealth of Nations and her acceptance of the King as the symbol of the free association of its independent member nations and as the Head of the Commonwealth."

In one fell blow, Nehru had accepted subservient status to an ejected colonial power by acknowledging the British monarch as head in perpetuity of an organisation of which India was one of dozens of past and present exploited British colonies. Without India the Commonwealth is a motley collection of invasive white settlements (Australia, New Zealand, Canada), former British African colonies (Kenya, Nigeria, Uganda) and islands scattered across the Pacific and the Caribbean. India forms 55 per cent of the Commonwealth's population. Along with Pakistan, Bangladesh and Sri Lanka, South Asia accounts for nearly 75 per cent of the Commonwealth.

Modi's views on the Commonwealth are ambiguous. While he seeks greater trade with post-Brexit Britain through an FTA, he has largely ignored the Commonwealth, giving its desultory summits a miss. The late Queen Elizabeth II was expected to be the last head of the Commonwealth though the 1949 Declaration mandates the British monarch will always head the Commonwealth. That should no longer be so now that King Charles III has slipped effortlessly into the role of head of the Commonwealth. If India unwisely decides to remain a member of what is a perfectly pointless institution, future heads should be chosen democratically—a quality the Commonwealth prizes but, in this respect, flouts.

Has Brexit led to a confident "Global Britain" ready to trade with the rest of the world as an independent entity, unshackled from the EU's bureaucratic regulations? Or has it shrunk Britain into "Little England"—back to the isolated island it was before it set off on its colonial quest in the 1700s?

A post-Brexit Global Britain is a fantasy the British are fond of indulging in. As *The Economist* wrote cuttingly: "The British establishment has always been ambivalent about the European project, partly because it was on the winning side in the second world war and partly because it has historically seen Britain as a global power, not a continental one. The ambivalence curdled into hatred in some sections of the Tory party as the EU acquired more of the trappings of a state. The Conservatives are profoundly divided over what to do about this crisis. Broadly speaking the Right of the party wants to complete the Thatcher revolution by deregulating markets still further and slashing taxes. For them, leaving the EU (was) a prerequisite to turning Britain into an offshore Singapore."

In 1707, Scotland—till then an independent nation—joined England to form the United Kingdom. The Scots in 2016 voted overwhelmingly to stay in the EU. Scottish nationalists are now seeking a second referendum on Scottish independence. In the first, in 2014, a small majority of 55.3 per cent voted to stay in the UK. The Scots have no love lost for the English. The feeling is mutual.

The Conservative government led by Prime Minister Rishi Sunak has ruled out a second referendum on Scottish independence. Scotland may have to wait till early 2025, when the next British general election is due and a Labour government—which too is currently against a second referendum—allows Scots to vote for an independent country. It could then apply to join the EU. The Republic of Ireland is already an enthusiastic member of the EU and has benefited from the EU's financial largesse. Its per capita income is higher than Britain's. Scottish independence and a reunification of Northern Ireland with the Republic of Ireland could lead to the unravelling of the United Kingdom. It is no longer as far-fetched a prospect as it once was.

A united Ireland is the ghost that frightens the British more than Scottish independence. Colonial Britain "populated" the northern part of Ireland with English Protestant migrants from the 1600s. Ireland's Catholic majority was gradually whittled down. The "United Kingdom of Great Britain and Ireland" was formed by the Acts for Union 1800. A year later, in 1801, the independent Irish parliament was abolished. It was not until a series of battles took place between colonial Britain and Irish patriots that Ireland gained full independence in 1922—but not without a parting kick: six counties of Ireland opted to stay with Britain, carving Ireland into mutually hostile Protestant Northern Ireland as a part of the UK and Catholic Republic of Ireland as an independent nation.

Over the decades, the population of Catholics in Northern Ireland has risen and now surpasses the population of Protestants. Sectarian strife between Protestants and Catholics and terror attacks in Britain peaked in the 1970s and 1980s. Today, an uneasy peace prevails. Brexit has raised the prospect of future unification between the two Irelands. It is a prospect Britain dreads. Were Scotland to seek independence from the UK and the two Irelands to seek a merger, that would spell the end of the United Kingdom.

As Jonathan Gorvett wrote[51] in *Foreign Policy*, quoting Jon Tonge, a professor of British and Irish politics: "Ask me if the UK will still exist in its current form in a generation, and I'd have to say—that's a very tough call."

Before 1707, England and Scotland were small and relatively poor nations on the periphery of northwestern Europe. Colonialism

---

[51] 19 July 2019.

and slavery, both enormously profitable enterprises, brought the English and Scots together in a formal union that, 316 years later, with colonial and slave revenues gone, makes little sense anymore to the Scots.

The fear of a shrunken England is shared by *The Economist*: "The link with Scotland is already looser than it has been for decades. There are very few Scots in the upper ranks of Britain's two main parties. England and Scotland backed opposing sides in the Brexit referendum."

Brexit could ironically turn out to be the trigger that eventually returns England to its modest island origins. It is a prospect Modi, in a putative third term as prime minister, will have to consider as he deepens India's trade and technology relationship with Britain.

Section Nine
PAKISTAN

TWENTY-EIGHT

A State of Terror

"PAKISTAN IS PRE-PROGRAMMED TO FAIL." WITH THOSE WORDS, MY father, a student of business management at the University of California, Berkeley, left a thin, gangling fellow-student, Zulfiqar Ali Bhutto, in a bad mood.

It was 1950. Bhutto went on to Oxford University to study law before returning to Pakistan. My father, management degree in hand, returned to India to join the family's manufacturing enterprise.

During his years at Berkeley, Bhutto tried hard to convince other Indian students what a great future his newly formed country Pakistan had. My father told him why he was wrong: a country founded on theocracy would eventually implode. More than seven decades after that conversation on a northern California campus, those words appear prophetic.

The terrorists Pakistan bred to bleed India by a thousand cuts are bleeding Pakistan instead. Balochistan is in ferment. So are Sindh and Khyber Pakhtunkhwa. Balochistan was an independent state named Kalat in the British Empire. It was not part of the instruments of accession at Indian Independence and Partition in 1947. In May 1948, the Pakistani army invaded and annexed it.

The Pakistani daily *The Nation* published a detailed account on 5 December 2015 of how Pakistan illegally occupied Balochistan, now the centerpiece of the China Pakistan Economic Corridor (CPEC): "Balochistan accounts for nearly half the land mass of

Pakistan and only 3.6 per cent of its total population. The province is immensely rich in natural resources, including oil, gas, copper and gold. Despite these huge deposits of mineral wealth, the area is one of the poorest regions of Pakistan. A vast majority of its population lives in deplorable housing conditions where they don't have access to electricity or clean drinking water.

"When the Dar-ul-Awam (parliament) of Kalat (Balochistan) met on 21 February 1948, it decided not to accede to Pakistan, but to negotiate a treaty to determine Kalat's future relations with Pakistan. On 26 March 1948, the Pakistan Army was ordered to move into the Baloch coastal region of Pasni, Jiwani and Turbat. Kalat capitulated on 27 March and it was announced in Karachi that the Khan of Kalat has agreed to merge his state with Pakistan. Jinnah accepted this accession under the gun. It should be noted that the Balochistan Assembly had already rejected any suggestion of forfeiting the independence of Balochistan (Kalat) on any pretext. So even the signature of the Khan of Kalat, taken under the barrel of the gun, was not viable. The Balochistan parliament had rejected the accession. The accession was never mandated by the British Empire either which had given Balochistan in dependence even before India. The sovereign Baloch state after British withdrawal from India lasted only 227 days. During this time Balochistan had a flag flying in its embassy in Karachi where its ambassador to Pakistan lived."

Like Balochistan today, Sindh too is restive. While lawless Karachi has been partially tamed by the Pakistani Rangers' concerted action over the past few years, the movement for an independent Sindh remains strong. Further north, the restless tribal areas of Khyber Pakhtunkhwa are riven by violence and corruption. It is not the Pakistan founder Muhammad Ali Jinnah had envisioned. Jinnah, like Bhutto, was a reluctant Muslim. A Gujarati Shia Khoja, he married a Parsi. Bhutto married an Iranian and at Berkeley had partied hard. Neither man would have fitted into the fundamentalist Islamic version of today's

Pakistan, fractured internally by political and religious battles.

After the 9/11 terror attacks in the United States in which Saudis and Pakistanis were the principal culprits, Pakistan turned from a rentier state to a vassal state. The George W. Bush administration had warned President Pervez Musharraf in a telephone call before launching the "shock and awe" missile blitzkrieg on al-Qaeda in Afghanistan in November 2001 that if Pakistan didn't cooperate in the war against terror, America would bomb it "into the stone age".

Musharraf cooperated. But like every Pakistani General before (and after) him, he ran with the hares and chased with the hounds. The US paid Pakistan an average of $3 billion every year to fight terrorism in Af-Pak. The Pakistani army, which controls a third of Pakistan's GDP, used most of the money to fund its jihad in India and salted the rest away in foreign bank accounts. Former chief of army staff (COAS) General Qamar Javed Bajwa and his family, it was reported in November 2022, had assets valued at ₹1,200 crore. The report was denied but few in Pakistan doubted its accuracy.

Taliban-ruled Afghanistan has meanwhile turned out to be a poisoned chalice for Islamabad. Afghanistan has been a graveyard for three empires: British, Soviet and American. The Chinese don't want to be the fourth empire to be sucked into the quagmire of Afghanistan's competing warlords. Instead of providing Islamabad with strategic depth, Taliban-ruled Afghanistan presents it with a strategic liability. One reason why Pakistan sought peace with India on the Line of Control (LoC) is the belated recognition that the Pakistani army has its hands full on its western front. A radicalised, Pashtun-led Talibanised Afghanistan will eventually create greater radicalism in Pakistan which already has a large restive Pashtun population.

Pakistan is a failed state not just because it is a terrorism hub: it has failed its citizens across economic and social parameters. In 1950, Pakistan's per capita income ($643) was higher than

India's ($619). Sixty years later, in 2010, India's per capita income ($3,372) in purchasing power parity (PPP) terms had overtaken Pakistan's ($2,494). The gap in 2023 widened further. Pakistan's GDP in 2030 is projected to be less than one-twelfth of India's.

Pakistani society has splintered into several disparate bits. The army, a giant financial corporation and terrorist organiser. Till former Prime Minister Imran Khan's open rebellion in 2022, nobody defied it or its spy agency ISI. The mullahs control their madrassas and meticulously radicalise impoverished Pakistani youth.

The judiciary and civil society form the more rational sections of Pakistan but many judges themselves are now radicalised. Religious murders based on blasphemy are tolerated by the judiciary. It doesn't dare prosecute an army officer for corruption in the manner it prosecuted former Prime Minister Nawaz Sharif. Despite the army's reduced power, civil society is so fragmented and weak that no one in Pakistan pays it much attention anymore. The media tries to be robust but murders of several journalists over the years by the ISI has made it toothless and fearful.

Faced with a domestic terror backlash that has consumed thousands of Pakistani lives, Islamabad has placed all its remaining bets on China. With the US reducing its annual aid to Pakistan, Beijing has emerged as a saviour. It is though in reality one more step for Pakistan towards the abyss. With China's own economy slowing, Beijing may lose patience to endlessly fund Pakistan.

*

The Indian air strikes on Balakot deep inside Pakistan in retaliation for the Pulwama terror attack changed the calculus of the 2019 Lok Sabha election. Rahul Gandhi made a tactical error by converting the 2019 general election into a quasi-presidential contest. Gandhi's daily attacks on Modi, muted temporarily after the Pulwama terror outrage, attracted the law of diminishing returns. Modi had mastered the ability to turn personal attacks on him to his political advantage. With every attack on him, Modi seemed to grow electorally stronger.

Congress MP from Thiruvananthapuram, Shashi Tharoor, had handed the BJP electoral leverage ahead of the 2019 Lok Sabha poll with his attack on Modi, who he said was converting India into a "Hindu Pakistan". Why was Tharoor's "Hindu-Pakistan" remark both inaccurate and ill-timed?

First, Pakistan doesn't just discriminate against minorities as Tharoor euphemistically claimed in his full speech. It kills them. Ahmadiyyas are hunted down—the law allows their persecution. In India, even after 15 years of BJP rule under Vajpayee and Modi spread over three decades between 1998 and 2023, minorities receive rights that often exceed those accorded to Hindus.

Second, in Pakistan, despite Imran Khan's blistering challenge, the army still controls the country though its authority has eroded. In India, the army in contrast suffers routine vilification at the hands of sundry politicians, activists and NGOs.

In February 2021, Pakistan's Director General of Military Operations (DGMO) spoke on the hotline to the Indian DGMO. He requested an urgent cessation of cross-LoC firing. Despite a 2003 agreement, ceasefire violations were frequent, especially after Modi took office in 2014. Pakistan invariably instigated these violations but suffered heavily in men and material from retaliatory Indian shelling. It finally sued for peace in 2021. Rocked by internal strife and a collapsing economy, Islamabad has tactically lowered the temperature across the LoC. The ceasefire has held for well over two years.

Pakistanis have long been fed on a diet that the core dispute with India is Kashmir. The last thing Pakistan's army generals want is a solution to the Kashmir dispute. The Pakistani army lives off the Kashmir dispute. Take that away and the Pakistani army would lose the enormous fortune that a low intensity, low-cost conflict in Kashmir delivers.

Consider the facts. Pakistan's GDP is around 10 per cent of India's. Yet its defence budget is nearly 25 per cent of India's.

Surplus funding is siphoned off by the army's top brass. On retirement senior army officers get large land holdings as gratuity. The best business in Pakistan is the business of the Pakistani army. Even junior officers are well looked after. The Pakistani army is an outsized entity for a relatively small country. It has a total strength of 6,50,000 soldiers with another 5,10,000 reservists.

The Pakistani army functions like an illicit military organisation. It commits genocide in Balochistan, arms terrorists in Kashmir and outsources vast swathes of its territory to China. The longer the dispute over Kashmir continues, the more it profits the Pakistani army. No one in the Pakistan government questions the country's dubiously large defence budget. The army has succeeded in making the majority of Pakistanis believe in its indispensability. Without an "enemy" (India) and without a "core dispute" (Kashmir), that aura would diminish.

Moreover, an all-out war with India's superior conventional forces would expose the Pakistani army's carefully nurtured image among ordinary Pakistanis of its invincibility. Rawalpindi doesn't want a repeat of Bangladesh 1971 or Kargil 1999. A slow-burning insurgency in Kashmir, following the reading down of Article 370, suits it better. Unemployed young men from poor families are used as terrorist cannon fodder in the Valley. When killed by the Indian Army or the Border Security Force (BSF), their families are generously rewarded with land and money.

The Indian government has begun imposing a cost on the Pakistani Army. Water has long been an underused weapon. Hydro-electric projects in the Valley are being fast-tracked. Under the Indus Waters Treaty (IWT), India is legally entitled to a higher quota than it has been using for decades. Less water to Pakistan as a result of the new hydro projects in Kashmir will impose a cost on Pakistani agriculture. Only when the price of abetting terrorism becomes unaffordable will the Pakistani Army be compelled to change its behaviour.

Defence Minister Rajnath Singh declared publicly years ago that the only subject of discussion henceforth with Pakistan – once it ceases sponsoring terrorism against India—will be Gilgit-Baltistan and Pakistan-occupied Kashmir (PoK). His statement that India's no-first-use nuclear doctrine is no longer cast in stone has further unnerved Islamabad. By responding with nuclear jingoism, Pakistan has exposed Islamabad's paranoia.

∽

Not everyone in India is happy with the liberation of Kashmir from the chains Article 370 had bound it in for 70 years. In a democracy, dissent is both welcome and necessary. A plurality of voices helps lend nuance to every issue. Let's examine two such voices. The first is Pratap Bhanu Mehta, former vice-chancellor of Ashoka University. Mehta wrote an op-ed[52] in *The Indian Express* criticising the Supreme Court's anodyne reaction to several petitions filed with it against the abrogation of Article 370: "Our legal abdication on liberties is a sign that we are not ready to treat Kashmir is as ordinary Indians and that we are willing to debase ourselves in the face of an executive that is acting more colonially than a colonial power."

Mehta is wrong. Parliament reflects the collective will of the people, a point the Supreme Court too made during the hearing it gave the petitioners. For Mehta to portray an empowering legislation that nullifies Article 370, approved by both the Lok Sabha and Rajya Sabha, as worse than the action of a colonial power exhibits prejudice, not principle.

The second example is equally telling. Brown University professor Ashok Varshney wrote in the same daily[53]: "Only in one democratic sense—democracy as a system of electoral power—can the decision to change Kashmir's status be called potentially legitimate. In all other democratic senses, we have

---

[52]17 August 2019.
[53]*The Indian Express*, 17 August 2019.

witnessed severely anti-democratic conduct. It was electorally-enabled brute majoritarianism."

The speciousness of this argument is obvious. Democracy is not a malleable concept. If majoritarianism is bad in the rest of India—and it is—it is bad in Kashmir as well. Varshney can't have it both ways: good in Kashmir, bad in the rest.

Article 370 gave J&K special status and laws. Revoking it had three significant implications. First, it opened Jammu and Kashmir to economic development from across the country. Restrictions applying to Indians outside the state were rendered null and void—they can settle in J&K, buy land in J&K, invest in J&K and make J&K a normal part of the Indian Union. Second, the Valley is now open to new influences—financial, social and cultural—from the rest of India. Movie theatres, banned by Islamists since 1990, returned to the Valley in September 2022. Third, with Indian security forces strengthened in J&K, terrorists are no longer fought with one hand tied behind the back. The malignant support to stone-pelters and local terror modules that bled J&K for decades has eroded.

The government did not technically revoke Article 370 in the Constitution. It used Section 3 in it to effectively nullify it. The revocation did not therefore need a constitutional amendment. This is what Section 3 of Article 370 says: "Notwithstanding anything in the foregoing provisions of this article, the President may, by public notification, declare that this article shall cease to be operative or shall be operative only with such exceptions and modifications and from such date as he may specify: Provided that the recommendation of the Constituent Assembly of the State referred to in clause (2) shall be necessary before the President issues such a notification."

In one stroke, this eliminated J&K's discriminatory laws on minorities, gender equality, land rights and other provisions that had landlocked the Valley for decades. In their place, the laws of India that give reservations to Dalits and others apply here too.

The Valley had for decades been used as a vassal by its feudal ruling classes. Two families—the Abdullahs for three generations and the Muftis for two—created an ecosystem where the people they professed to serve lived in shambolic conditions while they themselves amassed wealth. That era is history

❧

What precisely is the United Nation's role in J&K? Is the recurrent demand by the Pakistani government for a plebiscite in J&K justified? On 13 August 1948 the United Nations Commission for India and Pakistan (UNCIP) adopted a resolution. The resolution required Pakistan to vacate PoK before a plebiscite was considered. Since this UNCIP resolution has been frequently cited by both Pakistani leaders and analysts to justify a plebiscite in Kashmir, it's important to reproduce the relevant UN resolution in full:

PART I: Ceasefire order

A. The governments of India and Pakistan agree that their respective high commands will issue separately and simultaneously a ceasefire order to apply to all forces under their control and in the state of Jammu and Kashmir as of the earliest practicable date or dates to be mutually agreed upon within four days after these proposals have been accepted by both governments.

B. The high commands of the Indian and Pakistani forces agree to refrain from taking any measures that might augment the military potential of the forces under their control in the state of Jammu and Kashmir. (For the purpose of these proposals forces under their control shall be considered to include all forces, organised and unorganised, fighting or participating in hostilities on their respective sides.)

C. The commanders-in-chief of the forces of India and Pakistan shall promptly confer regarding any necessary local changes in present dispositions which may facilitate the ceasefire.

D. In its discretion and as the commission may find practicable, the commission will appoint military observers who, under the authority of the commission and with the cooperation of both commands, will supervise the observance of the ceasefire order.

E. The government of India and the government of Pakistan agree to appeal to their respective peoples to assist in creating and maintaining an atmosphere favourable to the promotion of further negotiations.

PART II: Truce agreement

Simultaneously with the acceptance of the proposal for the immediate cessation of hostilities as outlined in Part I, both the governments accept the following principles as a basis for the formulation of a truce agreement, the details of which shall be worked out in discussion between their representatives and the commission.

A.

1. As the presence of troops of Pakistan in the territory of the state of Jammu and Kashmir constitutes a material change in the situation since it was represented by the government of Pakistan before the Security Council, the government of Pakistan agrees to withdraw its troops from that state.

2. The government of Pakistan will use its best endeavour to secure the withdrawal from the state of Jammu and Kashmir of tribesmen and Pakistani nationals not normally resident there in who have entered the state for the purpose of fighting.

3. Pending a final solution, the territory evacuated by the Pakistani troops will be administered by the local authorities under the surveillance of the commission.

B.

1. When the commission shall have notified the government of India that the tribesmen and Pakistani nationals referred to in Part II, A, 2, hereof have withdrawn, thereby terminating the situation which was represented by the government of India to the Security Council as having occasioned the presence of Indian forces in the state of Jammu and Kashmir, and further, that the Pakistani forces are being withdrawn from the state of Jammu and Kashmir, the government of India agrees to begin to withdraw the bulk of its forces from that state in stages to be agreed upon with the commission.

2. Pending the acceptance of the conditions for a final settlement of the situation in the state of Jammu and Kashmir, the Indian government will maintain within the lines existing at the moment of the ceasefire the minimum strength of its forces which in agreement with the commission are considered necessary to assist local authorities in the observance of law and order. The commission will have observers stationed where it deems necessary.

3. The government of India will undertake to ensure that the government of the state of Jammu and Kashmir will take all measures within its powers to make it publicly known that peace, law and order will be safeguarded and that all human political rights will be granted.

4. Upon signature, the full text of the truce agreement or a communiqué containing the principles thereof as agreed upon between the two governments and the commission, will be made public.

PART III

The government of India and the government of Pakistan reaffirm their wish that the future status of the state of Jammu and Kashmir shall be determined in accordance with the will of the people and to that end, upon acceptance of the truce agreement, both governments agree to enter into consultations with the commission to determine fair and equitable conditions whereby such free expression will be assured.

Since Pakistan has not withdrawn its troops from PoK—as Part II of the UN resolution reproduced above requires it to do as an immutable precondition—the remaining steps in the resolution are rendered invalid. A plebiscite in J&K, the 1972 Shimla agreement notwithstanding, is therefore ruled out until Pakistan vacates PoK.

Pakistan has long been a state sponsor of terrorism. No other nation has used terror so ruthlessly as an instrument of state policy as Pakistan has done for decades against India. The Financial Action Task Force (FATF) consigned Pakistan to the greylist between 2018 and 2022 for money laundering and terrorism financing. Islamabad exited the greylist only after a show of compliance with FATF guidelines.

To maintain the fiction of Kashmir being the core issue between India and Pakistan, Pakistan recognises that terrorism must be accompanied by effective communications. The ISI has a well-trained cadre of people who use mainstream and social media to spread disinformation about how the Indian Army brutalises ordinary Kashmiris. They appear regularly on Indian TV debates, accompanied by retired Pakistani armed forces officers and relatively unknown Pakistani journalists. Reputed Pakistani editors, who do not function as ISI ventriloquists, are rarely fielded in these debates. They have independent views. The ISI shuns them. Inexplicably so do most Indian TV channels.

Indian channels instead provide oxygen to Pakistani analysts who are briefed before each debate by their ISI handlers. Instead of inviting Afghan, Baloch and Bangladeshi journalists who can counter the Pakistani Army's narrative, Indian channels allow themselves to become platforms for the ISI's propaganda. Some in the Indian media genuinely believe in the India-Pakistan "blood feud" myth. Others are simply vulnerable to the money on offer. Track-2 meetings are a special attraction. These seminars are organised by obscure "peace" organisations but function under the watchful eyes of ISI handlers.

Indian politicians have long fallen for the rakish charm of Pakistan's leaders. Indira Gandhi was blindsided by Zulfiqar Ali Bhutto into returning 93,000 Pakistani prisoners of war (PoWs) after the liberation of Bangladesh. Every successive Indian prime minister has succumbed to Pakistan's trickery. Atal Bihari Vajpayee, Dr Manmohan Singh and Narendra Modi—in his initial years in office—have each tried and failed to appease Pakistan with Kashmiriyat, Insaniyat, Punjabiyat and offers of friendship. Each failed to understand the Pakistani Army's mind: it wants trade and diplomatic engagement with India as part of a package deal that includes state-sponsored terrorism.

TWENTY-NINE

"Terror and Talks Can't Go Hand in Hand"

NURSING A SORE THROAT, PRIME MINISTER NARENDRA MODI SAT DOWN
to do a television interview just before campaigning for the
2014 Lok Sabha general election ended. His voice was hoarse,
but the message clear. When asked about his Pakistan policy by
interviewer Arnab Goswami, then editor of *TimesNow*, he said,
"Terror and talks can't go hand in hand." Speaking in Hindi,
he added words to this effect: "Can you hear each other over
the sound of gunfire?"

Modi's policy on Pakistan has gone from conciliatory to
confrontational to resolute. With China emerging as India's
principal adversary across the LAC, Pakistan is now seen by
the Modi government through a Beijing prism. Brainwashed by
anti-Indian history books in school and anti-India propaganda in
the media, most Pakistanis fear Indian hegemony. Equivalence
with India, however mythical, is what ordinary Pakistanis crave.

Despite protestations of peace with India, Pakistan continues
to develop nuclear warheads at rapid pace. Reports suggest it
will have over 350 nuclear weapons within ten years—more
than France or Britain. In a country beset by home-produced
terrorism, there is always the danger that some of the small
tactical nuclear weapons will fall into terrorists' hands and be
used against Pakistan itself. Rawalpindi has a secure nuclear
command and control centre. But breaching these safeguards by
disgruntled elements with terrorist links can't be entirely ruled

out. This potential nuclear risk is a standard ploy Islamabad has used for decades to prevent the West from sanctioning it over its support for terror groups.

A declassified Central Intelligence Agency (CIA) document revealed that former Prime Minister Indira Gandhi had mulled launching an air strike on Pakistan's nascent nuclear weapons programme in 1983 before abandoning the plan. According to one report, Israel offered, "as late as 1984", to bomb Pakistan's principal nuclear facility in Kahuta if India allowed "its jets refueling assurance, but India demurred."

There are three myths in the India-Pakistan relationship that the Pakistani army, ISI and the civilian leadership of Pakistan carefully nurse. They need to be dispelled.

Myth 1: "Pakistan, like India, is also a victim of terrorism."

Pakistan is the victim of its own terrorism; India in sharp contrast is the victim of Pakistani state terrorism. India doesn't send terrorists across the border to kill Pakistani civilians. To equate the two countries is a standard manufactured response of the Pakistani establishment—for instance, citing Indian involvement in Balochistan without providing evidence.

The Pakistani Army meanwhile continues to commit genocide in Balochistan. It does not need India to spark an insurgency among the Baloch—they have been fighting Pakistan's occupation of their country which Rawalpindi forcibly annexed in May 1948. Balochistan comprises 44 per cent of Pakistan's total land area and is rich in minerals.

Myth 2: "Jammu and Kashmir is disputed territory."

It is, but not in the way Pakistan thinks. As seen earlier, the key August 1948 United Nations resolution requires Pakistan, as a first step, to vacate Pakistan-occupied Kashmir (PoK). Once

Pakistan does that, all issues related to Jammu & Kashmir would be on the table. But the soft, porous border proposal discussed between General Pervez Musharraf and Prime Minister Dr Manmohan Singh over 18 years ago was a non-starter. If implemented, it would have given terrorists a free pass to J&K. Over time Pakistan would have occupied the entire state with a "creeping" strategy. It is fortunate Musharraf was removed from office before he could pull further wool over Dr Singh's eyes.

Myth 3: "We are the same people".

We are not. Pakistan has over 220 million people: 110 million Punjabis, 50 million Sindhis, 35 million Pashtuns, 15 million Baloch, and 10 million others. Punjabis dominate the army, civil service and business. In India Punjabis form less than 5 per cent of the population. No, we are not the same people.

After every terror attack on India from Pakistani soil, a rash of articles appears in Indian newspapers. Some are carried on the front pages of well-known dailies, others on the editorial page. All stress caution. Don't blame Pakistan yet, they chant in chorus. Simultaneously, television studios erupt with choreographed debates. Panellists urge viewers in dulcet tones not to jump to conclusions about Pakistani involvement in the latest terror strike.

This orchestrated campaign has a single-point objective: dilute the perception that Pakistan, "the state", had anything to do with the terror attack on India. It places the blame squarely on "non-state" actors over whom, Pakistan's army Generals claim, with a straight face, they have no control.

For a rogue state like Pakistan, mired in internal political chaos and terrorist violence, perception matters disproportionately. Islamabad bases its existence on being the antithesis of India. And yet it obsessively craves attention from India. With China,

Pakistan's relationship is that of a vendor. It provides geostrategic real estate to Beijing.

The ISI's mandate is to play a dual role in India. Its principal task is to fund terror groups against Indian civilian and military targets. Its parallel role is to build a cabal of Indian opinion-makers who will provide credible alibis for Pakistan after terror attacks by the jihadi groups the ISI has nurtured for decades.

Who are these opinion-makers and how are they subverted? In the first tier are journalists and retired army officers. They can be relied upon to defend Pakistan in newspaper columns and television debates. In the second tier lie filmmakers, artistes and writers who constantly seek people-to-people contacts and sporting links with Pakistan—irrespective of its terror strikes on India. In the third tier lurk opposition politicians who are quick to find excuses for Pakistan-sponsored terrorism ("but Pakistan is also a victim of terror") while criticising the Indian government's response. In the fourth and final tier dwell former Indian diplomats. They are track-2 specialists who eagerly attend peace seminars in the Doha and Bangkok.

The ISI nurtures its Indian apologists as generously as it nurtures its terror groups. India's chattering classes remain susceptible to Pakistani wiles. In the 1980s they thrilled to pre-satellite TV serials from Pakistan. In the 2000s no international leadership summit in Delhi was complete without a swaggering Pervez Musharraf or supercilious Imran Khan.

Most card-holding members of the Indian elite come from inconspicuous backgrounds. They host networking parties where politicians across the ideological spectrum mix with the rest of Delhi's nouveaux riches. Till a few years ago, before the Uri and Pulwama attacks, Pakistani guests were often invited: human rights activists from Karachi, TV anchors from Islamabad, retired army officers from Rawalpindi, cricketers from Peshawar and social butterflies from Lahore. That has ended since Uri and Pulwama.

However, the fact that Pakistan and increasingly China have

still managed to subvert a significant section of India's opinion-makers reflects poorly on successive Indian governments. During the ten years of UPA 1 and UPA 2 the atmosphere was especially congenial for the ISI to make deep inroads into the country. *Aman ki asha* soirees and cultural exchanges were the flavour of the decade, rudely interrupted by the 26/11 Mumbai terror attack. But even that was a temporary setback.

The Modi government's initially inconsistent policy on Pakistan-sponsored terrorism emboldened those in India who continued to speak for Pakistan. Modi's two back-to-back speeches in Kerala in September 2016 soon after the Uri terror attack were warmly received by India's "peace professionals". They said, in delighted unison, that Modi was finally advocating the sensible line they had been recommending for years: "strategic restraint".

What precisely is strategic restraint? In essence, it means responding to Pakistan-sponsored terrorism without serious military or economic retaliation. The benefit to India from such restraint? Uninterrupted economic growth. But the US and Israel—to cite just two examples—have shown that economic growth and military action against terrorism are not mutually exclusive.

Those disappointed with the PM's nuanced speech, though it was filled with duality of intent, had expected Modi to deliver a tough, unambiguous message to Pakistan after the Uri terror attack: enough surely was enough? Red lines had been crossed. Pakistan must be taught a lesson. They regarded Modi's direct call to the Pakistani people to fight a "war on poverty and unemployment" as a cop-out. They expected direct military action for the Uri attack, not a homily on poverty and unemployment. That reminded them of ten years of former Prime Minister Manmohan Singh and his apologetic statement on Balochistan at a summit in the Egyptian resort Sharm el-Sheikh.

Modi's speech was, of course, widely misread as events three days later, on 29 September 2016, proved when Indian commandos struck in PoK to destroy multiple Pakistani terror camps. The first 95 per cent of Modi's Kerala address had in fact strongly condemned Pakistan's abetment of terrorism. It was the closing 5 per cent of his address, when he spoke of competing with Pakistan in the war on poverty and unemployment, which India's small but influential community of *aman ki asha* activists seized upon as an expression of strategic restraint – code for doing nothing in the face of Pakistani terrorism.

The 29 September 2016 surgical commando strike and the 27 February 2019 Balakot air attack on Pakistan made Modi's intent clear. Between war and strategic paralysis, India demonstrated that it had several options which could impose a severe cost on Pakistan's abetment of terrorism.

MEDIA

THIRTY

Shining the Light on India

SLUMDOG MILLIONAIRE, DIRECTED BY BRITISH FILMMAKER DANNY BOYLE, was a rage abroad. The one stomach-churning scene in the movie starring Frieda Pinto, Anil Kapoor and Dev Patel, where a child falls into an excreta-filled sewer was played and replayed on foreign television networks with feigned horror. (The excreta was, in fact, a mixture of peanut butter and chocolate sauce!)

Books receive the same treatment. Katherine Boo's *Behind the Beautiful Forevers: Life, Death and Hope in a Mumbai Undercity*, which retells her experiences living in a Mumbai slum for three years, sparing no gory detail, was published to international acclaim in 2012.

Arundhati Roy's *The Ministry of Utmost Happiness* received an equally rapturous welcome abroad as it wended its laborious way through India's graveyard of troubles: Kashmir, Maoism, poverty, communalism, violence. Roy's sense of bitter hopelessness about India enthralls foreign publishers.

Sujatha Gidla's *Ants Among Elephants: An Untouchable Family and the Making of Modern India* tells the story of her uncle Satyamurthy, a Maoist leader who fought the Indian state from the jungles of central India. In a gushing review, *The Economist*[54] described Gidla (a Dalit Christian) as heralding the "arrival of a formidable new writer". The magazine added: "*Ants Among Elephants* is an interesting, affecting and ultimately enlightening

[54]29 July 2017

memoir. It is quite possibly the most striking work of non-fiction set in India since *Behind the Beautiful Forevers* by Katherine Boo."

The names trip off the tongue nicely: Boyle, Boo, Roy, Gidla. *The Economist* didn't exult over Shashi Tharoor's excellent book – *An Era of Darkness: The British Empire in India* – which exposed Britain's atrocities during its colonial occupation of India. Even the British edition of Tharoor's book was retitled to make it less offensive to British sensitivities. *An Era of Darkness* became the anodyne *An Inglorious Empire: What the British Did to India*. In an interview with the BBC for the book's British launch, one of the panelists was dismissive of Tharoor's detailed description of the brutalities of the British Empire and the financial ruination it brought upon India.

Should criticism of India matter? Emphatically not. India has many flaws—violence, poverty, rape, corruption, communalism, casteism. It is right for journalists and authors, Indian and foreign, to shine a light on them.

It is equally right for filmmakers to show the underbelly of India – from the coal mines of Dhanbad to the slums of Mumbai. Sunlight is a disinfectant. Shine it mercilessly on India's imperfections. Only then will change take place. The problem though is balance.

Where are the films on the brilliant "Team Indus" in Bengaluru which was making a robotic spacecraft to land on the moon's surface as part of a $30 million global competition sponsored by Google? Team Indus was one of only five teams, including those from Japan and Israel, which made it to the finals but fell short at the last hurdle. These stories, like the excellent web series *Rocket Boys* on pioneering space scientists Homi Bhabha and Vikram Sarabhai, too, need to be told by Indian (and foreign) writers and film-makers. Where, too, are the stories of India's technology startups which form the world's third largest hub of tech-driven innovation? You won't find many in the pages of *The New York Times, The Guardian* or *The Economist.*

Rocket Boys, tracing the life and work of Bhabha and Sarabhai, is an exception that proves the rule: positive, uplifting stories about India don't make the cut in film or literature. Indians though, are over-sensitive about how India is portrayed globally. Americans didn't care how their country was portrayed during the decade-long Vietnam war, the illegal invasion of Iraq, the historical crimes of African slave trading, the lynchings of African-Americans by the Ku Klux Klan as recently as in the 20th century and the frequent gun violence in schools. The British don't care how their country is portrayed as a brutal former coloniser. The Chinese don't care that their country is projected as an international law-breaker and abuser of human rights by most of the world.

Criticism is the lifeblood of media. Good journalism delivers news and opinion based on facts. The plurality of opinion in a democracy evens out the narrative. If facts are twisted, the market will punish the newspaper, website or television channel. The Modi government, like any other government in the states, must be held to account. The criticism should be fierce and fearless. That is the hallmark of a liberal democracy.

৵

Why does India get bad press internationally? The answer lies within complex layers of history and culture. Global media coverage of Kashmir is an example of how inaccurate and biased Western reportage on India can be.

Exhibit one: *The New York Times*[55] editorial board wrote: "The Indian government's decision to revoke the semi-autonomous status of Kashmir, accompanied by a huge security clampdown, is dangerous and wrong. Bloodshed is all but certain. The United Nations recommended holding a referendum to let Kashmiris decide their fate, but that never happened."

---

[55] 5 August 2019.

Note the confidence with which *The New York Times* makes the assertion: "Bloodshed is all but certain."

Worse is the newspaper's reference to the United Nations "recommending holding a referendum", without mentioning the fact that the UN had set a pre-condition for Pakistan to vacate PoK before any referendum could even be considered.

Exhibit two: Reuters reported[56] that "Police used tear gas and pellets to fight back at least 10,000 people protesting Delhi's withdrawal of special rights for Jammu and Kashmir in its main city of Srinagar on Friday, a police official and two witnesses said."

What were Reuters' sources? An unnamed police officer and two anonymous "witnesses". The report of "a crowd of 10,000" protestors was disproved by on-ground accounts from credible, independent Indian journalists. Reuters' reportage did not meet the standard of professional journalism.

The New York Times editorial board has often been forced to apologise for inaccurate commentary. The BBC and *Al Jazeera*'s editorial coverage of Kashmir is equally tendentious. Neither sufficiently stresses Pakistan's malignant role in abetting terrorism in Kashmir. Without context, such journalism sets a low professional bar.

India remains a tempting target for foreign media. A large, diverse democracy, it has multiple mutinies, as the late V S Naipaul wrote, going on raucously at the same time. These provide easy pickings for Western journalists. They have learnt their lesson the hard way after the French magazine *Charlie Hebdo* was attacked by Islamist terrorists, several of its staff killed and the publication eventually forced to change ownership. The lesson learnt? It is safer to criticise India. Indians don't hit back.

India, in fact, provides Western media an invaluable additional resource: Indian journalists. These editorial recruits can be

---

[56] 9 August 2019.

inveigled to write how viscerally casteist and communal India is. Were Western journalists to write the same articles, they would be accused of racism. Indian journalists serve as useful surrogates. The Indian government has compounded the problem by not holding daily briefings to provide timely information on key political and economic issues, allowing international media to misinform and distort as it does routinely in its reportage on Kashmir.

India presents an awkward problem for the West. Rising China can be excoriated for its totalitarianism. But India, a diverse, noisy, still-poor democracy, is different from everything the West has encountered since it constructed the current world order after World War II. Think-tanks like Chatham House in Britain and the Heritage Foundation in the US know from detailed projections that India will be the world's third largest economy well before 2030. The post-pandemic growth trajectory of India is irreversible, whichever political coalition is in office.

Despite the growing importance of the Quad and relentless efforts by Western leaders to draw India into its geostrategic orbit, influential lobbies in Washington are wary of a rising India: Asian, democratic and diverse, India's rise, without resorting to colonial plunder, centuries-long transatlantic slavery and genocide of indigenous people in other continents, unsettles them. Their own rise was not free of these atrocities.

The US has always been transactional and pragmatic. It needs India to counter the rise of Communist China as well as deal with the threat of the China-Russia axis. After spending seven decades fighting the paranoia of a potential domino effect of Soviet communism spreading in Indo-China and elsewhere, Washington is now confronted with the prospect of China dominating global economic and technological power supported by a militarily aggressive Russia as alliance partner.

The West used to look upon India as an unreliable, Nehruvian, nose-in-the-air, non-aligned, left-leaning country after

Independence. It gravitated towards Pakistan, the geostrategic gun-on-hire. The rise of China and the shadow of Russia have concentrated Western minds. The West needs India to help police the Indo-Pacific. It accepts that India's consumer market will be the largest in the world in the next decade, ahead of even China whose population has begun shrinking and ageing. The changing balance of global power and the impending loss of its centuries-long global hegemony, undermines the West's historical self-image.

Salvatore Babones, an associate professor at Sydney University, analysed the root cause of the antagonism of the West's academic elite towards a rising India[57]:

> Why does the West hate India? Hate is a strong word, and to be fair, many Americans, Europeans, and Australians love India. Even more of them know nothing about India. But whatever individual Westerners may think of India, "the West" is thoroughly anti-Indian, and that institutional hatred is getting stronger by the hour.
>
> Indians will be very familiar with this from their school textbooks, which are full of stories about the anti-Indianism of the colonial era. To be more accurate, British (as well as French and Portuguese) colonisation was specifically anti-Hindu, a tendency that ultimately led to the violence of Partition.
>
> For the first half century of modern India's Independence, Western anti-Hinduism was relatively muted. But lately it has broken out in places like Leicester, Toronto, and New Jersey. In all three places, the root cause is the same: an informal alliance between global Islamists and Western elites. Groups linked to Islamist extremism have convinced anti-Hindu Westerners to support their aggression toward Indians and India.
>
> Many Indians see the hand of Pakistan (or even China)

---

[57]*Firstpost*, 7 November 2022.

behind this unholy alliance. This is to misunderstand the arrow of influence. Western elites are not being duped by Islamist militants into hating India. Western elites are using Islamist militants as the shock troops for their own anti-Hinduism. We've seen this all play out before. Western elites have long harboured a small but vocal anti-Semitic minority among their ranks. After the horrors of the Holocaust, overt anti-Semitism became unacceptable in the West. This forced anti-Semitic elites to change their rhetoric. Instead of spouting anti-Semitic slurs, they switched to anti-Zionist and anti-Israel language. They found ready political allies for their opposition to Israel in the Arab world and Iran.

Today, on university campuses throughout the English-speaking world, you will find anti-Zionist, anti-Israel protests being organised by a strange alliance of Western secularists and militant Islamists. People who disagree vehemently on progressive social issues like women's rights and gay marriage work side by side to vilify Israel and prevent Israelis from speaking on campus. Together, they have organised the boycott, divestment, and sanctions (BDS) campaign targeting Israel.

And now they have a new target: India. As with Israel, the Islamists target India mainly for political reasons. They have been targeting Indian nationalism for more than a century, and they are not necessarily anti-Hindu. They have political goals, and they are prepared to fight to achieve them. The banned Popular Front of India (PFI) is representative of this kind of anti-India militancy. It is not anti-Hindu per se; its anti-Hinduism is driven by its political goals, not by irrational personal prejudice.

The motives of Western anti-Hindu intellectuals are very different, but the respectability they provide is crucial for the success of anti-India movements. For example, the overtly political **2021 Dismantling Global Hindutva** conference was co-sponsored by dozens of university research institutes. The conference organisers obtained statements of support from 40 professional associations and "60+ community organisations". It was in no sense a normal academic conference. It was an organised anti-Hindu jamboree. The main information sheet published by the conference organisers emphasised that "calling out Hindutva is not anti-Hindu". The parallel with the anti-Semitic trope that "calling out Zionism is not anti-Jewish" is crystal clear. The tactics are the same because the institutions—and many of the individuals—are the same. The Western elite anti-Semitic template has been adopted by anti-Hinduists, who (just like anti-Semites) mobilise institutional endorsements to bring the mainstream news media onto their side.

Hindu civil society organisations rightly called out the Dismantling Global Hindutva conference and the anti-Hindu sentiments that motivated it. These organisations have, however, missed the trick on anti-Hinduism. They have, instead, attached the label "Hinduphobia" to these slurs, on the model of Islamophobia. But anti-Hinduism is not a phobia. Many people really are afraid of Muslims; they are not afraid of Hindus.

Anti-Hindu Western intellectuals do not fear the rise of India; they resent it. Just as Western anti-Semites are offended by the success of Israel, Western anti-Hinduists are offended by the success of India. They can't accept the idea of a strong and independent Hindu-majority country. They would much rather keep India weak and poor, just as their ancestors did centuries ago.

∽

Weeks before Modi became prime minister in May 2014, a spate of articles appeared in the Western media bitterly critical of him. It would appear that a plague was about to visit India on 26 May, the day of his swearing-in. Roger Boyes wrote in the London *Times*: "It looks as if India is embarking on a sea change. We can and must respect their democratic choice. We can also warn our Indian friends, *in case they haven't worked it out for themselves,* Mr Modi is potentially big trouble."

Note the superciliousness: "...in case they haven't worked it out for themselves." It revealed Boyes' condescending, racist reflex.

Amol Rajan, *The Independent's* Indian-origin editor, wrote: "The charge sheet against Narendra Damodardas Modi is familiar and well-founded: the stench of Hindu nationalism covers him."

Being brown, Rajan served as a useful surrogate.

The Economist's infamous cover story on Modi in the middle of the 2014 Lok Sabha election campaign advised Indians: "We do not find the prospect of a government led by Congress under Mr (Rahul) Gandhi an inspiring one. But we have to recommend it to Indians as the less disturbing option."

The contrast with the Western media's coverage of the Congress is stark. Its 10-year tenure, laced with serial UPA scams, was lightly treated. The Gandhi dynasty – including the suddenly wealthy Robert Vadra – was treated with kid gloves by the Western media. No hard questions were asked about Vadra's land deals. No probing stories have yet been written on Sonia or Rahul's secretive trips abroad or the opaque acquisition of the property-rich *National Herald* newspaper, 76 per cent of whose shareholding is owned by Sonia and Rahul Gandhi. That's absentee journalism.

Why might this be so? The Anglospheric media continues to be disproportionately influenced by its clubby sources in India's old establishment, comprising a left-leaning cabal of academics, journalists, lawyers, NGOs and activists. This motley group rarely got outraged over the UPA government's corruption or farmer suicides in Congress-governed states. It reserves its anger – transmitted to sympathetic global ears – for the "danger" Modi poses to Indian democracy. Indians lambasting India is a post-colonial sport with eager local recruits seeking a foreign byline.

Disconnected India-born celebrities provide more ballast. A letter in *The Guardian,* signed by a group that included Salman Rushdie and Anish Kapoor, warned Indians that a Modi victory in May 2014 "would bode ill for India". On cue, a clutch of Bollywood B-listers issued a statement urging people to vote for a "secular government".

As one American journalist, David Cohen, wrote: "Like the US, India has cultural elitists who seem to desperately crave the approval of their former colonial masters in Europe. The Indian cultural elite despises Modi every bit as much as the American cultural elite despised (Ronald) Reagan. They look down their noses at Modi, cringing at the thought of being led by a common tea seller who can barely speak English. (Can you imagine Chinese or Russian citizens, proud of their own heritage, being ashamed that their leaders don't speak English?)

"Modi takes a tough stand against Pakistan-sponsored terrorism. In this regard, Americans would do well to remember that the Islamists are not fighting against the 'West'. Islamists are fighting against all non-Islamic societies. India is very much on the front lines of what we used to call the War on Terror, before our leaders lost the nerve to name it. Modi with his assertive posture against Pakistan – reminiscent of Reagan's stance against the former Soviet Union – should be a valuable natural ally."

I wrote in *The Times of India* on 18 April 2014, weeks before the general election: "Washington and London would like to do business with an economically liberal Modi government, but in Modi they could be dealing with a man who will introduce qualitative changes in India's political, economic and military relationship with the West. A Modi-led government will, for example, encourage technologically-capable Indian companies like the Tatas and Mahindras to develop indigenous defence equipment, saving billions of dollars in foreign exchange on fighter jets, submarines, artillery guns and other advanced weaponry. Foreign defence purchases, where made, will be transparent, the process swift."

That is exactly what has come to pass nearly ten years later. India's presidency of the G20 affords a glimpse of how the new world order is taking shape.

∾

Social media has enabled the prime minister to largely bypass the Indian and foreign media. This though has made the relationship with traditional media even more fraught. Being ignored does not endear journalists to a prime minister seen as remote and aloof.

How should the Modi government respond to such bias? It shouldn't. The government must instead communicate its policies through a structured daily media briefing, especially with the spotlight on India during multiple G20 meetings leading up to a global summit hosted by India. The scrutiny will be intense.

Each key ministry must have a designated spokesperson who briefs the media by rotation. Dissent is the foundational principle of democracy. In the absence of a structured daily information protocol by the government genuine achievement risks being ignored while errors of judgement are magnified by Indian and foreign media who resent that they have limited access to the top.

Foreign correspondents understand the reality. India's democracy has so many octopus-like arms among the media, bureaucracy, NGOs, activists, Opposition-ruled states, the police and public intellectuals that dissent is in no danger. But their editors back in New York and London want stories that work on the principle that bad news about India makes good global headlines. Indian journalists writing for American and British newspapers give their editors what they want: stories of rapes, riots, casteism and communalism. Indians though are wrong to worry about what foreign media writes.

Colonised, benighted India in 1947 had a literacy rate of 12 per cent, an average lifespan of 32 years and a tiny GDP of ₹2.70 lakh crore. Today literacy in India is 79 per cent, average lifespan 70 years and GDP over $3.75 trillion, larger than the GDP of former colonial power Britain. It wasn't meant to quite work out that way, write bemused Western journalists. Global tech and consumer firms now line up in Delhi to invest billions of dollars in foreign direct investment (FDI) in the world's fastest-growing consumer market bursting with world-class tech startups.

The old entitled Indian elite looks at India with the eye of the intellectually colonised. It is invariably on the wrong side of history – eulogising Pakistan-funded terrorists like Burhan Wani, being apologists for China, and undermining India at international conclaves. India is a noisy, open democracy. It gives everybody an opportunity to defame it. That is as it should be. It is the true strength of Indian democracy.

THIRTY-ONE

A Simmering Anger

THERE WAS AN UNPRECEDENTED TORRENT OF INTERNATIONAL CRITICISM of the Modi government following the 2020 Delhi riots. Britain's left-leaning *The Guardian* was incensed. It declared: "The immediate causes of events are the fallout from Narendra Modi's unjust Citizenship (Amendment) Act, the dangerous rhetoric employed by the ruling Bharatiya Janata Party in Delhi's city elections this month, and the mob incitement by BJP leaders like Kapil Mishra, to violently remove a group of Muslims who were blocking a road in the capital's north-west to protest against the legislation."

The Wall Street Journal's three correspondents—all of Indian origin—reported: "(Intelligence Bureau officer) Ankit Sharma was returning home when a group of rioters started throwing stones and charged into the street near where his house is located, his brother said."

The WSJ journalists then supposedly quoted Sharma's brother Ankur Sharma: "They came armed with stones, rods, knives and even swords; they shouted 'Jai Shri Ram'". In an interview with India's national broadcaster Prasar Bharati, Ankur Sharma disputed the WSJ report: "I never gave such a statement to *The Wall Street Journal*. This is a ploy to defame my brother and my family. *The Wall Street Journal* is lying."

Most international journalist haven't either read the Citizenship (Amendment) Act or haven't understood it. The fault though lies at least partially with the Indian government. It phrased the CAA with a dog-whistle paragraph that mentions six religions eligible for fast-track citizenship, leaving Islam out. The reason for Islam's exclusion has been laboriously explained by the government—principally that a law aimed at stateless non-Muslim refugees from three Muslim-majority countries, Pakistan, Afghanistan and Bangladesh, already living in India (pre-31 December 2014) can't obviously cover Muslims, persecuted Ahmadiyyas and Shias notwithstanding.

The CAA has nothing to do with existing Indian citizens, Muslim or non-Muslim. It has to do with non-Muslim refugees from abroad. The government's intent though was always clear: To single out foreign Muslims from three neighbouring Islamic countries. And thereby send two domestic messages: One, to Indian Muslims; two, to Indian Hindus, the BJP's voter base.

Matters now become more complicated. The sting in the CAA's tail is meant to right a perceived historical wrong. For 500 years, Hindus have quietly (and often not so quietly) watched as first Mughal invaders and then British colonists subjugated them. They were punitively taxed, suffered constant public humiliation, and had violence inflicted upon them under both the Mughal and British Empires.

When freedom came, the Congress, in an attempt to unite a country wracked by communal riots during Partition, bent over backwards to appease Muslims who chose to stay behind in India. They were allowed to keep Sharia, their personal law, even as Hindu personal law was codified. The 80 per cent Hindu majority was too divided by caste, language and region to argue effectively at the time that India was the only country in the world where the majority community was discriminated against in jobs and education while minorities were favoured.

Moderate Hindus are slow to anger. But after 200 years of Mughal depredations, when thousands of temples were destroyed, another 200 years of British colonialism when India's economy was severely damaged, and finally after 55 years of Congress governments that titled towards Muslim-first secularism, even moderate Hindus had had enough.

That is the pathology of Modi's landslide victories in 2014 and 2019. Moderate Hindus, who in the past had voted for the Congress, saw in Modi a Hindu leader who would deliver to them the justice and respect that was their due in their own country and which had been denied them not only by both Muslim and Christian invaders but by their own post-Independence governing elite.

In a sense, therefore, the rise of Modi is a quiet uprising of the moderate Hindu of Naipaul's *Wounded Civilisation*. The frontlines may contain the extremist Hindu fringe. But the silent majority backing them is made up of the ordinary Hindu. That is why the BJP and its NDA allies collectively won 45 per cent vote share in the 2019 Lok Sabha election—higher than even Jawaharlal Nehru's 44.99 per cent vote share in 1952.

Four pillars are needed to hold up a structure. Take one away and the structure tilts. In a democracy, the four pillars are the executive (government), the legislature (Parliament and state assemblies), the judiciary and the media. Each of these pillars has had its moments of turbulence: the executive and the judiciary during the Emergency and now increasingly over the Supreme Court's collegium system of choosing judges; and the executive and state legislatures through the decades when state assemblies were routinely dissolved and President's rule imposed.

The media, before and after independence, has faced several challenges as well. Under colonial rule, mainstream newspapers often toed the British Viceroy's line. Many others though were nationalistic and suffered colonial anger. After independence, the Emergency marked a new low point. Most newspapers lost their nerve and bent their spine.

The late 1970s and 1980s were the golden period of Indian

media. The Emergency was gone. New publications were launched. Specialised Sunday papers made their appearance. So did specialised magazines. In the 1990s, television was nascent but neutral. News had not yet fallen hostage to vested political and business interests. When did media's fall begin? The seeds were sown in the late 1990s when the first BJP-led government took office. It was around this time that Sonia Gandhi displaced Sitaram Kesri as Congress president.

In 1984, the BJP had two MPs. In 1999, it had 182. In 1984, the Congress had 414 MPs. In 2014, it had 44 and in 2019, 52. It is within these numbers that lie clues to the schisms that have developed over the decades. The media was drawn into this political vortex. Senior editors in the 1980s and 1990s were politically (relatively) neutral. The concept of paid news was notably absent. I launched my first media company, Sterling Newspapers Pvt Ltd, in the 1980s. Our journalists researched, interviewed, wrote and edited without fear or favour and without government interference. Very few editors in the country during that period fell prey to external influences: political parties, business houses, foreign intelligence agencies and power brokers.

The real change came in the 2000s. By then the *Indian Express* group had acquired Sterling Newspapers with our staff of nearly 100 editors, writers, designers and marketers. I set up a new media firm soon after that and began recruiting a new generation of young editors and correspondents.

But things had changed. In 2004 the Congress-led UPA government returned to office. More and more journalists had begun to cosy up to politicians and business houses. Between 1998 and 2004, when the NDA was in power and LK Advani home minister and then (from 2000) deputy prime minister, it did not occur to me to seek an appointment with him though he had been a regular columnist in one of our publications for over ten years. That was the arm's length approach to politicians we had always maintained.

Shortly after the Congress-led UPA government took office in May 2004, we found ourselves receiving invitations to interview UPA ministers. Finance Minister P Chidambaram conveyed to our Delhi bureau chief that he would be happy to accede to our request for an exclusive interview. We did the interview in Chidambaram's North Block office. This was followed in the next few months and years by exclusive interviews with then industry and commerce minister Kamal Nath, former petroleum minister Mani Shankar Aiyar and the then chief minister of Jammu and Kashmir Mufti Mohammad Sayeed, who hosted us to lunch at his Srinagar residence along with daughter Mehbooba. Not once did we attempt a further meeting with any of them beyond what was professionally required.

But on every trip to Delhi—and Srinagar—from 2005 onwards, I noticed a distinct change in the interaction between journalists and politicians. It is around this time that the scourge of paid news became an epidemic. Many journalists became PR intermediaries for political leaders. It was inevitable that PR would overwhelm journalism. The Radia tapes were recorded in 2008–09. Unofficial versions were circulated in early-2010 and finally published by two weekly magazines, *Outlook* and *Open,* in November 2010. They revealed the nexus between politicians and journalists.

The nexus has only grown stronger. It has also—since Prime Minister Modi took office in May 2014—become more toxic. The masks have slipped. Pretence has been dropped. Embarrassment at violating the principles of ethical journalism has evaporated. Paid news and private treaties are not the issues any more: they are far too common to even bear mention. The real cancer is the politicisation of journalism. Several television channels have become mouthpieces of the government.

∽

Modi has not been the perfect prime minister. Far from it. Early in his premiership, I wrote this: "The most successful leaders surround themselves with people smarter than themselves. Modi, in contrast, is surrounded by people who are not smarter than him. That is, perhaps, the biggest failing of his prime ministership."

Modi has failed to get the law ministry to speed up prosecution of allegedly corrupt opposition leaders. Cases are allowed to meander because government-appointed public prosecutors either don't turn up in court or advance weak arguments at hearings. What does all this add up to? Wilful delays by an old ecosystem that still has the power to block Modi's anti-corruption agenda? Complicity between that old, corrupt ecosystem and the new ecosystem that Modi has created but lacks full control over? Or something even more sinister?

Whatever the truth, this state of affairs can't go on. Modi believes that macro-economic policies matter less electorally than micro-economic schemes. He is the archetypal executor. Give him a project—new or old—and he will pursue it to completion with frequent reviews and micro-management. The results across domains have surpassed critics' expectations.

Modi's attention is fixated on the 2024 Lok Sabha election. He believes a combination of welfare benefits for the poor, large-scale infrastructure projects, foreign policy leadership and muscular Hinduism will deliver him a third term. He may be right. The Opposition privately thinks so too. Hence the anger. The vitriol comes from the top: Rahul Gandhi who stands to lose the most from Modi's continued electoral popularity.

The Indian media meanwhile remains divided: on one side is the supplicatory media that constantly flatters Modi; on the other is the viscerally hostile media that rages at him. A critical eye obviously needs to be cast on the Modi government's performance but an eye free of bias.

Amartya Sen, the Nobel laureate, wrote in a leading daily shortly after the BJP-led NDA's landslide victory in the 2019 Lok Sabha election: "There has been widespread criticism in the news media across the world (from *The New York Times*, *The Washington Post*, *The Wall Street Journal*, *The Guardian*, *The Observer*, *Le Monde*, *Die Zeit* and *Haaretz* to the BBC and CNN) of the ways and means of securing the BJP's victory, including instigation of hatred and intolerance of groups of Indian citizens, particularly Muslims, who have every right to be treated with respect (as under the Gandhi-Tagore understanding)."

Sen's remarks reflect a mind that genuflects at the feet of Western opinion. It is in thrall to what the foreign media writes about Indian politics, Indian democracy, Indian elections and Indian society.

Since the advent of social media, readers and viewers have become real-time arbiters of editorial opinion. Ivory tower editors, long used to a one-way discourse, are unsettled by this democratisation of the media. Factual errors are called out online in hours, forcing newspapers like *The New York Times* and *The Washington Post* and television networks like CNN and BBC to apologise editorially and post corrections. And yet these still are the media that Sen and his ilk in India pay obeisance to.

In a healthy democracy, it is as vital to have two strong national parties as it is to have two strong, duelling opinions on the left and right. The problem India now faces is that the marginalisation of the Congress has left the BJP with a monopoly on governance and legislation. Regional parties act not as a check but as disruptors.

The BJP's success can presage failure just as Indira Gandhi's did in the late 1970s. Power is never permanent – nor should it be. The BJP, however, is not driven by dynasty. The leadership of the BJP or the RSS does not pass from parent to son or daughter. There is no Narendra Modi dynasty. There is no Mohan Bhagwat dynasty. That too, though, is not an adequate safeguard to protect democracy. India needs a strong Opposition. The

Congress, as long as it is run like a family enterprise, can no longer provide such an Opposition, despite Rahul's resurgence.

Mahatma Gandhi foresaw this when he said shortly before Independence that the Congress should be disbanded. What he meant was the Congress must abandon the pre-eminence of individual leaders which served it well to evict the British, but would not serve democracy quite as well. He was right. It needed to be recalibrated to serve independent India.

As India prepares to elect the eighteenth Lok Sabha in May 2024, Modi stands on the cusp of history. If he leads the BJP to victory, he will become only the second prime minister since Nehru to win three successive general elections for full five-year terms.

Index

9/11 terror attacks, 165, 369

Aam Aadmi Party (AAP), 8, 13, 106–107, 130–133
style of politics, 133
Abdullah, Farooq, 60
Abdullah, Omar, 100, 280
Abdullahs, 60, 66, 100, 280, 306, 375
Abedin, Syed Zainul, 274
Abhishek (Mamata Banerjee's nephew), 126
Acts for Union 1800, 362
Adams, John Quincy, 122
Adityanath, Yogi, 41–42, 94–96, 98–99, 116, 130, 273, 284–285
80:20 division, 289
2022 UP assembly election, 288–289
crisis management, 96
criticism against, 293
infrastructure projects, 97
law and order, 97
second-term as chief minister, 293–294
welfare benefits, 97
Advani, Lal Krishna, 4–5, 7–9, 11, 72, 99–100, 127, 404
Rath Yatra, 100
Advita Ashram, 27
Affordable Care Act (Obamacare), 150

Afghanistan, 61
Soviet invasion of, 204
Taliban-ruled, 369
African-American slaves, 62
African slavery, 169, 251–252, 257–258
African slave trade, 251–252
Agastya, Rishi, 220
Agnihotri, Vivek, 305
agricultural tax reform, 185–186
Ahmadis, 279
Ahmadiyyas, 371
AI-IA merger, 173–175
AIMIM, 42, 308, 345
treatment of Muslims, 292
Air Arabia, 174
Air India, 90, 172–175
airlines traffic rights case, 174–175
Airports Authority of India (AAI), 173
Aiyar, Mani Shankar, 405
Aiyar, Swaminathan, 92, 171
Akbar, M. J., 164
Alibaba Financial, 182
Aligarh Muslim University (AMU), 75
All India Majlis-e-Ittehadul Muslimeen, 319, 345
All India Muslim Personal Law Board (AIMPLB), 303–304
Al Nahyan, Prince Mohammed bin Zayed, 247

al-Qaeda, 242, 266, 369
Altemeyer, Robert, 340
Amazon, 176–179
Ambedkar, Babasaheb, 102,
   301–302
American Jews, 312
American–Mexican war (1846-48),
   251
America's invasion of Iraq (2003),
   266
Anand, Aakash, 126
Anglosphere nations, 236
Anna Hazare anti-corruption
   movement, 3, 8, 171, 187
Ansari, Hamid, 81–82
   role in Iran, 82
anti-corruption movement, 3, 8,
   89, 171, 187
anti-Hinduism, 396
"anti-national" controversy, 108,
   322
Arab-Western coalition air strikes,
   241
Arkwright, Richard, 161
Articles of Indian constitution
   Article 14, 24, 290
   Article 19(1)(a), 291
   Article 21, 290
   Article 25, 290
   Article 25(i), 291
   Article 370, 32, 101, 372–375
Art of War (Sun Tzu), 52
Arunachal Pradesh, 50, 198, 207,
   215
ASEAN, 48–49, 248–249
Asian Institute of Management
   (AIM) Policy Centre, 123
assembly elections, 2023, 117
Associated Journals Ltd, 137–140
Association for Democratic
   Reforms (ADR), 4, 10
AUKUS, 49, 211–212, 218, 237

Ayushman Bharat scheme, 75, 88
Azad, Kirti, 105
Azad, Vinayak, 41
Aziz, Sartaj, 60

Babones, Salvatore, 394
Babri Masjid demolition, 30, 55,
   72, 100
Backops, 170
Baghel, Radhelal, 117
Bahujan Samaj Party (BSP), 94,
   132, 344–345
Baig, Mahboob Ali, 303
Bajpai, Kanti, 198
Bajwa, Qamar Javed, 369
Balakot air attack (2019), 19, 69,
   134, 370, 385
Balakrishnan, Ajit, 161
Balkan wars, 194
Ballmer, Steve, 163
Bandaranaike, Sirimavo, 254
Banerjee, Mamata, 15, 68, 85, 100,
   105–106, 126, 132, 308, 333–334
   electoral target, 107
   Jyoti Basu strategy, 107, 309
   victory in assembly poll of 2021,
   131
Bangladesh, 50, 284, 372
Bangladesh war (1971), 254
Barooah, D. K., 64
Barrackpore incident (1857), 311
Barton, Dominic, 159
Basu, Jyoti, 107, 309
Basu, Prasenjit K, 196
Battenberg, Lord, 354
Battle of Palashee (Plassey, 1757),
   265, 355
Bay of Bengal Initiative for Multi-
   Sectoral Technical and Economic
   Cooperation (BIMSTE), 237
Beckett, Samuel, 115
Belur Math, 26, 28

Bhabha Atomic Research Centre
(BARC), 221
Bhabha, Homi, 232–233, 390–391
Bhagwat, Mohan, 8
Bharadwaj, Abhishek, 128
Bharadwaj, Rishi, 220
Bharat Heavy Electricals Limited
(BHEL), 158
Bharatiya Janata Party (BJP), 4–5,
11, 18, 25, 29, 43, 73, 86, 96,
106, 130, 293, 297, 308, 320,
324–326, 345, 407
contenders against, 106–107
criteria for prime ministerial
candidate, 11
defection of senior leaders, 117
electoral armoury, 44–46
electoral victory, 29, 66, 84, 94,
100
foreign media on, 297
high command, 116–117
Hindi heartland states, 133
Hindu-first nationalism, 313
Hindu nationalism project, 55
Hindu votes, 30–31
leadership, 284
majoritarianism, 283, 298
membership, 45
power hierarchy, 43
surrender to farmers, 126
sycophancy, 43, 64
upper caste vote, 31
vote share, 30–31, 45–46
welfare benefits, 46–47, 86
Bharatiyata (Indianness), 112,
275
Bharatiya Vidya Saar, 220
Bharat Sanchar Nigam Limited
(BSNL), 90
Bhushan, Prashant, 133
Bhutan, 50, 207, 216
Bhutto, Benazir, 254
Bhutto, Zulfiqar Ali, 367, 379
Biden, Joe, 48–49, 235, 253

Biju Janata Dal (BJD), 42
Bismarck, Otto von, 339
black money, 91
Blair, Tony, 62
Bloomberg, Michael, 164
Border Road Organisation (BRO),
91
Bose, Subhas Chandra, 102
Boyes, Roger, 397
The Bradley Mine, 169
Brahmins, 30
Brexit, 93, 259
Briand, Aristide, 339
BRICS, 237, 287
Brihanmumbai Municipal
Corporation (BMC), 38
Britain, 250–251, 380
Brexit referendum, 361–363
British women, status of, 253–
254
colonial debt to India, 349–351
contribution to India, 352
Global, 361–362
massacres of Aborigines, 257
plunder of Indian wealth, 358
racism in, 354–355
reparations by, 351–352, 358
Royal Family, 352–354
tax revenue from Indian, 355–
356
transatlantic African slave trade,
355–356
British Commonwealth, 359–361
BSP–SP–RLD mega-alliance, 29
Buddhism, 47, 248, 264, 276
Burt, Alistair, 242
Bush, George W., 123, 369
Bush, Jeb, 123
Business Maharajahs (Piramal),
170
Cabinet Committee on Security
(CCS), 19, 68
Cameron, David, 93–94

Canterbury Tales, The (Chaucer), 219
carbon dioxide (CO₂) emissions, 167
carbon neutrality, 168–169
Carter, Jimmy, 123
caste system, 34, 265, 268, 277
casual violence, 33
Central Police Organisations (CPO), 149
Chadha, Raghav, 133
Chahal, Iqbal Singh, 38–39
Chandra, Naresh, 58
Chakravarty, Praveen, 134
Charles III, King, 353
Charlie Hebdo, 279, 392
ChatGPT, 162
Chatham House, 393
Chatterjee, Basudev, 357
Chaudhary, Dipanjan Roy, 209
Chiang Kai-Shek, 226
Chidambaram, P., 137, 143, 153, 299, 405
China, 63, 192, 225, 249, 254–256, 393–394
  aggression along LAC, 21
  aggressive policy across Asia, 52–53
  agricultural productivity, 183–184
  alliance with Russia, 52
  average per capita income, 205
  Belt and Road Initiative (BRI), 53, 194, 216
  carbon dioxide (CO₂) emissions, 167, 169
  Chabahar port development, 216
  chip-making ecosystem, 216
  crackdown on Hong Kong, 210
  Cultural Revolution, 208
  demographic dividend, 154–155
  demographics, 197
  economic reforms, 204, 216

  economy, 155, 159, 196, 200–201, 203
  ethnic tension in, 197, 211
  fertility rate, 154–156
  GDP, 200–203
  greying of, 154–155
  Hong Kong's value to, 222–223
  household per-capita income gap, 205
  incursions along the LAC, 50
  infrastructure and education, 205–206
  intellectual property rights, 220–221
  intelligence services, 222
  labour costs, 84
  militarisation in South China Sea, 194, 211
  Muslim Uighur minorities, 197
  nuclear programme, 232
  one-child policy, 154–155
  "One China" policy, 194
  prosperity, 205–206
  Qing dynasty, 207
  relations with UK, 210–211
  salami-slicing of India's border, 51
  scientific revolution, 220
  self-imposed economic wounds, 160
  social tensions in, 224
  spending on R&D, 219
  Tibet paranoia, 207–208
  total population, 53, 62
  urban-rural ratio, 206
  views on India, 210
  working-age (15–59 years) population, 54
  yuan-dollar rate, 201
China Agricultural University, 183
China-Pakistan Economic Corridor (CPEC), 197, 367

China-Pakistan nexus, 50
Chinese Communist Party (CCP),
    191–192, 198, 207–208, 222
Chinese products, ban on, 39
Chinese universities, 206
Chitra, Rachel, 181–182
Chopra, Nikhil, 39–40
Chowdhury, Adhir Ranjan, 286
Christianity, 264, 266, 274, 276–
    277, 280, 301
Churchill, Winston, 267, 339
Cipla, 39
Citizen's Action Committee (CAC),
    13
Citizenship (Amendment) Act
    (CAA, 2019), 23–25, 33, 36, 50,
    76, 326, 402
    clause 2, 23–24
    clause 3, 24
citizenship rights, 23
climate justice, 169
Clinton, Bill, 58, 283
Clive, Robert, 355
Cohen, David, 398
Cole, WA, 357
College of Physicians and
    Surgeons (CPS), 151
Colonial British "nationalism," 112
communalism, 121, 310, 313
communal polarisation, 280
communal violence, 67, 263,
    295–296, 298, 305
Communist Party of India
    (Marxist) (CPM)
    treatment of Muslims, 292
Congress party, 55, 65, 98, 134,
    320–321, 345
    alliance with JD(S), 29
    defeat of, 130
    gathbandhan, 29
    gaushala-friendly policy, 282–283
    general election of 2019, 18, 31

problems facing, 106
rule from 1947 to 2014, 16
saffronisation of, 282–283
target audience, 310
treatment of Muslims, 292–293
UPA government led by, 3, 8
victory in general election of
    2009, 5
vote share and seats, 42
    1970s to 1990s, 30
    in 2019, 31
Convenient Action: Gujarat's
    Response to Challenges of
    Climate Change (2011), 168
Cook, Michael, 316
COP26 and COP27 climate change
    summits, 166, 168
corporate culture, 162–163
corruption scams, 3, 7, 14, 77,
    182
cost of holding elections, 91–92
Countering America's Adversaries
    Through Sanctions Act
    (CAATSA), 217
Covid-19 pandemic, 18, 36–37,
    64–65, 76, 84, 96, 150, 152, 156,
    159, 161, 194, 213, 272, 297–298
    epicentre in Wuhan, 214
    GDP growth, 37–38
    lockdown, 37
Covid vaccines, 297
criminal justice system, 147–149
Criminal Procedure Code (CrPC),
    346
Cromford Mill, 161
crony capitalism, 170, 205
Cruz, Ted, 235

Dalai Lama, 50, 195–197, 208–209,
    217, 236
Dalits, 30–31, 45, 94, 120, 122,
    265, 270, 278, 319, 344–345,
    374

Dandavate, Madhu, 9
Daruwala, Keki, 263
Daruwala, Maja, 149
Deane, Phyllis, 357
Delhi riots (2020), 36, 401
Democracy and Accountable
  Governance, 10
*Democracy On the Road: A 25-
  year Journey Through India,*
  128–129
demographic changes, 62
demographic dividend, 153–154
  China, 154–155
  India, 153–154, 156–157
  Japan, 155
demonetisation, 17–18, 37–38, 67
"Deng Theory," 191
Deng Xiaoping, 204, 216, 339
Denyer, Simon, 35
Desai, Morarji, 46
Dharam Jagran Samiti, 263
Dhumal, Prem Kumar, 127
Die Zeit, 407
digital agriculture, 187
digital e-commerce ecosystem, 178
digitalisation, 153, 177
digitisation, 65, 116, 326
Dikshit, Sheila, 164
direct tax code (DTC), 47, 90
discrimination, 75
Dismantling Global Hindutva
  conference (2021), 270, 395–396
Disraeli, Benjamin, 339
dissent, 108, 322–323, 399
Doklam standoff (2020), 210, 236
dollar-rupee exchange rate,
  201–202
Doval, Ajit, 68, 101
Dravida Munnetra Kazhagam
  (DMK), 42, 66, 106–107, 309
Durant, Will, 358
dynastic politics

in Britain, 123
in India, 123–126, 128–129
relationship between dynastic
  politics and poverty,
  Philippines study, 123
in United States, 122–123

East India Company, 161, 251,
  356–358
e-commerce, 48, 176–179
economic reforms, 90, 95
  farm laws, 90
  labour laws, 90
  land acquisition bill, 90
  macro-economic reforms, 91
  privatisation of loss-making
    government-owned companies,
    90
Economic Times, The, 92, 321,
  323
Economist, The, 111, 279, 300–
  301, 334–335, 397
  editorial policy, 340–342
  liberalism, 334–337
  manifesto, 335
electoral campaign
  chowkidar chor hai, 18
  garibi hatao, 118, 313
  Haath Se Haath Jodo outreach
    campaign, 130
  by Modi, 7
  sabka saath, sabka vikas slogan,
    285
el-Sisi, Abdel Fattah, 248
Emirates Airways, 173–174
employment data, 175–180
entrepreneurship, 162, 171
  Mudra loan-financed micro-
    entrepreneurs, 180
European "nationalism", 110
Europe–China ties, 194

Facebook, 162, 196
Face the Press programme, 10
farmers' agitation, 96, 185, 187
Financial Action Task Force
    (FATF), 378
First Earth Summit, 167
first-past-the-post (FPTP)
    parliamentary electoral system,
    30–31
first-term prime ministership of
    Modi, 16
    economic growth, 17–18
"Five Eyes" intelligence network,
    236
Flantzer, Susan, 353
Flipkart, 48, 176–179, 182
foreign direct investment (FDI),
    34, 87, 158, 178, 334, 400
Foreigners Act (1946), 24
France, 49, 54, 95, 98, 104, 119,
    123, 193, 218, 234, 237, 242–
    244, 253, 257, 266, 295, 380
free trade agreement (FTA), 54
Fukuyama, Francis, 343
Fundamental Rights Committee,
    302

G3 summit, 199, 256–257
G7 summit, 193, 234, 255–259
G8 summit, 193
G20 summit, 48, 73, 100, 108,
    146, 188, 199–200, 237, 287,
    399
Galbraith, Ambassador, 232–233
Galden Namgey Lhatse Monastery,
    Tibet, 209
Galwan Valley clashes (2020), 39,
    41, 51, 64
Ganchi Muslims, 71, 298
Gandhi dynasty, 123–126, 128–
    129, 397. see also Gandhi,
    Indira; Gandhi, Rahul; Gandhi,

Sonia; Gandhi-Vadra, Priyanka
Gandhi, Feroze, 70
Gandhi, Indira, 9, 36, 43, 46, 66,
    70, 121, 131, 158, 231, 233, 254,
    263, 293, 323–326, 379
    1980 election victory, 77
    assassination of, 89
    Bangladesh liberation war
        (1971), 284, 324
    economic and governance
        legacy, 119
    economic socialism, 17
    Emergency era, 65, 71, 135, 321
    garibi hatao slogan, 118, 312
    as "*gungi gudiya*," 118
    Jayaprakash Narayan civil
        disobedience movement
        against, 64–65, 325
    plan to launch an air strike on
        Pakistan's nuclear weapons
        programme (1983), 381
    politics of povertarianism, 170
    post-Emergency loss in Rae
        Bareli, 283
    socialist government, 74, 171,
        313
Gandhi, Mahatma, 101–104,
    109–110, 408
Gandhinagar, 5–7, 12, 79
Gandhi, Rahul, 5, 12–13, 18–19,
    31, 33, 67, 85, 105, 107, 115,
    124–125, 129, 133–134, 136–137,
    140, 170–171, 269, 282, 296–
    297, 299–300, 307, 370, 406
    2019 Lok Sabha election, 283
    advisors, 68
    attitude towards poverty, 118
    Bharat Jodo Yatra, 106, 115, 118,
        284
    criticism against Modi, 67
    disqualification from Parliament,
        116

electoral target, 107
Hindutva tactic of, 67
management duties, 85
popular support, 115–116
"saffron-lite" strategy, 282–283
soft Hindutva, 75
Gandhi, Rajiv, 5–6, 31, 46, 89,
  118, 124, 170, 231, 284, 298
Gandhi, Rajmohan, 331
Gandhi, Sonia, 3, 5, 12–13, 84,
  98, 105, 115, 124–125, 134,
  136–137, 140, 293, 323, 327,
  397, 404
  gungi gudiya, 118
  management duties, 85
  maut ka saudagar comment, 98
  presidency of, 134
Gandhi-Vadra, Priyanka, 5, 42, 98,
  115, 124, 126, 397
  2022 UP assembly poll, 125
  management duties, 85
Ganguly, Anirban, 281
Gates, Bill, 163
Gati Shakti National Master Plan,
  116
Gautier, Francois, 35
gender equality, 253–254, 337,
  343, 374
General Election
  of 2019, 247
  of 2024, 293
  of 2029, 43
Gen Z, 161
geopolitics, 250, 253, 255
George, David Lloyd, 353
George V, King, 353
German 'nationalism,' 110
gig economy, 89, 175–176, 179–
  180
Giuliani, Rudy, 164
global power, 50, 63, 166, 192,
  234–256, 360–361, 394

global warming, 167–169
GMR, 173
Godhra
  railway station incident (2002),
    71
  riots (2002), 6, 71
Goods and Services Tax (GST),
  17–18, 38, 88, 116, 152
GooglePay, 178
Gorvett, Jonathan, 362
Goswami, Arnab, 380
governance, 74, 91, 94, 128,
  256–257
Govindu, Venu Madhav, 349
Gowda, HD Deve, 46, 106–107,
  308, 310
Guadalupe Hidalgo treaty (1848),
  251
Guardian, The, 33, 401, 407
Guizot, François, 339
Gujarat Assembly election
  of 2012, 5
  of 2017, 282–283
'Gujarat model' of economic
  development, 66, 152
Gujarat riots (2002), 4, 66, 71–72,
  98, 100
Gujral, IK, 9
Gulati, Ashok, 186
Gulf war (1991), 245–246
  war-related deaths, 246
GVK Industries Limited, 173

Haaretz, 407
Harder, Anton, 227–228
Harris, Kamala, 236
Harrison, Benjamin, 122
Harrison, William, 122
Hasina, Sheikh, 254
healthcare amenities
  Maharashtra, 151
  private, 150

in towns, 150
in villages, 150
health insurance scheme, 88
HelloPay, 182
Heritage Foundation, 393
Hickel, Jason, 358
hijab controversy, 290–292
Himalayas, 12, 27, 43–44, 57, 76, 99, 207, 286
Hinduism, 268, 273, 276–278, 281, 301, 307, 319
Hindu–Muslim unity, 101–102
Hindu nationalism, 55, 67, 82, 109–110, 397
Hinduphobia, 271–272, 279, 396
Hindu Rashtra, 272–274, 338
Hindustan Aeronautics Limited (HAL), 158
Hindustan Times, 53, 74, 162, 174, 183, 357
Hindu, The, 4, 10, 92, 233
Hindutva, 72–73, 77, 100, 133, 271–273, 275, 279–280, 293, 299–301, 307–308, 395–396
Hindu vote, 30
Hitler, Adolf, 110, 252
Hodeidah, port of, 242
Hollande, François, 247
Hong Kong, 222–223
House of Commons, 93–94, 123
Houthi rebels, 241–242
humanitarian assistance and disaster relief (HADR), 22
Hurriyat, 306
Hussein, Saddam, 244
hybrid working model, 161–162
Hyde Chen, 205

illicit money laundering, 74
inclusive growth, 104, 187
India, 247, 255
Act East policy, 47–48, 248

agricultural sector, 183–188
alliance with France, 237
average lifespan, 400
British colonial rule in, 251
carbon dioxide (CO_2) emissions, 167–168
China policy, 197–198, 207
contest with China, 48–49
democracy, 33–34, 206
demographic dividend, 153–154, 156
dependency ratio, 156
diplomatic outreach, 256
education, 256
entry into Nuclear Suppliers Group (NSG), 53, 59
female fertility rate, 156
as G20 leader, 146
G20 presidency, 48
geopolitical challenges and opportunities, 21–22
industrialisation in, 167–168
intellectual elite, 121
literacy rate, 34, 399–400
malnutrition, 156
Middle East policy, 243
military-technical agreement with Russia, 218
nuclear test, 57–59
population, 45, 53, 153–154
startups, 181–182
tax-GDP ratio, 185
tax system, 160
ties with European Union (EU), 247
Total Fertility Rate (TFR), 156
traditional role as Tibet's main ally, 196
working-age (15–59 years) population, 53–54
India–China relations, 198–200, 209, 217–218, 228

border disputes, 215–216
Doklam standoff, 210, 236
Ladakh standoff, 195–196,
    209–212, 236
India–EU trade, 194
Indian Administrative Service
    (IAS), 74
Indian Airlines, 173
Indian American Muslim Council
    (IAMC), 82
Indian bank NPA crisis, 143–146
    impacts, 145
    NPA classification rules, 145–146
Indian bureaucracy, 146–147,
    170–171
    remoulding, 147
Indian cities
    Delhi, 164
    Mumbai, 164–165
Indian Civil Service (ICS), 74,
    146–147
Indian diplomacy, 58
Indian Express group, 404
Indian Express, The, 136, 139,
    291
Indian Institute of Science (IISc),
    221
Indian Institutes of Managements
    (IIMs), 17, 158
Indian Institutes of Technology
    (IITs), 17, 158, 221
Indian Mujaheedin (IM), 279
Indian Ocean Region (IOR), 210
Indian Premier League (IPL), 127
Indian public health, problems
    with, 151
    maternal and infant mortality
        rates, 151
    shortage of specialists, 151
Indian Railways, 352
Indian rupee, 201
Indian science, 220–221

Indian Science Congress (ISC),
    2019, 220
Indian secularism, 55, 295
Indian Space Research
    Organisation (ISRO), 221
Indian Union Budgets, 157, 187
India–Pakistan relationship
    ceasefire order, 375–376
    myths in, 381–385
    truce agreement, 376–377
India–Pakistan war, 103
India's economy, 17, 88, 145–146
    aviation sector, 172–175
    economic reforms, 204–205
    GDP growth, 120, 153, 172,
        201–203
    'Gujarat model' of economic
        development, 152–153
    liberalisation of, 153, 205
    merchandise trade deficit, 201
    Nehruvian rate of growth, 121
    per capita income, 104, 120
    purchasing power parity (PPP),
        202
India–Taiwan trade, 198
India Today, 43–44
India–US civil nuclear deal (2008),
    258, 280
India–US ties, 218
India Versus China: Why They Are
    Not Friends (Bajpai), 198
The India Way: Strategies for an
    Uncertain World, 21
Industrial Revolution, 219
Indus Waters Treaty (IWT), 17,
    372
Infosys, 221
Insolvency and Bankruptcy Code
    (IBC), 47, 90, 205
Institute for Defence Studies and
    Analysis (IDSA), 20
insurgent groups, 108

International Solar Alliance (ISA), 287

Inter-Services Intelligence (ISI), Pakistan, 83

investment opportunities, in India, 86

I-PAC, 13

Iqbal Singh Chahal: Covid Warrior, 38

Iran, 254–255

Iranian revolution, 204, 245

Irani, Smriti, 31, 107, 269, 283

Iran's influence in Middle East, 242

Islam, 264–265, 276–277, 301

Islamic State-Khorasan (IS-K), 267

Islamism, 63

Islamist fundamentalism, 274

Islamists, 267

Islamist terrorism, 165, 299–300, 305, 313

Islamophobia, 61, 279, 396

Jainism, 276

Jain, Satyendra, 133

Jaishankar, S., 20–21, 23, 147, 199, 321

Jaish-e-Mohammed (JeM), 68, 267, 300

Jaitley, Arun, 14, 19–20, 32, 132, 160
  Union Budgets, 90

Jammu and Kashmir (J&K)
  evolution of, 32
  Jammu and Kashmir Reorganisation Act (2019), 326
  Reorganisation Bill, 23, 33
  special status of, 76, 373–375

Janata Dal, 308

Janata Dal (Secular) (JD(S)), 29, 42

Janata Dal (United) (JDU), 132

Jan Dhan-Aadhaar-Mobile trio, 88

Japan, 257
  demographic dividend, 155

jati, 277–278

Jet Airways, 172

Jewish communities, of India, 264

Jharkhand Mukti Morcha (JMM), 131

Jinnah, Muhammad Ali, 100, 102, 302, 368

Jio, 176

Jiomart, 179

Johnson, Boris, 94, 165

Joshi, Deepak, 117

Joshi, Kailash, 117

Joshi, Murli Manohar, 8

Kailash Mansarovar, 307

Kalam, Dr APJ Abdul, 280

Kapoor, Anil, 389

Kapoor, Anish, 398

Karma-Kargyu sect, 209

Kashmir dispute, 371

Kashmir Files, The (film), 290, 305–307

Kashmiri Muslims, 274, 305, 307

Kashmiri Pandits, 32, 305–306
  exodus of, 290, 305–306

Kayasths, 30

Kejriwal, Arvind, 8, 13–14, 68, 85, 131–133, 164
  criminal defamation case against, 132
  health care and education, 164
  against Modi, 14
  transformation of, 14

Kennedy, John F, 232, 235

Kennedy, Ted, 123

Kent, Michael, 354

Ketkar, Kumar, 4

Khan, Aamir, 305, 313

Khan, Ayub, 233

Khan, Imran, 63, 370–371, 383
Khan, Sadiq, 165
Khan, Salman, 305
Khan, Shah Rukh, 306
Kharge, Mallikarjun, 65, 85, 115, 125, 130, 286
  Haath Se Haath Jodo, 106
Khehar, JS, 303
Khilafat movement, 102
Khomeini, Ayatollah, 204, 244–245
Kishore, Roshan, 53
Kishor, Prashant, 13
Kissinger, Henry, 7
Korean War, 226
Krishna, Arvind, 162
Ku Klux Klan, 391
Kumar, Anand, 126
Kumarappa, JC, 350
Kumaraswamy, HD, 126
Kumar, Nitish, 132

Ladakh standoff, 195–196, 209–212, 236
Lashkar-e-Taiba (LeT), 267, 299
Lehman Brothers, collapse of, 174
Lekhi, Meenakshi, 210
Le Monde, 407
liberal Hindu civil society, 319
liberal Hindus, 289–290, 313, 319
liberalism, 289, 334–337, 340–342
  economic, 337
  five axioms of, 338
  gender equality, 337
  Indian left-leaners, 339
  liberal governance, 343
  liberal society, 343
  modern, 342–343
  sexual orientation, 338
  social, 339
Liberation Tigers of Tamil Eelam (LTTE), 81, 118
Licence Raj, 170–171

Lieber, Charles, 213
Life Insurance Corporation (LIC), 90
Line of Actual Control (LAC), 19
Livingstone, Ken, 165
Lok Sabha elections
  in 1971, 325
  in 1996, 30, 308
  in 2004, 81
  in 2009, 81
  in 2014, 5–6, 124, 280, 309
  in 2019, 19, 67, 69, 84, 91, 107, 126, 280, 283, 286, 297, 345, 370, 406–407
    BJP-led NDA's landslide victory, 29–31, 42
    impact of terror strikes, 68–69
    reasons for BJP's victory, 31
  in 2024, 41–42, 64, 70, 73, 106, 108, 117, 130, 146, 157, 188, 293–294, 324, 326, 345, 406, 408
  in 2027, 129
  factors influencing outcomes of, 308, 345
    Supreme Court ruling, 344–346
love jihad, 95, 269
Loya, B. M., 68
Lutyens' Delhi, 84, 127, 326–327

Macaulay, Lord, 35
Maddison, Angus, 278
Maharaj, Sakshi, 344
Maharaj, Swami Atmasthanandaji, 27–28
Maharaj, Swami Madhabanandaji, 26
Mahindras, 398
Maiorano, Diego, 119
majoritarianism, 55–56, 283, 298, 333, 343, 374
Maldives, 50

Mann, Bhagwant Singh, 133
"Mao Thought," 191
Mao Zedong, 155, 207
Marino, Andy, 6, 12, 25
  Narendra Modi: A Political Biography, 6, 25
maritime security, 22
Masani, Minoo, 302
Masani, Zareer, 119
Mathai, John, 247
Mayawati, 15, 96, 126, 132, 344
Mayflower Pilgrims, 61, 63
May, Theresa, 94
media portrayal on India, 391
  antagonism of the West, 393–395
  global media coverage of Kashmir, 391–394
  of Modi, 396–399
  social media, 399–400
Mehta, Pratap Bhanu, 291, 373
Meloni, Giorgia, 95
Menon, Menon, 217
Menons, 30
Merchant, Minhaz, 15, 43–44
micro-economic reforms, 89
middle class, 86–87
Mint, 38
Mishra, Abhishek, 290
Misra Commission, 269, 319
Mission R&AW, 82
Mittal, Varun, 182
Modi, Narendra, 131, 214, 284, 286, 296, 321
  age, 66
  attack on Nehruvian politics, 121
  biography, 71
  BJP's membership, 45–46
  campaigning for BJP, 7
  campaign promise, 146
  character and political future, 25–28
  China policy, 236–237

criticism by foreign correspondents, 33
criticisms levelled against, 64, 67, 83–84, 322–323
as a decision-maker, 38–41
demonisation of, 71
disappointments of first five years, 90
economic prescriptions, 158
economic reforms, 90, 95
foreign policy, 47–52, 65–66
ideological trajectory, 73
India's nuclear triad, 60
innovative economic initiatives, 84
leadership, 15–16, 68, 284–285
macro-economic management, 47
majoritarianism and Hindutva, 55–56, 333
Middle East policy, 243
Modi 1.0, 326
Modi 2.0, 326
Modi 3.0, 326–327
as the new Vajpayee, 99
outreach to Arab world, 248
outreach to Southeast Asia, 47–49
personal popularity, 76
policy on
  China, 197–198, 207
  Pakistan, 380, 384–385
political targets, 66
practice of inviting global leaders on Republic Day, 247–248
as prime ministerial candidate, 7–9, 63
relationship with family members, 77–80
religion as an electoral scimitar, 44–45
as RSS pracharaks, 57

secularism, 55–56
single-minded vision for India,
   293
soft secularism, 75
strengths, 66
tax reforms, 66
understanding of Indian mind,
   76
vote-pulling charisma, 130
welfare projects, 46–47, 86–89,
   108
winning vote shares, 46
monetary policy, 143
Monopolies and Restrictive Trade
   Practices (MRTP) Act, 74
Moral Re-Armament (MRA), 331
Mor, Nachiket, 183
Mountbatten, Lord Louis, 353–354
MSP law, 188
MTNL, 90
Mudra loans, 176
Mufti, Mehbooba, 126
Muftis, 66, 306, 375
Mugabe, Robert, 128
Mughals, 320
Mukerjee, Pranab, 160
Mullick, BM, 233
Mumbai Press Club, 3–4, 10, 15
Munshi, Kanhaiyalal, 302
Musharraf, Pervez, 369, 382
Muslim-first secularism, 313
Muslim personal law, 268–269
Muslims, 66, 75–76, 120–121, 270,
   277, 296, 312–317, 319, 344, 359
Muslim Women (Protection of
   Rights on Marriage) Act (2019),
   326

Nadella, Satya, 162–163
Nageswaran, V. Anantha, 202
Naidu, Chandrababu, 126
Naipaul, V. S., 252

Nairs, 30
Nal-Se-Jal (water from tap), 88
Nanak, Guru, 281
Nandi, Shreya, 177
Nandy, Ashish, 109–111
Narain, Raj, 65, 325
Narayana Health, 151
Narayan, Jayaprakash, 64, 312,
   325
   "total revolution" movement, 312
Narayen, Shantanu, 162
Nath, Kamal, 117, 405
National Commission for
   Minorities, 81
National Conference (NC), 42, 66,
   345
   treatment of Muslims, 292
National Democratic Alliance
   (NDA) government, 4
National Health Service (NHS),
   150
National Herald, 70, 136, 397
   alleged misappropriation of
     assets case, 136–140
   closure of, 137
   scam, 77
nationalism, 73, 109–110
   Colonial British, 112
   European, 110, 259
   Gandhi's, 110
   German, 110
   Hindu, 110
   Hitler's, 110
   Indian, 110–112
   real, 110
Nationalist Congress Party (NCP),
   42, 55, 319
   treatment of Muslims, 292
National Population Register
   (NPR), 24
National Register of Citizens
   (NRC), 23–25

National Security Commission (NSC), 148

NATO, 192, 218

Naxal terrorism, 32

Nehru, Arun, 170, 217

Nehru, Jawaharlal, 16–17, 36, 43, 46, 50, 70, 73, 102, 109, 120, 123, 137, 146–147, 158, 169–171, 227, 231–232, 236, 247, 270, 293, 295, 302, 318, 323, 326, 408
  assessment of China, 217
  blunders, 226–231
  foreign policy, 227–228, 230
  Rasgotra's views on, 231–234
  views against nuclear tests and nuclear weapons, 232

Nehru Memorial Museum and Library (NMML), 228

Nehruvian consensus, 120–121

Nellie massacre of Bengali Muslims, in Assam, 72

Nepal, 50

nepotism, 126–128

The New Clash of Civilizations: How the Contest Between America, China, India and Islam Will Shape Our Century, 279

New Education Policy, 322

New India (Bharat), 86

New York, 164–165

New York Times, The, 33, 95, 224, 242, 297, 392, 407

Ngawang Lobsang Gyatso, 209

Nivedita, Sister, 281

Nixon, Richard, 254

non-aligned movement (NAM), 226, 236

Non-Performing Assets (NPAs), 14

Noorani, AG, 227

North American population, 61–62

nuclear non-proliferation treaty (NPT), 59

Nuclear Suppliers Group (NSG), 234

Obama, Barack, 49, 121, 247, 342

Observer, The, 407

One-China policy, 51

O'Neill, Jim, 258–259

One-India policy, 51

'One Nation, One Election' work, 91–94

'one nation, one law,' 302

One Sun One World One Grid (OSOWOG), 287

One Year of Modi Sarkar, 15

Open Network for Digital Commerce (ONDC), 177–178, 327

opinion polls, 11, 67`, 115–116

Opposition in India, 94

Opposition, The, 8

Ottoman Caliphate, 102, 266, 318

P2P (peer to peer) platforms, 162

Pahlavi dynasty, 244

Pahlavi, Mohammad Reza, 244

Pahlavi, Mohammad Shah, 244

paid news, 404–405

Pai, Nitin, 224

Pakistan, 51, 63, 69, 100, 367–370
  ceasefire violations, 371
  discrimination against minorities, 371
  GDP, 371
  insurgency in J&K, 204
  Kalat's relations with, 368
  nuclear test, 60
  occupation of Balochistan, 367–368
  Pakistani army, 372, 379
  Pakistani society, 370

per capita income, 369–370
purchasing power parity (PPP), 370
as terrorism hub, 369
Pakistan-occupied Kashmir (PoK), 204, 268, 373, 378, 381
Pandey, Mangal, 311
Parikh, Vasantbhai, 25
Parrikar, Manohar, 19–20
Parthasarathi, Ashok, 233–234
Parthasarathi, G, 232, 234
Parthasarthy, Ashok, 217, 232
Parthasarthy, G., 217
Passport (Entry into India) Act (1920), 24
Patel, Dev, 389
Patel, Praful, 172, 175
Patel, Sardar Vallabhbhai, 99, 196, 303
Patel, Urjit, 145
Patil, Shivraj, 299
Patnaik, Naveen, 132
Patnaik, Utsa, 356–357
patriotism, 111–112
Patten, Chris, 210
Pawar, Sharad, 85, 126, 131
Paytm, 178
Peng Liyuan, 215–216
Pen, Marine Le, 95
People's Democratic Party (PDP), 66, 126, 307, 345
People's Liberation Army (PLA), 51, 195
Permanent Account Number (PAN), 185
Phadnis, Aditi, 196
PhonePe, 178, 182
Pichai, Sunder, 162–163
Pinto, Frieda, 389
Pitroda, Sam, 300
plural society, 343
PM Gati Shakti Master Plan, 91, 153, 327

Pokhran nuclear test, 57–58
Pokhran-II, 60
Western media reportage, 58
polarisation, 36, 55, 96, 280, 313, 343–344
anti-CAA sentiment, 25
police reforms, 147–150
appointment of DGP, 148
Police Complaints Authority (PCA), 148
Police Establishment Board (PEB), 148
selection and placement of Chiefs, 148–149
tenure of officers, 148
Popular Front of India (PFI), 82, 101, 395
Prabhu, Suresh, 175
Pratibha, 127
Premji, Azim, 313
private industry, 74
privatisation of airports, 172–173
production-linked incentive (PLI) scheme, 84, 326
productivity dividend, 154
pseudo-science, 220
public intellectuals, 33, 109, 399
Pulwama terrorist attack (2019), 19, 68, 300, 370–371, 383
electoral impact, 68–69
purchasing power parity (PPP), 52, 104, 202, 370
Puri, Hardeep Singh, 175
Putin, Vladimir, 192, 287

Qatar Airways, 173–174
Quad, 49, 237, 258, 287, 393
Quraishi, SY, 92
Quran, 276, 303, 314–316
burning of, 266
Qurayza, Banu, 316

racism, 393
Radia tapes, 405
Radical Islam, 63, 266, 271, 313
Rafale fighter jet deal, 18, 67–68,
  237, 297
raja dharma, 71
Rajagopalachari, C, 102
Rajan, Amol, 397
Rajan, Raghuram, 143–144
raj dharma, 73
Raju, Ashok Gajapathi, 175
Ramakrishna Mission, 26–27
Ramakrishna Mission Mutt, 79
Ram Mandir, 30, 33, 36, 38,
  44–46, 64, 68, 76, 282, 284, 324
Ram, N., 4
Ram temple, 33, 36, 38, 45–46,
  68, 72, 76
Ranade, Ajit, 4, 10
Ranganath Misra Commission, 269
Rao, K Chandrashekar, 132
Rao, PV Narasimha, 46, 81, 121,
  153, 158, 272, 284, 323
Rasgotra, Maharaj Krishna, 231,
  233–234
Rashtriya Janata Dal (RJD), 42, 66,
  126, 319, 345
  treatment of Muslims, 292
Rashtriya Swayamsevak Sangh
  (RSS), 11–12
  ghar wapsi programmes, 263,
  269
Ravi, K. Vyalar, 175
Ray, Siddhartha Shankar, 65, 325
Reagan, Ronald, 38
Reddy, YS Jagan Mohan, 85
Rediffusion, 161
Regional Comprehensive Economic
  Partnership (RCEP), 48, 248
Reliance, 158
religion and religiosity, 76, 320
  conversions, 265

freedom of, 291
religious teaching, 219
Remdesivir, 39–40
renewables, 166
Representation of the People Act
  (1950), 137
Republic of Ireland, 362
Research and Analysis Wing
  (R&AW), 82
Reserve Bank of India (RBI), 91,
  143–145
retail market, 178
revolt of 1857, 310–312
RIC, 237
Right to Education (RTE)
  legislation, 322
Rig Veda, 221
Rise and Fall of Nations, The,
  159
Rizvi, Ali A, 314–315
robots and artificial intelligence
  (AI), 216–217
Rocket Boys, 390–391
Rogoff, Kenneth, 216
Roosevelt, Franklin, 122
Roosevelt, Theodore, 122, 339
route rationalisation, 173
Rubio, Marco, 235
Rudd, Amber, 354
Rushdie, Salman, 298, 331–333,
  398
  Midnight's Children, 331
  Satanic Verses, The, 298, 332
  Shame, 332
Russia, 192, 254–255
  annexation of Crimea, 193
Russia-Ukraine war, 23, 54, 64–65,
  87, 146, 192–194, 209, 236, 250,
  252, 272, 287
  collateral outcomes of, 253

Sachar Committee, 269, 319

SAD, 42
safety of Christians and Muslims
   in India, 265–266
Sahih Muslim, 316
SAIL, 158
Samajwadi Party (SP), 42, 55,
   66, 94, 96, 126, 132, 263, 319,
   344–345
   treatment of Muslims, 292
Sanatana Dharma, 264
Sangh Parivar, 273, 324
Sangma, Mukul, 105
Sarabhai, Vikram, 390–391
Saran, Shyam, 101–104
Sardesai, Rajdeep, 15–16, 43, 285
Sarma, Himanta Biswa, 116
Saubhagya, 88
Saudi coalition, 241–242
Saxe-Coburg-Gotha, 103
Saxon-Slav proxy conflict, 252
Sayeed, Mufti Mohammad, 306, 405
scientific revolution, 219
Scindia, Jyotiraditya, 175
Scindia, Madhavrao, 99
Scottish independence, 361–362
secularism, 55, 119, 270, 273, 282,
   295, 298, 301, 303, 313, 318
   definition, 295–296
   Nehruvian, 270
   real, 270, 299
secular liberals, 344
Securities and Exchange Board of
   India (SEBI), 91
sedition, 108
Sen, Amartya, 322–323, 406
Shah, Amit, 23, 32, 98, 101, 127,
   285, 299
   handling of J&K issue, 32
   as home minister, 32
Shah, AP, 298
Shah Bano case, 1985, 269, 298
Shanghai Cooperation

Organisation (SCO), 200, 207,
   237, 287
Shankar, Uday, 4
Sharif, Nawaz, 14, 370
Sharif, Raheel, 241
Sharma, Dinesh C., 220
Sharma, Mahesh, 280
Sharma, Ruchir, 159
Shastri, Lal Bahadur, 70
Shaw, George Bernard, 339
Shekhar, Chandra, 81
Sheridan, Gavin, 235
Shetty, Devi, 150
Shia–Sunni relations, 244–245
Shiv Sena, 55, 345
Sikhism, 289
Singapore, 48
Singapore Fintech Association, 182
Singh, Ajit, 175
Singh, Arun, 170
Singh, Kanishka, 299
Singh, Khushwant, 332
Singh, Manmohan, 13, 15, 36, 46,
   121, 134, 153, 158, 269, 323,
   379, 382
Singh, Prakash, 147–148
Singh, Rajeshwar, 263
Singh, Rajnath, 6, 11, 32, 127, 373
   role during long standoff in
   eastern Ladakh, 32
Singhvi, Abhishek Manu, 137
Singh, VP, 46, 81
Sino-British agreement (1984),
   210–211
Sino-Indian war (1962), 17, 50,
   233
Sioux tribes, 250
Sitharaman, Nirmala, 20
   macro-economic reforms, 91
Slumdog Millionaire (film), 389
Smart Cities
   definition, 165

economic development and
  activity, 165
governance of, 166
technological platforms, 165
social discrimination, 33
socialism, 119
solar power, 166
South Asian women leaders, 254
South China Sea, 23, 48, 188, 192,
  194, 199, 211, 216, 249
Soviet communism, 258, 393
Sri Lanka, 50, 216, 249, 254, 360
Srinivasan, Rajeev, 277
Stalin, MK, 131
State Security Commission (SSC),
  148
Sterling Newspapers Pvt Ltd, 7,
  404
strategic autonomy, 236
Strategic Culture Foundation
  (2018), 241
strategic self-interest, 218
streetlight effect, 134
Students Islamic Movement of
  India (SIMI), 279
Subramanian, Krishnamurthy, 7,
  20, 128
Sunak, Rishi, 94, 355, 361
Sunni fundamentalism, 274
Sun Tzu, 52, 54
Super conducting Super Collider
  (SSC), 219
Supriyo, Babul, 105
surgical strike across LoC (2016),
  20–21
Suri, Navin, 181–182
Swachh Bharat, 88
Swamy, Subramanian, 5, 136,
  138–140
Swaraj, Sushma, 19–20, 32
Swiggy, 176

Tagore, Rabindranath, 112
Taiwan, 51, 209, 222
Taliban, 61, 267, 332
Talibanised Afghanistan, 267
Talwar, Deepak, 174–175
Taseer, Aatish, 354
Tata Consultancy Services (TCS),
  221
Tata Group, 21, 158, 175
Tata Institute of Fundamental
  Research (TIFR), 221
Tata, JRD, 153, 169–171
Tatas, 398
taxation, 16
Team Indus, 390
Teamlease Services, 176
Tehreek-i-Labbaik Pakistan (TLP),
  267
Telecom Regulatory Authority of
  India (TRAI), 91
Telegraph, The, 164
Telugu Desam Party (TDP), 126
terrorism, 204
Thackeray, Uddhav, 131
Thakkar, Jagdish, 3
Thakurs, 30
Tharoor, Shashi, 7, 59–60, 125,
  333, 351, 371
  An Era of Darkness: The British
    Empire in India, 390
  The Inglorious Empire: What the
    British Did to India, 349
Tibet, 51
Tilak, Lokmanya, 102
Times of India, The, 136, 398
Tocilizumab, 39
toilets, 87
tokenism, 118
token Muslim, 279, 296, 313
Tonge, Jon, 362
transatlantic slave trade, 1830s,
  252

Trevelyan, Charles, 235
Trinamool Congress (TMC), 29,
    42, 55, 105–107, 126, 132, 285,
    308–309, 319
  target audience, 310
  TMC-UPA alliance, 107
triple talaq law, 97, 298
Trudeau, Justin, 342
Trump, Donald, 33, 49, 298
Truss, Liz, 94
Tsai ing-Wen, 198, 210
Tuschman, Avi, 339–340

Ujjwala, 88
Unified Payments Interface (UPI),
    88, 116, 327
Uniform Civil Code (UCC), 84,
    299, 302, 304
United Kingdom of Great Britain
    and Ireland, 362
United Nations Commission for
    India and Pakistan (UNCIP)
    resolution on Kashmir, 375–379
United Nations Human Rights
    Council (UNHRC), 109
United Nations Population Fund
    (UNFPA), 155
United Nations Security Council
    (UNSC), 212, 218, 226–227, 257
  Nehru's refusal of US offer,
    227–231
United Progressive Alliance (UPA),
    174, 397
  UPA1 government, 81, 84, 205,
    299, 384
  UPA2 government, 7–8, 84, 143,
    187, 205, 299, 384
United States, 250, 256
  African-American descendants,
    234
  Anglo-Saxon colonial settlement,
    251

economic and political power,
    235
  foreign policy, 254
  governance, 256–257
  Hispanic Americans, 234–235
  policy actions towards Iraq, 246
  policy in Asia, 253
  US policy on India, 236
  as white-minority country, 234
UP assembly election, 2022,
    41–42, 126
Uri surgical strike (2016), 21, 68,
    134, 383–384
US–India alliance, 49
US–UK real-time intelligence
    sharing alliance, 236

Vadra, Robert, 77, 125
Vaishnaw, Ashwini, 147, 321
Vajpayee, Atal Bihari, 4, 11,
    30, 46, 57–58, 71–73, 75, 82,
    99–100, 120, 127, 236, 273–274,
    283, 379
Varshney, Ashok, 373
Vasudhaiva Kutumbakam, 21
Verma, JS, 271
Verma, Richard, 86–87
Vijaya Lakshmi Pandit papers, 228
Vijayvargiya, Kailash, 117
Vishva Hindu Parishad (VHP), 301
Vishwas, Kumar, 133
Vivekananda, Swami, 25, 27, 72,
    79, 281, 288
Vora, Motilal, 137
voter turnout, 92
vote share, 41–42
  NDA's, 323
  TMC, 107
  winning, 46
  women, 97
  youth voters, 97

Wadhwa, Vivek, 162
Wall Street Journal, The, 401, 407
Walmart, 178, 182
Wani, Burhan, 400
Warsaw Pact, 193, 218
Washington, George, 122
Washington Post, The, 242, 297, 407
water frame, 161
weapons of mass destruction (WMDs), 245
West Bengal assembly election (2021), 54
Western journalists, 33–35
Western media, 241–242
White Anglo-Saxon Protestants (WASPs), 235
Wilson, Woodrow, 339
wind power, 166
Windrush affair, 354
Windsor, Lady Gabriella, 354
Wipro, 221
work from anywhere (wfa), 161
work from home (wfh), 161
work-life balance, 162
World Population Prospects (WPP) data, 2022, 53
World War I, 243–244, 353
World War II, 244, 252, 350, 355, 393
Wounded Civilisation (Naipaul), 403
Wray, Christopher, 221
Wuhan, 214
Wuhan National Bio-Industry Base, 215
Wuhan University of Technology, 215

Xi Jinping, 48, 52, 155, 191, 195, 206, 212, 214, 223–224, 246
  endorsement of Russia's invasion of Ukraine, 191
  modification of China's Constitution, 223–224
  stance in South China Sea, 192
  support of Pakistani terrorism, 192
  zero-Covid policy, 215
Xi Zhongxum, 206

Yadav, Akhilesh, 126
Yadav, Lalu, 126
Yadav, RK, 82
Yadav, Yogendra, 133
Yanqing Ye, 213
Yechury, Sitaram, 273
Yeltsin, Boris, 192
Yemen genocide, 241–243
Yemen war, 241
Young Indian Pvt Ltd, 136–140

Zafar, Bahadur Shah, 136
Zaidi, Nasim, 344
Zaosong Zheng, 213
Zenz, Adrian, 208
Zhang Yijiong, 195
Zia, Begum Khaleda, 254
Zoroastrians (Parsis), 264
Zuckerberg, Mark, 162

www.ingramcontent.com/pod-product-compliance
Lightning Source LLC
Chambersburg PA
CBHW020447100426
42812CB00036B/3479/J